MUSIC IN AMERICAN LIFE

MUSIC IN AMERICAN LIFE
*A list of books in the series appears
at the end of this book.*

Fred Waring and the Pennsylvanians

VIRGINIA WARING

FRED
WARING

AND THE

Pennsylvanians

Foreword by Robert Shaw

University of Illinois Press   Urbana and Chicago

First Illinois paperback, 2007
© 1997 by the Board of Trustees of the University of Illinois
Manufactured in the United States of America
1 2 3 4 5 C P 5 4 3 2 1

The Library of Congress cataloged the cloth edition as follows:

Waring, Virginia.
Fred Waring and the Pennsylvanians / Virginia Waring ; foreword by Robert Shaw
p.   cm. — (Music in American life)
Includes bibliographical references and index.
ISBN 0-252-02295-5 (alk. paper)
1. Waring, Fred, 1900–1984.   2. Choral conductors—United States—
Biography.   3. Pennsylvanians (Musical group)   I. Title.   II. Series.
ML422.W3W37   1997   782.5'164'092—dc20   [B] 96-25186   CIP   MN

PAPERBACK ISBN 0-252-07444-0 / 978-0-252-07444-8

To Our Children . . .

DIXIE

FRED JR.

BILL

PAUL

MALCOLM

Contents

Illustrations follow pages 66, 230, 260, and 338

Foreword

Robert Shaw

I FIRST met Fred Waring when he came to Pomona College to film scenes for the motion picture *Varsity Show*. A goodly percentage of the student body worked as extras in that film. I happened to be leading the Pomona College Glee Club at that time due to the rather extended absence, by reason of illness, of the faculty member whose duty it had been for years. Pomona had a long tradition of superb glee club singing (due entirely to Professor Ralph Lyman), and I had not had the glee club long enough to destroy that tradition. Fred was kind enough to come to a glee club rehearsal. He heard the chorus, and generously gave us some of the Pennsylvanians' arrangements for our annual "Home Concert."

A year after *Varsity Show* I wrote Fred in New York, saying that I was beginning to consider music as a possible career and asking if he might have a place in his organization wherein I might work for a year to experience something of professional musical life. He wrote back, asking me to come to New York and organize a male glee club as an independent complement to his orchestra. (Heretofore members of the Pennsylvanians had doubled as singers and instrumentalists.)

I arrived in New York at the end of the summer of 1938, heard some five hundred voices during six weeks of auditions, rehearsed the twenty-four survivors for a few additional weeks, and the "Fred Waring Glee Club" went on the air that fall.

Basically, Fred was warm and generous. In those days he was also not without "temperament" and exacting performance standards. That these occasionally issued in frazzled nerves—his own as well as others'—should not surprise anyone. His musical intuition was remarkable. With regard to the American popular song, in particular, he sensed unfailingly how best to interpret melodic contour and emotional content. He was confident of these natural abilities, and felt no need to blazon them.

I can recall three major contributions that Fred made to my own musical growth. One had to do with the sense of elapsed musical time. (Here I'm not talking about dramatic or interpretative "timing.") One simply became very sensitive to *elapsed* sums of musical minutes and seconds, and to the possibility of "making up" fifteen seconds here or "spreading" thirty seconds there—tastefully.

A second contribution was the exposure to the speed with which musical ensemble disciplines could be effected under necessity. If, for example, it became necessary to alter a carefully rehearsed program and substitute another musical selection, it was not inconceivable that this could be done within a few minutes of actual air time—given disciplined rehearsal procedures.

In the third instance, within his self-created style Fred was undoubtedly a perfectionist. Erratic enunciation, for instance, simply was not tolerated. And, while one might have some personal reservations as to the aesthetic "richness" or "depth" of the repertoire or "gloss" of performance style, there simply could be no doubt about its technical cleanliness and discipline.

Fred enormously spurred choral technique, choral repertoire, and the public acceptance of choral music in the United States. It was he who first demonstrated on a national scale, and to the average listener's satisfaction, that choruses could, in fact, be understood. The choral sonorities he developed, with concurrence and contributions by Roy Ringwald, Hawley Ades, and others of his arrangers, were both diverse and distinctive. For instance, he achieved rich harmonic texture through a remarkably wide range of male voices, and brought forward the principal melodic voice through strategic octave doublings.

Almost alone, Fred "popularized" choral sound and the choral instrument. This is not a negligible or unimportant accomplishment. Though the later tours of the Robert Shaw and Roger Wagner Chorales dealt mainly with a more traditional, classical, and sacred repertoire than the basically entertainment repertoire of the Fred Waring Glee Clubs, it is certain to me that tours in the United States of the Bach *B Minor Mass* and the Mozart *Requiem* would not have been possible had not Fred Waring stimulated and helped to create an audience for choral music.

As for Fred's contributions to my own life: In addition to those elements mentioned above, had not Fred been interested enough in the work of a young Pomona College student to ask him to come to New York, that young man would surely have found his life's work in an entirely different direction. And in that sense Fred's specific invitation at that unlooked-for moment has made all the difference.

Acknowledgments

I OWE a bountiful debt of gratitude to the Pennsylvanians and friends, past and present. Their thoughts and remembrances provide the assurances of validity to this book.

Assembling the material and writing this book was an intriguing challenge. My dear friend Alex Dreier suggested I contact editor Jane Humphries. She transferred my reams of handwritten pages onto her computer, and thus began months and months of wading through the text, shifting and cutting. As the manuscript was passed back and forth between Jane and me, Alex offered periodic suggestions.

Marlowe Froke of Penn State went far beyond the latitude of friendship. He and his daughter Dana faithfully read every word of my seven hundred page manuscript, offering their insights and understanding.

Writer Rosalind Friedman provided invaluable advice, as did Frank Egan.

I am grateful to Sanford Thatcher of the Pennsylvania State University Press for submitting the manuscript to Judith McCulloh, the very capable executive editor of the University of Illinois Press. Judith felt it might fit into their Music in American Life series and has been most patient, along with Patricia Hollahan, in guiding and counseling me on the importance of footnotes.

Throughout the entire process, Peter Kiefer, curator of the Fred Waring memorabilia at Penn State, and Ruth Sibley, a forty-seven-year executive Pennsylvanian, have with cheerful diligence helped me check and recheck all requests for precise dates, names, photographs, and recordings.

I am humbled by the patience of all and grateful to them beyond measure.

Prologue

The Man Who Taught America How to Sing

IN 1943 I was the Morley half of the two-piano team "Morley & Gearhart" when conductor Robert Shaw heard us play and invited us to audition for Fred Waring. Bob had been Fred's choral assistant on the nightly Chesterfield "Pleasure Time" radio show since its inception four years earlier, and he said, "I don't know whether Mr. Waring can use you, but I would like him to hear you."

We had just signed a long-term contract with Columbia Artists for annual concert tours, so we were feeling quite smug. Even though Fred had been on the air ten years, we weren't interested, since we were insufferable musical snobs as only the young can be, and our career was set. We didn't need Fred Waring, or so we thought.

The audition took place at New York's Vanderbilt Theater immediately after Fred's first evening broadcast. He performed twice a night five nights a week in those days, from 7 to 7:15 P.M. on the East Coast and again at 11 P.M. for the West Coast. At that time Fred's Chesterfield shows had the largest audience that had ever been known to tune in to a network program from coast to coast. When the theater cleared, we went onstage, were introduced, and sat down at the pianos lined up side-by-side. I remember glancing up to see Fred leaning on the piano, chin in hand, listening intently and watching us with those penetrating blue eyes. He was only forty-three years old, yet so assured was his presence and manner, he could have been twenty years older. We had scarcely played our last note when, to our great surprise, he said, "How soon can you start to work?"

He was not exactly overjoyed to hear of our Columbia contract. But we compromised by becoming part-time Pennsylvanians, appearing as soloists whenever we were not touring.

Livingston Gearhart and I were newly married at the time, and we remained off-and-on Pennsylvanians until the early fifties. But by then many personal problems had arisen between us. We divorced and the piano team dissolved. Later in 1954 Fred and I were married, a union that lasted until his death in 1984.

During his senescent years, Fred would mutter from time to time about the book he was going to write. But he knew, I knew, and those around him knew that a man who hated to talk about himself, who loathed the confinement of boring meetings, and who carried around suitcases of unanswered mail was not about to spend cloistered months recapturing his past with its ups and downs. And so I've decided to have a go at it even though I'm a musician, not a writer. Some of you may say, "Stick to your keyboard." But having observed Fred as a professional musician for ten years and as a wife for thirty years, I do believe I knew and understood him better than anyone.

Fred Waring's life is a one hundred percent American tale that covered eight and a half decades. His professional life encompassed every aspect of show business—dance, theater, vaudeville, recording, radio, movies, television, and concerts—racking up many "firsts" along the way.

Before Fred came along, the use of voices was generally limited to operas, church choirs, and college glee clubs. Fred Waring was the first to have a singing band, the first to use megaphones, to feature vocalists with an orchestra, to combine an orchestra with a glee club, to originate the show choir concept, to make a full-length musical talking picture, and the first to present weekly musical spectaculars on television. Because the composers respected him so, Fred was the first, at their request, to introduce more new songs to the world than anyone, songs by such luminaries as Harold Arlen, Irving Berlin, Hoagy Carmichael, George Gershwin, Jerome Kern, Cole Porter, Richard Rodgers, Arthur Schwartz, Harry Warren, Richard Whiting, and many more. He taught a new way of singing so the listener would hear, as he emphasized so many times, "all of the beauty of all of the sounds of all of the syllables of all of the words."

Fred has three stars on Hollywood Boulevard for his accomplishments in three major entertainment media—radio, movies, and television. This then is the story of a man who started out as a teenage banjo player and was later honored by his peers and by adoring audiences. What are those personal characteristics in a man that enable him single-handedly to hold together a large musical organization for sixty-seven years? To change the face of American choral music by moving it from churches and schools to the popularity charts, later receiving a gold medal of Congress for these efforts?

Fred was an enigma for most people. He was open and comfortable onstage but a mixture of contradictions offstage. Here was a man of energy and vision who perfected the Waring Blendor®, which not only revolutionized the eating and drinking habits of America but was used by the cosmetics industry and in medical research. He was a golf nut who designed and laid out golf courses. He ran an empire of enterprises.

Throughout his life, Fred was the epitome of the clean-cut American. In the twenties and thirties, he exuded a collegiate, sexy, yet wholesome aura. With each decade he garnered more and more respect with his steadfast patriotism and meticulous shows until finally in the eighties he was regarded as an endangered species, a pure, apple pie, honest-to-God *Amurican,* as Wendell Wilkie used to say—one who, from the time he became a Boy Scout in 1912, believed in God and Country with such steadfast and eloquent fervor that no one dreamed of questioning his sincerity. He always gave an audience his very best. His fans sensed this and remained loyal to the end.

Everything Fred became as a man can be found and recognized in his formative years—a blueprint, as it were. In it you see the entrepreneuring, the determination, the bright and inventive mind, the shyness, the quick tongue that caused him such trouble, and the tempestuous relationships of two talented siblings—Tom and Fred—who, as their mother said, "couldn't get along *with* and couldn't get along *without* each other."

You also see his small-town musical background, the heavy-handed religious ambience that Fred later rejected, the great, great pride in his American heritage, the incredible love and devotion shown to his mother, which was also later bestowed on his personal and working families and friends, and the drive for perfection that made him so loved and so hated.

I shall start at the beginning.

1

The Victorian Warings

FREDERIC MALCOLM WARING was born June 9, 1900—the beginning of a new century. He arrived during the Victorian era, and he died eighty-four years later in the computer and space age. He grew up in the small, closely knit town of Tyrone, Pennsylvania, located precisely in the middle of the state fifteen miles northeast of Altoona. The population in 1900 was around five thousand, about the same as today. Tyrone was an important railroad center with its roundhouse and yards full of tracks and freight cars. It also counted on the paper mill, dirty and malodorous, for its economic health. But when the rail terminus was closed and the mill stopped functioning, the town became a peaceful, quiet community where retirees and commuters to this day choose to live.

Fred's mother, Jesse Calderwood, and his father, Frank Waring, were twenty and twenty-one when they married. Frank was a banker, the kind who loaned money based on a person's character. His salary was fifty dollars a month. Five children were born to Frank and Jesse, all two years apart: Helen, Monroe (Bud), Fred, Tom, and Dolly.

"We were all born in a small house that my father built on Washington Avenue," Helen said. "When Fred was about five, a most pretentious estate came up for grabs, which Father got for a low down payment. We went from a seven-room house to a twenty-seven room house full of gables, bay windows, and turrets. It had two bathrooms with even a foot bath. We lived on 'top street,' I'll tell ya!"[1]

The Waring property, in the middle of town next to the high school, included an orchard, a vineyard, an enormous stable, and an icehouse. Frank converted the stable into four apartments. Then he remodeled the icehouse into a home. Later he divided the original house into two homes. He did most of the work himself, Fred handing him the bricks. It only seems natural that in the forties when Fred acquired the Worthington property at Shawnee-on-Delaware, Pennsylvania, with its hotel, golf course, and summer houses, that he would choose a carriage house with an adjacent icehouse to remodel into our home.

The Waring children were raised in a strictly disciplined home surrounded by a number of narrow-minded, old-fashioned Methodists on both sides of the family. But the Warings had their share of eccentricities.

Tom Waring tells the story of his dad's brother Uncle Waldy. "Sadie, his wife, used to get the itch to go someplace, and she'd often just go. Once when she'd been gone for about a month, she came back and decided he wasn't giving her enough money, so she took him to court, and the judge said, 'You either pay her money or you go to jail.'

"Waldy said, 'She doesn't keep house for me. I will not pay her, and I will go to jail. Besides which, I have a whole big stack of books that I've never had a chance to read, and I would just relish that.' So he went to jail for thirty days. The proud Warings were completely upset and hid in shame. Mother was the only one who went to see him. She thought it was wonderful."

The Waring household was quintessentially Victorian. Frank was the patriarch and his word was law. He was a doer and an organizer who raised funds, decorated the church and home at Christmas, and played the leading parts in talent shows. He was also a champion roller skater—his children remember seeing him jump over six barrels on his skates. "Our winters were severe in those days, and we did a lot of indoor skating," Fred said.

Frank soon had Fred onstage in the town productions. His first two appearances weren't exactly S.R.O. events. When Fred was five, he was dressed as Cupid in a suit of long johns dyed pink, holding a bow and arrow, and astride a horse. And while his father sang "Cupid Is Captain of the Army," the nervous horse defecated. When Fred was six, he sang, "Little Jack Horner sat in a corner, eating a Christmas pie. He stuck in his thumb and pulled out a plum . . ." Frank had a special pie made for him so that he could pull out the plum at the right time. "I stuck in my thumb, searched frantically, couldn't find the plum and wet my pants," Fred said.

Frank, a rabid prohibitionist, sang duets with his wife Jesse at rallies and conventions. By now Fred was twelve. "Dad was a smart cookie. He knew how to get a crowd, so he thought having a young boy up there singing with him would be great for audience appeal.

"In those days brewery trucks were all pulled by teams of horses. The song we sang was called 'The Brewer's Big Horses Can't Run over Me.' Dad contrived the idea of making a noise like a locomotive. He made sand blocks for me to rub against one another—choo-choo-choo. I kept doing that with the sand blocks and then we'd sing:

> Oh . . . No . . . Boys . . . Oh . . . No!
> The turnpike's free wh-ere e-v-er I go.
> I'm a temp-er-ance enjine
> Don't choo see,
> The Brewer's big horses can't run over me!
> Choo—choo—choo.

"We got a tremendous hand," Fred said. "Today we'd say we stopped the show." When the Volstead Act was finally passed, over a presidential veto, one of the pens used to sign it was mailed to Frank for his efforts in bringing about the measure.

Frank had a razor-sharp sense of humor, but never cracked a smile when joking. Tom and Fred inherited his wit. "One time when I was quite small, Dad was holding a baby, and someone cooed, 'Oh, he's *so* content,'" Fred said. "And Dad replied, 'Oh, he's *soa*-ken wet!' I never heard my father swear, and was always delighted when he got really mad and said, '*Con sarn it!*'

"However, discipline prevailed at the dinner table. Everybody sat in place with hands clasped, the little finger on the edge of the table, and waited until Dad said the blessing. Then we could unfold our hands and start eating. But we dared not touch anything until after the blessing. If we didn't wait, it was upstairs without your dinner. Or, most often, we got thumped—a snap of the finger on the side of the temple. Dad was an expert at it."

Helen added, "If we didn't like what was on our plate, it didn't matter. We had to eat it or we didn't get anything else. Father told us to do something only once. That's the way our house was run."

· · ·

Fred's mother Jesse was spunky, witty, and feisty by nature, but completely submissive to her husband. She molded herself into the Victorian woman's role—the unwavering center of a household organized to serve the needs of everyone, especially the patriarch.

Cousin Tot Fisher, thirteen years older than Fred, knew the inner family well as a result of baby-sitting and helping with chores during the children's formative years. "The children respected their mother and took her advice," Tot said. "Jesse was smart—nothing she couldn't do. She was a marvelous cook and housekeeper, and a fine musician, but she had one of the toughest lives I think anybody could ever have. My mother used to say that some people are born to trouble, as the sparks fly up."

"She was a submerged character only where my father was concerned," Tom added, "because she felt that was the way it was supposed to be. She told my sister Dolly that she never went out with another man in her whole life."

Besides caring for her five young children, Jesse had to contend with visiting ministers who stayed at the house. She was obliged to feed them breakfast, lunch, and dinner. Frank often brought home drunks and put them in freshly made beds in the guest room. Jesse went along with it, but she had to do the cleaning up. She got everybody off to Sunday school, dressed, went to church, sang in the choir, stayed for rehearsal afterwards, came home, and prepared dinner for the family as well as the usual visiting ministers.

Fred never wanted to go to bed when guests were at the house. He had to take in everything. He hated to go to bed, a habit that stayed with him to his dying day.

Fred's younger brother Tom was ill most of these early days. He was a blue baby and had trouble breathing. Jesse had to carry him around on her hip because he couldn't lie down. When Fred was five or six, he contracted rheumatic fever. "Two people would hold two ends of a sheet and carry me to the bathroom. All I had to eat was juice, which I loved, butter thins, and a cracker." Jesse said that to have one invalid was bad enough, but to have two was a terrible strain. "One winter we all came down with diphtheria," Tom said. "The doctor came with the antitoxin, spread us all out on a bed, and with the needle punched one, two, three, four, five right down the line. The drug was very new at the time. Dad was quarantined out of the house. Not only did we get diphtheria, but the pipes froze and burst, and the ceiling came down in the parlor."

When Jesse had an infected knee, according to Tot, "Frank, who was not too sympathetic with illness—I don't think he was with anybody, as far as that goes—he was a very self-centered person—went off every morning to work, and she was left alone."

"Mother was in bed a month," Tom said. "Of course, we did nothing but fight. The only way Mother could have some peace was to keep us out of her room, and the only way she could do this was to use her horsewhip. It just reached to the door. Any of us who put our foot over the threshold got the horsewhip, and for me that was the worst thing she could have done—not to have us near her."

"Some people thought Jesse was a little too strict, but I think it paid off," Tot said. "They adored her. I think she was a wonderful mother and her sense of humor never left her. One time the doctor came to see her, and the preacher happened in at the same time, and she said, 'Well, this is just fine! All we need now is the undertaker!'"

"It was Mother who helped the boys when they were getting started," Dolly said. "She mortgaged the house many times to get them over the low period. I remember someone called, and I heard Mother saying, 'Oh, no, not again!' She didn't resent it—it was just that the repeated bank visits were a little embarrassing."

Within the Waring patriarchal family, a pronounced inequity existed in the way the boys and girls were raised. The female members were supervised, restricted, and controlled. Jesse, with little or no power of independence, was often overburdened with the rearing of five children. In today's vernacular, the Waring family probably would be termed dysfunctional because of the internal imbalances.

Helen, the eldest, was blessed with a fine mind and a wonderful disposition. Everyone adored her. The press referred to her as "plump and jolly," and that's what she was—forever smiling, laughing, and serving up delicious meals. Her life, however, told a different story.

"I wanted to go to college, but my father was against my having an education," Helen said. "It broke my heart. He was very old fashioned in his ideas. He thought a woman's place was in the home. He said that people who went to college became snobs—affected and lazy. He didn't like phonies. I went to nurse's training nearby. I do remember I was allowed to go to one dance at the hall, but my father came and took me home. That's how carefully we were guarded in those days."

Helen's life was full of heartaches and sorrows, but her bright spirit never faltered. No bitterness, no resentments—an amazing lady.

Bud, next in line, was, according to his younger sister Dolly, "a very happy-go-lucky fellow—strong and healthy. He looked after Fred and Tom like a protector. He loved animals and rode a horse as though molded on it. He used to scrub his teeth with Dutch cleanser."

Tom recalled that whenever there was trouble, "Bud usually got the licking. There's always a whipping dog in every family—and that was poor Bud. One time when Fred was about five, he built a fire on the playroom floor. Bud was blamed and was sent to bed without his supper. Father wasn't too sure about Bud's guilt, so he went to Fred and said, 'Fred, how did you get the matches?' And Fred said, 'I put the chair over by the wall (we had gas lights), climbed on the chair and got the matches.' Dad said, 'Why didn't you tell me you lit the fire?' Fred said, 'You didn't ask me.'"

"I remember Dad was going to spank me for something I deserved," Fred added, "and Bud stood up to him and said, 'Don't hit him,' so Dad turned around and spanked Bud instead."

"When Bud came back from World War I, he had been gassed and was shell-shocked," Fred continued. "His whole personality had changed. Things preyed on his mind. He built up a hatred of Mother and threatened to kill her, but she stuck with him throughout the whole thing. She was the mother of a soldier, and nobody was going to do anything to her boy. He straightened out to some degree later. He got married, but around Christmas in 1929, he was driving across the railroad track in the middle of town and was killed by a train." It was a sad time for the family.

Fred, born third of the five, didn't have any of the middle child syndrome of feeling left out or overlooked. He, too, was blessed with high intelligence, but unlike Helen was given leeway to explore and follow his inner drives. His superb agility and reflexes placed him high on the list of a father who was the local tennis champion and could jump over six barrels on roller skates.

I have briefly mentioned Tom, the blue baby. Physical weakness hovered over him from day one. Thomas Lincoln Waring, co-originator of the Pennsylvanians, was born February 12, 1902—two years after Fred. Their relationship was a classic sibling tragedy formed by hereditary, environmental, and musical differences. Tom was sickly and weak from birth; Fred strong, nimble, and forceful. Both were sensitive and creative, with goals pointed in opposite directions. Tom was permanently affected by his father's abhorrence of physical weakness and his mother's overprotecting counterbalance. Fred was a busy doer and achiever, manipulating and charming his way through life—nonintrospective and never questioning people's underlying motives.

"Tom was born prematurely," Helen said. "There were no incubators in those days, so Dr. Loewry ordered a silver spoon of whiskey when Tom's breathing was bad. For Father, a drop of liquor was a mortal sin, and if he was against something, he was against it the whole way. [He never knew that Tom was being kept alive with alcohol.] Tom took constant care—it was asthma and his heart. He was so very white—no color on his face or lips—and every day he lived was an achievement. The doctor said, 'If we can raise Tom until he is seven, then we'll be able to get him to fourteen.'"

Tom spent so many months, adding up to years, in bed that he had to learn to walk four times. "Each time I got up, my legs were weak and I didn't know what to do with them, so they had to teach me," he said. "Sunday walks with Father was a *must*. It was also a form of discipline. I wanted to go but my legs were weak. I was going into boyhood with flat feet and unprepared legs. When I was about eleven, the first little hike I went on was a twenty-mile walk. Mother rose up in anger over that. I wanted to join the crowd. So I uncomplainingly plowed through the thing. I could barely move when I got back. But I remember on that day my father said something to me. (My attitude is liable to paint the fact that I didn't like my father, because he didn't like me. My father was a complete stranger to me.) By then I was top-heavy (slightly fat) and he said, 'You will never walk the straight path.' In other words, he meant that somebody would have to help me. All the time which, of course, has been true. I thought he was selling me short. But it is true. Later on, when I was studying piano seriously because I wanted to do concerts, he asked me what I was doing. I told him I thought I would try the concert field because I hated being a Pennsylvanian, and he said, 'You'll never make it! You cannot go alone!'"

Tom used to make doll clothes and other things for his sisters. "All of Tom's activities were associated with the women of the household," Helen said. "Fred and the boys were not mean to Tom—he just couldn't keep up with them. If you are not strong, you are sort of discarded. Tom was never strong—never!"

When he was four, Tom would stand in front of the piano, so small he couldn't see the keys. "But I reached up and picked out a familiar melody on the black keys. From then on, I was at the piano all the time, and I played only on the black keys. Later, I took some lessons, but I never could learn to read music. I could look at a page, go through it once, and have it in my mind. I was unable to watch the music and play at the same time. It drove my teachers crazy."

Tom was restricted to the house for years, in and out of bed. One day after Fred and I were married when Tom was having breakfast at our home, I asked his opinion of some wallpaper I was considering. He confessed that he hated wall coverings because of the endless hours he had spent in bed tracing designs with his eyes day after day.

Jesse was Tom's protector throughout her life. Just before she died, she told her daughter Helen that Tom was now *her* responsibility.

In the Victorian days, an unspoken code prevailed that if something was unpleasant and you didn't want to think about it, then if you ignored it long enough, it would settle itself. Fred showed traits of this early on. When asked about the uncomfortable relationship between Tom and his father, Fred explained, "I usually disregarded all these undercurrents." He remembered nothing about his mother and the horsewhip. He had closed it completely out of his mind. In later years, such an attitude made it difficult for his employees. Unfortunately, unpleasant things just don't go away when you're running a huge enterprise.

Dolly, the youngest, was her father's favorite. She was cute, lively, and a tomboy. When the boys went tobogganing, she never used a sled. She went "belly gutter." She was forever tagging along, getting in their games, even though the boys told her to go away. "I ran and jumped and everything else they did," Dolly reflected. "I thought I was equal to them, and wanted to be with the boys all the time. When Tom played every Saturday night for dances, I wasn't allowed to go."

• • •

Two other people were important in Fred's early life—his great-grandfather and his lifelong friend Roland (Poley) McClintock.

Fred's great-grandfather William Griffith Waring was born in England and came to the United States around 1830. He became a farmer, teacher, school principal, and horticulturist, the only surveyor to be found in the Centre region of Pennsylvania in the 1850s, a flute player, stenographer, master of four languages (Latin, Greek, French, and German), contributor to many farm journals, and later editor of the *New York Tribune*'s horticultural department. He is best remembered as the first administrator of the Farmer's High School (later Penn State University), a job he never wanted and found uncongenial.

Being first administrator meant William Griffith Waring was in charge of clearing the land, burning scrub, and hauling away stones. He was also responsible for the erection of farm buildings. Waring laid out the original plans of the campus and supervised plantings. He wrote: "My retiring nature and independent, unyielding way, plain, candid, and unceremonious, soon got me into trouble with other members of the faculty, and with the boys."[2] Truly, seeds of Fred Waring. On campus is a Waring Hall and, in town, a Waring Avenue, both named after William Griffith, not Frederic Malcolm.

"My great-grandfather lived a block away from us," Fred recalled. "I remember his house—a bay window in which he sat in his rocking chair, and the smell of nasturtiums and geraniums and the apple pie that Aunt Mary used to make. Great-grandfather was ninety years old, and he decided that my schooling was going to be his responsibility. I remember, as though it were yesterday actually, the first day I went to school, the Park Avenue School. He took me in (I was just five) and made sure the people there knew who I was, and I was supposed to get treated as though I was six years old.

"And then I remember later, when we had moved up to Lincoln Avenue, he came up and fussed around until darned if he didn't get away with having me skip a grade. Consequently, I finished high school fairly young."

Fred's playmate Poley McClintock was born in Tyrone, in September of 1900, three months after Fred came into the world. Theirs became a touching friendship that lasted until Poley's death in 1979. Poley was a warm, lovable, shy man who developed a comedic talent and a frog voice that was later copied in a Hollywood cartoon character. As kids, Poley and Fred ran all over town chasing fire engines, hiking, camping out, and visiting the ice caves, but it was the formation of the Boy Scout movement in 1910 that sealed their close friendship.

"Of all the kids in town, Poley and I were the most enthusiastic," Fred said. "We had read up on Boy Scouts, and we were ready for it. We were the first ones down there, but were told that we couldn't join for two years when we became twelve. We must have bothered them to death, because they finally made us mascots or forerunners of Cub Scouts. Our wait was the most torturous of my memory, but finally the day came for me to join, and, lo and behold, I realized Poley would have to wait three months, and they just wouldn't break their rules, so I waited, and on Poley's birthday we both joined."

As a Pennsylvanian, Poley played the drums, and even though Fred later became "Boss" of the band, he not only remained Poley's friend but became his protector as well—always watching out for him.

•   •   •

Church in the Waring household was a normal routine. "We had no resistance to church customs—Sunday school and prayer meetings," Fred said. "But there were several things about the Methodist set-up that kind of got my goat—you couldn't play cards or dance, and they wouldn't let us read the funny papers on Sunday. Aunt Anne, Mother's sister, always bought the Sunday paper, so we'd sneak out in the afternoon to her home to read the comic strips. Our favorites were 'Katzenjammer Kids,' 'Happy Hooligans,' 'Hair Breadth Harry,' and 'Little Nemo.'

"Every time they had one of these Methodist conferences, we housed ministers—and a more boring group of people I don't think I could possibly meet up with. They would sanctimoniously put their hands on our heads and tell us what fine young people we were going to be. Then they would criticize us for something we would want to do or had done. As long as I've lived, I've had a strong resentment for this type.

"The minister's son was a very close friend of mine. He used to stay at my house one night, and then I would go to his house another night. We would have a marvelous time at my house. We laughed and had fun. But when I would go to his house, there was so much restriction and discipline that I felt sorry for that kid. We had quite a bit of discipline but we were a laughing house. I couldn't understand why there shouldn't be more happiness mixed with religion. Sure, I knew the Twenty-third Psalm, the Apostle's Creed, and all those other things as well as anybody else. I was a good Bible student, and I won my little mementos and prizes along with the rest of them, but I couldn't find anybody really happy—enjoying life in its fullest—who was close to this religious movement.

"After Poley and I joined the Boy Scouts, I began to realize that whoever had put together the Scout Oath had found the key to the good life. There's nothing in the Boy Scouts that would say you shouldn't have a good time, because to smile is part of the 'Scout is cheerful!' And do a good deed daily—well, that's part of your Bible teachings. A revelation struck me that nothing about being a good person had not been thoroughly covered in the Boy Scout creed or code. I decided these were the fundamentals I would try to live by." That, in essence, was the religion of choice for Fred Waring. In 1912, when Fred joined, one of the first scoutmasters was John Porter, who lived in Tyrone and became the best known scout leader of the day. "We called him 'Uncle John,'" Fred said. "He took an interest in all the kids. We would drop by, loaf around, and run errands. He was a special human being—sometimes called us 'scallywags.'"

"Uncle John had more influence on Fred and Poley than any other person except our mother," Helen added. "Fred's character was formed by that contact. His belief in things national and his belief in the land were the governing factors of his youth."

· · ·

The Waring household was a busy one. Frank spent time with his children but usually in an instructional way. "We took afternoon walks practically every day," Fred recalled. "He had a pedometer and barometer. We would climb a mountain, and he would tell us exactly in feet how high we were."

The Waring children's interest in athletics was fostered by the Pennsylvania Railroad, which subsidized a professional baseball team that supplied Philadelphia athletic teams with players. "The Pennsylvania Railroad thought so much of their team that they built a splendid athletic plant in Tyrone—a gorgeous baseball field, fine tennis courts, and a wonderful swimming pool, and later on, a golf course and a track," Fred said. "The town was agog with athletic events, track meets and state tennis matches. I used to go out in the morning, play five hours of tennis and walk back, and finally my feet just broke down—but that's how much I loved the game."

Every summer when school was out, the family went down to Iroquois and stayed for two months on the Juniata River. It was at Iroquois that Tom found the one sport in which he could excel—swimming. "I had been fooling around with water wings for a year or so. Bud came along and said, 'It's ridiculous—you can swim.' He threw me into the pool and walked away. I suddenly realized he was right. I could swim. From then on, I swam like a fish. But I was never good in any kind of team sport." Years later when Tom bought a house in Shawnee, he became a much-loved community member of the town of Stroudsburg, Pennsylvania, and supported the baseball and softball teams. It was his way of finally participating in team sports.

• • •

Saturday was chore day. Each week the children were given different jobs—keeping the furnace going, carrying coal to the kitchen stove, chopping wood, and helping with the housekeeping—dusting and so forth. "We were expected to work and didn't expect to be paid for anything we did," Fred said.

"Saturday was a battleground, as Father worked in the bank that day," Helen added. "No one wanted to do anything and there was always a fight before the day was over. Bud was an aggressive bombastic sort, Fred was quiet, Tom was not at all aggressive."

Tom's recollection was that "Fred and Bud didn't fight a lot—only every waking hour. To show the wisdom of Mother, she got a stick and sent them out on the lawn in the backyard. The houses were all around, so all the women put up their windows to watch what was going on, and when they wouldn't fight, Mother would hit them a crack to make them fight some more and exhausted them. They never fought outside any-more."

"Poley and I loved each other, we worked together," Fred recalled. "But we had a terrible fight one time. I don't recall what the hell it was. I think I was trying to bend his will. I beat him black and blue. Mother kept me in the house for three days. I remember one time when there were a couple of piles of bricks, and Tom and I got to tossing them back and forth. We were throwing them farther and farther, and suddenly he forgot to duck, and one hit him on the head. I was always accused of deliberately throwing a brick at him to hurt him. It was a very friendly thing. We were practicing dodging bricks. Another time Dolly, who was a rather obstreperous youngster—a real tomboy—was chasing me, and I made a sudden stop and gave her the stiff arm, and she ran into it. And, of course, it shocked and embarrassed her, and she went screaming to Mother, and everybody said I hit her. She just used to nettle the devil out of me."

Fred was the champion corset-tightener. Even Aunt Ann used to get him to lace her snugly. The women would stand in their camisoles, and Fred would brace himself and pull the laces around the steel hooks. Fred also worked the sewing machine foot pedal by hand when his mother stitched.

The children had baths Saturday night, from head to toe, and were only allowed to go out on Saturday nights to the Bijou for five cents. "Father didn't approve of movies because a boy in Dolly's class had ruined his eyes at the movies," Tom explained. "They neglected to say the kid was there every night and sat in the front row."

• • •

Cherished memories for the Warings were two things: delicious food and festive holidays. Everyone agreed that Jesse was a superb cook à la Pennsylvania Dutch cuisine, although today the amount of butter, salt, and sugar she used would not be condoned.

Frank was no slouch in the kitchen, either. He regularly made scrapple. "I can see him doing it, grinding the meat and adding the cornmeal," Helen said. "The oyster stew became a Christmas ritual. The strawberry shortcake was one whole meal. Huckleberry shortcake and peach shortcake—the entire meal."

"When my father made anything in the kitchen, you couldn't find an inch of space," Tom added. "He got everything out that there was."

To please Fred years later, I occasionally carried out the tradition of strawberry shortcake for a complete meal (or most of it.) It's not your usual sweet cake with whipped cream, but a large, rather thick, warm square of biscuit cut in half, buttered, and then placed in a deep bowl. Generous helpings of smashed sweetened strawberries are placed on the bottom half and on top of the upper half. Cold milk covers it all, and it's eaten with a soup spoon. Sometimes on a summer evening at Shawnee, we would sit outside in our pretty courtyard with friends and enjoy Fred's famous frozen daiquiris, a clear soup, and the Waring strawberry shortcake. An odd meal but tasty.

With this constant reference to all the great food that filled the Waring household, the big joke in our marriage was that I have managed to get through life without cooking at all! At least my daughters-in-law are spared having a formidable mother-in-law who's a fantastic cook.

· · ·

Christmas was the big holiday event for the Warings. "We had a huge house," Tom said. "Both parlor and living room had a big bay window from floor to ceiling. We therefore had a tree with candles that touched the ceiling. Friends came over on Christmas Eve to help trim the tree because it was so big, and then they got the kids up to open their presents. After they put us back to bed, the grownups supped on Dad's oyster stew." I grew up in a family where no one dreamed of opening a present before Christmas Day. Fred and I compromised—some on Christmas Eve, and the rest the next day.

"We decorated the church, we decorated the house," Helen remembered. "In later years, no matter what Fred's schedule was, we all tried to be together. The emphasis was being together with festive food and drink. The other big celebration was the Fourth of July. Five thousand people lived in town, and everybody was in the parade. Father was community minded. He provided fireworks on our big front lawn for everyone to enjoy." Later, in the forties, when Fred bought Shawnee Inn, he too carried on the tradition by giving the local citizens an impressive display of fireworks each year.

· · ·

Parties for young people were planned, with ice cream, cake, and games such as "post office" and "spin the bottle." However, dancing and playing cards were taboo for Methodists. "Street car rides were a great recreation but they were costly," Fred noted. "A nickel a ride, you know. That was pretty expensive. Neilmont and Altoona—an important ride because that was fourteen miles. Dad would take us up there to buy our suits and shoes.

"We had a very, very secret society called MLIC—the Missing Link Indian Club. Our clubhouse was a deserted pigeon coop. It wasn't very big, so our members were a select few. The rules and technicalities of the weekly track meets were all made behind the closed doors of that shack. We were bothered a lot by Doll, who insisted on sneaking in and disrupting it. Freddy Buck led the singing, which must have sounded pretty terrible to anyone who happened to be passing by outside the clubhouse. Even now I can hear very faintly the sound of 'I Want a Girl Just like the Girl Daddy Used to Have,' when of a night we were permitted to take an oil lamp and have an evening meeting."

An invention of his father's was the subject of one of Fred's first memories. He was four. "I remember he built a derrick for us," Fred said. "It had a coal scuttle and a very tall pole (to us it was very tall), probably only ten or fifteen feet high. He would put us kids in the coal scuttle, pull us up in the derrick, and turn us around in it. It was quite a thrill!"

When Frank moved his family to the twenty-seven-room house, Fred appropriated a round (ten feet in diameter) steeple room with windows all around that sat above the three floors below. It became his experimental workshop hideaway. "I read in *Popular Mechanics* how to make a glider," Fred recalled. "My cousins owned the planing mill, so I went there and picked up some scrap lumber. I knew the lumber had to be light, but unfortunately it was not good. I made the glider and decided to try it by jumping off the porch roof. I jumped. The glider fell apart because the lumber wasn't strong enough and the air was too heavy for it. The frame broke and I landed on the ground. I hit my chin on my knee and bit my tongue." Of course, I wondered if he broke any bones, and Fred said, "Just the glider and my desire to make one. Then I built a wireless radio set. I was getting messages. It hit the national newspapers.

"My next project was a searchlight. I got some carbons, some wire and a coffee can and one of those lamp mirror reflectors that they used to put on oil lamps. It was the most fantastic light you have ever seen. How I avoided burning the house down. . . . I blew fuses, and the wires would get red hot. I could shoot this searchlight a mile away. I used to scatter the lovers clear across town. They hated me."

"When we were eleven, Fred appeared one cold winter's day with something he called the 'red go-devil,'" Poley said. "It was a bright red sled with only *one* runner, bicycle handlebars, and a seat. He announced it would go faster than any sled built, and that only he would be able to ride it."

Fred admitted fifty years later that it was a miserable thing and one of the toughest to ride.

As a twelve-year-old Boy Scout, Fred invented and made himself a belt in first aid that later became standard equipment. This was a pattern that Fred followed for the rest of his life. He was always dreaming about, working on, or creating something—usually gadgets for the home to make life easier.

. . .

Around 1918 Frank received two blows to his self-esteem that resulted in a fragmentation of the Waring family. When Bud returned from World War I and refused to comply with his father's unreasonable demands on his personal life, Frank was shaken by the realization that his power over his sons was weakening. At the same time Frank was pushed out of the bank he had helped create fifteen years before.

"When Dad was crowded out of the bank, it broke his heart because it was his own baby," Helen said. "His health deteriorated, and the doctor said he had to work at something in the fresh air because of his asthmatic tendencies. He got into real estate. He would buy a plot and sell it for more. Buy and sell, and that's how he acquired the land around Harrisburg where he built his first golf course. Ninety-nine percent of Dad's work was around Harrisburg, a day's drive from Tyrone. At first he would come back once a week. Later, every two weeks. But then he began to come home less and less, and finally after a few years, he didn't come home at all." As a result, Frank Waring entered a new lifestyle that fed the gossip mill of Tyrone, Pennsylvania. His actions mortified the family, but the hurt was especially deep for Jesse, the deserted wife.

When I joined the Pennsylvanians, no one ever talked about Fred's father, who had died in 1939. After we were married, neither Tom nor Fred mentioned their father when we were chatting about family. I knew only that he had left home for good about the mid-twenties, but no one would talk about it. Not wishing to disturb what seemed to be a deep wound, I never probed until finally in 1980 I called Fred's sister Helen and said, "I need to see you and ask some questions."

"Fine!" she said. I drove to the country club in York, Pennsylvania, which she was still running at age eighty-four, and there she greeted me with a big smile and a warm hug. I set the tape recorder on the table and said, "Now! What happened to your father?"

Without any hesitation, she said, "A woman! Of course!"

We both laughed, and then Helen continued: "When he didn't come home and we heard he was seeing a woman, we were shocked. He had been so exemplary before. He never got a divorce. It wrecked Mother because she was crazy about Father."

"Did you ever meet the other woman?" I asked.

"Oh, yes. Very nice. Not educated, but very kind to him. As his asthma worsened, she took good care of him, drove him to Florida several winters. She was thirty years younger." Frank Waring would have been around fifty in the mid-twenties, which made her barely twenty.

"Tom and Fred were absolutely marvelous to Mother. Tom once said, 'My mother was badly hurt, and I made myself a committee of one to relieve that hurt.' Tom and Fred overwhelmed her with care and kindness to offset her heartbreak, and they did a beautiful job. I'm proud of both of them.

"Once when Dolly was complaining about Fred and his behavior (women, of course), I said, 'Dolly, listen, I'll never forget how marvelous he was to his mother. Whatever sins of any size, shape, or form that stand out, *that* washed them away.'

"At first Fred and Tom didn't treat Father very nicely, and rightly so, because of Mother. But when Father became ill, I went over to Harrisburg. I felt sorry for him. All I tried to remember was how marvelous he was and his attitudes to poor people and to black people, and his skills. He was as talented in banking work as he was in agricultural and architectural things. He could have had a profession either way."

Fred: "One of Mother's last confessions to me was that it was she who had been at fault. She could have avoided the whole thing if she had not been so blindly stubborn."

2

Entrepreneur

TODAY with music bombarding us in restaurants, elevators, stores, malls, and airplanes, and from radios and videos, one forgets that at the beginning of the twentieth century the only music heard, except for a few primitive recordings, was that made by people themselves. Growing up as he did in a small town far removed from cities, Fred's musical background was not as arid as one might imagine.

"Father and Mother had gorgeous voices," Helen said. "They sang everywhere for weddings and all sorts of gatherings. Everybody used to go to funerals to hear them sing. They would come home and tell what happened, like the iceman who, not realizing what was going on inside, came to the back door and yelled '*Ice*' at the top of his lungs. Or the ambitious young undertaker addressing the deceased family and friends at the end of the service and informing them he was going to use a new 'lowering device' and urging everybody to come out to the cemetery and see how it worked.

"Father couldn't read music, but Mother had some piano training, and they would work out the program for each Sunday with three or four people, sometimes three or four hours into the night. Then, if it didn't suit Papa, they all came back again. But when they got up there at church, it was a joy—Father's precision. Fred has every bit of it."

A quote drawn from an article in Penn State's magazine *Town and Gown* states: "Frank Malcolm Waring sang in the 'Thousand Dollar Quartet' at the Methodist Church in Tyrone, Pennsylvania, so-called because the first member in line had straight legs and the other three were bowlegged."[1] Fred must have inherited his father's tendency because he said, "Poley and I were so bowlegged as kids that we wore steel braces on our legs."

·   ·   ·

In many ways, the Waring home was Tyrone's musical mecca. "We had the first phonograph, and Dad made our house the musical center of town by giving concerts on Sunday on this Edison with its cylindrical records," Fred recalled. "I can still hear him announce 'The Edison Military Concert Band'! We also had local talent recitals in that room. If we kids were good we could stay up a little late sitting on the steps listening."

Those Sunday night concerts made a deep impression on Fred as he peered from behind the banisters, listening and absorbing. He reproduced that scene many times during the five years of the General Electric shows in the early fifties. I represented Emma Voght, the town pianist, playing an upright piano with its back to the staircase, just as Fred remembered it.

·   ·   ·

From the start, Fred was entrepreneuring, bossing everything and anything that interested him. He probably was born that way, but his physical stature, I'm sure, had much to do with his drive to succeed. He was only five-feet-six and one hundred and twenty-eight pounds when fully grown.

According to family and friends, young Freddy Waring was always observing, always thinking of new or better ways of doing something, planning ahead, and then *doing* it. He had an iron will. Actually, with his charisma, good looks, brains, and determination, he could have ended up a complete scoundrel. Fortunately, his small-town moral Boy Scout upbringing helped keep a balance.

I asked Helen what Fred was like as a little boy. "Closed up but very aware. I can see him yet when the house was full of people. Very quiet, but his eyes were talking. He'd grin. He was always on the outside of the crowd, was never crazy about parties as a teenager."

"He was always quiet," Dolly added. "You never knew what he was thinking. He's never been an easy person to talk to."

When Tot was asked if Fred were shy, she (giving a derisive laugh) said, "You can be shy as well as pretty doggone smart."

And Tom added, "Well, let's put it, he was *method* shy. That could be one of the reasons he always got what he wanted. The three of us boys had the third floor. There were two double beds. Fred was the skinny one,

Bud was fat, and I was hefty. Bud and I always had to share one double bed, and Fred always had the other one. Why? Because he was Fred, I imagine. Even at that age. Oh, yes, definitely!"

And the future entrepreneur was also orderly. He always folded his clothes perfectly, whether they were clean or had to be washed. "There Bud and I would be on our side of the room with our clothing scattered all over the place—we just *dropped* everything—and across the room, Fred's knickerbockers would be folded, his long black stockings carefully hung over the footrail of his bed, his shoes exactly in place, and he would be sound asleep—with his eyes open," Tom said. "We used to crawl over and peek at him to make sure. His eyes wouldn't ever be quite shut. In the morning the bed we slept in looked just awful. When Fred got out of bed, you could just see where he was—not a wrinkle or rumple in the covers. He never moved." The half-open eyes I never saw, but the bed—yes—its unblemished appearance in the morning attesting to the totally immobile occupant—it was a mystery that anyone could sleep so quietly.

When Fred, the entrepreneur, became a Boy Scout at age twelve, he saw the need for a drum and fife corps. The older kids and the big shots weren't doing anything about it. "Here was a great opportunity," Fred said. "So I went to work. I went up to Mr. Anderson, head of the paper company, and told him we needed drums. He gave us drums. I got Poley to teach the drums, and another friend, Freddy Campbell, to teach the fife. That left me nothing, so I went and made myself a baton out of an old curtain rod of Mother's, and decided I would be the drum major. It was a wooden curtain rod with fine brass ornaments on each end."

During an interview with columnist Jack O'Brian in 1980, Fred said, "Our drum corps was in all the parades—my thirteenth, fourteenth, fifteenth, and sixteenth years. I had so much experience bossing—"

O'Brian: "—that you've never given it up!"[2]

Fred also became a patrol leader, and immediately organized and rehearsed his troops until they were experts at signaling. "We knew every code, and were tops in first aid. We built a truck cart in which to carry our stuff to camp. Our tent was immaculate. In fact, morning inspection would call for a maximum of ten points for a perfect tent. Day after day we would be eleven, and sometimes twelve points for our innovations." The perfectionist, at age twelve.

Poley interpreted Fred's actions in another way, calling him a good leader with a way of handling the boys, but Fred noted the price that leadership brings even at that tender age. He said the other troops were jealous and resentful, and consequently were taunting and teasing all the time.

"I was cocky; had a sarcastic tongue, and they cut me down constantly. I was the smallest patrol leader of all the whole sixty-four kids, yet nobody ever struck me—an amazing thing."

. . .

In 1912, when Fred was twelve, the high school hired a superintendent named J. L. Gaunt, who happened to be a fine musician. He formed a glee club "out of sheer boredom." As he said, "A teacher in a small town like that is under the microscopic inspection of everybody, and there was little else for me to do. There was a lot of interest in music in Tyrone, because the Pennsylvania Railroad had a band and it was located there. The railroad company put sixty-five men on the payroll as timekeepers, mechanics, and so on. They wandered about the shops in the morning, and in the afternoons they would rehearse in the YMCA auditorium. They had some very fine professionals; seven or eight of them were Sousa men. When we had high school entertainment, we merely asked for as many musicians as we needed, and we got them for nothing."

Fred started playing a three-quarter-size fiddle when he was nine. "I enjoyed playing until I was forced to play in the high school orchestra," he said. "They appealed to my father as a member of the school board to have me play in the orchestra because evidently I was a fairly good student. I went to a rehearsal and I couldn't stand it. They played so badly out of tune. Just imagine, I'm thirteen years old and talking about inferior musicians. I didn't go back any more.

"The principal went to the superintendent, who went to my father and said, 'We need Fred in the orchestra,' which was embarrassing to my father, who thought I'd been going to rehearsals all the time. So Dad had a heart-to-heart talk with me—he did all the talking—which wound up this way: 'Either you play in the high school orchestra or you give up the violin.' That night I put the violin on the shelf, and I have never played a note since. My reasoning was this: if I must be forced to play in surroundings which are distasteful, then I don't want any part of it. Music, to me, was always something which should be enjoyed."

Although Fred's formal training on the violin was short-lived, he probably didn't spend long hours practicing. With his fantastic ear and flexible fingers, he probably played well with very little effort, just as in his studies—with a prodigious memory, he could glide through school without ever hitting the books.

"I enjoyed school," Fred said. "It was easy for me, but I hated to study. I liked to get into a project where I could work with my hands and work and work and work to do it. But where it requires making notes and studying formulas and things like that, I don't like it. I hated languages because you had to memorize; I hated history. I was an excellent mathematics student but I disliked making full reports.

"I reported to the high school glee club and was immediately accepted. I sang first tenor my freshman year, second tenor my sophomore year, baritone my junior year, and bass my senior year. I always sang where I was needed. Our glee club was great. J. L. Gaunt, our teacher, who had a splendid baritone voice, knew how to train kids. I was excited! This was doing music which got response! The rest of my music had just been participation. Now we're onstage, now we're doing concerts, now I'm entertaining people! It was a tremendously exhilarating influence. I give Mr. Gaunt credit for inspiring me into going into glee club work. In my junior year, we organized the Scrap Iron Quartet. Walter Harmer was top tenor, Squee Cherry second tenor, I was baritone, and Freddy Buck was bass. We were the four they pulled out of the glee club for special entertainment. I was president of the glee club for two years. Our glee club was state champion."

"I remember Fred as a very sober, serious kid—more or less a lone wolf," Gaunt recalled. "He had intense interest in mathematics and science. I thought he was going to be an electrical engineer. When we started a chorus, Fred was my greatest support in getting people interested. He was my secretary. He was a shy, intense boy. But not timid. He had a keen sense of time and a deep love of melody. He rehearsed himself relentlessly and insisted that others do the same."

• • •

Meanwhile, Fred could not escape his leadership role—whether staging banquets, setting up track meets, or launching the Pennsylvanians on their destined orbit. When Fred was a high school senior, he was appointed banquet chairman. "I wanted to be certain that this was a banquet everybody would remember, so I got a history of all other class banquets, and I did it up in brown," he said. "I decorated the place and had everything in fine shape. We had a tremendous turnout. But many people at this banquet didn't eat their food. We had the banquet on Friday and I had chosen roast pork. A number of Catholics and Jewish people were in our class, and I was unaware of it."

Then came the amateur Olympics. "Fred used to stage Saturday afternoon track meets around the house," Tom said. "He dug a pit for jumping and pole vaulting. He used to line the track up every Saturday morning and get it all set up. He entrepreneured everything he got into sooner or later."

One maneuver of Fred's that Tom did resent concerned a little piano/drum combo that he and Poley had started. It was the embryo of the future Pennsylvanians, and there are two versions of what happened.

"At first I didn't sing at all," Tom said. "I was the piano player in the family. In our early teens, Mrs. Beaston started a dancing class, and Poley and I went. Everybody finally got tired of dancing to records, so somebody said, 'Why don't you play for us?' Since I knew all the songs, I sat down and played them, but I got bored doing it by myself, so I decided Poley had to help out. That was the beginning of it all. I sang and played the rhythm. We thought we were pretty great stuff." However, it wasn't a very profitable arrangement for Poley, who had only a snare drum and had to rent a bass drum. He and Tom got fifty cents apiece a night to play, and Poley had to pay fifty cents for the bass drum.

"But pretty soon we were making a little money—just Poley and me," Tom said. "Fred and Freddy Buck, a Tyrone pal, had learned to play the ukulele and, without so much as a 'May we?' or 'May we not?' they sat in. They muscled in and sat down. What we had for the two of us we had to split for the four of us. Poley and I had about one season before Fred moved in."

Fred's version of the birth of the Pennsylvanians was slightly different: "The year was 1917. Tom was fifteen, and I was seventeen. A dance band was needed in town—but how could an older brother who had taken dancing lessons and who had played violin and been leader of the Boy Scout corps and was president of the glee club and in charge of the Scrap Iron Quartet sit by and let Tom and Poley make mistakes? So Freddy Buck and I *volunteered* to go in and help them. They were willing to take Freddy, but they weren't too sure about me. I said, 'Why don't I help you, because I know how to dance and I know the right tempos?' I was sincerely anxious that they not make any mistakes, and I felt they were a little young. I was two years older and knew more about it.

"When Freddy Buck and I joined Poley and Tom, we both were playing ukuleles. Then I struck upon the idea of getting a banjo. We had heard a visiting Negro band from Columbus named Guy Hall. The leader fascinated us because he was a banjo player who played all four strings at the same time. The only banjo we had ever heard was like a mandolin, just a guy playing melody. Suddenly, here's a fellow who plays a swinging beat in full chords that gave life to the band. Well, that just knocked us out. I borrowed an old five-string banjo with a long neck that Poley's father had. I used only four strings and played it more or less like a ukulele. Freddy Buck got hold of a tenor banjo, which is strung like a violin; he was a very good violinist.

"Guy Hall's wife played piano. They had a bass player and a violinist. They played and sang this haunting melody, and Mrs. Hall sang a beautiful obbligato. That's when I decided we should always have a glee club in our band. That was the development of the two banjos, piano, and drums. So the Banjazztra combo started playing for dances." Banjazztra, incidentally, is a contraction of *banjo jazz* orche*stra*. It was Fred's idea, I'm sure. Some forty years later he thought Virginia Junia would be the perfect name if our expected child were a girl. Fortunately, we had a boy.

The newly formed Banjazztra was gaining confidence as it played for an occasional dance. One was an annual party at Lakemont Park. "Here we were, the four of us, in our beautiful, skin-tight white trousers, blue shirts dyed by Tom, and white ties," Fred recalled. "It was an open air place, and *wham!* came the worst thunder and lightning storm you have ever seen or heard. The rain went right through the roof. Our banjos got soggy—couldn't get any sound, and then, to make matters worse, the heads broke. Here we were—piano and drums. Freddy Buck and I had nothing to play, and so we sang every number. We made a real big hit and were booked to play somewhere a little farther away. We got over twelve dollars that night—three dollars apiece. That was the beginning of our career—July 1, 1917."

• • •

Fred's teenage goal was to attend Pennsylvania State University (then Pennsylvania State College), a relatively small institution just over the mountain ridge from Tyrone. Although engineering would be his major, Fred's number-one priority was to become a member of the glee club. But his relationship with Penn State was not an easy one. He had to struggle just to get there and once there was treated rather harshly—a love/hate affair that lasted nearly forty years.

After receiving his high school diploma, Fred recalled approaching his father with eager anticipation. "I said, 'Well, Dad, I've decided where I'm going to college,'—you remember he was a banker."

"He said, 'Well, that's fine.'

"I said, 'I'm going to Penn State.'

"He said, 'Well, that will be nice to have someone in your generation go to Penn State. How are you going to do it?'

"I said, 'Aren't you going to send me to college?'

"He said, 'Of course not. Anyone as bright as you who gets through high school as easily as you certainly can get through college the same way.'

Fred was a bit rebuffed and upset. So he tried another tactic. "I said, 'Will you loan me the money?'

"He said, 'No sir!'

"I said, 'Will you help me borrow the money?'

"He said, 'No.'

"I said, 'How can I go to college if I don't have any money?'

"He said, 'Earn your way. Get a job. Make sure you deserve a college education.'"

At the time Fred thought it was a little unfair but he didn't give up. He asked his father, "Will you help me get a job?"

Frank, enthusiastic at last, said, "You bet I will."

Frank immediately obtained a job for Fred and his buddy Poley in the bakery division of the Hoffman Ice Cream Factory. At a salary of ten dollars a week, they felt that the dream of a college education seemed far away. "I would be in the bakery, greasing bread pans very early each morning—six o'clock," Fred said. "And then I would catch the bread as they pulled it out of the oven. You had a little hot pad in each hand, and these fellows would have their long scoops and pull these four loaves at a time on a hot metal thing, and as they slid the loaves out of the oven and into the air, you had to catch them with these pads. And if you dropped either of your pads, you really got it. Sometimes they would deliberately change the timing so you would be caught coming up just about the time the pans of hot bread would be coming down. [Fred used this tactic later on to keep the Pennsylvanians on their toes—changing the timing every night.]

"I learned to do everything in the bakery—greasing pans, kneading the dough, making ladyfingers, macaroons, and charlotte russe—in addition to driving the bread truck. Then I was given the bread route. You recall the war was on, so we got the old war bread. It was horrible stuff, and the bread business went to nothing as far as the delivery to homes was concerned. I built up that darn business about twelve hundred percent. I hustled. I was getting ten dollars a week. And then I'd work overtime and I would get two dollars extra in my envelope. I got charge of five trucks within a period of a few months. I learned to swear. I tell you, there was no one who could outswear me, because again it was the stature thing. All the rest of the truck drivers were big."

In the winter the most arduous truck-driving chore was allotted to the two teenagers. They had to go out into the country and collect milk from the farmers for the ice cream vats. "I well remember many times we'd leave at five in the morning and get back at nine in the evening on a route that usually took an hour and a half," Fred said. "I can recall times when I'd be going along driving the truck with Poley riding in the rear end, and find he had fallen off and was hundreds of yards back in the deep snow. As I was progressing, I thought I was pretty important—a big shot, you know. So I wrote a note to Mr. Hoffman one day (after I got my twelve dollars and was exhausted) specifying that I felt it was time I got a raise—that I'd increased the bread business over a thousand percent, and surely I was entitled to at least one percent of that thousand. I got a note back: 'Who asked you to increase the route business?'

"I was terribly brought down. In the meantime, the government had started to build an acetone plant in town, and the union crowd had marched in. They were paying carpenters' helpers five dollars a day. So I left and went right up and got a job at the acetone plant." But Fred was to learn another lesson about the inequities of life. He found to his dismay that good intentions and industriousness are not always received with acclaim. "I had been working fourteen hours a day and hard, and I reported for this job—signed all the necessary gadgets and punched the clock—and went to my foreman and he said, 'There's one thing I want you to do. Punch that clock every day in and out, and then stay out of sight.' It took me a while to figure out that this was one of those cost-plus things. The more they make it cost, the more the contractor makes. This, to me, was stealing from the government in a time of an emergency, and it was just awful. Here I am, a Boy Scout, and I'm just full of trying to do right things. . . . I want to work! I fought with those carpenters every day because the foreman was giving them hell for letting me do anything. I quit the job in one week and went back to Dad and said, 'Dad, I need another two hundred dollars. Will you loan it to me?'

"He said, 'No sir!'

"I said, 'Will you go on my note?'

"He said, 'No.'

"So I went to Dad's competitor bank—a man with whom Dad had had some real miserable dealings. He was a real enemy. There were only two banks in town. Would he loan me the money to go to college? You bet your life he would! So I took my two hundred dollars, went to college, and entered the class of 1922 in 1918."

3

Penn State

FRED, the perpetual optimist, arrived at Penn State supremely confident that he could liquidate his bank debt. He and Freddy Buck immediately joined the Alpha Chi Rho fraternity. "I waited on table and did other odd jobs, worked in a camera shop, and tried to book engagements—not knowing how to do it—but pretty soon we were getting ten dollars apiece instead of three," Fred said. "Booking the band kept me up quite late at night writing letters on the typewriter. I ran up some large phone bills, and sometimes there were cancellations. It was hard work! Poley and Tom came over on weekends to play for dances, and they lived with us at the fraternity house and were kind of adopted."

"For me at the start it was a means to get an education. I was meeting people, and every time we played in a college town, I died because they were going to school and I wasn't," Tom said. "I was sixteen when all this started. I was working at a toggery shop and one time ordered two suits wholesale. They came Thursday. Fred came home Friday to play a dance on Saturday. My two suits went back to college with him. Fred needed them more than I did. It was an act of necessity. Fred and I were thrown together in a common interest. He naturally took over, which was fine—entrepreneuring. I had no particular resentment at the time because I hoped it was all temporary. I still had my mind on greater things."

Since Fred and Freddy Buck weren't able to play with the band during the week, there had to be two replacements—Bud Rapsey on sax and Kibe Freeman on banjo. They changed the name from Banjazztra to Waring/

McClintock Snap Orchestra. "Bud played a C melody saxophone and it sounded awful," Tom groaned. "In order to play with me, since I was still playing in sixes and sevens [the keys of G and C flat], he had to pull that mouthpiece out so far he had to wrap paper around the horn. It was never true."

"With all the excitement that I felt I had caused in Tyrone in high school in the quartet and glee club, I thought I would be a smash in college," Fred said. "The only thing I wanted was to be in the glee club. It was *the one* thing I wanted. I went up for the trials and they turned me down. I was crushed because two fraternity brothers who had never had any experience made the glee club. I was devastated. They told me to come back at the end of the semester for another tryout. I did, and I was turned down again. This had a terrible effect on me because it really was one of the main reasons I had come to college. I wanted that outlet. College glee clubs were big in my life. I just thought it *had* to be a part of my life."

Penn State's Glee Club's rejection of Fred was a deep and bitter blow. He never got over it. Decades later every once in a while he would hear a choir and say, "I didn't make the Penn State Glee Club." It still rankled him. I'm sure it was then that he set that firm jaw of his and silently vowed he would show them all what a pitiful mistake in judgment they had made.

One often finds similar motivating influences in other famous people. A crushing blow to a young ego sometimes never heals but festers throughout a lifetime. Franklin D. Roosevelt's relatives said he felt left out and mortified when rejected by Harvard University's most exclusive Porcellian Club. They all agreed that when he became president and attacked Wall Street and was hostile to bankers like Morgan and Whitney, he was "getting back at them."

In retrospect, Fred viewed his putdown as insidious "college politics." He saw that "the students catered to the leader, to get what they wanted. The accompanist for the glee club played piano in a dance band, but ours was so much better than his, I'm sure. He was jealous of us." Thirty-five years later when Fred returned to Penn State to conduct a music workshop, the same fellow was head of the music department. "He never even came to one of our sessions. He was still jealous."

Now I realize that Fred had not recognized the real obstacle, the faculty member who directed the Penn State Glee Club, Clarence Robinson. Many years later, still reluctant to give Fred credit now that he had become famous, Dr. Robinson claimed Fred had "made his money on jazz," then "hired 'experts' to give him those better musical effects and train his glee club." He wondered if Fred had "enough taste" to conduct sacred music, and he hadn't "noticed any difference between Fred and any of the other boys that tried out for the glee club."

I'm perfectly sure that the problem was that he *did* notice a difference. He had apparently picked up some vibes that identified Fred as a strange weed in the Halls of Ivy. To Dr. Robinson, Fred was a potential rocker of the serenely self-satisfied boat of which he was the captain.

But then Fred had a second thought: "I guess I was an awfully fresh kid. I don't suppose my habit of trying to run everything helped any— but I didn't realize for a while that personal characteristics could have so much to do with decisions of that sort. My introduction to college politics was abrupt and painful. Established campus politicians don't like upstarts. An aggressive freshman who had already attracted weekend attention with his lively dance band would be regarded as a special threat. I was never any good at personal politics, and I've always been unable to disguise my passion for changing things when I think they can be improved." The last straw was the rejection by the Thespian Club and the Penn State orchestra. However, Fred gleaned some satisfaction from the total triumph at every appearance of Waring's Banjo Orchestra. The entire student body of Penn State took a proprietary pride in the unique combo, which played for all the important dances.

It was a musical gag that enabled Fred to get back at his nemesis, the Penn State Glee Club. Fred had learned to play a saw—an ordinary carpenter's saw played with a violin bow, no less! The saw is placed vertically between the legs with the serrated edge facing inward, while the bow is drawn across the smooth edge. One paper reported that Fred had inadvertently sawed through a pant leg during his rendition of "Meditation" from *Thaïs*.

"The glee club was in dire straits," Fred said. "They had no novelty act for their Christmas tour. Somebody told them about me playing the saw, so they asked me if I could go with them on tour. I said, 'Only if I'm part of the glee club. I can sing all the notes as well as anybody you have there.' So the glee club leader said, 'Sure, wait 'til you learn the music.' "And I said, 'I know every damn number you're singing.' They reluctantly took me in. I went to a couple of rehearsals to prove to them that I knew the stuff. When they lined us up on the risers, they put me in the second row in back of a tall guy. Nobody could see me."

In the eighties, I asked Fred about this incident. He said, "Finally they called me to do my solo. I was offstage, and there was this pianist Hum

Fishburn to accompany me. He said, 'What are you going to play?' and I said, 'Bells of St. Mary's.' He said, 'What key?' I said, 'Any key you want.'

"So they announced my name, and from the wings I threw the saw out on the stage. It made a hell of a racket. That got a big laugh. Then I went out, got my chair and sat down." He put a yardstick between his legs to show how he played the saw, and started humming "The Bells of St. Mary's."

Fred: "And it stopped the show—cold."

I asked if it was because he played it so well.

"They had never heard a saw before." Fred's bushy eyebrows went up. "What do you mean, 'well?' 'Course I played it well."

"So then what happened?"

"Then I left the stage—and they are applauding and applauding and applauding, and I take a bow and leave."

"And never came back?"

"And never came back."

In later years at his concerts and workshops, Fred took great glee in mimicking the gestures of stuffy choral directors who, I regret to say, for the most part remain today just as humorless and pedantic as ever. "I imitated the college glee club conductors, the way they ran their concerts," Fred went on. "You know their opening number is going to be something like Hindemith or [beating time] something like this, dah-de-dah. You know they are going to sing the Dartmouth 'Winter Song.' They don't change from year to year, and they go through all this dramatic stuff.

"So I represented the leader in his white tie and tails. The kids would walk in one at a time, and I would portray all of them coming in—the little scared freshman finding his place, and saying hello to his father and mother in the audience. And the guy coming in next to him and pushing him aside, and so on. I went through the whole bit. After they all filed in, the conductor would come in very erect—tap the baton—and all the boys would stand up straight, and he would turn around and give them the inspection. Finally, he would look at the accompanist who had one lousy note to play, and he would give him the cue, and the pianist would damn near fall off the stool doing it—hitting this one note. I think it was the best pantomime I've ever done."

. . .

"When Freddy Buck and I entered college," Fred reflected, "the war was on and, oh my gosh! What a mess it was. We had the largest freshman class in the history of the college, over a thousand students. Very few upper-classmen because of the war. So the freshman class really ran the college that year. The upperclassmen were unable to control this class, and I was, of course, practically the ringleader. We all had been inducted in the SATC (Student Army Training Corps). Our fraternity was a barracks, and the president was a 'sergeant-in-charge.' I'll never forget my roommates. One was six-feet six and a half, one was six-four and a half, and the other was six-two, and here I am—five-six—and trying to boss these other guys all the time. Since I had been turned down by the glee club, I decided to break my neck to become a sergeant. They made me a corporal fairly soon be-cause they could see I had experience. I had charge of my squad. We had a regular army colonel in command of this regiment—a nice fellow."

One day early in the fall of Fred's freshman year, the major who com-manded the trainees called for volunteers for officers' training. Fred, the patriot, was the first in line. The recruits were to leave Penn State, spend several months in training camp, then be sent to Siberia for three years. Fred resigned himself to giving up the band and his engineering studies. He was scheduled to leave in mid-November, 1918; the armistice was signed on November 11. He was in the army eleven days.

"I first majored in mechanical engineering and then realized I preferred architecture, and switched in my second year. I worked hard. Of course, I was a little special because I brought over these kids on the weekends to play dances and things. I was beginning to earn money.

"I also became one of the assistant managers of the football team—we were really gofers. One of our jobs was to keep the uniforms clean. We had the muddiest field in the world. The only system they had for get-ting the mud off uniforms was to bake them dry and then knock the mud off. I had the players remove their shoes and walk in the showers with their uniforms on when they returned to the locker room after a game or a practice. It was simple. The mud went down the drain, and our job was done. I can see now that if I had gone to college with money to spend I would have been a horrible person. As it was, I had to watch myself. I was *unbearable* at times, I know.

"We had to be in chapel at 8 A.M. every morning. It was held in Schwab Auditorium. There were thirty-five hundred students when I was at Penn State. Schwab Auditorium was the center of campus. Freshmen had to wear jackets, ties, and a cap. *Always.* They were not allowed to walk on the grass, and had to speak to everybody who passed, especially upper-classmen. If you didn't follow these rules, you were marked and got a whack.

"In 1918, when I entered Penn State, the university had just built an eighteen-hole golf course and was organizing its first golf team. I took up golf because I was never physically large enough for contact sports. My teacher was a fellow named Herb Ewer. We called him Horseman (short for horse manure). I didn't have time to play on the team but I did become a golf addict."

.   .   .

Everyone had an opinion on the subject of Fred Waring and women. His older sister Helen said flatly, "Fred liked girls and they liked him."

Cousin Tot added, "Fred was a *beautiful* child. He's one person who's carried his looks right straight through."

Fred admitted he had crushes on girls in high school but didn't have any girlfriends: "I was too afraid of them. The first dance I went to was the junior prom. I was still wearing short trousers, which they did in those days until you were a senior. I invited a cute little freshman from Neilmont, and I was so excited. Mickey showed up at the prom with a white stand-out short dress and a big hair ribbon. She looked like a ten-year-old, and I was embarrassed. People made fun of us all night. They said we were a cute couple."

Fred may have been a little afraid of girls, but it's certain he never had time for romance with the schedule he kept in his late teens and early twenties. He was either working to earn money or studying or rehearsing the band or playing with the band on weekends when most of his peers were out partying. These were the years he *should* have been sowing his wild oats.

It was the time, though, that Fred met the girl who would become his first wife. She was a tiny, perky little lass at the Birmingham Prep School near Tyrone. Helen said, "The school was a pretty fancy place. The aristocracy in England didn't have it any better than they did there." The young lady, Dorothy McAteer, came from a wealthy family in Pittsburgh. Everyone agreed Dot was vivacious, charming, and full of personality.

"I used to deliver bread to the Birmingham School, and the wife of the headmaster took a liking to me," Fred said. "She watched out when I would make deliveries, and darned if one day she didn't introduce me to some of the girls who went to the school dances. This one girl later was chairman of their prom committee. She wrote me a letter and offered us $65 to play their prom—which we did. It seems I was permitted to dance one dance with her, and romance began that way. Dot was a spark. She was a dynamo . . . very intelligent. We had a lot of fun together."

In the winter of 1922, while Fred was finishing his last year at Penn State, he booked the band—now ten strong—for a two-and-a-half-month tour starting in January. They had to go without him. This little jaunt was referred to later as the Starvation Tour. "We got twenty-five dollars a night *when* we got it," longtime Pennsylvanian trumpet player Nelson (Nels) Keller said. "Tom was never able to handle problems, so the responsibility of collecting was given to a banjo player who turned out to be a little underhanded. This was our starvation tour. We were on percentages, and nobody came to the dances. When we played Jamestown, New York, we were the biggest flop on earth. Honest to Pete, I don't believe there were more than four couples. At the end of the tour when we got back to Penn State, we were starved! Heavenly days! We were *emaciated!*"

Fred said, "Each boy got off the bus and said, 'I'm quitting! This is my last date!' They said that unless I would quit college and go with them, they would no longer do it. I went to Dean Warnock, who was one of our fans, told him my story, and asked his advice. He said, 'Fred, a lot of people go to college to learn a trade or to learn what they are best suited for in life. If, at this time, you have learned that your calling is orchestra business, then you've completed your college education. Go out and make a success of it. I'm rootin' for you.' Dean Warnock wrote to me, watched everything we did, and was very proud."

So Fred Waring left school in March, 1922, without his degree in architecture.

4

The Brash Kid from Tyrone

DURING our married years, Fred always referred to Paul Whiteman as his idol. He became upset when books and articles came out about the big bands of the past, as they did between the fifties and the seventies, with nary a mention of Whiteman, who had been known as "the king of jazz." Whiteman was ten years older than Fred and firmly established. They became acquainted while Fred was still in school.

"Everybody knew about Paul Whiteman," Fred said. "He first played at the Ambassador Hotel in Atlantic City and was a sensation there when Atlantic City was the most important resort in the United States. And then he went to the Palais Royal in New York, which was really built around him. He was the darling of the rich. He weighed three hundred pounds at one time. Whiteman also produced great records for Victor. His effect on music was immense."

Fred, the budding entrepreneur, decided his band was ready for more exposure, and so, in 1921, he called up his idol Paul Whiteman. The brash kid from Tyrone asked for an audition—and got one. Between frantic practice sessions Tom hurriedly dyed some new shirts a vivid blue and saw to it that the skintight white pants and white ties were freshly laundered. Funds were scraped up, and the group set off for the Great White Way by day coach. They registered at the McAlpin Hotel and had a swim in the pool, then a novelty among New York hostelries. It was a big day!

In the dim afternoon light, the empty dining area of the Palais Royal seemed cavernous. The bandstand, cluttered with instruments, ashtrays, and the usual disorder of rehearsals, looked big enough for a symphony orchestra. Whiteman, a genuinely warm and friendly man, introduced the country boys to his musicians and showed them where to dress. What the Whiteman band thought of the boys' costumes when they reappeared is not on record, but Tom's attachment to the black keys was well remembered. "We had already played in three states by then," Tom said. "We were Waring's Banjo Orchestra."

"When Whiteman heard us, we became friends immediately," Fred said. "I remember how impressed I was. He took me to his office, which was all fixed up with satin-quilted walls, kind of silvery. I remember his calling Victor and telling *them* that he had a new song that he wanted to record. That impressed me terribly. Imagine his being able to tell them that he was going to make a certain record. It was called 'Stumbling.' He played it for us. That night he invited us to the Palais Royal as his guests and then, of course, he played all his stuff. But he pointed that one out especially to show why he wanted to record it."

And then Paul Whiteman offered Fred Waring a job. Whiteman was sending out bands under his aegis to play for debuts and other big parties, and for dances. Fred had hoped that the audition would lead to work—but not exactly the kind Whiteman offered. Here was steady employment and a name Fred would be proud to be associated with, but he found himself saying, "No, thank you!" This would have meant oblivion for the Banjo Orchestra.

"We needed it, but Fred wouldn't take it," trumpet player Nels Keller marveled later. "It was a stroke of genius!"

A year later the Keith Circuit offered the Banjo Orchestra a fifty-two-week engagement doing a single show in vaudeville. "I turned it down," Fred said. "I felt to do only one act a solid year would not be productive. So we chose the movie theater career, which meant you needed a new show every week. Instead of performing twice a day we performed four and five times a day. I decided I wanted to be as prominent as Paul Whiteman and as productive as he, but I didn't want to do the same thing. I reasoned it would be foolish to try to build a band as fine as his, so I built the finest band I could and then added singing. We were the first with a singing band."

In spite of the competition, the two became fast friends for life. What a picture they made—Fred, five-feet-six, one hundred and twenty-eight pounds, collegiate from head to toe; Whiteman, over six feet tall, three hundred pounds, slicked-back hair, pencil-thin mustache, and always in white tie and tails. "Whiteman knew he was great," Fred added. "He wasn't arrogant but he enjoyed his success. He was accepted instantly."

Later, Fred became very close to Paul Whiteman's father. Wilberforce J. Whiteman was director of music education for the school system of Denver, Colorado. Paul's six-foot-tall mother Elfrida was a singer. Fred was fascinated by the elder Whiteman's conducting, "using very small hand motions, almost like mute language." Fred added that "he took the time to show me but I was never able to use the same method. It was unique. He was the only one who did it."

John Royal, "a true giant of show business," who "ran all NBC radio and television programs for decades,"[1] tells of his first contact with Fred Waring:

"In 1920 I was running the very big Cleveland Hippodrome and, being a former manager and press agent, my name had been in the trade papers. About 1920, I started getting letters from a young man at Penn State telling me that he had this great orchestra and that he had ideas! Well, it was the word *idea* that intrigued me because at that time we were up to our necks in all kinds of jazz bands—big ones and little ones—but not many of them had *ideas*.

"Fred and I corresponded for a long time. I gave him suggestions on how to get bookings, but I didn't know what he looked like. The appeal was that he was a youngster and that he had enough gumption to start writing out to the wide open spaces to find out what could happen, and it only cost him two cents to send out a letter. We became pen pals. I found later he not only had ideas—but above all—taste.

"All during the twenties and thirties we would talk on the telephone or he would write me and discuss his plans. I didn't realize then that he was really telling me things he proposed to do. For example, years and years before he bought that golf place—Shawnee—he outlined his plan for a music school there. It didn't materialize, but it shows he was always thinking."

In those days, although Fred booked the band and handled the finances, he was not the leader. He played the banjo along with Freddy Buck. Nels Keller: "The pay was divided evenly. Fred had a tremendous business ability which we lacked. After discussion, it was he who hired the new musicians as we added them one by one."

Fred's method of hiring musicians was not the same as that for the rest of the Waring organization. For the musicians, it didn't vary throughout the Pennsylvanians' career. He operated mainly on an extrasensory gut feeling. He had an uncanny ability to detect talents that often didn't come through at auditions. Besides talent, he was looking for intangibles. How would they fit in? Were they team players? Attractiveness and personality were assets. Ungainly performers weren't compatible with a fast-paced stage show.

For the moment, no nonmusicians were on staff. Fred was handling all the bookings, which required endless phone calls, telegrams, and letters. But soon the band hired a college roommate of Fred's, Spike McHugh, as a bookkeeper. He traveled with them and kept everything in a portfolio. Years later, when his organization expanded, Fred hired competent nonmusicians for various jobs but then gave them no directives, as Fred, to the end, improvised the business side.

Nels Keller remembers his "audition" in 1921: "I was seventeen when I joined Fred. I didn't have much training, but I was a worker. Man, I just loved that horn so much, I just wanted to play so bad. I had played in Philly with Art Horn on sax who was with Fred, and they decided they wanted a trumpet player. Fred came to see me in Philadelphia. We went and had lunch. Trolley car stuff—no taxis—heavenly days, no! We then went to a show and saw Will Rogers. Fred went back to Penn State—*never heard me play*. Just took Art's word for whether I could play or not." Fred, you see, had made the trip to size up Nels's personality.

"Then I got a telegram which said: JOIN US AT THE FORT WHEELING (I thought they were playing in a fort) ON JANUARY 5, 1922. I jumped on a trolley car and left my horn on the seat when I changed to the El. When I got to the train station, I raced back to wait for the trolley car and, so help me, there was my cornet—B flat! I went back home and said nothing.

"A couple of days later, I got a blistering telegram from Waring: WHERE ARE YOU? WHAT HAPPENED? MEET US IN JOHNSTOWN! So a few days later I went to Johnstown and played at Zack's Auditorium. I played but I had *no* idea of what I was doing because Tom was playing in nothing but the black keys, and for trumpet, that is *horrible!*" Nelson Keller remained for nearly twenty-five years.

Two English-born Canadian musicians, fiddle player Bill Townsend and alto sax man Curly Cockerill, were playing in a dance band at Toronto's Royal Connaught Hotel, when they heard that a small American group was booked for two nights at the Alexandria Dance Hall. When they asked the manager of the Alexandria what he knew about "Waring's Banjo Orchestra," the sage replied, "I don't know anything about 'em. They were cheap. Anyway, a band from the States will draw a crowd."

Bill and Curly hung around the hotel lobby until the Waring band arrived. Their jaws dropped. "They were the funniest looking bunch of rubes I've ever seen!" Bill wrote twenty years later. "It was our first look at the current American collegiate styles. They wore long overcoats that almost touched the ground, five-button jackets with every button buttoned, hats down to the eyebrows and turned up in front, trousers much too long, and huge galoshes open and flapping! Curly and I decided we'd go hear them—if only for laughs. When we arrived, they were doing an arrangement of Canadian Capers, and it was a honey! Then the management announced they would play two hours' extra. The crowd went wild. Then they all sang in harmony, and later Tom sang a solo with muted banjo. The effect was terrific.

"The next day this young chap came in while we were playing and listened attentively. He was very good looking, slight with brown wavy hair. He invited us out to dinner and then offered us a job." Bill couldn't see at the time how Fred could use a single violinist but, in spite of the Pennsylvanians' paltry income, Fred was far more interested in how the group should eventually sound than in the possibility he might go broke en route. The two young Canadians were enchanted with the thought that Curly's alto sax and Bill's fiddle were the first stage in the band's becoming, as Fred so simply expressed it, "better than Whiteman's."

In the late teens and early twenties, jazz—as it was then defined—was considered vulgar. Critics all over the country held a low opinion of all jazz bands. Old press clippings offered such descriptive adjectives as "blatant and blaring"; "a conglomeration of noise"; "the blare, squawk and whine"; "the weird noises," and so forth.

When Fred entered the jazz scene with his peppy eleven, the critics were surprised: "Waring's Pennsylvanians are simply too good to be true. Jazz becomes almost music in their hands."[2] "That dandy band! Here are musicians who look like human beings and play like them." "They prove a revelation to those who believe that jazz should be relegated to a bottomless pit."

These were white critics talking about white musicians playing popular music. The pure jazz greats like Louis Armstrong and Duke Ellington were still playing in small clubs in Harlem, Chicago, and New Orleans. Their full acceptance and exposure came later in the thirties.

.   .   .

When Fred left Penn State to go with the band, they had only one date booked, which was for the University of Michigan J-Hop. "We were getting two hundred dollars for the date, and we didn't have enough money to get there, so Mother supplied the train fare for Ann Arbor," Fred remembered. "We were all broke. I hate to think how many times she mortgaged the house to tide us over these low periods. Since I was leaving college, I figured this was the one thing I'd bet on. I didn't realize they had already engaged two huge bands to alternate in the large new gym. Rubenstein and Pasternack (Carmen Lombardo was one of their saxophone players) augmented to thirty pieces was at one end and O. S. Wright, the leading Negro orchestra of the country, was at the other. Next to the new gym was the old gym, which held, at most, a thousand people. That is where we were."

"At first there were only five or ten couples in our gym—nobody," Nels said. "We were listening to this tremendous band next door, and, really, it was annoying to hear, it was so loud. We had this little ten-piece tinkly rhythmic band. All of a sudden people started coming around. We started to sing our zing-zing dance rhythm. They loved it. We were sensational!"

"Nobody was paying too much attention to us, but then a young debutante, Julie Henkel, brought her partner and danced right in front of our band all evening, and where Julie Henkel went, everybody went," Tom added. "People started deserting the two big bands. We had to use megaphones to be heard. They started to troop in until they couldn't breathe in that little place. Before the evening ended, we must have had ten thousand in our little gym. We stole the show!"

This event was a major morale booster for the budding young band. "However, now we were stranded, and somebody said, 'Why don't you go over to Detroit and try to get on radio?' Fred said. "The station manager, Bill Holliday, turned out to be from Tyrone. He booked us into the Kunsky Theaters, and that was the beginning of our stage production. We didn't return to Pennsylvania for six months."

In the early twenties, bands played only for dances; no groups entertained with choreographed action, props, and novelty numbers. Fred knew that in a theater they would be observed, not danced to. Thus, as they frantically rehearsed, he began to build action into each number. The Waring Banjo Orchestra perfected precision drills with brightly painted megaphones that flashed under the stage lights. They played and sang everything with a flip and twist, rushing full flight through set routines, cutting off applause, taking a minimum of bows, speaking no words, and generally raising hell with most of the customs of show business. If the applause that followed them offstage did not last well into the newsreel, they felt they had done a bad show. They studied every performance, no matter how well received, probing it for flaws. They rehearsed with fanatic intensity because they had no backlog of repertoire, and a new show was required every seven days.

All through high school Fred had sung and performed as part of a group. Even while in college booking the band, he was merely one of the boys, playing his banjo. Still, some of his potential charisma must have been evident to Bill Holiday, who persuaded Fred to throw away his banjo and become their leader. Fred went to the group and asked, "What do you want to do? Do you want to split the money or do you want to go on salary?"

Nels: "I was all for splittin' the money, but the rest of the guys agreed to go on salary. That's when Fred became boss! Clear back then in 1922. That's when it started."

Fred: "I asked Bill Holliday's lawyer to draw up a contract which guaranteed the boys fifty weeks' work a year at a minimum salary of one hundred dollars per week . . . ten men. He drew it up but said I was crazy. I said, 'No, that's the way I wanted it.' Look what it did for me. It put me on a spot where I just *had* to get that work. So I signed them up. It was as scary as hell. It took an awful lot of guts."

Fred Culley: "Even though Fred was paying salaries and was figuratively the Boss, he was still part of the orchestra. We never went anywhere without Fred. We played golf together. We took vacations together. There was no jealousy—we were friends. Fred was not the conductor offstage. He was a member of the gang. I can still hear Nelson saying, 'Fred! Goddamn it! You did that lousy on the show! Why don't you learn how to conduct so we can follow.' But they all had terrific respect for his ability."

Bill Holiday also persuaded Fred to change the name of the band to Waring's Pennsylvanians. In just a few short years, the name had gone from Banjazztra to Waring's Banjo Orchestra to Waring's Pennsylvanians. "When I became a leader, I discovered the value of personality and began to try and cash in on what I had and to develop it," Fred said. "I also decided to cash in on the personalities of the rest of the boys. We found many in the band had the ability to do certain stints which we developed with surprising success. I knew we were building for the future."

From the beginning, Fred was quick to perceive that if you didn't grab the audience in the first minute or two, you had an uphill climb. "I ran all over the place to make people think I knew what I was doing. Actually, I didn't know anything. We were the fastest band in the world, and I was running around the stage at a fantastic tempo. We played our opening number, 'Stumbling,' so fast that we'd be halfway through the piece before the curtain reached the top."

But by the forties, Fred had perfected his technique of moving quickly about the stage without lifting his feet from the floor. "He had a way of shifting his feet back and forth, and would seem to glide across the floor," Nels said. "He would move from the center mike, then over to the floor of the orchestra in the front of the glee club. You didn't really realize he was moving and he did it quite rapidly."

The band was in Detroit for eighteen straight weeks, moving from one theater to another—the Madison, the Capitol, and the Adams. But Fred, never one to rest between shows, busily wrote booking agents and theater managers for future engagements. In his first letter to the Chicago theatrical barons, Balaban & Katz, he naively added, "P.S. Kindly return enclosed clippings." B & K said: "No date." Undaunted and with supreme intrepidity, Fred launched a barrage of letters throughout the Midwest—Toronto, Cleveland, Milwaukee, Minneapolis—that requested: "Kindly let me have your decision by wire since I'm contemplating other engagements at the same time."

The newly self-appointed boss was getting a little desperate. But just as their long engagement in Detroit was ending, a field agent for Balaban & Katz caught their act and wired their home office. (Today's ubiquitous telephone didn't seem to be used in those days.) The fledgling band was offered a date at one of the great movie palaces in Chicago, the Tivoli.

Arriving in Chicago in 1922, they checked into a first-class hotel where they could sign room and board chits for everything. "We could never get out because we spent our week's salary ahead and everybody was broke," Fred said. "Each week we paid the last week's bill, and then we couldn't get out because the current bill was due." They virtually starved the final week.

After checking in, Nelson and Fred visited an even grander theater, the Chicago, sat in the balcony, and watched the stage show. "Fred said, 'Boy! We're going to play here sometime,'" recalled Nels.

"I said, 'Are you kidding? We'll *never* hit this place—don't give me that stuff.'

"He said, 'We'll be here!' And do you know that son-of-a-gun Waring never told us we didn't have a job at the Tivoli. I found out later that actually the first show was only a tryout!"

On July 24 the band arrived at the Tivoli for the first show, nervous and excited. The marquee billing was a disappointment. The movie title and the organist's name were displayed in large letters, but Waring's Pennsylvanians hardly were seen. Backstage was no better—the stage crew played pinochle and totally ignored them—the boys had to drag out their own trunks and set the stage. Fred, the former manager of the football team at Penn State, used the same tactics as the coach did in the locker room to get the adrenaline flowing in his neophytes. After all, they were *the* collegiate band. Rah! Rah! Rah!

"From that first show, we were a sensation!" Nels exclaimed modestly thirty-eight years later. "You couldn't believe it unless you were there. We all felt that oneness that we were going to do something—when you heard that applause!" After the first show, a large sign JAZZ BAND RIOT gave the Pennsylvanians top billing, and the stagehands from then on couldn't do enough for them. "Later we used to take those fellas out to lunch when we would come to Chicago to show our appreciation," Nels said.

The world began to look bright again. A. J. Balaban, who would become Fred's lifelong friend, was impressed. He booked the Pennsylvanians into the Riviera and then the Chicago—just a few weeks after Fred had told Nels so confidently, "*We'll be there!*" They remained in Chicago fourteen weeks; then Milwaukee, St. Louis, and back to Chicago.

Newspaper clippings from 1922 tell the story:

> Waring's Pennsylvanians made one of the biggest hits the past week to be made thus far in the big Chicago Theater.[3]

> The greatest jazz band in the world, "Waring's Pennsylvanians." Comparing this band with some other so-called "jazz bands" is like comparing chicken salad to chicken feed. Direct from nine weeks' Chicago run. They play and sing—and how they play and sing, Oh boy![4]

And all this praise just five months after the Starvation Tour! The Pennsylvanians were becoming matinee idols, creating the same sort of excitement that was to follow Sinatra, the Beatles, and today's rock stars.

· · ·

Every spare minute was spent in frantic rehearsal for their weekly shows, but no amount of preparation can eliminate the unforeseen mishaps, boo-boos, and catastrophes that are endemic to show business. Fortunately, Fred—the irascible, volatile conductor—was unflappable, calm, and reasonable in emergencies. That one strong forte would help sustain him through sixty-seven years of constant performances.

Fred recounted a couple of incidents that happened those first weeks in the Chicago environs: "We had these special presentations, and one was called 'On the Levee.' All of us were in blackface. Bales of cotton and hay were strewn around the stage. Tom had written a song, 'Where Am de Moon Tonight?' A big moon was going to come up over the cotton bales and us, the quartet. You should have seen us [Fred singing], 'Where am de moon tonight.' Freddy Buck had the solo. Poley, Tom, and I were the obbligato, ta-dee-dee, ta-dee-dee, ta-dee-dee.

"Freddy had false teeth, and the third time he gets to the word 'tonight,' he opens his mouth wide and his uppers drop down on his lowers and make a big click. On the fourth time, they fall clear out! Freddy digs down on the floor looking for his uppers, while we're trying to sing. Poley and I were sobbing with laughter. We finally had to quit because we were laughing so hard. Tom was furious because it was his song. He finished the quartet alone."

When I heard this story, I was flabbergasted and asked if Freddy Buck really had false teeth when he was only twenty. Fred replied, "We had some lousy dentists in Tyrone. They let teeth rot."

Then Fred continued on another saga: "We were in Milwaukee in an old-fashioned theater where four floors of dressing rooms were in one end up the backstage stairway. There were four rooms to a floor, and at the end of the hallway of each floor was an opening where they would pull the performers' trunks up to the dressing rooms. So these doors were always left open.

"Onstage a lineup of sixteen chorus girls preceded us in a dance number. Their dressing rooms were all on one floor—four girls to a room. They had just finished, and we were now onstage, standing around the piano. Tom was singing the solo to 'Pretty Blue Eyed Sally' while we sang the accompaniment, when suddenly the girls started going to the john, one at a time. The commode not only was very noisy but was located beside the open door of the trunk opening, which made the sound audible to everyone. As the water gathered speed, it went *tinkle, tinkle, gurgle, gurgle, glub, glub,* AGAH, AGAH, ABAHABAHABAH, WAWAAWAWAAAAH! It was so loud the audience could hear it.

"Tom was singing delicately—'Pretty Little Blue Eyed Sally'—*tinkle tinkle glub glub* AGAH AGAH ABAHABAHABAH AWAWAAAAAH! We got to giggling so much we couldn't sing. Tom was getting madder and madder. After each eight bars, *tinkle . . . glub . . . etc.* We realized every girl was going, so we began counting out loud: '. . . twelve . . . fourteen. . . .' Tom was livid. He finished alone. We sang out '. . . *sixteen!*' The audience roared."

Waring's Pennsylvanians were popular, busy, and working, but after nearly twenty weeks of shows, Fred was faced with one of the inflexible axioms of show business—once an act is priced, it's stuck with that price unless something unusual happens or a costly holdout is held for a higher figure. Ten men with one hundred-dollar weekly contracts and an income of a thousand dollars a week was pushing the eleventh man into bankruptcy. Now, as well as then, people in the trade know the fees and, like a cartel, will keep it that way for their own protection.

But Fred lucked out again. His first break had been the J-Hop; the second came a few weeks later, giving the boys' career a needed boost. Sid Grauman was opening his magnificent Metropolitan Theater in Los Angeles on January 23, 1923, and it was reported, in typical Hollywood style, to be "the most beautiful theater in the world." True or not, it was one of the largest and most costly. A Michigan booker wired his friend Grauman in Los Angeles and said: "Sid, the Waring band is an act you want. These kids are sensational!"[5]

Grauman wired back: "All right, Jack, if you think so, send them along."[6]

Fred wired Grauman that their fee was $2,000 a week for six weeks, and requested, with some cheek, I must say, that Grauman send them an advance for transportation to the coast. All was agreed upon, but then Grauman wired that the opening would be delayed a week and asked Fred to fill in the date elsewhere. Fred replied he would try but might not be able to get the full fee at such a late date. CAN YOU MAKE UP REASONABLE DIFFERENCE? Fred wired.[7]

Grauman, bless his heart, wired back: EVERYTHING SATISFACTORY ACCORDING TO YOUR LAST WIRE. TRANSPORTATION HAS BEEN SENT. HOPE YOU RECEIVED SAME. WILL TAKE CARE OF AMOUNT YOU LOST ON WEEK'S BOOKING. PLEASE WIRE ME WHERE YOU CAN BE REACHED UP TO THE TIME YOU LEAVE FOR THE COAST. REGARDS SID GRAUMAN.[8]

With that good news, everyone went home for a short break. They had been away nearly seven months. Fred planned to spend part of the time in Pittsburgh to see Dot McAteer. Because of her family's attitude toward him, their courtship had been uneasy, and he hoped to gain their approval. But it didn't quite work out that way. "One time her parents got me cornered in their house and told me that I was corrupting their child," Fred said. "They didn't want her marrying any musician. I wasn't good enough for her. That's all the McAteers had to do to make me mad enough to marry Dot—just to spite them! It upset Dot, too. Dot was a spark—a dynamo! An intelligent girl who was fun! You could never tire her out. We were so right for each other in those growing-up days. We could go out and stay up late and that was great with her." The dance of the Roaring Twenties was gaining momentum, and those two were doing a fast two-step. They decided to get married in spite of her parents' opposition.

The boys reconvened in Pittsburgh to rehearse and play one concert before setting out for the West Coast. The concert manager was so thrilled that he wrote to his friend Grauman: "They were positively the biggest hit we ever had. We expected a thousand but the estimated crowd was more than ten thousand people—over eight thousand could not be admitted. Traffic was blocked for more than an hour. They are the liveliest bunch of young fellows you ever heard."[9]

Buoyed up by such accolades, the neophytes boarded the train for California, full of enthusiasm and hope. "On the last leg of that first trip to California, just east of Yuma, the train got stuck behind a wreck—for thirteen hours in the heat of the sun," Fred said. "We retrieved our instruments from the baggage car and walked about five miles from the train in the desert to rehearse our act. When we returned to the train, everybody said they heard every note—desert acoustics—no parallel walls. We finally reached California, and what a letdown. There wasn't a palm tree in sight, and it rained for fourteen days straight. We were met at the train by a dapper little guy from a phony little theatrical hotel. We slept with actors, midgets, and all sorts of circus people. And we rehearsed and rehearsed. I was keyed up—this thing *had* to go!"

The opening of such a splashy new theater was a major event in those days. On January 26, 1923, the *Los Angeles Times* and *Examiner* each devoted five pages to describing in detail the interiors and listing such invited guests as movie stars Gloria Swanson, Harold Lloyd, Wallace Beery, Monte Blue, Constance Talmadge, Jack Holt, and Sessue Hawakawa. It was to be a white-tie gala.

"Well, of course, the opening of this theater was a shambles, as is every opening," Fred said. "There were too many stars and too much stage show—the affair lasted until 1 A.M. They had built a shell for us which rolled forward. Because they were painting it, we never had a chance to sit in it to see if we all fit. We never got on that thing until about two minutes before the curtain opened. We squeezed ourselves on, and poor Poley had no place to sit behind his drums. I could see the back legs of his chair had to come off."

Fred, the boy scout, grabbed a saw, had one leg off and was sawing the other when the curtain went up, ". . . and there I am with a chair in one hand and a saw in the other. Everybody laughed. We did our show. Our act was twenty minutes long, and the audience applauded for twenty minutes."

Nels Keller: "Man! When that curtain opened, it was like somebody knocked you right in the head! That was it, boy! We were a stage band!"

The *Examiner* described others on the bill: "twenty-five dancers in diaphanous robes, a novelty number played by forty violins and eight harps, a rendition of the *Tannhäuser Overture* with one hundred singers, five hundred musicians and trumpets stationed at various points throughout the auditorium and a decidedly 'nifty' drill number put on by the usherettes dressed in Roman togas and high laced boots—every movement executed upon a gigantic staircase especially erected on the stage for this act."[10]

The concise, fast-moving, tightly knit Pennsylvanians benefited by the contrast of such corny opulence. Grauman was so pleased with Fred and his group that when they finished their engagement at the Metropolitan, he moved them to his Million Dollar Theater. "Sid Grauman took a great interest in my organization—was very kind to me—made sure I met all the important people in Los Angeles in the movie field," Fred said.

In less than a year, Fred had netted ten thousand dollars, faithfully paid his guaranteed salaries, and was able to show the snobbish McAteers that he had, indeed, become a Somebody. He was now faced with the fulfillment of his obligation: to marry Dot.

"But deep down in my heart, I'm afraid that I had lost my urge to get married," Fred admitted. "I really shouldn't have married. Here is this whole new field suddenly opening, and I was afraid to tie myself up. I was afraid of being buckled down with a wife and children. To tell the honest truth, I didn't know where I was going. I'd made up my mind that I would stay in show business for five years. I'd hoped to make a fortune and then go back to architecture."

In spite of his reservations and those of Dot's parents, who thoroughly disliked the entire theater atmosphere, Fred did what he thought was honorable (besides she *was* attractive) and persuaded the Pennsylvanians to telegraph Dot to come to California to get married—which she did, with her mother and father.

"We were at the Million Dollar Theater," Tom said. "Fred got married between shows. We had a dance team which worked in blackface. They wanted to go to the wedding, but they couldn't take the blackface off and make the wedding in time to get to the next show, so I told them to go as they were. They came and sat in the back pew. When Fred and Dot walked down the aisle, he and Dot exploded with amusement, but her mother just went to pieces. She just blew up. Everybody from the theater was there. We had to get right back to the show."

This is one pattern Fred kept for the rest of his life—staging his weddings between shows. All those early Pennsylvanians did likewise, but unlike Fred, they remained faithfully married throughout their lives. While playing in the Grauman theaters in Los Angeles, Poley fell in love with a starlet named Yvette. They decided to marry a few months later while the band was performing in Washington, D.C. Yvette came east by train, arriving at 9 A.M. They were married at 9:15, as Poley had to be onstage at noon. The date was February 1, 1924. Their union lasted until Poley died in 1979.

Fred's and Dot's union hit the *Los Angeles Times,* with the story ending: "The orchestra is going to San Francisco for an engagement and Mrs. Waring is going along on her honeymoon."[11]

Some honeymoon, while the Pennsylvanians did four shows a day! After the wedding, the newlyweds drove to Santa Barbara in Fred's first car—a Willys Knight Coupe Sedan. On the way he got pinched for speeding. For the rest of his life, Fred would get speeding tickets, until his stroke at eighty. By then he was so happy to be allowed to drive that he slackened up a bit. The next day as they left, an earthquake hit Santa Barbara. "We looked back, and our hotel was gone," remarked Fred.

In sophisticated San Francisco, the attractive young band was heralded with billboards all around the city displaying long red and white streamers that spelled out "Welcome Waring's Pennsylvanians." It was an encouraging beginning for the newlyweds. Fred remembered with joy, "We had a wonderful time there—just a marvelous time. I'll always love that city!" The press clippings from that era give some idea of what a young bride had to face, married to Fred Waring in the twenties. The working hours were bad enough, but those flappers! "Waring's orchestra fascinates women. They liked the way the leader jazzed up and down in front of his orchestra as he swung his baton in wild and weird directorial movements; and especially did the women like the Valentino staycombed hair of the handsome members of the new organization."[12]

Fred's lifelong paternalistic feeling for his Pennsylvanians shows in an early interview, when he was twenty-three years old:

> Fred Waring is just out of college. That youthful leader of Waring's Pennsylvanians now winning the plaudits of California theater audiences looks the part until you have a chat with him. Then he impresses you as a man whose experience spans many more years than he admits.
>
> Perhaps it was the struggle for success that matured him. And he did have a struggle—he will tell you that frankly. . . . The young leader spoke with a rather proud air of proprietorship when he referred to "my boys."[13]

Fred had to defend himself musically from the start. There were those who liked Fred's new syncopated music and others who could barely tolerate it. Any innovator is bound to have carping critics nipping at him, and Fred was no exception. He was different and worse—he took liberties and bent some of the rules. The first jab came in the middle of his honeymoon in San Francisco, from a reviewer who disdainfully started out: "Of course, being a chronicler of serious musical events, we shall never be reconciled to the usefulness of jazz playing in its accepted style. But, after all, we cannot be envious of the enjoyment of others who seem to take special pleasure in the manner in which these young Pennsylvanians 'put over' their kind of jazz playing."[14]

A totally different tone prevailed when the band returned to Los Angeles for a return engagement:

> In honor of Waring's Pennsylvanians, the entire *orchestra of UCLA* headed by the supervisor of music will attend the 11:15 P.M. performance. He believes that for those who are students of music of classic variety, syncopation, which has rapidly become the typical music of the American people, offers an interesting study. Fred Waring, manager of the orchestra, claims that syncopation is *not* jazz, and he contends that as much skill and musical genius is required in arranging and playing pure syncopated melodies as there is in doing the same with classical music.[15]

This statement would be Fred's leitmotif throughout the twenties.

.   .   .

A fervently devout blind organist in Philadelphia, Adam Geibel, author of more than five thousand hymns, wrote a piano concert piece called *Visions of Sleep*. Fred heard a small portion played by a black band from Columbus, Ohio, who came three or four times a year to Tyrone to perform for dances. (Columbus was the breeding ground for small black combos at that time.) They told him who had written it, and Fred went to see Dr. Geibel, who was delighted, and said he could use whatever part he wanted. However, Dr. Geibel did not think his name should be associated with it since theirs was a dance band. (One of the few nonsacred songs he wrote was "Kentucky Babe," which Fred recorded years later with Bing Crosby.)

Dr. Geibel's copyright was with Theodore Presser in 1893, and he said Fred could publish the portion he took. Tom composed a soprano obbligato and wrote the words to "Sleep." They spelled Geibel's name backwards as "Lebieg" so as not to embarrass him. But then the music publishing firm of Sherman & Clay went to Presser behind Fred's back and made a deal to publish the composition. They cut in one of their staff men who happened to be a bandleader, allowed him to write a lyric, and then published "Sleep" with his name on it—an out-and-out fraud to deprive Fred of his copyright. Fred fought them and finally, after twenty-eight years, obtained 50 percent of the copyright. This was a scandalous but typical example of the way copyrights could be manipulated. Fred had much to learn.

"Because of our huge success on the West Coast, we were asked to record 'Sleep,' our big number," he said. "We went down to Camden, New Jersey. I'll never forget that ferryboat ride at eight in the morning and the fog—we worked for three days recording until we got 'Sleep.' There was no way we could sing and play at the same time. Recording was done through inverted megaphones attached to a stylus which cut grooves in the wax by mechanical pressure. To prevent the wax from solidifying, the studio temperature was maintained at one hundred degrees and more. We had to stand up in front of the three horns. If we got up, there was nobody to play the instruments. Finally, Tom, Poley, Freddy Buck, and I sang. The recording manager played enough piano to oom-pa-pa for us. We yelled ourselves hoarse recording. The first week that record came out, forty thousand were sold in Baltimore where we were playing. For us, it was a sensational thing. But it was a real lousy record, I assure you." "Sleep" was the Pennsylvanians' theme song thereafter—for sixty-seven years.

• • •

Tragedy struck in 1923 with the sudden death of a young Pennsylvanian, Ward Campbell.

"Ward had been with us a year and a half," Fred said. "Here's a kid who was under eighteen—a remarkable musician, a great golfer, a real genius on the saxophone. Ward got the flu in Baltimore and stayed in his room for the matinee. After the matinee, I went out to the boardinghouse to see him and found him dead on the floor. That was perhaps the greatest shock I'd ever had. I was terribly fond of this boy; he was my pet! He played golf with me six days a week.

"I was so upset that we canceled our engagement at the Baltimore Theater and a couple of others [a move not acceptable to theater owners] in order to attend the funeral in Tyrone. Here we were, about twelve kids in our early twenties, terribly shocked at the loss of our beloved youngster. We were a tremendously unified team at that time. In the

Campbell house, they put all of us in a separate dining room. The service was held in the main parlor.

"I remember the minister, in the midst of his sermon, walking from the living room into the dining room where we were sitting weeping, shaking his finger, and pointing clockwise around the room at each of us, and saying, 'You *killed* this boy! *You!* By your lolly-gagging around the country, sinning and playing for dances and corrupting one another, you *killed* this boy!'"

As if the terrible blow of Ward's death weren't enough, the minister's outburst at the funeral devastated Fred and profoundly affected his attitude toward formalized religion. As a result, he withdrew from all church affiliations and did not enter a church voluntarily for many years.

5

Milk Trains

WHEN an engagement finished in a city, the Pennsylvanians, after the last show, had to pack their suitcases and instruments to catch an all-night train to the next city where they opened that day. Each Pullman car had open seats, plus one private compartment with sink and toilet. At night the porter would turn all the seats into lower berths, and the upper berths were pulled down from the ceiling. Two long, dark green curtains extended the length of the car with openings at each berth. One needed a ladder to get into the upper bed. The cars were never very clean. Trains that traveled at night, the "milk trains," stopped at every hamlet and crossroad and were sometimes shunted off to one side, then picked up by another engine going in a different direction. Sleep was nearly impossible with the constant jerks and stops.

Listed here is a ticket order in 1924 showing the cost of eighteen tickets. Five wives usually went along. Except for four men, all slept two to a berth, each scarcely wide enough for one. Two couples shared the one tiny stateroom—truly unmitigated togetherness.

1 stateroom	$ 13.50
4 uppers @ $3 ea.	12.00
5 lowers @ $3.75 ea.	18.75
18 tickets @ $12.58 ea	226.44
	$270.69

Buck—upper	1
Campbell—½ lower	1
Cockerill ½ lower	1
Culley—½ lower	1
Gilliland—D.R.½	2 (wife)
Horn—upper	1
Keller—½ lower	1
McClintock—lower	2 (wife)
Radel—lower	2 (wife)
Townsend—D.R.½	2 (wife)
Tom Waring—upper	1
Fred Waring—lower	2 (wife)
McHugh—upper	1
	18

But these minor inconveniences merely spurred Fred onward toward his goal of rising to the top. "I never had a lack of confidence in overcoming any responsibility," he said. "I was concerned with one thing. I knew we were up. I knew there was nobody bigger than we were, even Paul Whiteman. He was a few steps ahead of us, as well he should be, and I idolized him. I wanted him to be the first, but I wanted that our organization should be enough different from Whiteman's that there was room for two."

Fred's organization was different, to say the least. Whiteman had a thirty-piece orchestra, including twelve strings; Fred, a mere eleven men to his band. Whiteman, although a large man, was a natty dresser, and had a personality as flamboyant and expansive as his girth. Fred, too, liked clothes and had stage presence, but, more important, his Pennsylvanians were unique and on the rise. The February 3, 1924, edition of the *Washington Post* devoted two columns to the Pennsylvanians and concluded: "There has been no more significant musical development in America than the gradual evolution of the type of orchestra of which Waring's Pennsylvanians stands as a preeminent example." The *New York Evening World* added: "Paul Whiteman had best look to his laurels!"[1]

By the mid-twenties, that fussy, self-appointed guardian of musical standards, *Etude* magazine, instead of denigrating jazz as usual, decided to take another look:

> In its original form [jazz] has no place in musical education and deserves none. It will have to be transmogrified many times before it can present its credentials for the Walhalla of music.

In musical education Jazz has been an accursed annoyance to teachers for years. . . . the young pupil who attempts to play much of the "raw" jazz of the day wastes time with common, cheap, trite tunes badly arranged. . . . On the other hand, the melodic and rhythmic inventive skill of many of the composers of Jazz, such men as Berlin, Confrey, Gershwin and Cohan, is extraordinary. Passing through the skilled hands of such orchestral leaders of high-class Jazz orchestras conducted by Paul Whiteman, Isham Jones, Waring and others, the effects have been such that serious musicians such as John Alden Carpenter, Percy Grainger and Leopold Stokowski, have predicted that Jazz will have an immense influence upon musical compositions, not only of America, but also of the world.[2]

The press clippings of the twenties also indicate that Tom Waring was quite famous in those early years. His picture appeared almost as often as Fred's, which was constantly, and the critics were full of praise for his singing: "The warm voice of Tom Waring," etc. Yet despite his recognition in the theater world, Tom's deep-seated insecurities made him overly sensitive to any slights, real or imaginary.

After Fred and I were married in 1954, Tom came over many mornings a week for his favorite breakfast of chipped beef on toast and black coffee made by Elsie, our German housekeeper, who followed Jesse's recipe exactly! (Not the healthiest diet for anyone—let alone a man with a bad heart.) Tom regaled me with funny stories, and little by little I became aware of his notorious *list,* otherwise known as his shit list—a rather daring word in the fifties, at least in our circles—although Fred said his mother's spinster sister Aunt Anne used to say it when the occasion called for it. Fred's sister Helen always vowed that Tom was a mind reader. "He had developed what couldn't be developed physically," she said. "I wouldn't like Tom not to be fond of me."

When the Pennsylvanians played in Washington D.C.'s Crandall Theater in the twenties, Tom would drop in between shows to see his good friend Nelson Bell, head of publicity for the Crandall Theaters and theater columnist for the *Washington Evening Star.* "At least four afternoons a week Kate Smith sat on Nelson's desk," Tom said. "That was before she gave me the big snub, but I knew Kate Smith plenty! She was a dancer then, you know, a fat dancer, a tap dancer. She was wonderful! This was before she got tied up with La Palina Cigars and CBS. She was in a show with Eddie Dowling, who had been my friend for years, so naturally when I saw the show, I went backstage. Kate fell all over me and wanted to know how I thought she did, and all this and that. She was so thrilled to see me. Several years later she was 'Kate Smith on Radio.'

"One time I went out to the races with Floyd Bennet, and her car pulled up beside me. We all got out at the same time. I turned and looked her square in the face and said, 'Why, Kate! This is the first time I've seen you since Honeymoon Lane!'

"And she said, 'I beg your pardon! I don't know you.'

"I said, 'Well, I'm terribly sorry, but I'm conceited enough to think my face is very hard to forget! I shall remember you to Nelson Bell when I see him.' And that was the end of that.

"Later on when she saw me in the elevator at Columbia where we first worked on Madison Avenue, she remembered me and wanted to speak, and I wouldn't speak to her. That's the old business. You don't get a second crack."

.   .   .

Fred the golf devotee never let strenuous tours in America's movie houses deter him. He would tee up on the golf course at 6 A.M. in order to be back in time for the first show at noon. "It wasn't easy since we had four and five shows a day seven days a week," he said. "I'd phone ahead—had a wonderful rapport with all the pros. If one of my boys was unable to go, I would go out alone and religiously hit a hundred approach shots. I then would play, and it would take me two hours walking."

The newspapers in each city soon picked up Fred's obsession: "Fred Waring, conductor of the Pennsylvanians (the novelty orchestra) that is breaking all records at Crandall's Metropolitan, carries more than his leader's baton on tour. One of the most important parts of his impedimenta is his bag of golf clubs. Waring swings as mean a club as he does a 'blues.'"[3]

.   .   .

In 1924 Fred met songwriter Dick Whiting on a golf course during an extended Detroit theater engagement. "We played eighteen holes every morning for thirty crisp days in October," Fred said. "Dick was a gentle, retiring person with a round, cheerful face. I sometimes called him 'Foxy Grandpa.' We became good friends." Among the songs Whiting wrote were "Till We Meet Again," "Beyond the Blue Horizon," "My Ideal," and "Too Marvelous for Words."

Fred saw lyrics writer Gus Kahn as almost the reverse of Dick Whiting, although they worked well together. "He was rough, tough and anything but a beauty on the outside," he said. "But within, he had the humor of a Mark Twain and the sensitive warmth of a Stephen Foster, as captured in his lyrics—'It Had to Be You,' 'Carioca,' 'I'll Be Seeing You in My Dreams,' 'Yes, Sir, That's My Baby,' 'You're Nobody's Sweetheart Now.' Gus and I played golf, too, and he was a rare needler." It takes one to know one.

For two years Fred had struggled to get a New York theater booking. He enclosed copies of rave reviews in his letters but received only curt negative replies. Finally a request came from J. Plunkett of the prestigious Strand Theater. Everything was agreed upon until Fred read an appended note on the contract in Plunkett's handwriting stating he had the right to approve and change Fred's program. A quick, polite, but firm reply came from Fred saying, "Knowing my organization as I do, I believe I am in a little better position to judge the kind of program we will put over most effectively."

The Pennsylvanians arrived in New York, and while they were setting up the stage, Plunkett came in and demanded to see their act. One can imagine the stultifying effect of playing an afternoon audition before an empty house, save for two cold-eyed skeptical men who, God forbid, were smoking big black cigars. When Plunkett decided to re-routine the show and insisted they open with a short encore piece, Fred stood firm. The encore was a novelty number he had introduced in Baltimore, called "Mr. Gallagher, and Mr. Sheehan." Everybody was singing it: "Cost of living's gone so high that it's almost reached the sky / Absolutely, Mr. Gallagher / Positively, Mr. Sheehan." Fred cast Nels Keller's trumpet as Mr. Gallagher and Jim Gilliland's trombone as Mr. Sheehan. Their plaintive instrumental conversation, using trick mutes and mimicking voice inflections, delighted audiences. Fred refused point-blank to start his show with that encore. The battle between Plunkett and Waring waged long and loud, with Fred finally emerging the somewhat battered victor. After the first show, which was well received, nothing more was said. Later the two became friends.

Fred recalled a similar incident with another New York agent who was just as adamant: "Louis Sydney and I had a terrible battle—in fact he was quite vicious for a number of weeks, but wound up being a very dear friend. I think they must have just thought it out and decided that, after all, the only thing I've ever fought for was principle. I'm supposed to know my business, and the only difficulty I've ever had was when they were going to tell me how to do my show. It happened in radio and TV and everywhere else. I did not have as much success in maintaining my principle in TV as I did elsewhere—the time elements and the pressures are greater."

It was interesting to note in page after page of press clippings how, in 1924, little by little, the movie titles in each theater began to take a back seat to the Pennsylvanians: "Waring's Pennsylvanians are here. What need to say that there is also a picture?" "Any feature picture no matter how good is of only secondary importance." "Waring's Pennsylvanians billed as 'added attraction' have developed into *principal* attraction. Held over for 9th week."[4]

In the twenties Fred worked hard to maintain California contacts, and went after any opportunity he could find to perform there. "Once I was asked to come and teach Nancy Carroll and Buddy Rogers to sing a couple of songs," he said. "I knew songwriter Leo Robin and Oscar Levant, and I just went out and got involved. I usually flew. Transcontinental flights were just starting—DC-3s and smaller planes—Ford Tri Motors and Fokkers. It was a long flight to the coast.

"One time we were flying and ran into a storm. We had to land in a cornfield in Kansas. The temperature was a hundred and thirteen degrees. All the passengers walked about a mile and a half to a six-room hotel. I can't remember any hotter night in my life. The pilot had persuaded somebody to mow the field. We took off the next day and completed the trip."

. . .

Everyone talks about how squeaky clean the Pennsylvanians were in appearance and habits as compared to other band members and star performers of that era who were frequently overindulging or missing shows. For instance, when Bing Crosby was starting out with Whiteman in the twenties, he frequently missed engagements—he liked to drink and party. Through the decades, the lifestyle of many jazz musicians has not been conducive to promoting a "goody two-shoes" image. The young men in Fred's band were as they appeared: church-oriented, apple pie, cross-your-heart-hope-to-die, upright lads. As one newspaper announced, "That dandy band, Waring's Pennsylvanians, look like human beings and play like them!"[5]

. . .

In reviewing all the telegrams and correspondence he carried on during the twenties just to keep his bookings going and the Pennsylvanians' fee from stagnating, one can see why Fred, once he attained some help, shunned the business end of his operation for the rest of his life. In later years his secretaries unsuccessfully wheedled, cajoled, moaned, bullied, and used every tactic imaginable to get him to answer the mountain of letters that piled up daily.

In 1925, two years after the Pennsylvanians' first great run in Los Angeles, Fred, once again, was maneuvering to get his fee raised. He wanted $2500 a week for a return engagement at Grauman's Metropolitan Theater. After much quibbling and many letters, Fred stood firm and the fee was agreed upon. Sid Grauman heralded the Pennsylvanians' arrival in Los Angeles by entertaining them at his Egyptian Theater on May 28 and announcing a golf tournament in their honor. Fred won the tournament with what the newspapers described as "a sizzling 86." Then, while the band was playing at his Metropolitan Theater, Grauman built one of his characteristic extravaganzas for the Fourth of July week—a large and loud spectacle complete with full symphony orchestra and a living tableau framed high above, of the "Spirit of '76"—all to precede Fred's little band.

For the first few performances, Fred found he was being pinched in his backside during the blackout that covered the departure of the living tableau performers. Fred would receive the nip just as he made his appearance onstage. Resolved to capture his assailant, Fred lay in wait and grabbed the figure before he could escape. It was the boy of the tableau, a fresh, snub-nosed, black-eyed kid named Scotty Bates, ordinarily a pageboy in the house. He was such a wonderfully happy, irresponsible youngster of unfailing good nature and effervescent fun that Fred did not forget him, and when the Pennsylvanians were hired for the prologue of Harold Lloyd's spectacular picture of college life called *The Freshman* at Grauman's Million Dollar Theater, Fred sent over to the Metropolitan for Scotty Bates to be the frosh in their stage skits. "We hazed him—put him through a lot of things that had happened to me in college," Fred said. Poor Scotty was tossed four or five times a day in a blanket and otherwise set upon. "We adopted the most extreme sort of collegiate costumes—enormous broad trousers, loud sweaters and wide jazzbo ties. The University of Southern California asked permission to imitate our costumes, and invited us to the USC-Stanford game at the Coliseum and, with a hundred thousand people looking on, saluted us at half-time."

This record-long run in Los Angeles in the Grauman theaters enabled the band to get in so much golf that one newspaper took note of it:

Ah! Waring's Syncopators are "Golfopators" Also!
Why do Waring's Pennsylvanians wear golf costumes while playing at the theater? Not simply because they make a natty, summery stage costume, smiles Fred Waring, director of the Syncopators, now in their 5th week at

the Metropolitan. Fred confides that the real reason is a practical one. The boys are all ardent golfers and try to get in at least 9 holes every day, either before the show or after matinees. As time is very limited, they combine the apparel of the links and the stage costume into one. "Our working clothes are also our playing clothes."[6]

"Those were the days I got my comeuppance from some very good local golfers in each town who knew gamesmanship," Fred said. "I was a naive kid making a big name on the stage, and these golfers would invite me to play, and then take me time after time after time. We were on the road year round and I finally learned."

It was in 1925 that Fred's father, Frank, made an incredibly prophetic statement. He said, "Golf will eventually be one of the best and the biggest sports." His words proved to be true.

"Dad didn't play golf, but he believed fundamentally that no man should be denied the right to play just because he was poor—that any poor man should be allowed to learn how to play," Fred's sister Helen said. "And he made that possible. He started building a golf course in Harrisburg in the twenties. Then, in 1935, he bought a nine-hole course in York, Pennsylvania, and built a second nine. From the start, both courses were open to black players. Father said, 'There's no color line as far as I'm concerned—and never will be.' I can remember when his fees were fifty cents for a round of golf—eighteen holes. You could get a whole meal for fifty cents in those days."

. . .

Fred, the hard-pressed booker of the Pennsylvanians, was finally beginning to develop friendly relationships with certain theater managers and owners:

Office of
HARRY B. WATTS   April 27, 1925
    Managing Director
    Rialto Theater
    Omaha, Nebraska

Dear Fred:
    Was certainly glad to hear from you but very sorry to hear that you will not be available for this theatre until you return from the coast and on account of this I hope that while you are in California you all get the hoof and mouth disease.

I was surprised at you quoting that you are now receiving $2,500.00 per week as all the reports I have had on you the highest has been $2,250.00. . . .

. . . Hoping that no one has hidden your trumpet in the celesta recently, I am still fat and ill-natured and hope you are the same.

H. B. Watts

Dear Brother Watts:

It certainly was good to have a letter from yourself "personal" instead of through your hard-boiled agent and I'm hoping that we can conduct our future negotiations, contracts, slams, boosts, etc. in the same way. I don't object to seeing an agent getting a commission (as long as somebody else pays it) but your friend Woolfolk and I just naturally don't get along. That, of course, is between you and me and the gate post.

Incidentally, anent your surprise at the $2500.00 salary, McHugh read your letter and said he would prove that the reports were all wet. Hence the photostat print of last week's pay check. However, we'll talk about that a few months from now when we are ready to start on the return trip.

With kindest regards "from all to all," I remain

Sincerely,
Fred Waring

Dear Fred,

I owe you two apologies, but I have good reasons in both instances. Your letter from St. Louis enclosing a photo of a $2500.00 check has kept me awfully busy. I have tried every bank in Omaha and surrounding territory including Chicago, and I can't find anyone to cash it so now I have decided that the check is no good and will file it away with other mementos. I am still looking for your triumphant return to Omaha. Of course you will have to break your rule of buying a new car in every city and throwing it away after the engagement and get your prices down to a figure that there will be a chance to get in cash instead of Rialto Theatre Tickets. Let me know about six to eight weeks in advance when you think you can play Omaha.

Best wishes to you and the gang and hope that you are not waring.

Very truly yours,
Harry B. Watts

Dear Brother Watts:

The matter of reply will only take a couple of lines which saves the typewriter ribbon, carbon paper, the Corona, etc., a certain amount of wear and tear which we can ill afford. Also the secretary who is not much inclined to work as you may remember. The thing in a nutshell is this: give me a yes or no on the price. In other words, are you going to use us or must we sail through your beautiful city without stopping long enough to buy a new automobile (and your ideas on my automobiles are base slander because I haven't bought a new one in two years—that is until last week and it's a pip—I mean a Cadillac).

Sincerely,
Fred Waring

Fred was considered a master at programming. He said in the eighties that his premise was based pretty much on the old saw "Something old, something new, something borrowed, something blue." This was a credo that Fred employed early in his career. A Philadelphia paper noted in 1926: "Every program is carefully planned to please each member of their audiences, from the jazz music for the rabid flappers (who fill the front rows of every performance) to the sweetest and most musical of waltzes for the memory cherishing old folks, from side splitting comedy to the most beautiful tonal combinations and symphonic effects."[7]

All talented Pennsylvanians who observed it and learned, also incorporated Fred's basic principles throughout their professional lives. Even years later, the same phrases came out: "He taught us that variety and quality must prevail, what songs come where"—"How much of each"—"What tempo"—"The flow of the overall theme of it," and so on.[8]

The Pennsylvanians' stringent routine of incorporating fresh ideas and daily rigorous rehearsals brought them closer and closer to the top. A January 18, 1925, *Philadelphia Record* headline proclaimed: THE WARING BOYS COME BACK!

"We just kept going back and forth to all those places we had already played—Chicago, Detroit, Toronto, Los Angeles, Philadelphia," Nels Keller said. "In those days, time went slow. A year's time—it was amazing. You felt like you were out on the road five years."

. . .

Lindy's in New York was a favorite haunt where Fred and other theater people would gather at night to relax and joke with each other between tours. Fred loved to work with Harry Warren. They met at Lindy's to kick around ideas. Warren, who at the time of his death in 1981 had four hundred songs to his credit (including such hits as "Lullaby of Broadway," "42nd Street," and "Chattanooga Choo Choo"), shared a flair for novelty numbers with Fred, who enjoyed staging them. Poley sang "Where D'ya Work-a-John?" for years in his frog voice. Warren, who was Italian, once used the word "Aluta!" and Fred felt that word also would be funny, coming from Poley. So Warren wrote a catchy song in which the key word was "Saluta," and Fred and Poley made it a hit. But later on, Fred said, everyone went in different directions and their "paths never crossed." Fred went into movie houses and the others didn't.

"The movie palaces became the vogue when we were starting," he explained. "In Chicago you had the Chicago Theater, the Tivoli, and the Capitol; in St. Louis, the Missouri; in Minneapolis, the Minnesota; in Boston, the Metropolitan; in Philadelphia, the Stanley, the Fox, and the Earl; in Los Angeles, Grauman's Chinese Theater and the Metropolitan; and in San Francisco, the Granada, the Warfield, and the California theaters. Sometimes the old opera houses and vaudeville theaters were adapted to movie houses. We played in one in Milwaukee. There was a hole right in the center of the stage. To accommodate the movie craze, they had built an organ rise, and we had to play around the damn hole!"

When I was on the road in the eighties with Fred, he sometimes mentioned with sadness and regret the demise of almost all of the theaters he had played in the twenties. I listened with half an ear as he reeled them off. It wasn't until I started this saga and pored over the old yellowed scrapbooks and realized how many weeks and months and years that he spent in those theaters that I began to understand his nostalgia. He *lived* in those movie palaces. They were his home.

Their other homes were either hotels or boardinghouses. A favorite of the latter was in Baltimore. The owner, a southern lady, was a great cook but, according to Fred, "a pain in the ass—how rich and important she used to be and who tried 'like hell' to wish an eligible daughter on me."

The following gives some idea of hotel room costs:

April 14, 1925
St. Louis, Mo.
Inside room with bath at $3.50—E. C. Cockerill and Park Lytle
Inside room with bath and twin beds at 4.00—F. C. Buck and J. R.
    McClintock

Outside room, twin beds and bath at 5.00—Fred M. McHugh and Tom
  Waring
[Four couples:
Mr. and Mrs. G. A. Culley
Mr. and Mrs. J. B. Gilliland
Mr. and Mrs. W. I. Townsend
Mr. and Mrs. Fred M. Waring]
Outside rooms, double bed, tub bath at 4.50

.   .   .

"About 1925 we came back to Chicago," Fred told me. "We were billed
very high and Spitalny (Leopold, not Phil) had an eighty-piece symphony orchestra—in the pit! It was really something. He was a little miffed—
his nose was out of joint. Here we were, a little twelve-piece orchestra
getting all the attention from the press and production department who
were gung ho about us—especially Balaban & Katz. The usual sequence
was the orchestra overture and then the newsreel, and that gave the audience a chance to get settled back for our act, and then the movie. But
Spitalny contrived to have us follow the overture. His idea was to show
us up—so what overture do you think he picked? The '1812 Overture' and
he had cannons on the stage all around us. We were set up back of the
curtain and didn't know anything about the G.D. cannons. As you know,
the finale is cannons and fireworks. The curtain opened for us—smoke
all over the place and there we were. So we did our eight-ten-minute act
and then they put on the newsreel and people applauded all through the
newsreel for us."

"How did you resolve it?" I asked.

"They changed it. Spitalny and I became friends later. I won him over.
He respected our . . . integrity."

I had noticed that Fred was always extremely courteous and polite to
stagehands. No matter how tired he was when leaving the theater, he
thanked them and wished them well. Scriptwriter Jack Dolph said that
in his earlier days the stagehands' union, the International Association of
Theatrical and Stage Employees (IATSE), discovered Fred was "goosey
and on his first appearance every week he was goosed on every stage in
the USA. He would come on with a great big squeal."

John Royal mused, "Well, I must tell you that it is flattery when a stage-
hand from the IATSE will get that familiar with him. Yes, Fred was always
friendly—they liked to see him."

The Pennsylvanians will never forget that, in the beginning, life was not so easy. "We had to carry all the instruments ourselves," Tom said. "I always carried Poley's drum. I almost had curvature of the spine from carrying it. One time we were playing at Kenny Wood Park in Pittsburgh. We had come down as far as the bridge on a street where we were staying at the William Penn. Poley had ordered from Volkweins, the big music store in Pittsburgh, a folding bass drum which was supposed to be very classy and also smaller so I wouldn't have to walk curved. I used to have to catch the top of the drum on my hipbone and I had this heavy suitcase on the other side. Poley had two cases of traps.

"We got off the streetcar and started across the bridge, and Poley had been talking very loudly about how happy he was that the new drum would be there and he was going to pick it up. I asked him six times, 'Are you sure the drum is there?' He says, 'Oh yes, it's there. All I have to do is pick it up.' I said, 'All right, then! This is the last of this drum!' and I heaved it into the river. And he cried. He cried the whole way home. I actually was ashamed of myself. Fortunately, the other one was there. It was twice as heavy as the original, but at least I could walk straight."

The lugging of heavy suitcases and instruments affected them all. For the rest of Fred's life the right sleeve of his jackets had to be three-eighths of an inch longer than the left one.

Fred Waring, age three, 1903. This and all other illustrations come from the collection Fred Waring's America at Pennsylvania State University.

Fred Waring as a Boy Scout, Beaver Patrol, Tyrone, Pa., 1913, thirteen years old.

The original group, Waring's "Banjo" Orchestra, Tyrone, Pa., 1917. Left to right: Poley McClintock, Fred Waring, Tom Waring, Freddy Buck.

The Waring family, ca. 1918. Left to right: Bud, Helen, Tom, Dolly, Frank, Jesse, and Fred, in Tyrone, Pa..

Penn State coach Hugo Bedzek and Fred Waring, 1923.

Waring's Pennsylvanians, Detroit, Mich., 1922. Left to right: Fred Waring, Tom Waring, Curly Cockerill (behind Tom), Poley McClintock, Freddy Buck, Ernie Radal, Art Horn, Bill Townsend, Jim Gilliland, and Nelson "Nels" Keller.

Tom Waring, Jobyna Ralston, Harold Lloyd, and Fred Waring.

According to this 1925 marquee, Waring's Pennsylvanians provide an "atmospheric prologue, "On the Campus,'" for Harold Lloyd's comedy film, *The Freshman*.

Fred conducting, publicity photo, mid 1920s.

Fred Waring in the 1920s, in a shot which captures his bright eyes and impish grin.

Waring's Pennsylvanians, Hollywood, Calif., 1925. Joining the band, left to right, center row, are: Douglas Fairbanks Jr. (white pants, jacket and white tie), Esther Ralston (dark hat), director Mal St. Clair (center, dark suit), Florence Vidor (light cloche hat, white skirt), Tom Moore (polka-dot tie), and Ford Sterling (far right).

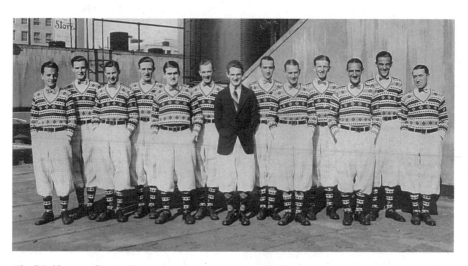

The "Golfopators," in Hollywood to appear with the film, *The Freshman,* 1925. Fred, the golf nut, devised these costumes so that the golfers of the group could get some play in between shows without changing clothes, weather permitting.

SALLE PLEYEL, 252, Faubourg Saint~Honoré

MARDI 3 JUILLET 1928 A 21 HEURES
(Ouverture des Portes à 20 h. 30)

A LA DEMANDE GÉNÉRALE
(à la suite de son triomphal succès du 18 Juin)

UNIQUE CONCERT SUPPLÉMENTAIRE
DU

WARING'S
PENNSYLVANIANS

FRED WARING, Director — TOM WARING, Soloist
en exclusivité sur disques Gramophone "LA VOIX DE SON MAITRE"

WARING'S PENNSYLVANIANS
COLLEGIATE ORCHESTRA INCOMPARABLE

21 MUSICAL MARVELS IN MIRACLES OF MELODY
FAREWELL APPEARANCE IN PARIS

PIANOS PLEYEL

PRIX DES PLACES : ORCHESTRE RÉSERVÉ 70 fr. ; Loges (la place) 100 fr. ; ORCHESTRE 1re SÉRIE, 50 fr.; 2e SÉRIE 40 fr.
PARTERRE 30 fr. ; PREMIER BALCON : Loges 40 fr. la place ; 1re Série 35 fr. ; 2e Série 25 fr.,
DEUXIÈME BALCON, 1re Série 20 fr. 2e Série 15 fr. (droits compris).

BILLETS : Salle Pleyel ; Durand, 4, place de la Madeleine ; Guide-Billets, 20, avenue de l'Opéra ; aux Ambassadeurs.

Agence Artistique des Champs-Elysées, 59, Avenue des Champs-Elysées
P.B. Arnaud et H. Lartigue, Directeurs — Filiale de William Moriss Agency, New-York

The cartoon was drawn in the style of John Held Jr. by an artist named Edouarde, Paris, 1926. It was used throughout the 1920s and 1930s in all kinds of promotion for concerts, shows, recordings, with and without the artist's name.

The Pennsylvanians in Paris at the Cafe des Ambassadeurs, 1928.

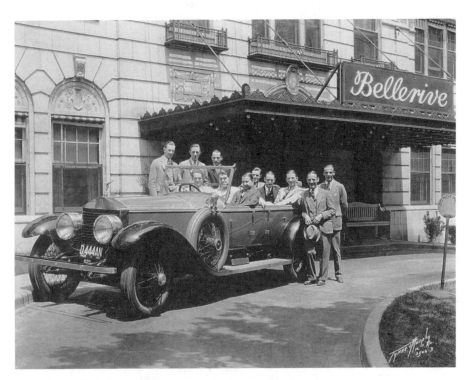

Fred and the Pennsylvanians in a 1925 publicity shot in front of the Bellerive Hotel, Kansas City, Mo. The car, still sporting the manufacturer's license plate, is a Rolls-Royce, a Pall Mall tourer on a Springfield (Mass.) Silver Ghost chassis. Information courtesy of Ken Karger, editor of *The Flying Lady.*

The Pennsylvanians, starring in their first musical motion picture, *Syncopation*, 1929.

Fred Waring and Dorothy Lee in *Rah Rah Daze*, 1930.

Fred Waring and Buddy
Rogers, Los Angeles, 1930s.

Evalyn and Fred, from a Warner Brothers short of "Alma Martyr," 1932.

Fred Waring in Europe, 1932, in Cadillac Phaeton.

Advertisement for the Old Gold Hour, 1933. This is a stand-up display, presumably used in tobacco stores; the same illustration appeared in printed ads.

New York marquee pairing Bing Crosby and Fred Waring, December 24, 1934.

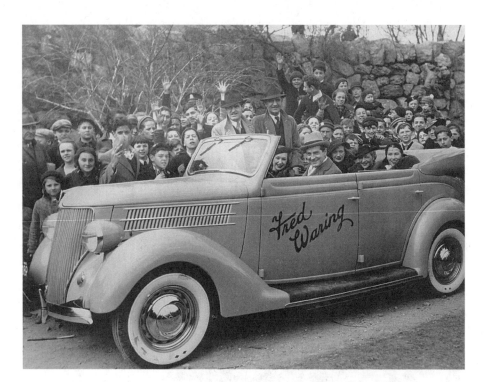

Fred Waring in the 1930s, when he was doing the Ford Hour. A Ford was supplied by the dealer cosponsoring the broadcast.

Fred Waring with (left to right) Rosemary and Priscilla Lane, ca. 1936.

Fred in a crummy back-stage dressing room, mid to late 1930s. The place could be any backstage of any theater of that era—the stairs, the hall radiator, the tiny dirty dressing room, the bulb lights around the mirror—were all typical.

Left to right (standing): Honey Perron, Jane Wilson, Donna Dae, Patsy Garrett, with Fred (seated), in a publicity shot from late 1930s.

Fred Waring, Priscilla and Rosemary Lane, and Dick Powell, in the finale of Warner Brothers movie, *Varsity Show*, staged by Busby Berkeley, 1937.

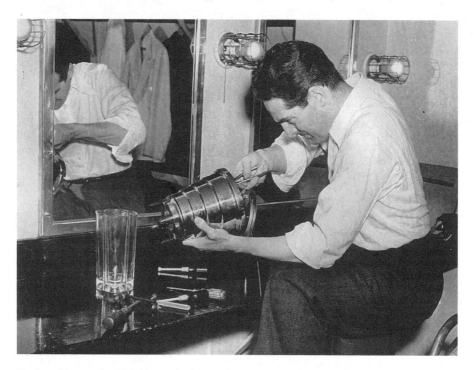

Fred working on the Blendor in a backstage dressing room, 1938–39.

The original glee club, performing on the Chesterfield radio show, 1939. Robert Shaw is in the second row, far right.

Pool champion Willie Hoppe with Fred Waring, in Fred's office, July, 1939. Fred had made a round billiards table, and Willie brought square billiard balls with him. Obviously a publicity stunt.

6

Stairway to Fame

IN THE early years, the Pennsylvanians had played by ear. "We had no music—heavenly days, of course not, and it was difficult to improvise in Tom's ungodly key," recalled Nels Keller. Then still playing on the black keys, Tom began to write out simple arrangements for three trumpets, three saxophones, and two trombones, while he and Poley, on drums, simply filled in. "But," he said, "it was *very* hard because I had to do them all in one key and then transpose them."

When Fred Culley, a pit conductor in Toronto, first saw the band in 1925, he was impressed with those "little dudes, about the same age, the same background. They'd take a melody and enhance it, embellish it. It was amazing what they could do with trite tunes. They were little symphonies. These kids had freedom in their music." By the time Culley joined in 1926, everyone pitched in on arrangements. "They were called 'head arrangements,'" he said. "Fred would come in with a number, an old thing, say, like 'Tea for Two.' We would play the printed stock version, which was pretty bad—they usually were in those days. So then Nels would say, 'Well, gee, I can play this in here,' Freddy Buck would scratch out an introduction, maybe a first chorus with a few tricks in it, Tom would sing a section with maybe a little violin obbligato added, and then Fred would make a head arrangement for the last—change the melody around—just jazz it up. It was patchwork stuff. And Tom was still playing in all the flats."

But Fred knew that if he really wanted to compete with Whiteman, he had to enlarge the band and provide more sophisticated and higher caliber arrangements. Thus began the development of what was to come—the sound became more lush. "Fred never had liked a piano tinkling in the background when they sang—too much like a church choir," Culley continued. "Whenever the music called for a choral sound, the whole band put down their instruments, stood up and sang. And they sang often."

The deep schism and friction between Fred and his supersensitive brother Tom began when the classically trained musicians began to enter. It was Tom, after all, who had launched the whole thing ten years before with Poley. Tom's musical talents—songwriting, arranging, and vocal—were integral threads in the tapestry of the Pennsylvanians. According to early Pennsylvanians, Tom brought new and distinctive chords and sounds to those arrangements—a little ricky-ticky, perhaps, but intriguing and cleverly done with minimum instrumentation. "Everybody liked Tom as a singer because he didn't attempt to be great, and you could always understand lyrics when Tom sang," Nels said. "When he would write and play his own tunes, they were always a little different. Tom did have a soul and heart for music. He had a great personality—people liked him. He was terrific at a party. He could sit down and play all those old songs."

Tom had felt comfortable in the intimacy of the small band: "Our group was still like a bunch of fresh amateurs entertaining at home on the biggest stages in the country. We weren't overprofessionalized. We had enthusiasm and spirit."

Nels: "Everything was memorized with all the gestures. This is why the fellas had to play when we were sick, and I mean *sick!* I played a recording date with a sore lip that was about an inch out. I remember we carried Art Horn onto the stage in Detroit because he was so sick. Once in Philadelphia he was so sick the doctor said not to move him, but we took him anyway to make a recording with us. If anyone was absent, the whole show fell apart. There wasn't an inch of jealousy in that outfit—no jealousy between Fred and the players; absolutely not. We all did everything together—played golf together—took vacations together. When beds were few, I even slept with Fred—no one thought twice about *that* in those days."

But now, with Fred's vision of expansion toward pageantry, spectacle, and breadth of sound, Tom felt pushed aside, disenchanted, and at a loss. As the organization grew, he was humiliated by the more professional musicians who, by and large, were, and still are to this day, a pretty snobbish lot—ask any orchestral conductor. "The musicians started pushing me out of the band," Tom noted. "It was gradual. The Al Evanses, the Charlie Hendersons—they were always trying to reorganize the whole thing. Charlie was very competent, but he was another Harry Simeone—demanding. He found out we didn't read music very well, that some of us couldn't read at all. All of a sudden it became a law—you had to be an experienced reader."

Fred's and Tom's opposing professional aims in life—Tom's intimate, Fred's grandiose—caused them to battle ferociously, and since both had strong wills, it was a simmering situation that would boil up at intervals, bringing heartaches and sadness to them and those around them.

The first outside pianist/arranger, Paul Mertz, joined in 1927, along with a gifted vocal arranger, Fred Ahlert. By this time, one-third of the Pennsylvanians were named Fred. Fortunately, Freddy Buck was called "Petey" most of the time, and the lone business manager, Fred McHugh, was known only as Spike. Fred Campbell had been hired after his younger brother Ward's death. Fred Culley was never called Freddy, nor was Fred Waring, except by his sister, John Royal, and me. His mother sometimes called him Fritzy Boy, as did Frank Sinatra.

Anyway, Mertz said, "What an education I stumbled into. Ahlert would listen to the men sing and then pick out the half-dozen notes that were solid. He would then create that bell-like effect that Waring became known for. The guys would put down their instruments, the soft lights would come on, and then we'd sing. This went over great."[1]

Publisher/agent Danny Winkler: "Payola was very prevalent in the twenties. In 1926, I was with a firm called DeSylva, Brown and Henderson, as general manager. One of my important contacts at that time was Fred Waring. Not only were we close personal friends, but he was a very important man to the popular music publisher because he was what is known as one of the 'Great Plugs.' I remember one of our songs that he took and almost single-handedly made it a great big hit by putting on a presentation of it. It was called 'Tin Pan Parade.' He almost made a standard out of it. It was all due to Fred Waring.

"The only time we gave an actor or band a piece of a song was with the consent of the songwriter. Fred never asked for or accepted any money to perform our songs. He said, 'I'm playing these songs because they're good songs,' and as he told me and others—he was simply paying me back through the firm for giving him first crack at what was a sensational first two years in the publishing business. In those days, you recollect, practically all the big orchestras recorded for either Columbia, Victor, or Brunswick. There was always a battle, especially at Victor, who Fred was with at that time, to get the good songs in these first two years. De Silva, Brown and Henderson had three or four terrifically successful scores for shows that they had written. The minute that the show would open out of town, I would call Fred and say to him, 'These are the four songs I think will go.' As soon as I told him the titles of the songs, he would notify the recording manager at Victor, and he would put a hold on those songs. Rudy Vallee, a contemporary of Fred's at that time, was touring up like a house afire. I say a contemporary, but the only thing about it was that they were both on radio and both were name orchestras. Vallee, of course, in my book, was the guy that had his hand out for more dough. . . .

"I remember we had a show opening in Boston. I told Fred about it, and Vallee came stomping in. He had heard about the opening and he went into [Ed] King and said, 'I want to do these four songs from the show,' and King said, 'I'm sorry but Fred Waring has already spoken for them and we've assigned them to him.'

"Well, he came marching into our firm to find out what it was all about and why Waring always got the preference, and so forth. I told him that the reason I do it for Fred is because Fred returns the favors without any additional favors on my part. For years it became a gag. Every time Vallee would come in to see us, he'd come into my office and say, 'How is the *great god Waring*?' And I'd say, '*The great god Waring* is still the *great god Waring*.'"

"In 1926 we had been appearing in Washington and we took a sleeper to Buffalo," Fred said. "Tom had been taken off the train in Baltimore for an emergency appendectomy. Our train went through Harrisburg, and for some reason the baggage car was shunted off there, and we arrived in Buffalo with nothing but a handful of megaphones. No instruments, no nothing. We get to the theater, and the manager forced us to open the curtain to a full house without a darn bit of music, without an instrument except for the piano they rolled onstage. I got a megaphone. We faked a couple of songs and I looked off in the wings and saw a dozen guys standing there watching us. During a little interlude, I walked offstage and said, 'Who are you?' They said, 'Yale Collegians.' I said, 'What do you do?' 'Well, we played here last week.' I said, 'Do you have any instruments?' They said, 'Yes.' I said, 'Go get them, we need 'em.' So they went and got them and brought them to us onstage and we used them for the rest of the show.

"One of the fellows was very interested in our show and watched very carefully. His name was Rudy Vallee. Later on in his book he said he got his inspiration to become a leader by watching us in Buffalo. He said, 'If Fred Waring can sing through a megaphone—then I can.' Rudy was never much better than I was, but he was a good showman. He responded to adulation. Everybody thought he was beautiful and they loved the sound of his voice and that he was handsome. He responded. He did everything they expected him to do."

Because of Fred's innovative ideas and distinct style of stage presentations, he was a prime target for imitators, beginning in the twenties. John Royal said, "Christ! One act stole practically everything but the gold in his teeth." About another act *Variety* reported:

> The rawest "steal" in the stage show business for years around here occurred last week at the Pantages when "The Pennsylvanians" were billed as a 10-piece band with Harry Shannon Jr. featured.
>
> But the theatre and Shannon knew they were participating in a deception when lifting "The Pennsylvanians."
>
> Not only was the attempt a very bad one for the show business but the band was even worse. It played and tried to do "business" of a comedy kind upon the stage as though the members had just been thrown together out of honky tonks.[2]

By the end of 1926, Fred encountered once more a persistent old bugaboo: he couldn't persuade the bookers to elevate his stipend. He had wired everywhere frantically and had been systematically turned down. So Fred, the gutsy entrepreneur, decided to try out an entirely new concept. He would book the Pennsylvanians on a two-month series of one-night stands in dance halls and call it a Concert-Dance Tour. The idea was to play for dancing, perform a half-hour show at 10 P.M., and then resume the dancing. Promoters and sundry showmen said he was crazy. Was he? Well, let's see.

It was off-season, they insisted, the freezing months of January and February, when no one would leave their warm fires to attend a Waring show. Their nays, of course, only made Fred more determined. By this time, the Pennsylvanians were carting around twenty trunks for sixty or seventy instruments and eight personal trunks for seventeen musicians, which made the prospect even gloomier.

But Fred was right. After the first week, one reporter said, "If you haven't heard the Pennsylvanians in their new dance concert appearance, leave the dishes in the sink and take advantage to hear one of the greatest orchestras."[3]

Every week Fred inserted in *Variety* a clever announcement detailing their take and offering a nightly weather report, to boot. A reporter from *Variety* stated on February 2, 1927, that Waring's gross each week averaged $9,000! Fred's plan, contrary to the doomsayers, succeeded beyond even his expectations. The following months produced reviews and weekly grosses that were better than ever. The *Cleveland News,* for example, reported, "They play as few orchestras do. I know of but one in the theater that shows the directing skill shown by Signor Waring and that is his fat friend, Paul Whiteman."[4]

It had been ten years since they started—ten years of working seven days a week, creating new weekly shows, rehearsing, rehearsing and rehearsing, eating and sleeping in boardinghouses, and riding milk trains from city to city. But the boys never objected. "Because, after all, we were on the first team," as Nels expressed it. "Ours was recognized as the greatest stage show in the country. Oh, heavenly days, yes!" The *Baltimore News-Post* concurred: "It isn't fair to ask any ordinary moving picture to compete on a program with Waring's Pennsylvanians. The Pennsylvanians are a better attraction than forty-nine movies out of fifty. There is but one god of Jazz and Fred Waring is his prophet."[5]

Fred never let up on discipline—it was practice and more practice. The *Columbus (Ohio) State Journal* headlined an article: PARTIES NOT RELISHED BY WARING'S BANDBOYS. "It may be all right for a few hours, but Fred works them too hard the next day. They are wined and dined after a hard night's work and shipped back to their hotel about 4 A.M. No sooner have they hit the hay than Simon Legree in the form of Waring himself roots them out for practice and rehearsal."[6]

One critic, aware of the curt dismissal Fred had received when he wanted to join the glee club in college, mused, "I wonder what that director thinks when he sees Fred Waring step debonairly out to the front of the stage to conduct his breezy young orchestra." He added, "Today Waring makes $4,000 a week—a college graduate might make $5,000 in twenty-five years if industrious."[7]

On a philosophical note, Fred once said, "The stage is a selfish master. It is a hard master to beat, for it takes so much from one and gives him or her few moments of relaxation. There is fame, success and fortune, of course, for those who are gifted, but the path is difficult and full of heartaches. People in everyday lines of professional and commercial pursuits may take off an evening, enjoy a weekend in the country, run off to friends and parents during holidays or indulge in open air pastime for a length of time, but this is not the lot of the stage follower. One must give up lots of pleasures in order to study and prepare for the thing called stage techniques. We study, study, study, and then more study.

"In order to master a new number, we can think of nothing else but the selection. There's the orchestra, the tempo, the momentum, the novelty elements to be incorporated, the solos, the comedy elements and whatnot to be considered. Pleasure is a matter of secondary importance. We give up our pleasure for work, because we all love to do what we are doing."[8]

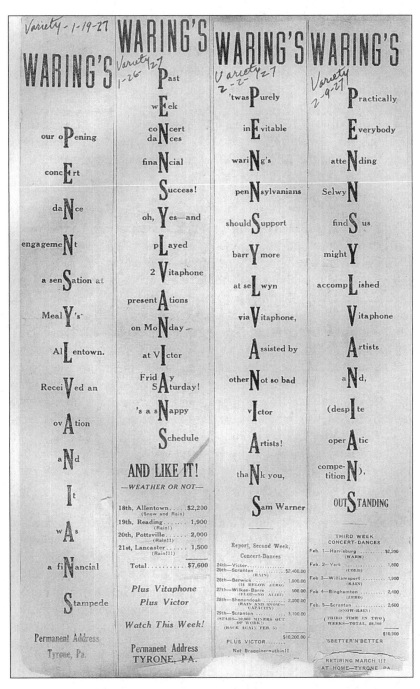

Ads for Waring's Pennsylvanians, *Variety*, weekly, Jan. 19 through Feb. 9, 1927.

During their improvising days, the band used any and all methods for amusing and diverting the audiences. A full-page spread appearing in the *Philadelphia Record* noted: "The brass team uses ordinary tin cans to produce a wa-wa in a blues number and produces the tremolo of a great organ with the same tin cans. Those cans held at the bell (aperture) of a trumpet or trombone result in an amazing replica of the human voice. A perfect imitation of a Scottish bagpipe is obtained by placing a salt shaker on the strings of a violin next to the bridge. Then Fred Waring says, with a grin, that the crusade for clean music is really responsible for his introducing a washboard into his orchestra."[9]

· · ·

In 1927 Fred dreamed up a new visual showstopper around a spirited and catchy tune of the day, "Dancing Tambourines." It was to be a ballet of lights on a darkened stage. Each Pennsylvanian would hold a light made out of a round tin baking pan with a flashlight soldered in it. Fred was making them himself while they were performing in Philadelphia. He said, "I remember the day—I took a trip to New York to get one last bit of equipment. It was May 21, 1927—the date Lindbergh landed at Le Bourget in France."

The tambourines were a hit. Once seen, no one ever forgot the impression it made on them. In 1980 when Fred celebrated his eightieth birthday and simultaneously "shot his age" in golf, as he put it, he received a letter from a fan who recalled seeing the tambourine number in the twenties at the Stanley Theater in Philadelphia. She wrote, "The stage was in total darkness when small lights began to appear until finally the stage was a myriad of lights—like fireflies. Then the lights grew bigger and began to dance."[10]

Because their movements were restricted, Fred devised a much more complicated scenario called "Dancing Dominos." This time he took an oblong cake pan, soldered in a flashlight, and covered it with shellacked linen marked with domino dots. (Dominos was a popular game in the twenties.) The men held one in each hand and not only had to press a button in either hand on a certain beat but also had to move around quickly on a totally darkened stage. Everybody worked but the piano player.

Every year the dancing domino sequence became more intricate and elaborate. A reporter described it four years later in the *Buffalo Courier Express:*

> The dominos . . . form dancing men whose legs dangle and kick to the rhythmic beat of the tune. Suddenly these figures fall apart and one mas-

sive dancing goblin takes up the center of the stage and wiggles through the chorus of the number with a snake-hip and rolling shoulder dance.

All this is done in a completely blackened stage and auditorium, while the music unmistakably is coming from the orchestra on the platform. . . .

If one were allowed to watch the Pennsylvanians rehearsing this electrical illusion, he would see a score of collegiate acrobats clambering over shoulders, passing the illuminated dominos from one to the other, all the counts of director Waring and every member of the orchestra of 20 alternating his movements with playing his portions of the melody.

If, by some stroke of fate, the house lights were flashed on in the middle of the routine, the audiences might see a cornetist flat on his stomach as he piped out his tones, while high up on the platform the trombone player would be seen mounted on the bass viol's shoulders frantically waving a quartet of lighted dominos, two in each hand.

Every movement must be timed accurately and measured to a fraction of an inch and all in total darkness. One slip, a misplaced foot or a slanting arm, and the entire number is thrown out of rhythm and the figures become imperfect.

The space allotted is just large enough to allow for the passage of a player, for musical instruments, chairs and racks fill up the platform, and the boys must circle around and in between these as they climb, stoop and jump to their places in the drill.

Waring first works out all his drills and musical tricks on paper, after which they are transferred to blueprints and a copy given to each member of the organization.

. . . a series of practice periods were worked with the players blindfolded. Once they became accustomed to the crosses and learned where every item on the platform was placed, the tempo of the tune was adjusted to synchronize with the men's movements. . . . Neither Waring nor his band uses makeup.[11]

*　*　*

For his last tour in 1983, Fred decided to revive a segment of this bit of nostalgia for his road show. He was obliged to use young singers instead of instrumentalists. They weren't disciplined in pushing buttons on a certain beat—a technique any horn or piano player could have accommodated. The skit was rehearsed every day for three weeks. Never having seen the dominos, I was looking forward to the dress rehearsal—but what an unmitigated disaster! The foot fell off; everything was disjointed. I could hear suppressed oaths as the Pennsylvanians bumped into each other in the dark. We in the audience found it hilariously funny, but Fred, like Queen Victoria, was *not* amused, and deleted it. Later, on the road, the drummer asked Fred if he could work with the group, and finally, after weeks of diligent rehearsals, it was put back in the show.

Fred's admiration for Paul Whiteman and his orchestra extended to others as well, especially some of the struggling new bands facing the same problems he and his men confronted.

"In 1927 when Dot and I went to a wedding party in North Carolina, a band called Hal Kemp was playing," Fred said. "It was an exciting band and I fell in love with the group. We first brought them up to Tyrone. Mother fed and housed them, and we found places for them to rehearse. We gave them instruments and costumes and tried to help them develop an act, since up to then they had been more of a dance band. Then I got them booked in Shea's Buffalo and Shea's Toronto and finally got them booked in the Strand Roof in New York where they had a long run."

The young promising band gave Fred an idea. "I remember one time when Fred said, 'Boy, wouldn't it be nice to have a small band sort of augmented with us,'" Nels said. "We would sing and have the band playing behind us and then both bands would play together."

"I remember Hal Kemp and his band coming in and being broke and hungry," Fred's sister Dolly said. "Mother fed them, and I can remember one of the boys coming out and saying, 'If you will just give me a piece of bread, a crust of bread, I am so hungry, I don't know what to do.' But that was typical in those days, you know, bands traveling all the time all over the country, and the poor kids not having enough to eat." Fellow musicians like the Dorseys, Kay Kayser, the Coon-Sanders band, and others often stopped at the Waring home for free room and board. Fred would tell them when they were hard up and between dates to stop at Tyrone. Poor Dolly and Jesse.

"We were always staying at Poley's or Fred's home, and eating at Fred's house all the time, and I never heard Jesse gripe at that gang of kids in there," Nels said. "Our rehearsals must have driven her crazy. I don't know how she stood it." Fred's poor mother. First the drunks, then the boys of the band, plus all sorts of itinerant groups passing through. It's a pity Jesse didn't complain, at least a little, or Fred might not have expected so much of his future wives! Dottie was never faced with that particular problem, since she and Fred never had a home.

• • •

Fred's career was gaining momentum, but his marriage was undermined by a flawed premise and aggravated by an impossible lifestyle, constant travel, and flappers. *Variety* reported: "PHILADELPHIA—A novel sight to the showmen of this town last week were the women, mostly flappers, waiting outside the stage door of the Stanley Theatre picture house, to see the boys of Waring's Pennsylvanians orchestra leave the theatre. This was a daily occurrence and is said to happen with the band boys everywhere."[12]

Few men can handle this kind of constant feminine adulation and not lose their perspective, and I'm afraid Fred was not one of them, although at this point his life was too hectic and transient for any serious "extra-curricular" activities. "Dot was a society girl—she rarely came around," Fred Culley said. "She was thoroughly disinterested in Fred's business—they had nothing in common."

"One night in New York after a play, Mother and I went up in an elevator with Dot and Fred," Helen said. "They looked like two antagonists. I thought the place would explode. When we got off, I said to Mother, 'It looks like they are going to have a fuss.' She said, 'A fuss—they're going to have a fight!' Dot was tiny but she was an explosive little girl—lots of personality but very positive. I thought then, if she ever bumps with Fred when he's in a mood not to be bumped, she's going to come out not on the same train. She didn't bend at all."

Fred: "At first we had fun together. But later we seemed to have as much fun with somebody else."

Yes, all they talked about was having fun, but then it was the Roaring Twenties—the era characterized by excess, dedicated to abandon, and preoccupied by sensuousness, a scenario played out with raccoon coats, rumble seats, and hip flasks.

The infant motion picture industry was beginning to attract Fred's attention in the late 1920s. "When talking pictures first came out, Warner Brothers began to grab leading artists," Fred recounted. "They wanted to make some shorts to be sure of their footing. We had a lot of novelty numbers in our act with choreography and cute things. Warner Brothers asked us to make the first short. Sam Warner lived in Brooklyn then. He was a dreamboat. They were very patient with us. We had never been under lights. I shall never forget the experience. Not only was it so hot that we could hardly tolerate it, but at the end of the day we had almost gone blind from the lights. We were all at the Warwick Hotel in New York, and at about 1 A.M., the kids began calling me saying, 'We're going crazy.' They had 'Kleig eyes' and didn't know what to do. Some were threatening to jump out of the windows, they were so frantic with pain. I called Sam Warner at 2:30 in the morning, asking what to do. He said, 'You stay where you are. I'll be there.' He got out of bed, went to a drugstore, and got some special eyewash, brought it to us, and went around to all the rooms of all of our kids and applied the eyewash for them to relieve them of this horrible, excruciating pain."

.   .   .

By 1928, in addition to the twenty instrument trunks, one thickly padded with sections for three violins, the Pennsylvanians were now transporting ten wardrobe trunks—but still only one business manager, Spike McHugh. "He was secretary, treasurer, box office," Tom remembered. "He carried all his business in a briefcase. We finally had to get a letter file for him to carry around. Spike always prided himself that he never made a mistake, until one day he couldn't find six cents. He damned near died. I used to room with him. When we would wake up in the morning, he would crack every joint in his body. *Oh gawd!!*" The band, now counting eighteen men who played more than forty instruments, with all their scores memorized, grossed around $4,000 a week. A ladies' slip cost 65¢ and a pair of boys' tennis shoes, $1.35. Their business address was still Tyrone, Pennsylvania.

In those days Fred never uttered a word onstage. As Nels Keller succinctly explained, "Fred didn't open his trap." The gracious and humorous emcee that radio and television audiences came to know, the man who loathed intermissions and had to come out in front of the curtain and kid around with the audiences, hadn't yet metamorphosed. When the band first started, an usher from the theater would come onstage with a placard showing the name of the next piece. Then Scotty Bates, besides being thrown around in a blanket, was given the job of bringing out the cards. He was a naturally funny pantomimist, a cute little devil and "mis-che*ev*ous," as Fred's manager Johnny O'Connor would say. He would get a laugh by bringing in the cards upside down. Once he accidentally tripped as he came running out and slid halfway across the stage. That brought down the house and Fred kept it in the show—bruised limbs be damned. Anything for a laugh. Fred was amused when the diminutive Scotty would be discovered backstage asleep in a bass fiddle case.

Scotty, not being a musician, became a gofer. He was quite irresponsible and did some crazy things. A few years later he married, and Culley said that he and his wife Lil were devoted to each other. But one time he hung her out of a hotel window by her heels because she wouldn't do something. Another episode involved a fire he built in the corner of his hotel room because he was cold. "He burned a rug—cost us a little money."

Although Fred never claimed to be a jazz exponent, he never hesitated to express his beliefs. In 1928, in a two-column Boston interview that included a full-length picture of Fred in an ankle-length fur coat, the headline stated: FRED WARING, CONDUCTOR OF "MODERN MUSIC," DECLARES HIS ART IS HARDER THAN SYMPHONIES:

> He claims that what symphony orchestras call jazz is simply modern music which they don't know how to play. He says that the eminent conductor of the Boston Symphony (Koussevitsky) or any other great conductor, with the one exception of his friend, Leopold Stokowski, of the Philadelphia Symphony, could not hold a theatre audience five minutes. I retorted, "But these men have no desire to play and compete in motion picture theatres."
>
> Waring: "This may be so, but it makes me mad when they say there is no art in what we do. Sure, a great symphony is a wonderful thing, but like Shakespeare, Browning and Milton, you can't feed on it all the time. You must have something more livable, something that makes people smile— that is the aim of our modern music. It is one hard job, and I know it."

The interviewer's final comment: "and all through the interview, the young leader never smiled."[13]

Meanwhile, the overzealous copycats continued to crawl forth:

> Just as Waring's Pennsylvanians began the recent fortnight engagement at the Palace Theatre on Broadway, a Chinese restaurant a few blocks north advertised a musical attraction called "Frank Weingar's Pennsylvanians." The similarity in names struck us as singular, but what stood out was the manner in which the Chink [sic] restaurant owner exploited his attraction. Small college pennants flew from the sidewalk canopy and a banner carrying the band's billing stared the passing pedestrian in the eye, coming north or south on Broadway. At a distance anyone might have accepted this as an announcement that Waring's Band was employed there, since Waring always employs the pennant style of advertising, and, as far as we know, was the first to play around here with the "Pennsylvanians" as a trade title for his musical group.
>
> Perhaps the Broadway theatregoing public recognizes the Waring outfit as Waring's Pennsylvanians, and when another musical aggregation comes along with this billing, the theatregoing public is bound to suffer through the confliction, and it looks from this spot as though the chop suey salesman has selected John Public.[14]

A newspaper announced: "Ha! Ha! It is to laugh! To compare this world famous Jazz Band, Waring's Pennsylvanians, with others who try to imitate them is like comparing STERLING SILVER WITH TIN FOIL."[15]

7

Paris

IN FEBRUARY of 1928, Fred an-
nounced that the Pennsylvanians had been booked in Paris for two
months at the internationally famous Théâtre-Restaurant des Ambassadeurs. The show was to be written by Cole Porter and performed by Clifton Webb, then known as a dancer, Morton Downey, and a bevy of pretty show girls. The Pennsylvanians and their wives were excited and
scurrying around for passports, steamer trunks, and French phrase books.
They were to sail on the *Ile de France,* an elegant new ocean liner.

Fred, always thinking ahead, was concerned about his boys being forgotten while they were away. "We had taken a big cut in salary to go to
Europe but I felt we needed a shot in the arm—'Just returned from Europe, etc.' I had a feeling it would increase our salary." He then prevailed
upon Johnny O'Connor, a small rugged Irishman—shorter than Fred—
who possessed an ever-constant imagination, to release a story about the
Pennsylvanians as often as he could (while they were in France)—anything to keep them in the public eye. O'Connor had been around the
block. Unless forced by necessity, though, he would never consider expos-
ing himself to the wilds of anything west of Hoboken, New Jersey. He was
"a former theatrical reporter, an alumnus of *Variety* and the *Morning
Telegraph,* and the author of *Broadway Racketeers,* a highly successful
exposé of the cons, gyps, molls, thugs and dips by an expert one-time
observer who *not only knows where all the headstones are but whose bodies they mark.*"[1] The *Telegraph,* an important amusement and entertain-

ment publication at that time, had on its editorial staff Bat Masterson, Gene Fowler, Ben Hecht, Westbrook Pegler, and Ring Lardner.

Johnny had just seen the Pennsylvanians perform and was impressed, and when he met Fred and Dot, he was entranced. So he agreed. He got in touch with Joseph Kennedy, then head of Pathé News, and arranged for newsreel photographers to film the Pennsylvanians in intriguing poses against the riggings of the *Ile de France* as they set sail for gay Paree. Because it was Pathé, the news clips were shown across the country.

While on the high seas, Poley, who was highly susceptible to the effects of alcohol, fell out of the upper berth in his and Yvette's cabin and sprained a big toe. Yvette was subsequently disturbed by a French nurse's persistent attentions to Poley. (All wives had been warned of the sexy behavior that could be expected of anyone whose national anthem was the "Marseillaise.") "That nurse couldn't leave him alone. She couldn't stop rubbing his toe with Baume Bengué. That's all I could smell in the cabin," Yvette related jealously more than five decades later.

O'Connor wanted to make a still bigger impression for their Parisian opening at Les Ambassadeurs. He dug out an old Blue Book, copied all the names that sounded French, and reported their ringside presence at the gala. The *New York World-Telegram* gave it a two-column spread.[2] Johnny learned later that most of the people he listed had died forty years earlier. Another O'Connor press release included Democratic presidential candidate Al Smith. It announced that all the children around Paris were singing and dancing to "East Side West Side," Smith's campaign tune, that Waring had played it for 2,500 guests at U.S. ambassador Myron T. Herrick's lawn party on Independence Day, and that the tune was sweeping Paris. Johnny added, "Needless to say, every Democratic paper in the country put it on the front page with a picture of Waring and Smith." It is true they played at the ambassador's party, where a medal was given to Lindbergh . . . by proxy.

"Cole Porter met us when we arrived and immediately took us to Montmartre to an Americanized restaurant where we could get scrambled eggs," Fred said. "The girls had to go to the bathroom. They went in on the left and the men on the right, but in Paris in those days it was pretty open on the inside to both sexes. I'll never forget standing there and a woman standing in back of me. The girls were soon screaming their heads off."

Fred's description sparks my memory of when, as a young woman newly arrived in Paris, I was walking down the Champs Elysées, surrounded by a troupe of boys and their counselor from Northwestern University, who had adopted me on the ship coming over. They took me everywhere before my day of registration at the summer school in the château of Fontainebleau, where I was to study piano with France's premier pianist, Robert Casadesus. On each block, I saw a small round structure on the wide sidewalk that looked like a kiosk but was actually a men's public urinal. I could see feet protruding below and sometimes a head above. For a young girl who had moved from a small town to an all-women's college, who upon receiving a scholarship to France had boarded a train alone for New York and Paris the night she was graduated, and who always believed necking implied "only from the neck up," these latrines were a bit of a culture shock.

At any rate, the five wives going to Paris had taken some French lessons before boarding the *Ile de France.* Yvette, speaking a few French phrases with me more than fifty years later, pronounced *merci* as *mercy,* as in "the quality of *mercy* is not strained." She could still repeat what she would call down to Poley at 2:30 A.M. when he would stand under her hotel window after the show and ask her what kind of sandwich she'd like. "*Jambon sans beurre,*" she'd shout (ham without butter). The one thing that miffed Yvette were the forty show girls—"hand-picked beauties," according to Bill Townsend, the Canadian. They had been brought over by Bobby Connolly, the most popular choreographer on Broadway. "They came over in inexpensive clothes and went home in mink coats," she sniffed a half century later.

The Théâtre-Restaurant des Ambassadeurs was a spacious odeum with trees growing inside and a movable steel roof that closed in inclement weather. The daily musical menu consisted of a French band, an Argentine band, a concert orchestra, and the Pennsylvanians, who played for tea dancing at 4 P.M. and for the Cole Porter show at 10 P.M. The Pennsylvanians were given star billing since theirs was the biggest name.

According to Tom, there were a few opening-night snags. "George Gershwin's sister was to sing a group of her brother's songs. It was Gershwin year in Paris due to Elsa Maxwell. While his sister Frances and I were rehearsing, I pulled a flub on the piano. George had just come in and said, 'If you come over to my apartment after rehearsal, I'll show you how to play these things.' I said, 'George, you don't seem to understand that I don't read music and no matter what you would do, it wouldn't help me. You'll have to play for her yourself, which would be a hell of a lot better anyway.' So he did. He played for her opening night, and nobody in God's world laid the egg this girl did. She opened and closed in one night, and I've never heard of her since."

Fred wasn't satisfied merely with conducting for the Cole Porter show. He wanted his Pennsylvanians to sing and play and do their show, too, after the 10 P.M. performance. The club manager wanted no part of it. He was furious and, according to Nels, "tore his hair. But we did it every night—pulled the piano out ourselves in this classy joint and did some of our stage numbers. The manager came around to all the men in the band and said quietly, 'You fellas want to play in Deauville? In the summer you can play Deauville and in the winter you can play here.' And we said, 'Oh, boy, sure!' Then he said, 'Not with *him*!' pointing to Fred. We could have done it, but it was like saying to us, 'Do you want to disown your mother or father?' It was just unheard of. Can you imagine a bunch of guys today turning down such a lucrative offer?"

Clifton Webb evidently had some perks written into his contract that Fred rather envied—such as dinner served in his dressing room every evening, champagne—"and things of that sort for which we had to pay tremendous fees."

"Everybody came to Les Ambassadeurs—everybody—English royalty (the duke of Kent sat in and played Poley's drums), Garbo and Grace Moore," Tom said. "Baron Rothschild loved us and was responsible for Fred's receiving a cultural honor—the Palm of the French Academy. At that time, only two Americans had been so honored. We played a benefit for the baron at his home, which looked like an annex to the Louvre."

Fred, always the sportsman, enjoyed lunching and hobnobbing with boxing champion Georges Carpentier and tennis champions Henri Cochet and René LaCoste, who had beaten Bill Tilden. The Pennsylvanians played at Adolphe Menjou's wedding to Catherine Carrer, which took place at City Hall at 10 A.M., and later serenaded the couple at the Gare du Nord when they departed by train for their honeymoon.

It was an exciting time for the little band of naive young men from Tyrone, Pennsylvania. "One night they had a Bastille Day celebration," Fred said. "Everybody was there. In those days royalty and French aristocracy were still taken seriously. Chevalier entertained. I have never heard such cheering and applauding. They were screaming. I couldn't understand it because to me he didn't have a voice. But he had such a charming personality. Obviously, he was a French hero. There was no question about his charisma and popularity. He sang and sang and sang and sang. They wouldn't let him stop. I met him later when he came to Hollywood.

In Las Vegas in the fifties, Danny Kaye and Chevalier came to see our show many times—sat down front and cheered us on."

When Maurice Chevalier came to rehearse for the Bastille benefit, he brought his two piano players over to Tom and said very graciously, "I would like, Mr. Waring, if you would show my men how to get a little American rhythm. That is all we lack. They thought maybe you could help them." Tom became very fond of Chevalier and said Jacques Frey was the sweetest guy on earth, but Braggiotti had the distinction of getting on Tom's shit list.

The Pennsylvanians gave two concerts at the Salle Pleyel. As reported the *Paris Herald Tribune*: "Fred Waring and his aggregation received the greatest ovation ever given in the French capital. There is sort of mob psychology behind the success of these Americans in France, and it seems to be Fred Waring's innate modest and unassuming manner of attempting the ultra in musical entertainment without making an effort at revolutionizing music."[3]

•   •   •

Fred and Dot and Morton Downey were sharing a suite at a new hotel called the Novarro, 44 Rue Blondelle, on the Right Bank of the Seine. They had all settled in for two months of fun. Downey, a well-liked, gregarious and highly motivated man, seemed to know everybody. "Mort and I were always pulling practical jokes on one another," Fred said. Mort would ring Fred's telephone, pretending to be Madame Bernhardt, Nijinsky, or Charles Lindbergh.

"On one particular day he taught the Argentine Tango Band some dirty words," Fred said. "They had taken our megaphones off the stands and had concealed them. We were compelled to perform without them. As we were about to go off the stage, we look over and see the Argentines holding our megaphones to their mouths and they say, '*Shit!*' We were terribly embarrassed since there were many Americans and English who heard it too. Fortunately, everyone laughed. That night we finished about 2 A.M. I decided instead of going out the stage door to go out the front, through the auditorium. It was dark and empty. At the checkroom I heard the phone ringing. I picked up the phone, and a voice with an extreme British accent, said, 'Hello, hello, calling Fred Waring. America calling Fred Waring.'

"I said, 'Oh, come on, Downey, don't try to pull another joke like that!' I hung up. Damn phone rang again. I said, 'Hello, Downey, what is it?'

"'Hello, this is the London operator. I'm trying to locate Mr. Fred Waring. This is an overseas call.' It was the first overseas call anyone had ever heard of around here.

"I said, 'Okay, this is Fred Waring. What is it?'

"'Hold the line please. Hello, America, I have Mr. Fred Waring on the line.'

"On the other end, '*Freddy!*' It was John Royal. He said, 'I'm in Cleveland. Just wanted to be the first to call overseas, to talk to you, to give you my love, and to see how you are and I want to book you into Cleveland in the Palace as soon as you get home.'

"I said, 'Okay, John.' So we booked the Palace."

Downey wasn't the only practical jokester. Fred remembered one played on Sid Grauman: "Sid used to hold auditions for new acts at his Chinese Theater. He would invite Harold Lloyd, Gloria Swanson, and me, and would swear and complain about the terrible acts. One night a bicycle act was especially atrocious, and Sid was especially violent. He was rather taken aback when he had ordered the bicycle out—never to come back—that the riders turned out to be Gloria and Harold."

•   •   •

Composer/arranger Leo Arnaud: "It was in 1928 that I met Fred in Paris when he was playing at Les Ambassadeurs. He heard some of the arrangements I had made for a band I was with, and a few days later offered me a three-year contract for $8,000 a year plus extra money for arrangements, recordings, radio, and *television.* In 1928 nobody knew about TV and this amount wasn't an everyday offer. It took me three years to get to America—because I applied for the 'Quota.' I arrived in August, 1931."

"Everybody in Paris knew about Leo Arnaud," Fred said. "He was gifted, brilliant—had studied with Vincent D'Indy and Maurice Ravel, and was a marvelous trombonist. I offered him a job, and three years later he called me while we were playing the Palace Theater in New York. He was in Canada. He had gotten married in order to pass customs. He had married a girl who had to reach America as well. They arrived in New York, and we put the girl in a few shows to get her started. They divorced as soon as he joined us and she was established. Her name was Ella Logan. She became a tremendous Broadway star."

In the fifties I became acquainted with Leo, that witty, energetic, volatile Frenchman, on one of our annual visits to the Los Angeles area. He used to make and drink his own absinthe. Although he bragged it would eat through varnish on his desk, it never seemed to affect his health. His teeth were unblemished and his thick hair remained black until his mid-seventies. He gave Fred a quart of absinthe, which was then poured into a cleaned-out apricot brandy bottle and tucked away. It tasted like licorice. Sometimes Fred would put a few drops in a Waring Blendor full of daiquiris, and it would give them a *je ne sais quoi* kind of taste—no one could figure out what made his daiquiris so special.

Fred's young and gifted musician Freddy Buck had been sent to Paris earlier to make arrangements of the Cole Porter music. He had worked long hours, and by the time Fred and the gang arrived, he looked terrible. His lifelong weakness for tuberculosis had caught up with him. Fred sent him to a famous TB sanitarium in Switzerland and paid the bills. Freddy remained there long after the Pennsylvanians returned to the United States.

Fred was involved in one little adventure that didn't endear him either to his wife or the Armenian manager of the Ambassadeurs: "There was a little girl in the show named Evelyn Hoey. A bandleader friend of mine made me promise to look after her in Paris. She was just a kid—about eighteen—a charming child, a nice talent and spark, but limited voice projection. I saw to it that she met the Cole Porter crowd. Her contract finished ahead of ours. I had to get her on a boat train at 6 A.M. (her mother was along too). I got her set on the train and happened to see my dear friend Al Kaufman. With him was Jesse Lasky. So being Evelyn Hoey's pro tem manager, I decided she should meet them. She was already on the train.

"I get back on the train and deposit her in Kaufman and Lasky's drawing room. They are delighted to see her. They think she's cute and I figure this could be a big professional opportunity for her in Hollywood. I'm shaking hands, and the doggone train starts. I try to get out, and no! You can't open the door. I figure I'll get off the next stop. It didn't stop until Cherbourg, some three hundred miles. I didn't realize I didn't have any money until I got off at Cherbourg. There was no train for hours, even if I did have money.

"I see a couple of chauffeur-driven cars lined up. I figure I'll bum a ride. I found one English-speaking chauffeur in front of an Hispano-Suiza town car. The owner said I could ride up front. I had no coat, no hat or anything, and it got cold! About halfway to Paris we came to a lovely hotel. The gentleman and lady go in (they are Americans). I realized they weren't getting a glass of beer because it took them three hours. I had already missed the afternoon tea dance. I was late for the nine o'clock show. The owner, Sayag, was already mad at me. Dot is *really* burning! She thinks I've eloped. I had no interest in the girl. What a tremendous to-do at the Ambassadeur.

"Months and months later we are in Jersey City in a theater, and I get word Cole Porter is coming to show me a new song he has written, 'Love for Sale,' for a trio of mine called the Girl Friends—my three untouched young singers. Cole comes to the stage door with a gang of people with him. One of them is Evelyn Hoey—ebullient, busting all over, laughing and laughing. The man with her, her escort, was the American guy in the car (coming from Cherbourg). Tremendous romance . . . but undercover. The money backing Cole's show, called *The New Yorkers,* was the woman who owned the car. She was from a big oil family and this same man was her paramour—also undercover. The pace was too fast for Evelyn— she committed suicide a few years later."

In 1928, even in Europe, jazz was still not an acceptable form of music in the eyes of many. Fred responded quickly when eminent British critic Ernest Newman wrote: "Jazz requires no brains. All the brains of the jazz exponents would not fill the lining of Johann Strauss' hat."[4]

"We play with our brains and we expect the audience to use their brains also," Fred asserted. "It is an easy thing to scrape across a violin, utter sounds from a throat or beat a tom-tom or a drum. It is simple and anyone can do it. But true syncopation, the basis of modern music, is not an easy accomplishment. Jazz demands finished technique as much as any other art. Syncopation can express any mood, but the orchestra must first determine what it desires to express, and that is why I say we play with our brains as well as hands."[5]

By the time they reached Paris, the marriage that shouldn't have been was finally drawing to a close. Cute, vivacious Dottie decided she would "live it up." She found it exciting to be escorted by titled Englishmen and maharajas while Fred was working—surrounded, of course, by chorus girls and stagestruck groupies. But when they returned to the United States, there were no elegant Frenchmen for diversion, just the same young women lounging around the stage doors. As one New York reporter related, "I encountered a flock of young women at the stage door of the Casino the other night where I went to see Fred Waring and I asked the door tender about them. Oh, them stage door Janes? They're waiting for the lads in the raccoon band."[6]

Tom was so frustrated and unhappy by the end of their stay in Paris that he, the cofounder of the Pennsylvanians, decided after ten years he wanted to get "out of the goddamned business." He went to Berlin for a week with Morton Downey. "We had a wonderful time—a ball. Downey is a great guy." Then he came back to Paris and accepted a solo engagement at the Paramount before sailing for home.

"I put on my tails and opened with 'My Blue Heaven' and was to close with 'Ramona,'" he said. "On the final strains of 'Ramona,' this girl was supposed to play the pipe organ for me which rested below the stage. She was to give me an introduction on the organ; I was to start singing; then she was to press a button and the organ would come up while I was singing, I would then climb on the organ and we would disappear together. She played the introduction and nothing happened. She kept pushing buttons and the thing wouldn't rise. This was the first show, and finally she forgot where she was and yelled out at the top of her lungs, *'For Christ's sake, sing!'* The audience, who turned out to be all English-speaking, roared! Just as she said that, the organ came up. I climbed on and we went down together. That was the first show.

"On the second day, a guy gets in the balcony with one of those whistles that you put water in that sounds like a canary bird. All the while I was singing, the whistle was going and a woman was talking to me from the pit saying, 'That son of a bitch with the whistle!' That went on for four shows. I thought I would die.

"I came back to the United States and tried to get into vaudeville as a single, at the end of 1928. I opened up in Newburgh and was practically stoned out of town. They didn't like any of our acts. Then I worked with Ken Murray, and we had a hell of a lot of laughs. He'd walk through my act and break up the audience. That lasted about six months." Tom, who never had any natural business acumen, found it tough going it alone.

In 1928 the Pennsylvanians were offered a chance to appear in a feature film. "While we were in Paris, a producer from Hollywood saw our show and decided to make the first *musical* motion picture for Pathé Pictures," Fred said. "It was to be titled *Syncopation.* Morton Downey and Barbara Bennett were to star in it with us. At the same time the New York producer George Choos asked us to star in his musical, *Hello Yourself.* We made the picture while in *Hello Yourself*—went out every morning to Long Island. It took four weeks and was a horrible experience. Everybody was fumbling around. They wrote it as they went along. There was so little experience in talking pictures—everything was, 'Hello Betty, Hello Joe'—open up a door for an entrance and then as they left, they had to close the door—saying, 'Goodbye Betty, Goodbye Joe'—that's the kind of picture it was.

"The Long Island studio had a creaky floor. Everyone was in a panic— sound! If a girl's bracelets jangled or dress rustled, they'd yell, '*Cut the scene.'* Or they would ring a gong, meaning no one could move in the whole damn building while they were shooting. During the making of the film, Pathé was dissolved. It had been bought by another firm—Radio Pictures. When the film was finished—Radio Pictures had been bought by Keith Orpheum and became RKO. Because of all this manipulation of the ownership of the film, the release of our picture was shelved for a year. Meantime *Broadway Melody* came out. It was made in Hollywood and made a big splash. Ours came out second, which was a bad break."

There were two hit songs in that ill-fated movie. The producer, George Choos, had thrown a number called "Jericho" out of *Hello Yourself.* Fred rescued it and put it in *Syncopation.* The other hit was "I'll Always Be in Love with You."

The trade was astonished to hear that Johnny O'Connor received $55,000 for Fred to be top billed in the new movie *Syncopation.* The *Morning Telegraph* wondered under a banner head—WARING AT $55,000—how vaudeville would be able to compete.[7]

· · ·

With the advent of *Hello Yourself,* two new girls came into Fred's life. They were brought from California by Choos, the producer, to be in his show. Evalyn Nair, an exotic, dark-eyed, long-legged dancer, was seventeen. Her mother came with her. Dorothy Lee, a "tiny package of dynamite," was fifteen.

"We started rehearsal for *Hello Yourself* and these two little kids were there—this beautiful girl in a black leotard was stretching and doing, you know, what girls do at rehearsal halls, along with this other cute little trick, Dorothy Lee," Fred Culley said. "They were friends."

Fred Waring's thoughts: "Dorothy Lee was an exciting kid—she stopped the show every night with her shenanigans. She was quite athletic—a bobby-soxer—the John Held type. [John Held created cartoon figures patterned after the Pennsylvanians' collegiate look.] Evalyn, the dancer, was good but not as vital as Dorothy Lee onstage. It turned out that Dorothy Lee was married. She was only fifteen. She turned up pregnant, had an abortion after the Saturday matinee and came back into the show that night. She had this very athletic routine and it didn't stop her at all." Dorothy Lee truly was indefatigable—she married at least six or seven more times.

Fred was more and more aware that he needed talented arrangers to help his musical growth. "I knew a shy little fellow, a Harvard graduate named Charlie Henderson, who came to New York and told me he wanted above all to meet Fred Waring," Danny Winkler said. "Fred was in *Hello Yourself*. I called Fred and told him all about the boy and his background. Fred said, 'Well, look, I could talk to him for twenty days and I wouldn't know anything about him. If he wants me to look at some of his work, give him our instrumentation, have him arrange something and at our next rehearsal we'll run over it. I can tell you then whether or not he's going to be any good to us.' Fred picked a song, Henderson arranged it, the boys got into it, and at the end Fred said, 'If you want to—you're working for me.'

"Henderson was with Fred for years and years, and told me later, when he came out to 20th Century Fox as vocal arranger and coach, that he was successful because of his early training with Waring." Most everyone who left said the same thing, even though at the time they often didn't understand Fred and some weren't sure they even liked him due to his stringent demands for precise stage performances.

After *Hello Yourself* closed in New York, it reopened in Chicago for a six-month run. While there, Fred became involved with some professional jai alai players who had been brought over from the Basque country of Spain. He spent every hour between shows at the fronton learning to catch and throw the rock-hard *pelota* with the long basketlike contrivance, the *cesta,* which players wear on their hand. Jai alai is one of the fastest games in the world, requiring exquisite hand and foot coordination. The Basques played with Fred almost every day, and at the end considered him one of the better players in the country. His *cesta* rests with his memorabilia at Penn State.

When Fred returned from Paris, he and Johnny O'Connor agreed to get together with nothing more formal than a handshake. The understanding was that O'Connor would take complete charge of the business and never interfere in the music or the programming. "I never attended a rehearsal in the whole twenty-one years that I was with them," O'Connor said. "And I was only in Waring's home five times—all funerals." One reason Fred and Johnny O'Connor hit it off well was the fact that Johnny didn't tell him *how* to spend his money. Johnny was smart and believed in Fred. "At that time his was the greatest entertaining band the theater ever had, which very few people remember or have seen in this generation," he said.

O'Connor had just opened a single-room office on the tenth floor in what was then known as the Hammerstein Building at Fifty-third and Broadway. After their verbal commitment to each other, O'Connor rented one more room for Fred. Fred remained in that building for twenty-seven years, adding rooms and floors as his organization grew.

Because of all the publicity that came out in the United States about Fred's Paris engagement, O'Connor realized he had a great opportunity to raise his salary. At first Johnny put Fred in vaudeville picture houses, but the next move was to motion picture theaters. "Vaudeville was now losing out," O'Connor said. "Only some of the top houses were still open and they were featuring pictures. The picture producers *owned* the theaters as well as controlled them, and they owned the studios. There was Paramount, Warner, and the First National Group. Joe Kennedy owned Pathé, and he came down to New York when Albee was gettin' tired and vaudeville was about to fold, and bought him out. Later it was called Radio Keith Orpheum—RKO—and then he finally sold to Sarnoff.

"The first big deal I made for Waring was at the Paramount for sixteen weeks: $6,500 net. They were to pay baggage hauls, union help, and all transportation including a forty-foot baggage car which Waring needed for trunks, platforms, music, etc. That's when I learned about pictures and Waring. They certainly did load him up with lousy pictures—but despite that, he was a draw."

The *Philadelphia Bulletin* confirmed Fred's success: "These eighteen collegiate musicians and their popular young leader are the holders of box office records in twenty-five of America's leading motion picture theatres. In other words, Waring's Pennsylvanians attracted more money to the box office of the theatre at which they were appearing than any other attraction offered at that house."[8]

"Later on, when Waring was in the $10,000 a week class, I always demanded a woman star," O'Connor said. "I wouldn't put him up against a male star."

• • •

After the closing of *Hello Yourself,* the format of an all-male band was changed. For the first time girls were included, and Fred, the late bloomer, seemed to start his delayed adolescence. Cora Ballard, his secretary and friend of many years, said later, "Fred's a sexy guy. I think he's sexier than a lot of men."

Yes, he was a sexy, charismatic man, all right. His eyes were blue and bright—never missed anything. His hair was thick, dark, and curly. He wasn't tall, but in those days was thin and agile—had marvelous reflexes. But what is charisma, anyway? Is it more energy and sex hormones than what others possess? Fred was the rock star of his day, exploding with enormous vitality all over the stage.

The inclusion of girls was the proverbial straw that put Fred's marriage in jeopardy. Between the hectic life of show business and the constant grind of vaudeville engagements back and forth across the country, plus Dot's lack of interest in Fred's professional life, their marriage really didn't stand a chance. His sister Dolly was most adamant: "I did *not* want the girls to come into the organization. I felt that when you bring girls into a group like that, it's the beginning of problems." Then she added smugly, "And I was right! I felt Fred was in the public eye and shouldn't have done the things that he did. I thought it was a reflection on us. I felt that with all the struggle and work and devotion and love and hope and everything we had back home, that there shouldn't have been *any* of that. I have always felt it. I do not know why he had to be like his father!"

Tom said simply, "Dolly is a prude. I was smart enough to dissociate myself from all that as much as possible. What I heard went in one ear and out the eyes."

In later years, I would hear Fred ask Helen sometimes, "Oh, by the way, how's *your* sister, Doll?" They always laughed about their private joke. Helen always remained loyal to Fred. She felt his good points far outweighed his unfavorable ones. But Dolly never forgave him.

Those first two teenage girls Fred added to the band couldn't have been more dissimilar. Evalyn, quiet and insecure, disliked the theatrical world from the beginning. It wasn't long before a handsome member of the band turned her head and persuaded her to marry him between shows. Dorothy Lee's vivacious personality enchanted most of the males of the band but she definitely set her cap for the unavailable Fred Waring. The general impression was that during the *Hello Yourself* period, Fred's marriage was broken up by his attraction for and to Dorothy Lee. There was no doubt their interest in each other furnished gay and amusing gossip to the press for several years. One publicity picture depicts Dorothy Lee sitting on Fred's lap cuddled up, with the caption, "Fred and Dorothy are shown above enjoying what might be termed, 'close harmony.'"[9]

But Dot Waring said, "By that time it was inevitable. I was terribly jealous all those years. I was on the road with Fred practically all the time. We had no permanent home. I hated show business." She described Fred much as did others: "He was so hard to know—so hard to be close to! Sometimes he seemed so remote you couldn't reach him at all. He just wasn't there."

That first marriage was doomed. Late in the year Fred and Dot were divorced. It had been six years. The press, of course, picked up on the divorce but Fred, the private person, made no public statement.

He did, however, continue his contact with the press to justify his position on the American musical scene, as in this interview:

"Do I regard my present career in music as an art, a profession or a business?" Fred Waring pondered. "I should say it is not a profession whatever else it may be. And it impresses me as something more than a business and not quite an art. Perhaps some day it may become an art because, after all, the thing we call 'jazz' is the most adaptable form of musical expression we have at present. Even though it has not reached perfection, it has been demonstrated that it can be suited to any mood, which is something that can not be said of the older forms of musical expression. They are set in precise and rigid forms fixed by rule and tradition.

"The passing of 'jazz' has been frequently predicted but it is here to stay. It may not retain its present form, but it is bound to color all our music in the future, both the lighter and the more serious compositions. No one has ever given a satisfactory or comprehensive definition of jazz. To me, it is the articulation of the mood of modern life expressed in terms of rhythm. And rhythm is an essential element of human life. If you don't believe it, watch how little children and primitive people respond to it. The older forms of music, including those we call the classics, have exhausted themselves and have nothing new to offer. The only hope of future progress lies in the wider application of the rhythmic principles revealed and developed by 'jazz.'"[10]

Shortly after Fred died in 1984, an album of the Pennsylvanians' recordings of the twenties was released. On the back cover, Will Friedwald stated emphatically, "The twenties were not called the Jazz Age for nothing. Fred Waring was behind one of the hottest bands in one of the hottest eras in American popular music."[11]

Fred was working constantly on stage technique and showmanship. He admired master showman George M. Cohan, and they later became good friends. Fred studied Cohan's performance skills, his timing of bows, and his use of the curtain at the end of the show.

"Until we started carrying our own lights, sound system, risers and props on the road, Fred used to fight like hell backstage to get something done that nobody believed in," Fred Culley said. "They'd say, 'What the hell do you want with that, it's a band, isn't it?' when he wanted special lighting effects. We saw an example in 1959. We had a day off, and we went to see a Tommy Dorsey show headed by Warren Covington, a handsome man and a beautiful trombone player. They had the original music and some of the original men. This was not for dancing; it was a stage presentation. Do you know what the musicians were sitting on? Coca-Cola boxes—which you could actually see from the audience! Some miserable tightwad didn't have enough brains to dress up the act which had so much going for it. This is what Fred always fought for."

And his efforts paid off: "We recommend that all collegiate bands and orchestras study Waring's Pennsylvanians for no other reason than to learn what showmanship does toward putting an outfit over. The eighteen men play over forty instruments, they sing equally well, they add an occasional touch of comedy, they stage numbers ingeniously, but lacking showmanship it would all go for naught. Fred Waring, with an ever-ready smile, makes the audience feel that the next number is the very song they have been waiting to hear."[12]

By August, 1929, the *Cleveland Press* noted that Fred had played ten thousand engagements and made two hundred records in six years. He and his band had recorded steadily for Victor since 1923. *Variety* noted that Fred and Whiteman made a twelve-inch concert disk together, each playing his own interpretation of "Ah, Sweet Mystery of Life" and "Chloe"— "and a corking try it is."[13]

Yet on the whole Fred was not yet recording the "greats"—Berlin, Porter, and Kern. A 1928 Victor ad in France, titled "La Voix de son Maître," showing the little dog listening to "his master's voice" printed a list of available Fred Waring disks:

Any Ice Today, Lady	*My Regular Girl*
Bolshevik	*Wob-a-ly Walk*
Hello Swanee	*Nashville Nightingale*
I've Got Some Loving to Do	
I Scream, You Scream, We All Scream for Ice Cream	
I Wonder How I Look When I'm Asleep	
I've Never Seen a Straight Banana[14]	

• • •

The Lambs club in the twenties, thirties, and forties was *the* prestigious organization of show business. All prominent producers, writers, actors, and musicians belonged. Johnny O'Connor decided, shortly after he became Fred's manager, to introduce him into that charmed circle. "The Lambs were to put on its annual gambol at the Metropolitan Opera House, which was the greatest theatrical event of the year at that time,

1929," O'Connor said. "I wired Waring to ship his platforms from Detroit. I had them painted and ready for him in the alley that Sunday. He had his boys looking spic and span—they made an ideal picture. It was arranged they would come on to open the second part of the show. The master of ceremonies appeared before the curtain after intermission and told the audience that he had a surprise attraction for them. He announced Waring's Pennsylvanians, and when the curtain went up, the boys looked, well, just marvelous. They were supposed to do twelve minutes, and they made them do at least forty. E. T. Albee, then head of the Keith's Orpheum circuit, was in one of the boxes close to the stage. I stopped at his box and asked him what he thought of the act. He said he thought it was great and would like to have him and I said, 'You've got him.'

"I went up to his office the next day and signed Waring up for twenty weeks for $5,500 plus transportation which at that time was a top salary for any band—in '29 and '30. One could live very well on $50 a week—a good hotel room would be had for $3, complete breakfast for 25¢, and a filet mignon at the finest restaurant was $1. I remember writing to Waring at Syracuse. They were going to make their first bow at the Palace—the following week—and preceding them, the headliner was B. A. Rolfe and his Lucky Strike Band—of fifty pieces. I wrote Waring a long letter advising him to notify his men that they had to use West Point deportment onstage because the Rolph crew were talking to one another during the show and pointing out to the audience and laughing among themselves, and it looked terrible.

"So Waring came in from Syracuse and opened at the Palace, which was the number one symbol at the time. As a result of that engagement, Waring received an honor which I doubt very much he realizes to this day its value among showmen of the era. It was customary at the end of the year for a lot of people to pick the top vaudeville bill, the top pictures, etc., but the one that everybody looked at for the ideal vaudeville show was Jake Lubin, who was general booking manager for the Loew's circuit. Lubin was a great showman; a fine, honest man. He knew vaudeville backwards, and practically devoted his life to the business. That year Jake picked Waring as the star headliner of his all-time vaudeville bill and for ten years afterwards kept Waring in that spot. I don't think Fred ever realized the value that meant in bookings, in dealings, and in selling."

8

Fred Loses His Shirt

DOROTHY LEE, after finishing a picture on the coast, rejoined the Pennsylvanians with her usual vivacity amid cheers, gags, and publicity. Evidently Dorothy not only looked like a flapper but she acted as wildly crazy as we are led to believe flappers were. She decided to focus her charms on Fred Waring and had the audacity to tell Fred's mother that she would capture him even if it meant landing a plane in his backyard. One can just imagine the tart retort from the notorious tongue of Jesse Waring. Dorothy, to the delight of newspaper people, furnished them with tales such as her "mistake book." She said that "every time I made a mistake, I wrote it down in my book, and every night I studied those mistakes and made sure I wouldn't make them again." Once she added she had been puzzled by finding an error in her mistake book!

By 1930 Fred was feeling confident and probably a little cocky. Since Hollywood was the new mecca of show business, he decided to produce a revue based on the Pennsylvanians' tried-and-true collegiate formula and call it *Rah Rah Daze,* to open in Los Angeles. He must have been pretty smitten by Dorothy Lee, because he wrote, produced, and sank every penny he had into the show that was built around her.

Tom was called back in to write the music and design the sets, but he was frustrated: "It was probably the biggest mess we ever got into. There were about four or five of us writing the book and the music, and none of us got along. The one song that survived the show, 'So Beats My Heart for You,' was the cause of most of the problems. I had written the melody but was having trouble with the bridge and let them in to help, and I'll never forgive myself because I think it's the worst bridge I've ever heard in my life. It was the eighteenth version. I had turned down seventeen that were worse by Henderson, [Fred] Waring, and Ballard."

Johnny O'Connor booked them across the country to cover expenses, and when they arrived at the Mason Opera House in Los Angeles, they rehearsed in the lobby, on the stage, in the aisles—right up to the last minute. They had a sellout the first week. "We broke the house record of $27,000," Fred said. "The second week we did $2,700. We have the theater for four weeks. Now we are into Holy Week. We do $2,800. I'm paying full salaries. I had to borrow from the stage door manager to get a bus home. Some Lambs club members, Charlie Winninger and Leon Errol, came in to help me out and the show picked up, but the theater option hadn't been renewed and there wasn't a free theater in L.A., Hollywood, San Diego, or San Francisco. So we had to close." Actually the reviews were quite good. They said the Waring act was a riot of fun and amusement, and was the best show to hit town in many a day, but everyone agreed it was the wrong town and the wrong time—1930—in the depression. Fred lost $160,000—no small sum in 1930. O'Connor disparagingly referred to the show as "Rah Rah Raspberries."

"Fred lost a pile of dough out there," Nels Keller said in disgust. "Man, he went broke! It took him about a year to pay us all back—little by little." This was the second time Fred had lost his shirt. Two music stores he owned in Florida plus a carload of uninsured pianos had been wiped out by a devastating hurricane in 1927. He lost $150,000 on that venture.

In an interview with the *Los Angeles Times* "over a plate of fried mush—all Pennsylvanians eat fried mush—Fred related his Horatio Alger story."[1] He was still eating fried mush thirty years later whenever he could persuade someone to prepare it for him.

"It was during our run in Los Angeles that Joe Kennedy showed up again," Fred said. "He was a stage-door Johnny, and every night he took out one of my cute little chorus girls in his black limousine. Twenty-five and thirty years later in St. Louis, the girl that Mr. Kennedy courted used to come to our concerts. She had become an alcoholic, but Joe always supported her.

"And as for Dorothy Lee, during *Rah Rah Daze,* she became involved with Jimmy Fiddler. She married him and later dumped him to marry the football star Marshall Duffield. She got married a total of seven times. During her fifth marriage she was pregnant and had a miscarriage, and in three weeks went out and won the club tennis championship. And a couple of weeks after that she had a baby—a twin." Dorothy Lee had no compunctions about leaving Fred after his fiasco in Los Angeles. He even made a trip back to Hollywood to negotiate a contract for her. Wheeler and Woolsey, comedians, wanted her in their pictures. "It was for a million dollars and like a damned dope I didn't exact any commissions," Fred said.

Tom, too, had decided to leave the organization again. "My going ended in a row which it always did. We were two stubborn people. I wanted to go, and Fred didn't want me to go. Mal St. Clair, the director, and his wife practically adopted me and wouldn't let me leave California. Still, it was hard going. I thought I had a lead in a picture, but at the last minute they told me I was too old—I was twenty-eight. Just one more disappointment. I made a few shorts, but not much else. Even so, I loved it there and collected a lot of good friends."

During the run of *Rah Rah Daze,* a New York producer, Ray Goetz, came west to see the production. He liked the material and asked the Pennsylvanians to star in a show to open on Broadway, *The New Yorkers.* Peter Arno was to do the sets, Cole Porter the score, and Clayton Jackson, Jimmy Durante, Hope Williams, Clifton Webb, and Libby Holman featured along with the Pennsylvanians. According to Poley, *The New Yorkers* was more of a revue. "The Pennsylvanians were all over the place—in the pit, on the stage, in cabaret scenes—taking part in the background, etc. Everybody had something to do except Fred."

"They brought in Al Goodman to conduct the pit orchestra," Fred said. "That was the final blow. I had done a lot of the staging of the show. I was to conduct our group onstage as well as share the pit conducting. But he cut me off—never let me conduct. One time though, when he was sick, I did, and everything went well. I knew the show backwards. Johnny O'Connor fought a losing battle trying to get me that. I wanted so much to conduct that show.

"I shared a dressing room with Jimmy Durante—what a wonderfully sweet man! We became very good friends. Every night there was a huge crowd backstage to see him. His great number 'Wood!' was in the show. Sensational!" As the *New York Times* described it, "When Jimmy hurls his paean of wood as the first act finale, shouts himself hoarse over wood's honorable career in the making of the American nation, and then, with his sweating comrades, crowds the stage with rhymeless exhibits of wooden objects—boxes, trees, doors, bars, violins, bass drums and finally that particular institution which made Chic Sale such a specialist (an outhouse), *The New Yorkers* is as overpoweringly funny as a weak muscled theatre goer can endure."[2]

"I was directly center and Jimmy was always trying to hit the bass drum," Poley said. "I got hit at least once a week and he'd come over and ask how much he owed me. He was always shelling out money."

• • •

But as the weeks went by, Fred became more and more frustrated. "I really got the blues," he told me years later.

So I asked Fred about this and he said, "Yes, I was really blue. . . . I even contemplated suicide."

"*You?!*" I said, flabbergasted. "Why?"

"I just felt I was a failure. I had failed on two shows. They had taken my material, my people, and left me nothing. They were destroying my identity—nothing was working right. I was living at the Barbizon Plaza Hotel on the thirty-second floor. I remember one night I had the blues so badly I looked outside and there was a sheer drop down into a . . ." I asked him if that was the only time he felt like that. He said, "Yes."

Fred's disclosure really stunned me, because in the forty years I had known him, there never was the slightest inkling of such a trait. Far worse things had happened to him after that, which he met with great resilience, determination, and guts. In retrospect, there were some other factors he didn't mention that surely added to his deep depression:

The divorce from his wife Dorothy was final, a sad episode in his life. Second, the divisive relationship with Tom always preyed on his mind. And then all his efforts for Dorothy Lee had been fruitless. It seemed to be all take and no give on her part. Last, but certainly not least, he had hit a stone wall for the first time in his career. In eight years the Pennsylvanians had risen to the top. Each success was always just a bit bigger than the last. But this recent combination of disasters truly shook his self-confidence. He told me he called his friend Buddy Rogers and offered to sell him the Pennsylvanians lock, stock, and barrel, arrangements and everything, for $150,000. "I contemplated going back to school and starting where I left off, and becoming an architect."

Shortly after the show opened, the *New York Telegraph* interviewed Fred and, as usual, he was touting his friend Paul Whiteman:

> "Paul Whiteman plays the best jazz music in the world," says Waring today as he sat, a lean dark bearded young man in a nattily plain blue suit in his Broadway theatre dressing room. "Every night, every bandleader in the country ought to remember Paul Whiteman in his prayers. He was the one that started this whole business."

Waring surprises you with his Main Street candor, a strange perplexing trait in a Times Square star whose orchestra is the highest paid attraction showing in a Broadway legitimate theatre.[3]

The interview continues:

"I realized I couldn't compete with Whiteman's music. Paul has done—instrumentally, I mean—everything that possibly can be accomplished with musical instruments.

"So I became a salesman—selling tricks. My boys are all good musicians. But they don't try to sell music. They all sing, dance and play solos. We have tricks with megaphones, chant cheers; make figures with lighted dominoes on a dark stage.

"I like Broadway. I like its crowds and lights and traffic symphony. It's false New York but I like its falseness. I hate night clubs and speakeasies. But I like Broadway."[4]

The cast of the show must have liked Fred in turn. The *New York Telegraph* reported, "Fred Waring was presented with a solid gold baton on June 9, his thirtieth birthday, with signatures of the cast of *The New Yorkers*."[5]

In spite of his melancholy, Fred hung in, probably because *The New Yorkers,* from Johnny O'Connor's point of view, was a full-fledged success: "It grossed $76,000 the first week. It had a good healthy run (six months). It was during the depression of 1931—they jammed them in." After *The New Yorkers* closed, O'Connor set up some recording dates and a tour of nearby theaters. The band "suitcased" New York—an old vaudeville term for playing dates sufficiently close to a major center to permit getting back every night.

• • •

In the early thirties, the Pennsylvanians were booked into nightclubs in the environs of Chicago, not knowing which ones were gangster-owned. "They were the only places to work then," Fred said. "Unfortunately, there was an epidemic of the mobsters, known as 'the boys' [an ironic euphemism], walking into stars' dressing rooms and holding them up. A lot of the gangsters loved my music. A few of them had come backstage to tell me so. In 1928 when *Hello Yourself* was playing in Chicago, one of 'the boys' (a thug) followed me in my dressing room. He looked threatening but I laughed at him and said, 'You're kind of silly, you know. Bugs isn't going to like this.' I had met Bugs Malone a couple of days previously. (He was a handsome man.) The guy turned white and ran."

"A couple of them came in one night and asked to see Waring," Johnny

O'Connor said. "I went down and could see by their clothes they were two-bit racket guys—shakedown bums. . . . 'We expect you to buy $5,000 worth of tickets; one of our boys is in trouble . . .' sort of thing. I told them to meet me next day at the Sherman House at 2 P.M. I had two Westside boys who were pretty well up in the racket headline and two newspapermen in the room. When the bums came in and saw the two Westside fellas in the room, they started backing away, apologizing. The guys grabbed these bums and said if they bothered Waring or me they wouldn't live. They never bothered us after that. However, one of Fred's trumpet players made the mistake of rushing one of the show girls. He was warned to stay away from her. He didn't and wound up with his face kicked in." Most bands of that era had experiences of shootouts during performances in Chicago. Two men in Guy Lombardo's band were killed.

The names of Bugs Malone and Bugsy Siegel cropped up, but the kicker came when Fred was playing the Stanley Theater in Philadelphia. "The U.S. Treasury department came backstage before the show and cautioned that there might be a disturbance during our performance and to be sure to keep playing to prevent a riot or panic in the audience," Fred began.

"I said, 'What is this?' They said, 'We are going to pick up a delinquent taxpayer.'

"I said, 'Is it a hoodlum?' They said, 'Yes.'

"I said, 'Hell, what if there's shooting?' They said, 'Well, we'll just have to take that chance.' I said, 'Thanks very much.'

"I had a feeling who it might be because I knew that Al Capone was crazy about our music. And sure enough it was he. He came in and sat in the back row. I could see his head silhouetted against the back even in the dark movie theater. I saw the agents moving in on him. There was no fuss whatsoever." Capone was sentenced to prison in 1931.

One night in the sixties while Fred was calling me from a hotel near the O'Hare airport in Chicago, I heard a huge explosion followed by an expletive from Fred, and then dead silence. For ten terrible minutes I feared he was dead, until he called back to reassure me he was all right. A day later we learned that an irate mobster with a vendetta against the new owner had blasted the entire side of the building. Fred happened to be lying on the bed farthest from the window, so was merely grazed by flying glass. As Fred was the only one registered in his wing, the entire hotel staff rushed to his rescue.

Meanwhile, still more copycats continued to pussyfoot around, never relinquishing their need to live off the ideas of others. Because of their actions, an agency called Variety Managers Protective Association was formed to prevent plagiarism. "The most recent case," a New York paper reported, "was Fred Waring against Benny Meroff who is now appearing at the Palace with his band. Meroff was using a megaphone drill that Waring claimed, and the VMPA upheld Fred Waring with Meroff taking out the bit."[6]

. . .

Johnny O'Connor, always working and promoting, was encountering the same vexing dilemma that Fred had faced throughout the twenties—trying to elevate the Pennsylvanians' weekly fee, set in place and jealously guarded by managers.

"After *The New Yorkers* had closed, I booked Waring on Loew's circuit for $8,500 net, transportation, etc., for twenty-eight shows and baggage hauls and everything I could think of," O'Connor said. "When he finished the Loew time, then things were slowing up, and I wanted to put him back on Warner time. They wanted him very badly, but they said that they had a manager's agreement now and they set their own prices—it was a price-fixing combine, and Waring's price was fixed at $6,000. I said, 'Who fixed it?' They said Louis Sydney, the chairman. I said, 'The son of a bitch just paid Waring $8,500 per week for fourteen weeks so he doesn't need him.' But I said, 'The next time he wants him it's going to be high. The deal's off. Never!'

"Eventually I was in Lindy's one day at lunch, and Marvin Skinks and Louis Sydney came in. Skinks says, 'We would like to have your boys for the Capital.' I say, 'Yeah—for what picture?'

"'Well, it's a picture you'll like because you always like a woman star opposite him. It's the wife of the great producer, Irving Thalberg.' I say, 'Well, you've got that cross-eyed dame starring—Yeah—you can have him. But I've got to have four weeks.'

"He says, 'A deal.' I say, 'Yeah—$10,000 net for twenty-eight shows.'

"That knocked Sydney and his price fixing. So we played a string of houses for Loew for $10,000 net.

"I would never book Fred in a town against another band. That was done once in Chicago. Lombardo was at the Palace Theater, and Waring was booked for the Chicago Theater. I jumped on a train and went to Chicago, and I lined up a minimum of two, and sometimes four and five radio broadcasts a day for Waring. Knowing all the newspapermen there so well, I had no trouble in arranging to have Waring's picture in at least one, and sometimes three and four papers a day, with an appropriate story. The result was, when Waring opened, he had practically a monopoly on the interview time on the air, and Lombardo couldn't get to first base. Waring never lost money for a theater promoter. Never! He was a tremendous draw."

Seasonal factors also affected Johnny O'Connor's booking rules. Thus, he "would never book Fred into Boston, Buffalo or Baltimore during Lent. Citizens of this trio of towns observe the 40 days of penance fervently. Caruso, the all-time top draw in his palmiest days, couldn't lure a nickel into the box office in these three cities in the Lenten season, and however explainable a flop may be, it lessens the chance of getting the same or bigger money for the next date."[7]

Of course, Fred had something else going for him—his uncanny ability to see into a situation and size up his options:

> The astonishing thing about Waring's success is not an immediate click that started him toward the top. This happens to all bands with any merit. It is that for 12 years Waring has maintained his rating in a business about as friendly as a tong war.
>
> Even among bandleaders who are a testy mob with few words for rivals and those bad, Waring is occasionally admired and generally envied for a business sense that probably would have carried him far in banking or commerce. He says his continued success has been due to watching the mistakes of others and profiting thereby.[8]

· · ·

Fred's imagination and farsightedness never took a rest. As early as 1931, he was contemplating television: "Television still may seem remote to the layman but, to one whose livelihood depends on anticipating public demands in entertainment, it's close enough to warrant serious attention. Fred Waring has been giving it serious thought for some time past. It may, he thinks, be better than present day radio, which incidentally, he believes has harmed more orchestras than it has helped."[9]

That same year he told Leo Arnaud that "electronic musical instruments will be the forceful trend of the future." In 1940 Fred brought out a revolutionary steam iron. He said the manufacturers made him change from light aluminum to heavy metal because they wouldn't believe "the scientific fact that it isn't weight but the heat that counts in ironing."

Fred also became interested in a rotary valve internal combustion engine and for several years poured nearly a quarter-million dollars into its development. Unfortunately, World War II brought a halt to both projects. The engine was showing great promise of replacing about fifty moving parts, but the automotive industry was not interested. "Maybe we were just ahead of our time," Fred recalled. He was right. The Japanese have since employed the rotary engine. And in 1946 Fred made a suggestion to a top General Motors executive that what they needed was a small second family car called "Kidillac." A corny name, but the idea, if followed, would have placed the company years ahead of the Japanese flood.

9

Ballet, Classics, and the Roxyettes

JOHNNY O'CONNOR booked the Pennsylvanians into New York's dazzling Roxy Theater for a six-week run starting January 1, 1932. This was no trivial engagement. In addition to leading his own band of eighteen, Fred was to conduct a sixty-piece orchestra in a classic overture; the Roxy ballet corps of thirty-four in a traditional ballet sequence; and the thirty-two Roxyettes—as they then were billed—in a popular number. He also had to provide all accompaniments for guest performers from Ernestine Schumann-Heink to acrobatic acts, plus design, rehearse, and prepare the Pennsylvanians' show— an entirely new routine every Friday.

"Fred and I must have auditioned six hundred men for the orchestra," Leo Arnaud said. "They all had to look like the original bunch—young, no mustache, be able to play jazz as well as symphonic music, and *sing a part.* We finally started rehearsing what was called the largest Synco-Symphonic Orchestra in the world."

Fred had to become a full-fledged conductor—overnight. And he amazed everyone. "What the hell did Fred know about those long scores?" wondered Johnny O'Connor. "Some of those overtures were eight to ten minutes long. But he got up there and directed sixty musicians from memory."

"He never put a score in front of him, not even a music stand," Arnaud added. "He made a few notes on his cuff—crosses and scribbles that nobody could read."

Fred Culley, assistant orchestral conductor, explained: "Fred had to learn from sheer talent. Nobody ever told him how to be a conductor. You can learn some refined motions, but you have to have the instinct for it. Fred was doing a better job than a lot of so-called big conductors like [Dmitri] Mitropoulos. That guy could get so bogged down with conducting, waving his arms around in a circle like a paintbrush, that the musicians in the back would say, 'What in the name of Christ is this man doing?' A small orchestra can *help* a conductor. Now, this Ray Block that conducts, I mean, he's a left-handed conductor and nobody ever knows where the beat is. But Block's always got a drummer, a fine first trumpet player, a bass player, and a piano player who *do* know where the beat is. Now these few people can put that show over. But with sixty men in the band, *you* must be the man. *You've* got to hold them together. If it's a bright tempo, it's got to be *your* bright tempo, and you've got to make them do it. It's not easy."

I once quizzed Fred about the Roxy engagement and how he managed to suddenly conduct so-called legitimate music when he was unable to read orchestral scores. And Fred replied, "I would memorize it. Toots Bryan, our first trumpeter, was my assistant. He would do the rough rehearsing, and I would do the dress rehearsal and the shows. Some of our toughest assignments were the ballets."

Russell Markert, creator of the Roxyettes, was amazed to discover Fred at 8 A.M. sitting by the piano in the rehearsal hall, listening and watching the dancers at every rehearsal: "The result was the most sensitive accompaniment the dancers had ever known—for here was a conductor whose first concern became the dancers and their timing rather than written cues on an orchestral score," he said. Fred was a perfectionist in all phases of his work. He may not have been overly fond of ballet and modern dance, but he had to give it his best. There are several reasons he would dislike it. Sitting in an airtight room full of hot, sweaty dancers could have been one of them. The dancers not moving precisely on the beat could have been another. This experience probably turned Fred against ballet forever. To please me, we once attended a ballet performance, but I sensed it was not Fred's favorite leisure activity.

The engagement at the Roxy was a smash and lasted an unprecedented four and a half months—a new show every week. "We were only two arrangers who practically lived at the Roxy feeding score pages to the copyists," Leo Arnaud said. "There were four shows a day, with rehearsals in between, except on Saturdays. The musicians ate in the cafeteria in the building where a meal cost fifty cents. My salary was $275 a week."

Fred had devised risers that rose from the pit while the orchestra was playing. Fred's podium was built on top of the organ, which had its own elevator, and when they all came up together, it was a most impressive picture with the gleaming brass moving in unison. "But one day the elevator got out of sync, Fred rose all by himself, and finally the orchestra, playing like mad, rose, too, but Fred disappeared for a while and then rose again as the orchestra descended," Arnaud said. "Most of the audience thought it was one of Fred's dramatic effects."

Two unexpected episodes put more pressure on Fred. John Philip Sousa died during their engagement. So the two arrangers worked all night on an overture using his tunes. Fred, with little sleep himself, rehearsed it and played it from memory—a few notations on his left cuff.

On the week of Lincoln's birthday, the famous Hall Johnson Choir came in with an original a cappella piece called "The Emancipation," a magnificently staged production. But Hall Johnson became ill after the first day, and Fred, who had never heard the composition before the first performance, had to take over. Later that year Fred recalled the event in a Boston interview: "We had one hasty rehearsal, and I want to tell you I was a mighty scared person when I stepped onto the conductor's platform. I almost fainted from fright. I was at least thirty-five feet from the singers and it seemed more like thirty-five miles. But somehow I got through it. The job was one of the most inspiring ones I've ever tackled."[1]

"Fred did a masterful job," Arnaud added. "I guess that's why Hall Johnson recovered in a hurry."

The trade papers were kind in their reviews of the weekly shows. *Variety* reported, "No other modern orchestra of such size has been seen on Broadway while musically there is nothing else for comparison."[2]

Evidently the staid tenured members of the musicians' union felt threatened by the popularity of the new Syncho-Symphonic orchestra at the Roxy, as the New York newspaper clippings of that era were full of their complaints:

> Union members will vote
> Resolved, that no employed musician should do incidental work
> Resolved, that no musician should *sing, recite* or *act* from a theater pit
> Fred Waring is unwittingly the focal point of the brewing storm. Waring, now at the Roxy directing a 60 piece Syncho Symphonic orchestra, has revolutionized theatre music.
>
> Before Waring went into the Roxy, ten weeks ago, an old line symphony orchestra had been there five years. This outfit was known as the "closed corporation" in bandland. Fritz Kreisler and his fiddle couldn't break in there.

Fred Waring's musicians sing, act and otherwise entertain. This unorthodox routine in the staid Roxy delighted patrons to the dismay of the old-school instrumentalists. Now the union is trying to drive out Waring.[3]

But the union didn't succeed. Fred remained at the Roxy two and a half more months. His weekly spectacular of superbly trained musicians who could also sing and entertain forced the musicians union to change its restrictive policy of tenure.

. . .

It was in February that a previous copycat reappeared, only he had changed the spelling of his name from Weingar to Winegar: "Frank Winegar and his orchestra recently used the title Pennsylvanians in a recent broadcast and Waring immediately took the matter up with the American Federation of Musicians who decided the trade name belonged exclusively to Waring. Winegar was told to drop the title or action would be taken."[4] Shortly after the article appeared in print, Johnny O'Connor placed this ad in the February 23, 1932, edition of *Variety:* FRED WARING HAS SOLE RIGHT TO THE TRADE NAME *PENNSYLVANIANS*.

Fred, the handsome, photogenic, unattached musician, was good "copy" generally in those nonradio, nontelevision days:

HAS brown wavy hair with a glint you'd pay a lot to get on your own . . .
grey blue eyes . . . strong chin . . . neatly cleft . . .
HAS marvelous musical memory . . . directs every program without
score . . .
SAID to be highest paid leader now . . .
VERY highly strung . . . restless . . . craves action . . . gets plenty.
DOES everything himself . . . never trusts anyone to do it just as well . . .
NOT superstitious . . . but strong on hunches in business . . . distrusts any
plan that makes him hesitate . . .
WILL go into big deals . . . like Roxy contract . . . on sheer nerve . . . then
stick out his chin . . . and win . . .
CAN'T . . . stand snobs . . . detests them more than garlic . . . would walk
miles to avoid either . . .
CONSIDERS himself outspoken . . . does spill painful truths . . . if necessary
. . . is really too reticent to volunteer criticism . . .
STRONG on fair play . . . but alas, his dry humor . . . barbed with sarcasm
. . . gets him into tough spots . . . means no harm really . . . can take it
himself well enough . . .
ADORES home cooked meals . . . exists almost entirely on restaurant food.
IS neat . . . favors sports clothes in season . . . wouldn't wear a colored shirt

for the Queen of Sheba . . . wears dark blue woolen socks exclusive
. . . all year through . . .

LOOKS ascetic . . . but don't let that fool you . . . is all there when it comes
to femmes . . . darn fickle in his interests . . .

WAS married six years . . . emotionally dented by the experience . . . not
adverse to remarriage . . . keen on raising a family . . . but hold on
girls . . . there's a very exacting mistress . . . who will come first always
. . . in time schedule anyway . . . *HIS WORK*.

IS more stubborn than any two mules . . . discouragingly undemonstra-
tive . . . a fast driver . . . steps on it for all it's worth . . . gets away with
accidents just like that . . . without a scratch.[5]

· · ·

Luckily for Fred, he was able to get along on very little sleep because
as he said, "On top of our grueling schedule, I was doing Harlem at
night—seeing Lena Horne and all the great people. It was a big custom
to go up there."

One night in 1932, Danny Winkler said, "Fred called and asked me to
go with him up to Harlem to the Cotton Club. I said, 'What the devil's at
the Cotton Club?' Fred was never much of a café man.

"He said, 'There's a guy opening up there that I want to hear play.'
When we got there Duke Ellington was playing. He turned to me and said,
'What do you think?'

"I said, 'Fred, I can't tell you that I like it because I don't. I'm considered
a pretty good two-by-four dancer, but I couldn't dance to that number.'

"He said, 'I want you to listen to it because it is the next trend.' I know
at the time he was the *only* one that was out shouting from the house-
tops about Duke. Fred was always a notch ahead of what his competitor
was doing."

According to the newspapers, Fred was not only performing four shows
a day and cavorting in Harlem late at night but also spending time with
les femmes. Louis Sobol, in his "Voice of Broadway" column: "Dorothy
Lee's contract is not renewed and she packs her personal lares and penates
and starts eastward where rumors of her secret marriage in Canada last
fall to Fred Waring, the orchestra leader, will either be definitely confirmed
or denied shortly." Walter Winchell: "Fred Waring and Mary Brian dance
with each other all evening, and people immediately jump to the conclu-
sion that perhaps this is romance." The *New York Morning Telegraph*:
"Dorothy not to be Mrs. Waring. She's decided to marry Marshall Duffield—says Waring is a nice fellow but really Duffield is the man for her."[6]

In the end, after his long engagement at the Roxy, Fred went to Europe alone, with only his new Phaeton Cadillac. It was cream colored with robin's egg blue leather seats and, according to Leo, it cost $5,000.

"I had lost an awful lot of weight and was exhausted," Fred said. "That's when my terrible hay fever struck again and stayed with me for the rest of my life. In Evanston, Illinois, the year before, I had my first attack while playing golf with Johnny Revolta and Dorothy Lee. I sneezed a hundred and five times. [Typical, that he would be counting.] Then that went away and I had no trouble until I got off the boat and was driving to Paris through all the lush green country, and I started sneezing again. I was in awful shape and was unable to see." Fred soon figured out that sudden temperature changes were deadly for allergic people. The abrupt shift from hot air to air conditioning or the touch of a cold glass set him sneezing.

Fred seldom spoke of that trip to France except to mention the fascination that passersby had with his snazzy convertible. Wherever it was parked, young and old would be standing on the running boards, examining every detail. He drove it all over France, and once when he took what looked like a shortcut through the Swiss Alps, he ran into hairpin turns so tight that he had to back his phaeton in and around each one for miles and miles. And even though he had found some friends to accompany him on all his trips, evidently he was lonely. His thoughts were focused more and more on the exotic, black-haired, black-eyed dancer Evalyn Nair, who, after her divorce, had left Fred's organization because she hated show business. Before he left for Europe, Fred asked Evalyn to marry him, but she refused. She didn't like the way the girls buzzed around him—or his obvious delight in them.

"He called me from the ship—he even called from Paris," Evalyn said. "He called me every single day for two months. He'd talk for an hour. My father was with the telephone company and it nearly drove him crazy. He would keep telling me to hang up, and Fred would say, 'I'm not ready to hang up,' and keep on talking. You know how he usually is. He calls you and then expects you to do all the talking? Well, not then! He tried to convince me that I had made a terrible mistake, and he wanted me to come right back and marry him. When I came back to California, I was finished. Through! My common sense told me that I didn't want any part of that life again." Her picture of Fred's "flirting around with everybody" was not what she conceived as her future. But Fred kept talking.

"In the meantime, I was miserable at home," Evalyn continued. "I was used to working, and I didn't know what to do next most of the time. And my family—I was in the way, really. When you go home to your family after being married and leading a busy life . . . well, I was sort of infatuated with Fred. Then, of course, I got letters every day, special delivery letters, and I began to wonder if he really did love me. I was *very* much attracted to him."

When Fred returned to the United States, he kept on talking (he can be very persuasive), and on September 29, 1932, the East Coast newspapers announced that Evalyn had taken off on a United Air Lines flight at seven in the morning that was due in Chicago at one the next morning (sixteen hours!). Fred, armed with the marriage license, met the plane and rushed her back to the Blackstone Hotel, where they were married by a judge.

"There was much publicity," Evalyn recalled. "We stayed one night at the Blackstone and took a train for New York the next night. This was our honeymoon. When we got back to New York, it was right back to work. The honeymoon was over.

"I wanted to get a little apartment and cook and be with Fred—just be together. Instead we took this house out in Bronxville. He put me out there with two servants and I was lost. I didn't know what to do with myself. I couldn't go out and cook in their kitchen. It was a miserable experience. Three months later I was pregnant. Fred often had to leave early and not get home till late."

When Fred returned from Europe, he pulled the band together and took to the road. After those six months of concentrated training in the lighter classics at the Roxy, the epitome of success for most young musicians would have been a move into the more (in their minds at least) rarified atmosphere of the three B's—Bach, Beethoven, and Brahms. Robert Shaw is a prime example. During the Chesterfield years with Fred, Bob could hardly wait to move on, out of the field of popular music. He spent hours picking any knowledgeable musical brain available—first my erudite piano partner Livingston, then Leonard Bernstein, and so on. Fred willingly and happily backed the Robert Shaw Collegiate Chorale until it became airborne, but felt no pull whatsoever in the direction of serious music. He was convinced that bringing entertainment to the masses was more important and more difficult than anything the so-called longhairs were doing. In 1932, the *Boston Globe* wrote:

> "It's more important to know psychology than it is to know music if you intend to be a successful orchestra leader," says Fred Waring. He tries to find out why an audience laughs when he does one thing and why it stays quiet when he does something else. Fred Waring is a quiet, slim, studious young man who wants to know when is the exact moment to turn on the

lights, when it is best to play in semi-darkness and why one number makes a big appeal in Boston and proves a flop in Brooklyn.

"There's psychology to everything connected with the stage," says Waring eagerly. "That's why the stage is so fascinating. I like to experiment with emotions, and when I am conducting my orchestra, I can change the emotions of the audience by the selections I offer them. There's a tremendous sense of power in being able to sway collective emotion from comedy to tragedy, from pathos to laughter. Everyone in public life must experience this feeling. It's heady—like champagne.

"There is a psychology of lights. I have to know that an audience will burst into applause if lights are flashed on immediately after a fadeout number. But if there is any delay in the turning on of the lights, then the applause is lost. I even have to time my own gestures. It takes me several rehearsals to learn when to turn from the orchestra to the audience.

"Every entrance and exit must be built up, and we can only learn the best way by trying several ways. And when the applause is consistently louder for one entrance or exit, then that is retained in the act."[7]

It was not only the imaginative planning but the hours and hours of rehearsals that promoted the Pennsylvanians' growth and ability to stay ahead of their contemporaries. Anyone lucky enough to see the hundreds of out-takes for a single Charlie Chaplin sequence can only wish a creative showman today could have the luxury of such unlimited time to polish his craft.

And Fred's demand for perfection continued to pay off. A *Billboard* columnist pronounced the Palace Theater show "one of the best staged and best lighted vaude [*sic*] shows that this reviewer has seen."[8]

10

Radio Days

TOWARD the end of 1932, Fred was making $10,000 a week and had plenty of work, but he wasn't satisfied. He began to envision the Pennsylvanians on radio. "Waring, the great perfectionist, went to some sound studios on Fifty-seventh Street and he made at least two hundred large transcriptions of the band," recounted Johnny O'Connor. "He directed the balance and everything himself to get the best styles of singing. He still did not have a separate glee club—the band did the singing. It was the consensus that Waring was to be seen and not heard—that for radio he wasn't worth a nickel. Waring wanted to prove to himself that they could be heard only. He went to that sound studio day after day, paid his men union scale, and made transcriptions over and over. He'd find the flaws and then perfect them. I think he was one of the first that used multiple microphones. He demanded them. He finally said, 'I think we can do it now.' He auditioned and auditioned, but nobody wanted choral singing. The sponsors all said, 'Glee clubs are for college kids, choirs are for churches.' We did an audition with Jack Benny, and they threw us both out.

"Finally in 1932, I booked Waring in Cleveland at the Cairo Hotel over the Christmas holidays. I got him $21,000 for seventeen days. I arranged for John Royal, who was then vice president in charge of programs at NBC, to give him an hour out of there on one night. John gave us a Saturday night. Together Waring and I framed up and wrote a program of our own based on a college idea. We thought of having some kind of good comedian as the professor. Now, of course, I had written a lot of vaudeville acts in my time, and I knew something about construction and the buildup to a line and how to cue in on songs, etc. I then sent out about a thousand engraved cards announcing the hour we would be on. I got these cards all out to every advertising agency, every advertising sponsor, and every industrialist in the country—so I built up a pretty sure audience for the broadcast. This was sustaining—no pay. We arranged with Ken Murray to play the part of the professor."

"We had a handshake agreement with Ken that if after our audition any sponsor wanted either of us without the other, neither of us should accept," Fred said. "Three days before we were to appear, Ken accepted another engagement and was unable to come. It put us in a terrible spot. He had gotten equal billing. I told Johnny to look up a young comedian I'd heard in New York. He said, 'Yes, he is available. His show closes tonight and he's driving home to Cleveland for the holidays.' The weather was terrible. He got as far as Buffalo, his car had broken down and he would be late. We were to do the broadcast at 10 P.M., and at 8:30 in he comes, exhausted, bedraggled—hadn't slept all night. He said he had written some stuff down. I was to be straight man. He didn't seem too interested. We did the show. We waited for the mail. Johnny called and said, 'Nobody liked the comedian. We have an offer for you—but no comedian.' I said, 'Turn it down because I made a deal.' The comedian was Bob Hope."

"I got four or five touches and one of them was Old Gold, which looked like the one for me," O'Connor said. "Whiteman had been on Old Gold for a year, and it had built him up to a hell of a big attraction. So we went on for Old Gold every Wednesday night on CBS. Waring had Babs and her brothers, the Smoothies, and Priscilla and Rosemary Lane. Bob Hope and Fred agreed to go their separate ways."

The challenge now for the Pennsylvanians was a totally new one—pure listening for an unseen audience—a basic reorientation for this highly visual organization. They never stopped their daily stage shows, and the commuting back and forth could not have been easy. "We did the Old Gold Show once a week in Carnegie Hall while we were playing daily shows at the Paramount Theater," Culley said. "We had to have a police escort to get us to the broadcast on time."

Carnegie Hall in the early thirties was still reserved for the classics. Fred's irreverent group caused comment from one New York newspaper:

> There was an unusual audience in Carnegie Hall last night. It was made up of the people who sit next to you at the corner movie, the lady to whom you give your seat in the subway of those who catch the 5:15—your neighbor and mine.

They were there to see the Fred Waring show. The 3,000 of them filled the great hall from orchestra to highest gallery. Their applause was quick and long. They needed no cues from studio directors. They were getting a glimpse of the land beyond the microphone.

Laborers sat on the aisles where only the chosen rich sit other nights.[1]

Another wrote that "Fred Waring's second broadcast from New York's Carnegie Hall had brought out the largest crowd ever assembled for a commercial program."[2]

When Fred added a radio show to his daily stage productions, his responsibilities increased and his life became more complex. It was reported he had forty-nine people on his payroll—thirty musicians, three arrangers, and two librarians, plus fourteen nonmusicians. His library contained 4,000 musical arrangements valued at $100,000. It was becoming a one-man musical repertory. The theater tours required six weeks of rehearsal. All the music for every stage show plus extra numbers were memorized so they could change an entire show for holdovers. Fred might prepare several numbers for the Old Gold Show, and not until the afternoon of the show would the group really know which one he'd use. Spontaneity was the key word of his credo: "When playing a medley of college tunes, Waring's men never know what melody is to follow which. As they play, Fred quietly calls the air that is to follow, and from their memories, the boys conjure up the complicated arrangements that are necessary. They must keep over 100 tunes at the tips of their fingers."[3]

"Well, the polls made Waring the top show all over," O'Connor said. "Then Old Gold started tinkerin' around with the show. They got a writer from the *New York Journal*—a columnist and they hired a colored woman named Magnolia to do comedy. This fellow got on, did his talk and talked with her. He was straight man for her. Then they decided they wanted something funnier. I got Joe Cook down there, I had Jack Benny, I had some of the best. Nothing worked. It was the agency that insisted on the guests. We never dealt with anybody but the agency. Of course, being an ex-newspaperman, I knew the relationship and respected it— between agency and sponsor. The shortest way to cut your own throat is to jump over the agency's head. The thing that threw Waring off balance was Bob Orr from the agency calling up on the day of the rehearsal saying, 'Take out that song and put in this.' I quickly stopped that. Waring never contacted the agency or went near the sponsor at that time. He kept the hell out of the business altogether, which was perfect. But I had to go down to those meetings."

Even the newspapers began to complain: "Sponsors of Fred Waring's practically perfect radio show have begun to tinker with it."[4] Finally, seven weeks before termination of the Old Gold contract, the Pennsylvanians performed alone for the first time. Three weeks later the national polls placed them at the top of all radio entertainment.

Radio was a medium made for Fred Waring. Instead of audiences of thousands, he was now reaching millions. His themes of family, country, and religion clearly matched those of the times. The Pennsylvanians would be heard continuously on the air for the next fifteen years. Fred Waring became a household name. It is ironic that two of Fred's major radio sponsors were cigarette companies promoting Old Gold and Chesterfield. He barely tolerated cigarettes but he absolutely loathed cigar smoke. He wasn't happy in a room where somebody *had* smoked a cigar (a not infrequent experience in theatrical circles). He never hesitated to make rather loud remarks—especially when someone was smoking in close areas like elevators (people did in those days) or in train dining cars. Fred seldom suffered in silence when subjected to cigar smoke and, unfortunately, his fanaticism brought him a goodly portion of enemies along the way.

The stories of Fred and cigar incidents go through the decades.

"The Boss could smell a cigar a mile away," reminisced veteran Pennsylvanian Stinky Davis. "Nobody could smoke a cigar in the theater, or he would raise Cain. One incident stands out in my mind while on the road and doing the Old Gold Show. We had an early morning rehearsal in Baltimore. Three spectators came to watch the rehearsal. There was only one thing wrong with it. They were all smoking cigars, and you might guess Fred's reaction to this. He had the building vacated and all the windows thrown open until the air cleared. The only thing odd about it was the fact that they were VIPs from the agency."

The *Washington Daily News* reported: "The one thing that is barred during CBS' biggest cigaret program [Old Gold] is cigarets. Fred claims it's bad for the vocalists." Although the papers reported that neither Fred nor nine of his group smoked, one added, "The cigarette sponsors of Fred Waring's band are taking a lot of kidding because several members of the band and Jay P. Medburg, master of ceremonies, coughed during the broadcast—smokers 'without a cough in a car load.' Their ads all say, 'As smooth as an Old Gold.'"[5]

On the other hand, if Fred admired and respected someone, he could be most diplomatic and tolerant. Puss Ronemus, another Pennsylvanian veteran, recalled, "We were doing a show in Atlanta, Georgia, and Fred took [singer] Leonard Kranendonk to the Masters Golf Club in the afternoon. That night after the show we asked Leonard how he enjoyed the afternoon. He said he was introduced to Harvey Firestone, and Harvey was smoking a big cigar blowing smoke all over the place. We asked him if Fred said anything, and Leonard said, 'Not a word!'"

"Fred was the speaker at a meeting in Washington at which four or five senators and eight or ten representatives were present," said Admiral Edwin Dexter, a longtime friend of Fred and the Pennsylvanians. "They were worried about certain matters concerning unions. Half of the group smoked big black cigars. Fred was genuinely allergic, but he told me to never mind the cigars. He stood there for thirty minutes giving an extemporaneous, impressive, extremely articulate talk in which not a sound was uttered by any of the audience present. He virtually turned green with all the cigars, but he stuck it out."

While on long tours in the fifties, Fred cut down cigarette smoking on the buses to ten minutes each hour, set by his wristwatch alarm. As he was years ahead on enforcing a nonsmoking rule, there was much grumbling and sneering behind his back, mostly from instrumentalists who weren't concerned about their throats and vocal cords. From the sixties on, Fred banned smoking on the buses altogether, but allowed a thirty-minute rest stop every two hours on long trips. Fred insisted his abhorrence of cigars stemmed from his early teen years when he babysat in tightly closed houses filled with stale cigar smoke. One whiff of a cigar to Fred was tantamount to a sniff of cyanide, and he would go reeling out of the room.

· · ·

In the early thirties, Bing Crosby was an eminent star on the Columbia network. In 1933, in the same week, one could hear on CBS Kate Smith at 7:30 P.M., Bing Crosby on the Chesterfield Show at 8, Lombardo with Gracie Allen and George Burns at 8:30, and Fred Waring at 9. On NBC Morton Downey aired at 8:30 P.M. John Royal decided to groom Tom Waring for a spot against Crosby. "He sent me to Cleveland to prepare for it," Tom said. "While I was there, Russ Columbo, a good friend of mine, went to New York and got the job. He apparently didn't need grooming. I was really upset; I told everybody off in the city of Cleveland. It was about this time my mother said to me, 'I think that the only thing for you to do is to change your name. Just drop the Waring. It's no good for you anyway.'"

On another occasion, Jesse said, "They can't do without each other. There are things Fred can do—Tom can't."

During these years Eddie Cantor became a star on radio. But one time "Eddie had a bout with the flu," Fred said. "He couldn't make it to his radio show, and asked Rudy to take over the hour at the last minute. The custom was that substitutes didn't get paid; they could either expect an exchange appearance on their own show or a handsome gift. When Eddie asked Rudy Vallee what he wanted, he said a boat: a twenty-seven-foot brand new Chris-Craft!

"Once Rudy invited me up to the lake. He was quite a host. One of his guests was the president of WOR radio station. Rudy put on a big show for us. He had off-the-air recordings of my material and he made everybody—all his guests—sit there and listen to my radio shows. The yacht Eddie Cantor had given him was out on the lake. First we had to stand around and catch medicine balls while Rudy did his exercises. After lunch, we all went out for a ride around the lake on the Chris-Craft. Rudy put on his admiral's uniform and had two flunkies dressed as sailors. I had sent him a Blendor for twelve-volt use, and we had to sit on the boat and drink daiquiris, because I was the guest of honor. His house was something else. Each bedroom was named for a star—Alice Faye, with whom he had worked, and others. Each bathroom had musical tissues which played the theme song of the girl for whom the room was named. When you pulled down on the roll, the music box would begin."

Columnist Jack O'Brian told Fred, "I remember Rudy Vallee was so popular that men resented him. Once John D. Wells, a reporter on the *Buffalo News*, said, during Rudy's huge popularity, 'Today there was a plot to kidnap Rudy Vallee, and some blame fool circumvented it.'"[6]

Tom rejoined and unjoined the Pennsylvanians all through the thirties—the friction never stopped. Danny Winkler, who was fond of them both, said, "It was kind of the talk of the industry that Tom and Fred weren't getting along, but *never* once did I ever hear Tom say anything disparaging about Fred or Fred about Tom. *Never!* I was always fond of both Fred and Tom for a reason that I was what's known as a 'mother's boy.' Fred used to call his mother frequently on the phone. After a radio show, he'd say, 'Well, Jesse, how was that?' He wanted to get her reaction. The reason he had variety in his show was because of his mother, and he stuck to what his mother wanted him to do. She emphasized, of course, religious music."

Promoter Balaban was impressed that Fred's mother had financed their first trip to Chicago in 1922. "Mr. Balaban warmed up to me because I had sought my mother's advice," Fred said. "Subsequently, I visited his mother and father."

In 1984 when Fred was putting his last show together, I asked him how he had happened to choose "Marcheta." He said, "I'm dedicating this program to our friends. 'Marcheta' was my mother's favorite song, and she was a friend of the Pennsylvanians." Fred and Tom were in good company. Douglas MacArthur, Frank Lloyd Wright, and presidents Franklin D. Roosevelt, Harry Truman, and Lyndon Johnson were all mamma's boys.

• • •

Toward the end of the year's contract with Old Gold, Johnny O'Connor was getting anxious: "We're getting $10,000 net a week plus transportation for our stage shows, and $3,500 for the Old Gold Show. I went to Waring and said, 'I'm afraid you're going to get the stink of cigarettes into ya and suffer the same fate that Whiteman did if we sign up again with these people, because Whiteman couldn't get a sponsor after Old Gold.' Whiteman was so well identified with Old Gold that nobody wanted him. Waring agreed—he always agreed. He said, 'Have you got anything in mind?' I said, 'No, you're at the top of the heap here. I don't think there will be any trouble. In the meantime you've got all the work you can handle and enough money.'

"The next day I went to a lovely luncheon meeting with Orr and Leonard of the same agency in the Chrysler Building. When it was all finished, I said, 'Well, do you want Waring for next year?' They said, 'Yeah—we can go to the office and pick up the contract.'

"I said, 'You know the terms?' They said, 'What are the terms?' I said, '$6,500.'

"One of them said, 'There's a place under the Fifty-ninth Street Bridge where they keep guys like you.' I said, 'Yeah, I'm goin' over there now. But if you want to get in touch with me, write the office.' They said, 'You'll be finished in February. You can't get that kind of money.' I said, 'Nevertheless, that's it or else,' and praying they wouldn't accept, and they didn't. We were due to get off the first week in February of '34.

"Roosevelt was now in the White House, and Prohibition was going out, so I thought the best thing in the world would be a whiskey sponsor, whether Waring liked it or not. He didn't smoke and he didn't drink, but he had ballyhooed cigarettes; now a little whiskey might help. I read that Lord Dewar was on his way over, coming into Boston, so I went up to Boston. I got a newspaper pass to go to the boat to see Lord Dewar.

"I was in the hotel when a knock came at the door and I let in a fellow named Paul Lewis from N. W. Ayer and Sons agency who said he understood that my attraction was going to be available in February. I said, 'That's right.'

"He said, 'We've got a client who I think would be interested in him.' I said, 'Who's the client?'

"He said, 'I can't divulge that.' I said, 'I have to know what kind of a product it is, because we can't accept every product.' He said, 'It's a motor car.'

"So I excused myself and went and looked in my agency book and saw their motor car was a Ford. I went out and I said, 'Mr. Lewis, I don't know anything about your motor car, but our price is pretty steep and I've got a client coming in on a boat, and I have practically closed the deal with him—it's just a matter of shakin' hands and drawin' up the contract.'

"He said, 'Can I know who it is?' I said, 'No, I can't divulge the client's name, but I can tell you the product—it's liquor.' He said, 'You are going to New York on the next plane with me.'

"I said, 'Do you know what you are buying? You are buying a hell of an expensive package.' He said, 'What is the price you set?' I said, 'The price is $12,500 or better.' He said, 'You're still getting on the plane.' So I went on the plane and went up to Ayer's office at 500 Fifth Avenue, and I was turned over to a big, powerful, good-natured giant named Doug Colter. I told him what the costs would be. He shook it off, although it obviously stunned him. I said there are some side prices to go in there. $500 for publicity, $100 for stamps, and so and so. I was going to throw in arrangers and everything else. So he said, 'Just sit down a minute.' He went into another room and apparently phoned and came back and said, 'You are hired.' He said, 'I just talked to Mr. Ford.' I said, 'Oh, is that who the client is?'

"I told him Waring is to have full control of the production—no interference from sponsor or agency insofar as the content of the program, other than the commercials. I told him why—how we had been hampered on changing songs at the last minute. He said that would be all right. We would have the privilege to travel, and they would arrange for the local and all the mechanical necessities of the program while we were on the road. I said, 'Secondly, you'll have to get a theater for us because we are too big for a studio.' They made Columbia get the Hudson Theater. I said, 'I want a five-year contract.' We settled for three years. But it was a year solid at a time. It was for '34, '35, and '36. I signed it and wired Waring in Pittsburgh. We closed for Old Gold on February 4 and opened for Ford on February 9 at $12,500. It was the highest ever paid and the first time a broadcasting company had bought a theater just for radio."

Fred was always amused by Johnny's deadpan gangster expression under his grey fedora hat and the happy gleam in his eye when he managed to get the best of a shrewd adversary. Johnny was equally amused by Fred's small-town ideals. As he once growled to Fred's secretary Helen Helwig, "You can take the boy out of the country but you can't take the country out of the boy." Still, he liked Fred's fearless "up and at 'em" heroic showmanship. They both loved a challenge: instead of making their shoulders sag, a whiff of opposition was like inhaling pure oxygen. Each was a real romantic and they understood each other.

No sooner did the Ford show take off than, according to the *New York Daily Mirror,* "the wild scramble of imitators began."

> Radio advertisers throughout the country began demanding auditions patterned after the Waring Brand of presentation.
>
> Vocal combinations were hastily formed and attached to orchestras, bands were broken up to make replacements with musicians who could sing, choirs were recruited from the amateur ranks. Former members of the Waring unit were to help direct new programs à la the Waring technique.
>
> But while they all carry the general essence of the Waring show, the odor of the rubber stamp and the ink pad is easily discernible. After all, it takes even the most scientific copyists more than a few weeks to successfully duplicate a technique and judgment of program pace that required fifteen or more years of research, labor, and practical experience in its development.[7]

Guy Lombardo wrote in his autobiography, "In 1933 one of our few rivals in popularity was Fred Waring's band featuring chorus and vocal groups. John Ruber, president of our agency, insisted we have singers, so we added eight voices. A stack of uncomplimentary telegrams from radio editors poured in—our band was no longer Lombardo, it was synthetic Waring."[8] Fred and Guy Lombardo nonetheless remained lifelong friends—never seeing much of each other but continually exchanging friendly barbs on the air.

•   •   •

Fred had a strong instinct—some called it a spark of genius—for perceiving latent talent in musicians and singers who auditioned for him. But his method of hiring those who worked behind the scenes continued to be haphazard, impulsive, and sometimes a drain on the organization, since he could not bear to fire anyone.

One example of impetuous hiring that did succeed was Hilda Cole, in the early thirties. Hilda, a recent high school graduate who'd joined the staff of CBS's publicity department, had interviewed Fred a couple of times for the network's news releases. "One day when I was taking a shortcut through the halls of Radio City, I met Fred," Hilda recounted. "He said, 'Hello,' and made one of his quick decisions. 'How would you like to do our publicity?' he asked. I said I would love to. I was a far cry from the established Broadway press agents; they were usually 'characters' and I was too young to be one, even if I had wanted to be. Also, I was probably one of the first, if not *the* first lady, to do advance publicity work for a road tour. My guess is that he never had liked the hackneyed or what is euphemistically known as the 'tried and true' route, and was drawn to people who might do something different because they didn't know any better. And so, maybe ten days later, I was following a redcap through Grand Central Station. He was carrying my big suitcase and my portable typewriter onto a sleeping car on a train headed for Chicago, the first stop of a big coast to coast tour." Some ten years later, Hilda left the organization to get married. Her first born were twin girls. She named one of them Freddy. After Freddy grew up, she married George Plimpton.

When Fred chose singers impulsively, he was on sure ground. Talent and personality were high priorities. Looks didn't hurt either. In 1932, two talented and pretty teenagers, Priscilla and Rosemary Magillicutty from Indianola, Iowa, came to New York with their mother. Once there, they changed their name to the Lane Sisters. As Fred came out of an agent's office one day, he saw Rosemary and Priscilla in the waiting room. "They were around sixteen or seventeen and looked as cute as buttons," recalled Fred Culley. "Fred stopped and said, 'Who are you?' and Rosemary, being the talkative one, said, 'Who are *you?*'—not recognizing the great Fred Waring. Since he always liked spunk, Fred soon had them singing and added them on—until Hollywood grabbed them five years later."

• • •

Up to this point in his career, Fred still hadn't talked onstage. But on radio he was expected to read scripts, a duty he found he enjoyed. Fred soon began making verbal contact with his live audiences and found that making them laugh was the most fun of all. His jokes were sometimes corny, but as long as the audience responded with laughter, he didn't care. He stated later that he was purveying corn long before Lawrence Welk could count to two. Pleasing an audience was always uppermost in Fred's mind. To the end, he said that music was written to be enjoyed, and if it meant making a "funny" sometimes between songs to keep things rolling—so be it. He worked hard to gain and keep the respect of his beloved audiences.

Bill Demarest, the great character actor and comedian, once remarked, "The best laughs you get were what we call 'find' laughs. You just find them; you just pick them up from the audience. For example, I'd say, 'Somebody call out an animal, any animal, and I'll imitate it.' Now what does some guy holler? 'Cockroach!' That's a 'find' laugh."[9] Fred's formula, as well, was to find humor in everyday situations, mostly centered around the Pennsylvanians. He helped cultivate latent comedic possibilities in his group, and sometimes used a Pennsylvanian as a foil. A prerequisite for the latter was to be feisty, quick-witted, and completely unafraid of Fred.

Fred's lifelong friend Poley McClintock was the first prankster. Martha Graham once said that the most important quality in humor is innocence, and Poley, that sweet, gentle, tongue-tied man, had this quality. Fred encouraged Poley to improvise. During a show, while Fred was giving a dignified performance, Poley often would clown around behind his back, trying to hit the pianist with a pea shooter, or waving a Confederate flag, if the Pennsylvanians were playing a southern city. He might suddenly change his voice into a basso profundo, make a froglike croak, and sing a silly song. Or Poley might come down front stage, tap out "Nola" on his teeth, and then spit out a mouthful of Lifesavers, which resembled broken teeth.

Fred knew that, in the Lane Sisters—young and fresh from Iowa—he had some potential fodder for humor. "One time onstage, Fred began kidding us about Iowa and the tall corn," Priscilla said. "It annoyed me. In fact it made me mad, so I began answering him in a hillbilly accent, saying, 'I'll say, kid!' It got a laugh, so he kidded all the more, and I got madder and started flipping him in the arm as I said it. The audience seemed to love it. Fred was a great producer, and he knew we were creating a dialogue. I didn't; I was just mad."

11

Henry Ford & Co.

SOON after the Ford dealers show started in 1934, the *Boston Traveler* reported, "My dear, haul up a chair: Paul Whiteman's crown as the heaviest paid bandleader passed to Fred Waring and his outfit last week when the Pennsylvanians grabbed $10,000 as seven days salary at a Broadway playhouse. Whiteman's best previous top had been $8,500. They also do the Ford show—for that they receive $12,500."[1]

Ford's first theme song was Fred's idea—Dick Whiting's "Breezin' Along with the Breeze." He also wrote his own announcements. The opening—"*Hello, everybody, and thanks for coming. This is Fred Waring and all the Pennsylvanians*"—became almost as familiar over the years as his theme song, "Sleep."

A new funding concept was proposed for the Ford program. Basic financing was to be provided by the Ford dealers, who contributed a specific amount for each car bought from the factory. It became known as the "Ford Dealers Program." Since the Pennsylvanians continued to play theaters throughout the country with the sponsor's approval and encouragement, the Ford-Fred Waring show on the road became a lively combination of show business and advertising—with Fred as traveling ambassador. The dealers were excited about the idea. Besides the fact that the show offered enormous publicity, each dealer could stage a special event when Fred was in his territory. Tickets to broadcasts were divided among participating dealers—a pleasant favor for prospective car buyers and a mammoth hassle for everybody else, as freebie tickets inevitably become.

A fleet of white Fords with, according to Jack Dolph, a "particularly nauseating" gold one for Fred, met the Pennsylvanians at the train as the band arrived in each town and hauled them through the streets. In the lead car, Fred and Priscilla Lane waved and smiled like conquering heroes in a ticker tape parade. The rear car contained a loudspeaker inviting one and all to come to the show. "Watch the Fords go by" was their advertising slogan, and the dealers benefited from all the hoopla.

Everyone agreed that the Ford period was the "Era of Hard Work." In the twenties, the Pennsylvanians sometimes performed no more than three theater shows a day—one in the afternoon and two at night—but now they were up to five and many times six a day, seven days a week. "We had no time to eat," Fred Culley said. The *Washington Herald* noted that Fred Waring "is hard at work from early morning until midnight. . . . When he has a few hours to himself he hies himself out to the country and knocks a golf ball around the landscape."[2]

Hilda Cole usually arrived in a city a week prior to the Pennsylvanians, in time to plant stories and pictures in newspapers and arrange for interviews with music critics or radio reporters. "Photographers and reporters often turned up at the station to meet the train with me," she said. "And poor Fred (it usually was the first thing in the morning) would come trudging off in his polo coat, wearing a patient expression. At the theater, the marquee lights were already shining to announce the first show. I would stay with the Pennsylvanians for a couple of days of their engagement to see through interview appointments I had made, then I would move on to the next city where they were scheduled to perform. . . .

"So I got to know something about the way Fred worked. What persists in my mind was that, if there was a crisis of any kind (and there were many), he would thoughtfully eat an apple, his favorite tranquilizer. I got to know exactly what his manager Johnny O'Connor meant when he'd say, 'There we were, three hours late in a blizzard, and we were sure as hell going to miss the first show. So I went to discuss it with Fred and he was eating an apple.'"

Johnny added, "When they played the theaters, those Pennsylvanians never had any worries. They traveled in class. They traveled with a forty-foot baggage car fully equipped, and they traveled in top-flight Pullmans. The veterans got the lowers and the newcomers got the uppers, and they never had to hop a taxicab. A fleet of them was always waiting for them at the depot—back and forth."

Soprano Jane Wilson recalled an incident that occurred shortly after she joined the Pennsylvanians. "In the private sleeping cars reserved for us, all the other female Pennsylvanians were assigned lower berths. I, being the 'new girl,' had an upper. After a few trips, I went to Fred and, in a very determined voice, asked, 'Why don't I have a lower berth as the other girls do?'

"He just looked at me for a minute, then said, "You've made a mistake! You should have started with, 'Would it be possible?' instead of 'Why don't I?'"

. . .

In September, during all this turmoil, Evalyn said that Fred barely managed to get home in time for the birth of their first child—a girl. "Shortly after, I ran into Bing [Crosby] in New York," Fred said. "He and his wife Dixie were in a taxi. I was crossing the street as he yelled out of the cab. I got in the cab and said, 'We just had a baby the other day and we're naming her Dixie for you.' She was tickled."

After Dixie's birth, Evalyn was granted her wish to live in a New York apartment. The family moved to 210 Park Avenue. "I thought it was a dream place," she said. "I wanted to cook and I was so happy. That's when Fred got Fred Lewis as a cook and valet in the office. That left me out of cooking and having any fun."

During a New York rehearsal, Fred walked in with Henry Ford and introduced him to the Pennsylvanians. The slim, gray old man smiled gently at the enthusiastic reception they gave him. Everyone expected him to leave soon, but Mr. Ford sat quietly for a long time, displaying a bright-eyed, lively interest in the musical activity. Henry Ford had brought for Dixie a little wooden desk from the McGuffey Schoolhouse. "When he held her on his lap, he said it reminded him of Edsel when he was little," Evalyn said. "She wet on him and he said, 'Oh, that's all right.'"

Meredith Willson, a good friend, was always instigating a friendly feud between Fred and himself, anything to "get Fred's dander up." In honor of Dixie's birth, Meredith sent Fred his anathema—a crate of empty cigar boxes. The card read, "Kindly fill and return."

In retaliation, Fred sent his office boy to the city zoo and all the livery stables in New York, with orders to fill the boxes with various manure specimens, then return them to Mr. Willson C.O.D. "Meredith had his secretary open them for him and there was, of course, a lot of screaming," Fred said.

"In 1934 Meredith was with a San Francisco radio station during one of our theater engagements. When I arrived, Meredith had beautiful linen handkerchiefs sent as a gift to my dressing room. I opened the box and embroidered on each handkerchief was 'Stolen from Meredith Willson.'

"Meredith had argued for years that the shrill sound of the piccolo would carry much farther than any other instrument. I said, 'Oh, no, the bass drum.' So we decided to fight it out. We would stage a demonstration. He collected all the paraphernalia and had all the station people there, the microphones, the announcers. One of us had to go to the island in the bay, Yerba Buena, and the other was to stay on the shore in San Francisco. Naturally, Meredith stayed onshore with his piccolo, and I had to go to Yerba Buena at 5 A.M. with a goddamn bass drum. We had it timed so that the microphone on my side was to pick up his piccolo, and the mike on his side was to pick up the bass drum. The only thing heard was the bass drum."

In the fifties, shortly after we were married, Fred and I were invited to dine with Mr. and Mrs. Willson at their home near Palm Springs, California. It had been many years since Fred and Meredith Willson's paths had crossed, so there was much friendly joshing and reminiscing. I noticed a rather large Band-Aid on our host's thumb and asked him about it. He replied that when he was in the process of creating, he would unconsciously rub the skin off that particular finger until it became raw. He was then working on *The Unsinkable Molly Brown*.

For the Ford show, Tom was back again with the group and not too happy, because his job was to sing duets with Rosemary Lane, sharing his music. "She ruined my memory because I had to keep my finger on the music for her," he said. "She could never find her place because she was always looking around at the audience and making bows. I had to nudge her every time it was her turn to come in."

He and Fred continued to have their usual blowups. They were always arguing about the various aspects of interpreting a piece of music—the tempos, nuances, crescendos, diminuendos, ritards, loudness, softness—the list is endless. The Pennsylvanians did it Fred's way. Tom often wanted to perform his own version, which didn't always set well with Fred's musical ear. "I remember one time in Pittsburgh when Fred blamed Tom for something—I'll remember it as long as I live," Jack Dolph said. "Tom went to the hotel and packed his bags. He was frustrated, angry, and hurt, all at the same time.

"I went to supper with Fred and I said, '*You're wrong*. You're just plain wrong; you're being unfair,' and he said, 'Do you really think I am?' This sort of thing never dawns on him. I said, 'Tom will be at the studio. You walk in and tell him you're sorry because you're wrong.' He did. Oh, brother!"

Tom's heart and asthma problems had plagued him all his life. He was never in robust health. But he wasn't the only one who had to take a sabbatical because of illness. Three other Pennsylvanians were afflicted with tuberculosis, a contagious, often fatal disease those days. (When I was growing up, no one spoke above a whisper when referring to TB.) One of the three, Freddy Buck, was released from a Swiss sanitarium and returned to the group for short periods, only to drop out. The last time he had worked a little was in 1932 at the Roxy. Then in 1934 the Pennsylvanians received word he had died. It was a sad day—one of the original four was gone. Freddy was only thirty-four. Curly Cockerill, the Canadian, died a few years later. Poley McClintock was lucky—he survived the dreaded affliction.

. . .

Fred was conducting four and five stage shows a day, seven days a week, plus the hourly Ford program, now in its second year. At that time the *New York World-Telegram* poll, a widely recognized popularity rating, placed Fred Waring at the top.

Fred Waring	104
Rudy Vallee	72
New York Philharmonic	66
Jessica Dragonette	48
Paul Whiteman	45
Philadelphia Orchestra	42[3]

And the road business throughout the Ford period was tremendous and highly lucrative. The trade papers reported: "Boston Metropolitan, $33,000—$11,000 over par!—New York Paramount SRO—15,000 hear Warings at Convention Hall, Philly; 3500 turned away!" and "Waring combines Boston, Buffalo, Minneapolis, Chicago and Detroit for 600,000 attendance and five house records."[4] These, of course, were the depression years—1934, 1935, and 1936.

At the opening of the Ford Rotunda in Dearborn, Michigan, Edsel had insisted that the Pennsylvanians come out and play for the inaugural ceremonies. To Fred's dismay, he saw that it was a circular building, all glass. "The acoustics were just plain horrible," Fred said. "There we had our big orchestra trying to play quietly enough so that it didn't scare anyone. We had just about run through our repertoire of soft music of which we had brought little, and lo and behold, approaching the platform is Stokowski with Henry Ford. Mr. Ford was giving his attention to Stokowski, as was his custom. He treated everyone with utmost respect and a desire to please. Stokowski practically yelled from at least a hundred feet away [and Fred imitates Stokowski]: 'Fred, Fred, *Fred Varing*, oh, isn't this vonderful?' and he came right up to the platform and said, 'You've got to play something for me.'

"And I said, 'Well, I . . .' I felt it coming. I had a feeling that he was going to ask the impossible. I said, 'You know, we don't have much here.' He said, 'Oh, I know you can play this—everybody can play this and you play it so vonderfully.' And I said, 'What is that?'

"He said, '*Tiger Rag*,' knowing damn well that if we played four bars of our triple forte brass arrangement of 'Tiger Rag' it would drive everybody out of the place. 'Well . . .' I said, 'now you *know* that "Tiger Rag" is out of the question in this situation.'

"Stokowski said, 'Oh, you must play it. Mr. Ford, don't you think he should play "Tiger Rag"?'

"Henry, who had always liked me, looked sort of nonplussed and said, not knowing what 'Tiger Rag' meant, 'I think you should play whatever Mr. Stokowski asked if you can.' I said, 'For the first time, I must say, I think you'll regret it.' So we started to play 'Tiger Rag' and sure enough . . . it was so loud and horrible. Stokowski walked away from the stand with a glint in his eye, realizing he had pulled a real good one on me."

· · ·

It was in this banner year of the Ford show that Fred received some disquieting news: the Ford Motor Company and N. W. Ayer agency executives had decided to use guest stars. Fred was disappointed because they seldom fit in. One can imagine his apoplexy when a guest on the show lectured for five minutes on dinosaur eggs or when the New York City Police Department was saluted for being the first with radio-equipped patrol cars. A dramatization of their speedy response brought six cops thundering down the aisles of the Hudson theater during a broadcast, brandishing their nightsticks. One got carried away, and as he approached the open microphone yelled, "What the hell is going on in here?"

Writer Jack Dolph was employed by the N. W. Ayer Agency and was assigned to the Ford program as a liaison between the agency and guest artists. He also wrote the commercials. He was expected to attend rehearsals and performances. One Sunday Dolph's chief at N. W. Ayer told him that Ford felt that Fred's novelty songs were undignified and wanted them off the show *now,* along with Poley McClintock and his frog voice. It was Jack's unhappy assignment to tell Fred about that order from on high—and see that he conformed. Jack knew that Fred Waring's chin didn't jut out like the Rock of Gibraltar for nothing. Dolph had a major problem on his hands, and he dreaded the confrontation.

He went to the Hudson Theater long before the rehearsal time and walked over to Fred's podium. He picked up the familiar yellow pad on which program, timing, cues, and notes were set down in Fred's distinctive blue and red crayon scrawl. Listed just above the closing number was "Annie Doesn't Live Here Any More." Dolph visibly flinched. "Annie" was a rollicking novelty song with Poley prominently featured in it. He had heard the Pennsylvanians going over it, and it was anything but dignified.

At noon, Fred drove up to the stage door in his shiny new Brewster-Ford town car, all set for the final rehearsal of the show to go on that Sunday night. Jack braced himself and intercepted Fred on his walk to the podium. He timorously divulged the sponsor's adamant demand for drastic surgery. Fred listened and, without a word, walked to the podium. Dolph lurked around the theater as the musicians entered, laden with instruments. The writer's heart sank as Fred announced that the first number to be rehearsed would be "Annie Doesn't Live Here Any More." Fred rehearsed it and rehearsed it and rehearsed it. Then Johnny O'Connor nonchalantly strolled in. Jack immediately went over and asked O'Connor to please intercede with Fred, that the sponsors were serious. Johnny's poker face turned deadpan. "There's a 'no interference' clause in the contract," O'Connor said calmly. "Ford and Ayer knew perfectly well what they were buying."

At the rehearsal break when the strains of "Annie Doesn't Live Here Any More" had mercifully ceased, Fred asked Jack if he'd like to join him for doughnuts and coffee. Jack hoped it was a sign of intention to cooperate but, after three cups of coffee and several doughnuts, no progress had been made. "*Ford* and *Ayer* both knew perfectly well what they were buying," Johnny said over and over—changing the words but never the tune. "They might as well hire any other band. Take away the novelties and we're not Waring anymore."

"I know, I *know,* I KNOW!" Now Jack was really sweating. An hour before the show he took a peek at Fred's big pad. "Annie" was still next to closing. Jack felt the tension tightening in his solar plexus as he walked into the control room and stationed himself near the engineer. He had decided to destroy a tube that would take the Pennsylvanians off the air when he heard the introduction to "Annie Doesn't Live Here Any More."

Suddenly it was time for the next to closing number. Fred gave the downbeat, and Jack nearly collapsed with relief. The orchestra and singers filled the air with a new and beautiful choral arrangement. Fred had taken pity on Jack who, from that moment on, became his staunch friend. What Jack did, in return, was to fly to Dearborn, Michigan, for a special meeting with the Ford executives. He persuaded them that novelty numbers were intrinsic to the Pennsylvanians' unique ability to go from the sublime to the ridiculous. The novelty songs and Poley's frog voice were reinstated. Jack mused, "I had apparently caught the occupational disease of most of the Pennsylvanians, past and present, of loving the guy and never quite being able to figure out why—like being a Marine—it was tough, but you were proud of it!"

· · ·

And still one more activity was added to Fred's busy schedule—that of music publishing. He was actually forced into it.

> In 1935 the American Federation of Musicians, a tough union now headed by tough Jimmy Petrillo, began to organize the arrangers working for the music publishers. The publishers promptly yelled bloody murder and AF of M blasted right back—started a boycott of all top songs of publishers who had not unionized their staffs.
>
> The publishers countered by informing all band leaders that if they persisted in their boycott, they would prohibit the leaders from making special arrangements of their (the publishers') copyright songs. This was a body blow. Special arrangements are the life blood of a band leader. They are what makes his band outstanding, give it style and personality.[5]

Fred already had a bone to pick with publishers. Two years before, *Variety* had noted: "In giving CBS carte blanche about inviting anyone it wanted to the party he threw at the Essex house last Tuesday, Fred Waring however stipulated that music publishers were not to be included among the invitees. Reason for the attitude was that while he played theater dates the music men paid little attention to him but now that he has the Old Gold Hour on the air they are all too ready to flock around him."[6]

"I investigated and found that the publishers were well within their rights to keep us from arranging their songs, so I called an immediate conference with Waring, Whiteman, Lombardo, Abe Lyman, and Jack Benny," O'Connor said. "We decided to buy a publishing company and found the Harry Engel catalogue was available so Waring, Whiteman, and I put up $10,000 apiece. Lyman and Lombardo each put up $5,000 and Jack Benny put up $2,500—$42,500. We paid $41,000 for the company. In it was a song, 'The Night Is Young and You're So Beautiful.' Waring made an arrangement and played it, but everyone else thought it was a dog. They wouldn't play it. Shows you how much bandleaders know about music. For six weeks nothin' happened, and then one Friday afternoon I came in the office and there were orders for about 80,000 copies. We had a hit. Waring kept sinkin' dough in the company—none of the other stockholders were asked to sink in it. Listen, this wasn't Waring's firm, for Christ's sake—he only had ten shares of stock, the same as me. But he took it and he ran with it."

The name was changed to Words and Music, and later Fred bought out the others. When he moved to Shawnee-on-Delaware, Pennsylvania, he changed the name to Shawnee Press. It eventually became one of the largest publishing companies in the world for choral and instrumental music, serving schools, churches, community choirs, bands, and orchestras.

Amidst all the excitement, the copycats continued to stalk Fred Waring. Horace Heidt, one of the most persistent of the breed, said when he graduated from the University of California, "I'm going to be a better Fred Waring."[7] His band was Horace Heidt's Californians.

"He stated it publicly and proceeded to do an absolute imitation of Fred Waring with megaphones and everything, except he added a bit with a police dog," John Royal recounted. "There was nothing Fred could do about it and it must have been galling, because for a while Heidt was soaring around the top."

Finally, after several years of this, on June 11, 1935, Heidt wired Fred: A WEEK FROM THIS THURSDAY WE WOULD LIKE TO PAY PERSONAL TRIBUTE TO YOU AND AS FOLLOW-UP, GIVE OUR INTERPRETATION TO "WAY BACK HOME." WOULD THIS INTERFERE WITH YOUR PLANS IN ARRANGING PROGRAMS AS WE ARE NOT ALLOWED TO REPEAT ANY NUMBER YOU DO ON YOUR SHOW? MY PERSONAL ADMIRATION OF WHAT YOU HAVE ACCOMPLISHED PROMPTS THIS AND IS FIRST OPPORTUNITY HAVE EVER HAD TO IN SOME WAY SHOW IT. WE ARE VERY HAPPY HERE AT DRAKE HOTEL AND FEEL FORTUNATE TO HAVE FINALLY GOTTEN WHAT YOU ALONE KNOW THE PROBLEMS A STAGE BAND HAS IN GETTING STARTED ON THE AIR. GIVE MY BEST TO TOM AND THE BOYS. SINCERELY, HORACE HEIDT.[8]

O'Connor wrote Heidt on June 20, care of the Drake Hotel in Chicago:

Your wire of the eleventh addressed to Mr. Waring was not answered because his program for the date you mentioned was not arranged until

Thursday morning. Your expression of personal admiration for the accomplishment of our organization is sincerely appreciated but your effort to publicly exhibit same in a special way seems a bit superfluous. Don't you feel that you are paying a personal tribute weekly to Fred Waring and his organization when you present a carbon copy slightly smudged but nevertheless a carbon of his program, arrangement, radio technique, comedy numbers and glee club right down to the rather mediocre impression of Poley McClintock's individual talent? I do.[9]

Heidt's response came on June 29:

Thank you very much for your courteous reply to my wire of the eleventh concerning my apparent misguided efforts to express admiration of our band for Fred Waring. The contents of your letter in particularly the sentiments expressed in your last paragraph were discussed with my present associates, the management of the Drake & Blackstone Hotels in Chicago, and with the officials of the Stuart Warner Corp. who suggested that I forward their reaction to you. These sentiments obviously intended as highly complimentary were considered particularly flattering by my present employers, so I am not unhappy.[10]

Johnny O'Connor decided he'd had enough. He sharpened his pencil, collected his wits and finished the dialogue:

Yours of the 29th arrived during my absence from the office over a holiday period. I note that your present associates, the management of Blackstone & Drake Hotels and the officials of the Stuart Warner Corp. considered my comments as flattering. My, oh my, isn't that marvelous! But after all, Horace, it's not surprising for every fellow who buys a secondhand suit likes to think he's the best dressed man in town.

In one of his few signed articles Fred Waring once declared, "Radio entertainment is either original or copied. There is no middle ground—if the whole of the industry is viewed through a glass that defines both professional and commercial value. In the upper brackets—individuals and groups enjoy popularity for the simple reason that they have brought something new and entertaining to the air. Bringing up a struggling vanguard are the second guessers who specialize in something 'just as good or just like it.' These are radio burglars against whom the creator has no protection either legally or by commission ruling. Originality's sole defense against the copycats rests in the public opinion support, published credits of trained observers and the facts that the copycats' efforts bear the unmistakable odor of the rubber stamp. The contrast between these two types of entertainment is that of a clean shirt and a dirty shirt.

The absence of the court of complaint for the protection of talent and material is unfortunate in a profession that plays with millions of dollars and individuals. Eventually something may be worked out to caulk the leaks. Until then the creative professional is ticketed as a legitimate target for the unethical sharpshooters of show business. The thermometer of public popularity, however, is a true gauge and the public, despite the machinations of the incapables, can always be depended on to note the differences between the clean shirt and the dirty shirt."

Now, Horace, read that little opinion over again, gulp a couple of times and go take a peek at your face in the mirror. Your efforts at satire are quite as futile as your endeavors, if any, to create something that would liberate you from radio's laundry bag. I do not question your versatility, for when a trouper can hobble through the gamut from animal trainer to maestro and still keep his name in lights, he certainly holds something and Horace, my boy, you have held, at one time or another, everything Fred Waring has introduced except the police dog. But you always seem to get them on the second bounce and even a class B outfielder occasionally gets one in the air. Since both you and your sponsors seem proud of your result as shirt model, it seems only fair that the radio be given an opportunity to applaud during your spasm of ecstasy and in order that both our opinions be properly aired I think it would be a good idea to release our correspondence for publication. Please give me your opinion about this.[11]

Johnny O'Connor had no intention of turning over the correspondence to the press. When Jules Stein called from Heidt's hotel, not only putting forth an inquiry but also indicating a fear that publication would follow, O'Connor assured him, "No, Julie—I wouldn't."

It was a tribute to Fred that the copycats followed him throughout his career. The last and most persistent of these was Lawrence Welk. Indeed, I would see him each year in the auditorium either at Santa Monica or Long Beach with his secretary and her stenographer's pad. Welk actually came backstage and talked about this and that gag or vignette or combination of songs that he had almost perfected. But Fred never took umbrage at his apers. "I think we are the best, the most musically alert and the most capable of doing the greatest range of music," he said. "You'll hear a lot of imitations of us—and I don't say that bitterly but with pride."

· · ·

The arrangers most responsible for creating the recognizable Waring choral sound were Roy Ringwald, Hawley Ades, and Harry Simeone. Fred heard Roy Ringwald in 1935 when he was performing with a quartet of three boys and a girl on the André Kostelanetz Show. When their contract was up, they moved over to the Pennsylvanians and Fred renamed them "Stella and the Fellas."

"That was in 1935," Ringwald said. "I did the arranging for the quartet. Shortly after I joined the Pennsylvanians, I asked Fred if I could make one arrangement a month for the group. He said, 'Good,' so I did. They were a cappella with only minor instrumental indications. For many rhythmic pieces, Leo Arnaud often merely sketched the bare harmonic outlines for the singers, and Fred, in rehearsal, improvised elaborate rhythmic effects in vocables, word repetitions, and the like—teaching them by rote.

"I was still performing and I just hated it," Ringwald continued. "I was self-conscious and didn't like jumping around onstage, and so I buckled down to the business of writing. Fred asked me to make an arrangement of the old pop song 'For Me and My Gal.' He gave me unusually detailed instructions on what he wanted—which soloists, which groups, what tempos, etc., etc., etc. I had followed through meticulously—on each and every detail. After he'd had the score a while, Fred approached me in the hall with an ominously down expression and was saying, '*I thought I told you.*' By that time I had snatched the score from his hand, croaked, 'That's the best I can do,' and was on my way to the nearby elevator. Fred was calling, 'Now wait a minute, Roy! Now wait a minute!' He was merely testing me. He never did that again!"

Roy Ringwald, a shy, gentle, introverted man, had a round face with a continually benign expression. He lived his entire life almost as a recluse—always working at night, sometimes all night.

"On one other occasion a few years later, I remember losing my temper when I thought that Fred, from the control room, was being unfair about a balance my 'twin-trios' (sextet) was trying to get on microphone," Ringwald said. "I spouted off. Fred didn't say a word, just put his head in his hands and waited me out. I have an idea he was hiding no little amusement. That was the last time there was *any* such yakking between us."

By the end of the first year on the Ford show, Fred had added another notch in his musical belt. The show still gave out a young, fresh, collegiate impression, but the choice of songs Fred had added and the way he performed them placed him beyond the simple term, *bandleader.* Cole Porter, Jerome Kern, Hoagy Carmichael, and many other writers who treasured their lyrics as well as the melodic lines of their songs considered Fred Waring an interpreter par excellence. Two factors made Fred a songwriter's delight—his huge media exposure on radio and, more important, his exquisite handling of a song, in ways such as diction, phrasing, and precision in group singing. Fred considered a creative person a precious commodity whose artistry warranted utmost respect.

"Most of our arrangements of Jerome Kern music were done by our arranger Roy Ringwald," Fred said. "Mr. Kern was always complimentary. When he'd hear one of his songs presented by us, he would always let me know he'd been listening. He wrote a song called 'And Her Name Is Russia' and called me to ask permission for Roy to arrange it. Roy did, of course, and then we recorded it for Mr. Kern. His graciousness is something I'll always remember."

In October, 1935, Fred performed a cavalcade of Jerome Kern songs. Kern, called to the stage from the audience that night, took a bow in tears—saying they were tears of joy. Fred described Jerome Kern as "a man of beauty, both in appearance and in mind. He was attuned to the beautiful things about us and expressed them in lovely, celestial melodies.

"Richard Rodgers and Larry Hart wrote *Jumbo,* which was to open at the Hippodrome Theater. They were anxious for us to hear the score and, naturally, to give it a push on radio and record it if possible. They had me over to a dress rehearsal and the opening night. It was a big to-do and a big fuss. They were always so appreciative. It was a joy to sing for them."

Cole Porter also spoke often of Waring performances of his music, such as the broadcast of the score of *Jubilee,* which he "so affectionately remembered."[12]

. . .

Much of Fred's success in his long career lay in two things—the strong familial sentiments generated by his concern for the Pennsylvanians' welfare, and the exhilarating pride of the Pennsylvanians in being part of a number-one team. On the road, Fred provided housing, transportation, all the amenities—everything but meals. Even today, most performers must look after themselves. Some have to set up stages, provide their own transportation to theaters, pay for and worry about many daily chores. When Fred made money, the Pennsylvanians made money. In the halcyon radio days it meant, according to Priscilla Lane, "terrific gifts for everyone" including stand-up steamer trunks and paid-up insurance policies. Years later some of the newer members were stunned to learn, after visiting the Lawrence Welk show on TV, that the Lennon Sisters were still being paid scale wages after starring for so many years. Fred was generous all his life. What's the use of having money if you don't spread it around?

"I arrived in the big, mad magic city of New York in 1935, fiddle in hand, to be greeted by a large family of friendly, wonderful people—with whom I was to coexist for the next thirteen years," Ferne Buckner said. "Their musical activity, I sometimes felt, was a secondary concern, being super-seded by the close, family-like devotion of the group to the group. Of course, disagreements sometimes occurred, particularly in the small re-hearsal room of Stella and the Fellas—Stella Friend, Roy Ringwald, Paul Gibbon, and Craig Leitch. Screaming and pounding shook the walls and rattled the door periodically, but as in the case of all families, the fights of fury were soon forgotten and absorbed."

"I got to join Fred and some of his cronies for a breakfast now and then, or a snack after the last show," Hilda Espy said. "During such impromp-tu chats, I learned that Fred was a staunch Republican. I was a red hot Democrat and I asserted I had voted for Roosevelt, my first and only vote up to that time. Fred didn't argue with me and took no reprisals except to refer from time to time to my political acuity—'Ask Hilda. She knows it all.'

"Fred noticed everything, and he noticed I was picking up some back-stage language. Billboards carried ads known as 'three sheets.' This led to the use of 'three-sheeting' to describe anybody who was showing off or talking big. I added that to my vocabulary, and one day Fred overheard me using a word I had just learned: *jerk.*

"'I wonder if you know what that means?' Fred inquired.

"'No, I don't. What does it mean?'

"'Never mind. But I wouldn't use it if I were you.'"

How times have changed!

Fred had not seen the last of Miss Dorothy Lee. In late 1935, the fol-lowing paragraph appeared in Leonard Lyon's "Lyon's Den": "Yesterday's papers . . . announcing Dorothy Lee's divorce from Marshall Duffield . . . stated that the movie actress may pick up the threads of her romance with Fred Waring. If the report is true, Miss Lee is a bit brazen in view of the fact that the bandleader presumably has been happily married for almost two years."[13]

No one was concerned. It was just another gem from the mischievous publicity-wise mind of Miss Lee herself, who thereafter went on her merry way.

12

The Legalities of Interpretation

ONE NIGHT in the spring of 1935, Fred was in New York chatting with several musical notables and newspapermen in Lindy's restaurant, their favorite after-show hangout, when someone complimented him on a broadcast of the Pennsylvanians he'd heard earlier that evening. Fred was puzzled, as he hadn't performed on the air that day.

It turned out that disc jockeys had started a practice of playing Fred's records they'd received from the recording companies without cost. They would air his music at the same time as the Ford show, for which Fred was being paid $13,500 per program. "I felt it was unfair for them to have our records playing in competition to us," Fred said, "and it was a growing menace to all performers."

So Fred, the white knight, his square jaw firmly set, looked into the legalities and found, to his consternation, that no law prohibited the kidnapping of talent. The United States copyright laws, which had not changed since 1909, gave protection only to writers and inventors. No rights of musical interpretation existed under the Constitution. Interpretation is an act of creativity. It is unique. Any musician who literally "reads" the notes of a composition is not playing anything interesting. Without the endless components of tempi, nuances, tonal quality, inflections, and timbre, it is merely sound—music in its embryonic stage.

After talking over the matter with such friends and fellow-sufferers as Paul Whiteman and Bing Crosby, Fred assembled other performing artists who were awakening to this realization of high-handed piracy, and formed the National Association of Performing Artists (NAPA) to bring about legislation restricting the use of their recordings.

Fred was asked to be president. For counsel, he turned to New York entertainment attorney Maurice J. Speiser, who represented such famous artists as Leopold Stokowski and Fritz Reiner, as well as his own law associate Walter Socolow. "We wanted to add to the copyright law *the Right of Interpretation*," Fred said. "The typical purchaser does not buy a record of just a song; he buys a record of someone's interpretation of that song. For example, there are three selections of 'Star Dust': one by Como, one by Waring, and one by Sinatra. Since the choice is going to be interpretation, the interpreter should get a reward—a tiny percentage of the money paid in.

"If you agreed with the copyright law, you would have to contend that you go to a concert to hear a composition; whether it is played by Eugene Ormandy or the Salvation Army Band doesn't matter to you! Fans pay thousands of dollars to hear Sinatra sing a number that all soloists are singing—it's what Frank or Lena Horne add to a song that makes people buy one of their records.

"Nearly seven hundred artists joined NAPA. We had a tremendous list of people—bandleaders and singers. We began bringing lawsuits in various areas to prove a right of interpretation." Fred filed a precedent-setting suit in his home state of Pennsylvania. Lawrence Tibbett, Don Voorhees, and Paul Whiteman took action in New York; Abe Lyman and Connie Boswell, in Chicago; Guy Lombardo, in New England; and Bing Crosby, Lily Pons, and Wayne King in California.

During Fred's lawsuit against station WDAS in Philadelphia, it turned out that one of the most persuasive pieces of evidence resulted from a farsighted defensive action of his, long before actual piracy had come up. "In 1932, Waring's Pennsylvanians had cut two songs for the Victor Talking Machine Company, for which the orchestra was paid $250 a side. The record sold at the standard price of the day—75¢. Fred anticipated the proliferation of radio and saw an implicit danger in the use of records without remuneration to the performers. Therefore he requested, and Victor agreed, to affix on every record label the warning "Not licensed for radio broadcasts."

Five years later, when the case of *Waring v. Station WDAS* was tried before the Pennsylvania Supreme Court, Judge Horace Stern relied heavily on that evidence. In his decision, he wrote: "There is no moral or legal difference between tapping telephone wires for the purpose of 'listening in' than there is in using for broadcasting a phonographic disk made by plaintiff in defiance of the maker's injunction written across that disk, to wit: 'Not licensed for radio broadcasting.'"

Judge Stern continued: "The aim of the law should always be to extend protection so as to adequately do justice under *current conditions* of life." He pointed out that "the advent of sound recording devices permitted the fixation of a single performance upon a disk or record which could be played and replayed and heard over and over again through an indefinite course of years." He asserted that it would be important for a musician to "protect his property against indiscriminate reproduction." He then asked, "Does the performer's interpretation of a musical composition constitute a product of such novel and artistic creation as to invest him with a property right therein? It must be clear that such vocal and instrumental artists as Jenny Lind, Melba, Caruso, Kreisler, Toscanini, by their interpretations, definitely added something to the work of the composers which not only gained for themselves enduring fame but enabled them to enjoy financial rewards from the public in recognition of their unique genius." And so he concluded, "A musical composition in itself is an incomplete work; it is the performer who must consummate the work by transforming it into sound."[1]

In 1981, some forty-four years later, the prominent *New York Times* music critic Harold C. Schonberg wrote, as though he had stumbled on a fresh idea: "I come to realize that the artist had everything to do with how the music sounded. Notes *alone* mean nothing. It is the performer who has to be the intermediary between composer and listener. Music, then, is an *interpretation of the mind of the composer expressed through the mind of the performer.*"[2]

In the courts, voluminous testimonies and discussions were produced in the Waring case. Because the subject was unprecedented and unusually interesting, tomes of statements by lawyers and experts are now filed in law libraries. They make *Gone with the Wind* look like a short short story.

"But our enemies began working on our members," Fred told me years later.

"Why?" I asked.

"To weaken them . . . to weaken their stand."

"Who were your enemies?"

"The broadcasting stations, the disc jockeys, the publishers, the record companies, and even ASCAP, who feared that we would invade their rights and split their take. Ours would have been an additional compensation, and deservedly. Jukeboxes, which cost a nickel to play, took in an estimated $500 million annually, playing our members' recordings. Each record was bought at cost and was played hundreds of times with no recompense to us.

"So we began bringing lawsuits in various areas such as restaurants, ballrooms, and radio stations who used our records at no cost. My suit against a radio station in Philadelphia was won for all of us. There were some successful suits in other lower courts."

However, Walter Socolow recalled, "As the radio broadcasters united in bitter opposition, progress through the courts became increasingly difficult, slow, and tremendously costly."

"We had planned for Paul Whiteman to be our banner suit in that he was the most important musical artist of the day," Fred explained. "His lawsuit was brought into federal court in New York. We felt that there was no way we could lose that key battle. To our utter dismay, it was learned during the suit that Paul Whiteman had unwittingly signed a contract with his recording company which, somewhere in the fine print, granted to the recording company all rights."

That was clearly the first ominous note and a staggering blow for everyone involved. The news of the judgment against Whiteman broke just as a trainload of prominent artists, led by Fred, was headed for a hearing in Washington. "A bill was being sponsored in our favor," Fred said. "But our lobbying suffered greatly after the debacle. Our bill failed to pass the House and therefore never reached the Senate. We were doomed for failure."

The setbacks might have been overcome if everyone had hung in with determination, but NAPA's enemies—those who employed their artists—had been working on the performers to give up the fight. Little by little they deserted. "The rats left the ship," Fred said, "and left me holding the bag."

John Royal added, "Fred had no support. He was trying to sweep back the ocean with a broom." And this, ironically, was when the organization was on the verge of making some real gains.

Fred: "Many of the jukebox people were friendly towards us and made offers to go along with us before the federal action. One jukebox owner who controlled thousands and thousands of them had offered to pay us a fee of $10 a year per box, which would have been, in those days, an income of five million dollars for our association. That was for jukeboxes alone. And eventually NAPA would have made a similar collection from disc jockeys—ten cents each time one of our records was played. It would have been so simple for them."

I asked, "Were they able to afford something like that?"

"Sure they were. Figure it out for yourself. How many records can you play in a day?"

The powerful Jimmy Petrillo, head of New York's Local 802 of the Musicians' Union, believed so much in Fred's ideas that he offered to leave his job and join NAPA. But when everyone began to drop out, he became disgusted and pushed through a law that enacted a fee from the recording companies. The fee benefited the musicians, but did not compensate the stars who made records.

Walter Socolow shook his head while recalling how Fred had "suffered substantially." He related how Fred had spent thousands of dollars and hours of his precious time in conferences and courtrooms and on the telephone with NAPA members. He had lost a fortune by refusing to record while the lawsuits were underway—a dry period of ten years from November, 1932, to January, 1942, when Fred refused to make any records of the Pennsylvanians.

I asked Fred if the NAPA suits had had any lasting effect in benefits for the performing artist. He shook his head. "We gained nothing except for the precedent and the long-winded testimony in law books." But it was Fred who paid in the long run, since he had initiated the organization and had triumphed over a radio station in the Pennsylvania Supreme Court; he was an abomination to all broadcasters. Thirty years later when Freddy, Jr., was on the road as an advance man for a concert tour, the disc jockeys scorned him. Freddy, who was born the year of NAPA but knew nothing about it, was puzzled, and asked them why they wouldn't play his father's records. They didn't know the reason either—only that Fred Waring was a dirty word and a no-no.

"One day I was in Howard Johnson's sitting near a jukebox when a man was changing records on the machine," Fred told me. "I asked him if he ever used any Fred Waring records. He said, 'No, the son-of-a bitch is trying to wreck my job.'"

However, it was not Fred's style to brood over losses and carry a grudge. He lost, but buried the hatchet and persevered. Finally, on January 7, 1942, he signed a contract with Decca, and the Pennsylvanians recorded upwards of seventy sides within a few months. But he had rankled many in the industry. Years after NAPA's ignominious defeat, Fred was startled to discover that his old enemies were still in influential positions—and still incensed. The issue popped up again and again for the rest of his life. Yes, he had won, but not conclusively. Fred had made the entertainment industry aware of the importance of interpretation. And, as he once put it, "the threat was still there, if someone had the intestinal fortitude to take on the big guns."

And Fred was right. Ten years later Tommy Dorsey, angered that he had received nothing from the thousands of airplays of his hit "I'll Never Smile Again," tried without success to change the law. In 1967 Stan Kenton, with Tony Bennett, Alfred Newman, Meredith Willson, and Freddy Martin, formed the National Committee for the Recording Artists. "It's ridiculous that we could still go with laws made in 1909 before there were radio stations which are still free to profit from our records," Kenton said. "The fee they pay goes only to the publisher and composer. The bandleaders and arrangers are left out."[3] Kenton didn't succeed either. It is now the last decade of the century, and the unfair copyright law remains intact—unfazed by an ever-weakening threat.

13

The Waring Blendor®

FRED was always a dreamer who accented some of his dreams with an extremely active mind. Given his inquisitive and farsighted nature, it is no wonder that he was highly receptive to an undeveloped and seemingly unworkable device brought to him by a man named Frederick J. Osius in 1936.

Osius had talked his way into Fred's dressing room after a radio broadcast. According to one report, the visitor was wearing striped pants, a cutaway coat, a dark blue woolen shirt, and a bright lemon-yellow tie. He told Fred of his idea for an emulsifying machine for which he had been able to secure a patent in 1933, even though his project was still in a germinal stage. Fred, not one to be put off by outward appearances, was intrigued and decided to help him with ideas, money, and marketing.

"As far as inventions are concerned, I'm sort of an editor," Fred liked to say. "Now, any editor can take your copy, rearrange it, take out a few words here and put in a few words there, and soon it comes alive. That's what I do with inventions that haven't quite come off."

Over the next few months Fred analyzed and studied Osius's prototype. He decided it needed sealed ball bearings for the bottom drive, propeller-like blades, and a cloverleaf-shaped jar to throw the contents back down. Fred persuaded a buddy at Chrysler Corporation to help him solve the ball-bearing problem, which he did secretly. Finally the Waring Mixer, as it was then called, was ready to be presented. Frederick J. Osius, unfortunately, did not live to see public acceptance of his brainchild, though the royalty arrangement was inherited in trust by his widow. The agreement was later changed when the war came and all production was stopped.

Selling the public on such a new concept was the major hurdle. Sophisticated market research and marketing techniques were still years in the future. Fred's approach was disarmingly simple—make the machine as visible as possible and persuade everyone to sample its products. He decided to use all his connections and show business flair. How Fred loved a challenge! He was a kid with a new toy, not put off one whit that scarcely anyone was enamored of the weird pulverized concoctions that emerged from his new mixer.

"One day Fred called me and said he'd like to take me to lunch," John Royal said. "He came to pick me up. We went downstairs out to Sixth Avenue and turned into Fifty-second street. I thought, 'Good, he's going to take me to the 21 Club.' There was a building near the parking lot. We went up the front steps into a God-awful place where the rats were running around. We climbed three flights of stairs, and on the top there were two or three men waiting. He took me in and said, 'I want to show you the working model of my Waring Mixer.' Now, this was before it had ever gone on the market. He gave me a little spinach soup and something else. That evidently was to be my lunch. I went back to my office and I asked my secretary to send out for a sandwich. I'm not a vegetarian!"

Ferne Buckner recounted her remembrance of the new device. "Interwoven in a mesh of network broadcasts, rehearsals, short tours, and whatnot, emerged a strong thread, incredibly new and shiny, its voice destined to drive us close to straitjacket stage before it finally settled back into the folded yardage of the Waring fabric. This *thing* was the first working model of the Waring Blendor, known then as the Mixer. It made its appearance in the late fall of 1936, and proved to be the only truly irritating new member inducted into the Waring ranks during my time as a Pennsylvanian.

"Its advent coincided more, or less, with the long tour. We left Grand Central Station with ourselves, our instruments, our identical white wardrobe trunks replete with initials and identifying colored stripes—Christmas presents from Fred . . . and the *thing*.

"The *thing* traveled in its own converted wardrobe trunk filled with lemon squeezer, can opener, cutting utensils, glasses, ice, strainers, and measurers. It was accompanied by another trunk containing canned goods ranging from sauerkraut to mangoes. At first we considered the whole affair a harmless foible—the sort of squirrelly therapy one expects a man of certain genius to contrive for his own amusement. Gradually we realized that we were involved, but hopelessly, in the role of collective guinea pig . . . and for a gadget that was becoming a monster! I remember watching Fred's face during a 10 A.M. stage show, an almost maniacal light playing in his blue eyes, as he dreamed of cranberries and cabbage churning to a pulp with a liquefier of buttermilk or borscht or library paste—a delicacy which, we knew only too damned well, we would be called upon to share . . . with unyielding insistence!

"All this went on for months, with everyone casing any and all alternative routes between stage and dressing rooms in each new theater in an attempt to avoid the *thing* and the strange fruits thereof. Finally, near the end of the long trip, we hit Atlanta and there, one morning, having exhausted all combinations of fruits, vegetables, nuts, and roots, Fred quietly determined to experiment with alcohol, a desperate decision for a man of clean habits to make! Having thus decided, he launched the mixer on its first alcoholic experience on one important mid-morning, beginning with the world's first mixer-made frozen daiquiri . . . and me!

"As taster for this historic episode, I stayed dutifully within range of the alcoholic barrage as he experimented frantically with more lime juice, less lime juice, more sugar, less sugar, more ice, less ice, more rum, less rum, and finally, less and less Ferne. By around 11:30 A.M. I was well aweigh for the day—and by virtue of my steadfast adherence to duty and the fact I was listing helplessly to portside, I was excused from further activity for the rest of the dim day."

Experimenting with alcohol was an about-face for Fred. He was thirty-six years old and had never touched a drop, much to the disgust of his feisty Irish manager Johnny O'Connor, who liked to play the horses and drink his whiskey. He complained that "Waring was too goddamned narrow-minded. For instance, he deplored the thought of me drinking. For Chrissakes, the biggest contract I ever had was sewed up in a saloon!"

Fred not only involved the Pennsylvanians in tasting his creations but in promoting them as well. You'd see some clarinetist or violinist setting forth carrying a black case; they were accustomed to carrying instruments, but this particular black case contained a Waring Blendor. Maybe the musician had never sold anything before, but he got up in Macy's, Gimbels, Bloomingdales, Wannamakers, and so on, cut up carrots and celery, tossed them into a whirling liquid, and told everybody how wonderful it would be to make fresh vegetable and fruit drinks.

No one was safe from Fred and his new mixer. An unwary trio had decided they had to meet and audition for Fred Waring. Pennsylvanian Hal Kanner said, "Daisy, Murray, and I were ushered into a rather lavish rehearsal room in Chicago, and very shortly Fred appeared. I recall electricity in the air as he entered. As the conversation began, I felt he was about the most charming individual I had ever met. Later I sat at the piano, and we performed some of our best arrangements. I thought Fred would say, 'Thank you,' and we would leave, but I was wrong. We were invited to visit his dressing room and watch his new Waring Mixer pulverize all the fruits and vegetables in sight. After we agreed that the machine was remarkable, we were politely forced to partake of the vile-looking drink it had created. Surprisingly, it tasted rather good, and since none of us turned green, Fred was convinced that we had enjoyed his concoction."

Fred himself was the Blendor's biggest promoter those early days. From appearances at the *Cleveland News* cooking school to interviews while on the road with the Pennsylvanians from Boston to Los Angeles, he and his gadget garnered healthy press. He loved to whip up six or seven frozen daiquiris in a couple of minutes and watch with glee the faces of the astonished reporters who came backstage in each city.

A January 24, 1938, radio interview, "For Men Only," with a Mr. Butell, went like this:

FRED: I've always been interested in gadgets ever since I was a kid. I've brought one of my own gadgets with me and I'd like to show it to you.

INTERVIEWER, describing it on the air: This is a gadget about fourteen inches high, has a polished metal base with a sort of clover shaped jar on top of it. What do you call that thing, Mr. Waring?

FRED: The Waring Mixer.

INTERVIEWER: And what does the Waring Mixer mix?

FRED: Just about anything. Would you like a demonstration? How would you like to drink a banana?

INTERVIEWER: Did you say, 'drink a banana'?

FRED: I'll make for you a chocolate milk shake with a banana in it. I pour in the milk, a little ice cream, a little chocolate, and at the bottom of the jar there is a little revolving fan-shaped thing—sort of like a propeller. It starts at the speed of eight thousand revolutions per minute—like this—now we step it up to twelve thousand revolutions per minute, like this. Now we drop in the banana, like this. We are now making three milk shakes at once.

INTERVIEWER: That mixer jar is uncovered, Fred, and nothing is splashing out.

FRED: That's because of the clover shape of the mixing jar. It sort of causes a downward suction.

INTERVIEWER: What else can you mix?

FRED: I can mix anything at all—I can fix a health drink that has celery, carrots, cashew nuts, spinach, pineapple juice, anything you—

INTERVIEWER (cutting in): You don't expect anybody but Popeye to drink that now, do you?

FRED (unrattled):—I can put together vegetables, fruits, ice cream, sherbet, you name it. All in nothing flat. In Florida the other day at a party I made some four hundred and twenty frozen daiquiri cocktails in about an hour and a half.

INTERVIEWER, with great skepticism in his voice: Well . . . I think your Waring Mixer might be useful to some people, Fred.

FRED: That's exactly how I feel about it, and I've formed a company to make these Waring Mixers, and if all goes well, we will put one out in circulation one of these days. In fact, we'll have a national distribution campaign.

INTERVIEWER (laughing derisively): We . . . ll, until then, Fred, we'll be dropping in at your dressing room for some of those *health* drinks and . . .

FRED: You're certainly welcome, Mr. Butell! Just ask for the old MIXTRO![1]

"Rudy Vallee and I were friends," Fred said. "He had become very, very popular and had just completed his engagement at the Paramount theater in New York, and we were to open there. I'd finished the Blendor and was demonstrating it on our tour. I had built a special trunk for it. Rudy had just got off a kick of drinking pink champagne. He had made a lot of publicity with that. Then he discovered the frozen daiquiri. That's all he wanted everywhere. The bartenders hated to make it because it was a tough job by hand . . . it took ten or fifteen minutes to make one.

"I called him and said, 'Rudy, if you have time will you come down to the Paramount? I'd like to see you very much.' He said, 'Well, I'm going to Hollywood at 3:30.'

"I said, 'Our first show is at twelve noon. Could you be here at a quarter to one in my dressing room?'

"He said, 'Yes, but I don't have much time. I have to make that plane. I'm going out to make a picture.'

"I said, 'You be there. I'll come off the stage at quarter to one and I'll be in my dressing room at fourteen minutes to one.'

"He said, 'I'll be there, but remember I'm in a hurry. What did you want to see me about?' I said, 'I'll tell you when you get there.'

"So I came off the stage and went to my room and there he was with one of his gofers. He said, 'What's this all about?'

"I said, 'I hear you like daiquiris, and I thought I'd make you one.'

"'Oh, you can't make it the way I like them. I like strawberry daiquiris and you can't make it.'

I said, 'Sit down there a minute, will you please?' I opened my trunk. I had already crushed the ice . . . the Blendor pops up. I poured the ingredients in the container.

"He said, 'What are you doing?' I said, 'Sit down there, will you please?' He was very impatient. He said, 'I'll tell you how to make this.' I said, 'No you won't. I'll make it my way.'

"He kept interrupting. I turned on the Blendor, and in one minute, I poured out this beautiful strawberry daiquiri—which, by the way, I had invented.

"He said, 'What is this?' I said, 'A strawberry daiquiri. That's what you wanted isn't it?' He said, 'Yes, but how did you do that?'

"I said, 'Taste it!' He said, 'It's marvelous. But what *is* that thing?' He went over to it and looked and found the name Waring on the front.

"He said, 'What is this?' I said, 'This is a Waring Mixer.' He said, 'I've got to have one of these right away.'

"I said, 'Be patient. Have another drink.' He said, 'I've got to go, but I must have one of those mixers.'

"I said, 'It's all set for you.' I picked up a little black case I'd had made in which was a mixer and an extra container. It had his initials on it . . . R.V. I said, 'This is for you.'

"'Oh,' he said. 'Thank you very much, but I have to have one for California and I have to have another one for my apartment here in New York.' [Rudy was notoriously parsimonious.]

"I said, 'All right, they'll be there.' He said, 'This is marvelous. I want to be your agent.'

"I said, 'All right, go ahead. You are my first salesman.' So he took his little case and left, and in a couple of weeks I got a phone call from him. He said, 'Where do you get these? I've sold a lot of them.'

"I learned how he was selling them. He would take that little case with him at night after his shows and go around to the various bars. He'd walk in the bar, step up, look very carefully to see if there were a Waring Mixer there. If not, he would say, 'I want a frozen daiquiri. Don't you have a Waring Mixer?'

"The bartender would say, 'No, what is that?' He would say, 'Well, I just happen to have one with me. I'll come back and make a daiquiri.' So he would go behind the bar and get the crushed ice and make a container full of daiquiris.

"People around the bar would say, 'Hey, I'll have one of those.' The bartender would get all excited. He'd call the owner who'd come and say, 'What's this?' 'This is the new Waring Mixer that Rudy Vallee has here.'

"The owner would get excited and say, 'We've got to have a couple of those here.' Rudy would say, 'I'll take your order right away,' and the owner would say, 'Order one for yourself.' Rudy ran up a stockpile of those.

"The next night he would go into a place where they already had a Waring Mixer in the bar. Rudy would say, 'What's that?' The bartender: 'A Waring Mixer.'

"Rudy: 'A Waring Mixer? What's that?' The bartender: 'Oh, it makes a frozen daiquiri wonderfully . . . banana, pineapple, whatever you want.'

"Rudy: 'I'll have a strawberry daiquiri.' He'd serve it to Rudy who would rave about it. Rudy would say, 'Hey, that's marvelous . . . a Waring Mixer. Where do you get those?'

"The bartender would call the owner, the owner would say to Rudy, 'We'll give you one.' He would give him a Mixer. Rudy wound up selling hundreds of them, but he also collected three hundred and fifty which were gifts to him. He gave them away as Christmas presents."

And so the Waring Mixer was launched. *American Business* reported that thirty-five thousand were in place by September, 1938. Thirteen found their way into the Waldorf-Astoria in New York City. Toscanini took one home to Italy with him.[2]

The Waring Blendors were assembled in Toledo, Ohio, by Air-Way Electric Appliance, a vacuum cleaner company, that used a motor easily adaptable to power the new mixing device. Fred employed Air-Way to supply the motors and assemble the Blendors. Other parts were purchased from various suppliers. Salesmen were sent out to spread the word. Mabel Stegner, a dietician, was engaged to develop recipes and help steer the Waring Blendor from bars to kitchens.

World War II was the major turning point in the affairs of the Waring Blendor. Due to rationing, production came to a halt, although small quantities of scarce materials were allowed to be used to build a few Blendors for scientific laboratories. But this situation became a millstone around the neck of the Waring organization and led to the decision to sell. Following a series of corporate reorganizations, Dynamic Corporation of America ended up manufacturing and marketing the Blendors under the Waring Product Division, and paying Fred a royalty on each unit sold.

The impact of the Waring Blendor reached far beyond food and drink. Years before antibiotics were in common use, Fred was asked to produce a sealed, stainless steel container for scientific laboratories. Two serums were needed, one for Rocky Mountain tick fever and the other for yellow fever. In both instances, live ticks and live canaries had to be pulverized—a horrible thought, but it did save lives. Also, a special Waring Aseptic Dispersal Blendor was used by Dr. Jonas Salk to prepare culture media used in developing the polio vaccine. And just recently I heard that a new medical term has been coined—the Waring Blendor Syndrome—a hemolytic anemia that sometimes follows the surgical placement of artificial cardiac valves, caused by trauma to the red blood cells. Finally, the Blendor completely revolutionized the cosmetic industry. Think of the homogenization of all those creams!

But it never pays to get too cocky. Fred tells the story: "One day in the forties in New York—we were at the height of our popularity. I was in a building waiting for an elevator. The elevator stopped. Five or six people were on the elevator. As I got on, Stokowski, who was also on the elevator, made a big deal over my entrance.

"'Oh! look who this is! Fred *Varing*, and I've been *vanting* to see you! I've *vanted* to tell you about the great joy you have brought into my home—just *vonderful* pleasure you have brought into my home!'

"Of course I began to puff up—because here was the great maestro paying his respects to a little maestro in public. Everyone on the elevator was all eyes and ears. He said, 'I can't tell you and I can't thank you enough for the *vonderful* pleasure you have brought into my home.'

"I expected, of course, for him to add something about last night's performance, but he went on to say, 'You know, that *Blendor* of yours is the greatest machine for anybody's kitchen!' Of course my bubble burst. I should have expected that from him because he had always done something of that sort to me."

And so the royalty payments rolled in for some thirty years until the mid-seventies, when suddenly the quarterly checks did not arrive. The parent company—Dynamic Corporation of America—went into Chapter Eleven bankruptcy and was using the profits from its little subsidiary, Waring Products, to pay off creditors. But someone neglected to read the small print on Fred's contract, which said that if the royalty is not paid within sixty days of date due, then all tools, dies, etc., revert back to Waring. Fred's lawyer, Walter Socolow, waited the time period and sent notice. The corporation retaliated by slapping a three and a half million dollar lawsuit claiming that Fred had had nothing to do with the Blendor. Long and expensive litigation ensued. Fred's victory was Pyrrhic—the bill for the battery of lawyers needed to defend him was astronomical and took years to pay off. And the new contract read that all royalty payments would cease at his death.

14

Burgeoning Empire

IN THE TWENTIES, Fred and his Pennsylvanians were a close-knit, relatively small organization of people who worked and played together. Their wives traveled with them, and Fred had no reason to feel lonely. But when radio came into the picture, the band and its enterprises proliferated. Fred's closeness with his group diminished, and confidences could not be exchanged so easily. It was not physically possible for Fred to be open or on call to everyone, as he had been before. I sometimes think that artists, musicians, and writers have antennae sticking out that pick up so many subtle vibrations of sounds, colors, temperatures, and moods that in order to keep their balance and sanity, they must withdraw to revitalize themselves. Fred was driven more and more into his office with the door closed.

In truth, several old-timers began to feel hurt and a little resentful of Fred's seclusion and lack of closeness. They missed the old days of the twenties when, although the Boss, he was still one of them. But as Fred Culley put it so succinctly, "Those working stiffs never had to worry about money." It was Fred who had to juggle and keep his burgeoning repertory company afloat. As the years went by and the pressure grew, Fred chose to make himself inaccessible as a means of survival.

By 1936 Fred and Evalyn had moved to a handsome apartment at 14 East Ninetieth Street. As was his wont, Fred had designed and made unusual and useful cabinets, shelves, and furniture. But he was infrequently at home. Between long absences on the road, new responsibilities as a member of the Lambs, production problems of the Waring Mixer, plus all the day and evening rehearsals for the radio shows, Fred was the central figure of an accelerating rat race. His social life in New York was a mixture of occasional public events, theatrical gatherings, or large parties he and Evalyn held at their luxurious apartment. Fred liked to entertain, but those who knew Evalyn and felt compassion for her said she was insecure and shy, and didn't know what to say or do at her own parties. These professional and business pressures started a chain reaction of unhappiness and discontent in Fred's personal life. He began more and more to center his life and his interests at the office. Evalyn seldom visited the Hammerstein Building when the band was not touring. Through the late spring of 1936, the Pennsylvanians saw almost nothing of her— she was pregnant again.

Fred's first wife, Dorothy McAteer, had stated: "Fred seemed always to be crazy about someone." Ten years later Evalyn, unknowingly, repeated it almost verbatim. There is no doubt that sometimes Fred had crushes on various girls in his organization—and for the most part they were exactly that, just crushes. It seems to me that Fred was not deeply committed to anyone. On the surface his family life appeared to be running along smoothly. Evalyn had hired a German nurse, Elsie Hess, to help with the children. (Elsie was still with Fred as housekeeper when we were married twenty years later. She still called him "Mr. Varing.") But marital stress was incipient and, underneath it all, Fred was a lonely man. Realistically, he and Evalyn had nothing in common. His life was show business. She hated it and wanted nothing to do with it.

After Freddy was born in June, 1936, Fred proposed to Evalyn that they go to Bermuda. She thought they would have a nice vacation together. "But right away he made friends with some people who were with us the whole time," Evalyn said. "I discovered that I would *never* be alone with him. I used to bug him about it. I was always dreaming of these wonderful things we would do together." Evalyn's dream of corralling Fred into cozy domestic bliss was as futile as trying to pour quicksilver into a bottle. And so they carried on, living a superficial and emotionally shallow life that, unfortunately, constitutes many marriages. In hindsight, it was a fragile union, but to the world in 1936, Evalyn had everything: a beautiful home, charming children, and a handsome, famous, and wealthy husband.

· · ·

Fred had now taken over the entire tenth floor of the Hammerstein Building. The business end was getting so complex that he hired a controller to run what was then "the Waring Corporation," producers of the

Waring Blendor. Up to this point, Fred had shown ingenuity in handling financial matters, but he never was interested in money per se and, once he hired Jake Cohen, a former CPA with the federal government, Fred slowly divorced himself from what he considered the boring aspects of his mushrooming empire.

After his years of service in a disciplined government atmosphere, Jake Cohen scarcely knew how to cope with Fred's individual and sometimes erratic system: "At my first meeting, Fred was calm, cool, casual. Whether I was employed or not appeared to be of no importance to him, while my butterflies were working overtime. Fred's personal casual attitude at my interview contrasted sharply with the office atmosphere as I became acquainted with it. Such energetic activity, with everyone seemingly running in overdrive all the time, was startling. My office was at one end of the tenth floor at 1697 Broadway, and though Fred's suite and the seat of power was at the other extremity and I had very little direct contact with him at that time, I soon learned that the influence of the boss emanated from him by a sensitive grapevine or sometimes by a kind of radar magic. Although more subtle and less visible than his waving hands onstage, it was just about as potent. While his personality and influence were felt throughout the organization, it came through in a very general way, subject to a variety of interpretations. As a consequence, people reacted differently, often running in different directions in response to the same signal. Since my function was to deal in dollars and cents, I found myself hard put to adjust and contribute in such an atmosphere. I discovered quite early that my notice of the importance of small numbers ranked as petty in the general scheme of things."

Because the bottom line was not high on Fred's list, all those who handled his money and were used to set business procedures had a difficult time adjusting. Cohen soon learned that if he wanted a message to be received seriously, "the gist of the matter had best be on one page—with plenty of white space."

The newspapers had begun to report on Fred's burgeoning empire:

> It is with some feeling of sadness and dismay that I report that the gay old days of jazz are gone forever and that music is now big business.
>
> To one who knew the music business when a dance band consisted of nine instruments and a gaudy old Cadillac with a special case for a bass drum, this is distressing news.
>
> *Fortune* magazine, usually interested only in dividends paid by International Harvester Corp. and such like is trying to expose the juicy figures

gathered in by Fred Waring Inc. To this, however, the Warings are not receptive. Like the Duponts and the J. P. Morgans, they have their secrets.

Waring, the president, is a grand executive, a hard worker; he doesn't drink, smoke or chew but he knows by instinct what is going to be popular and what isn't.[1]

Meanwhile, Johnny O'Connor was booking solid theater engagements. He had a product he believed in and his excessively self-confident method of selling seemed to work: "Probably because he is himself more or less quiet and mild mannered, Waring has an emphatic, decisive mannered manager. The contrast often is astounding at conference with Fred sitting quietly behind his desk munching graham crackers while his manager declares what *shall* and *shall not* be done, from a business standpoint."[2]

"I never sold Waring in my life," O'Connor said. "I made it so they wanted to buy him, and when they bought him, I wrote the terms. You can't go around with a poor mouth and sell an outfit like Waring's." Fred never had another manager who understood him and the workings of the business as well as Johnny O'Connor.

. . .

In 1936 the Ford Motor Company decided to stage an extravaganza to celebrate its fiftieth anniversary and show off its new cars. Fifteen thousand dealers would be transported to Detroit in eighty-five special trains, and housed, fed, and royally entertained by Ford. The person hired to produce this gala affair was not succeeding, so at the last minute the Ford people called Fred Waring. He had eight days to come up with a show. "They gave us a $40,000 budget," O'Connor said. "For Christ's sake, I could have brought in the Pope and the Sistine Choir almost for that."

Since Detroit did not have a decent amphitheater, Fred took an abandoned rotunda with a dirt floor and refurbished it. For three days hundreds of people in pageantry, beautiful girls, attendants, new cars, and ten of the best acts of the country rehearsed. Against this was the din of hammering, sawing, shouting, loaded trucks grinding up and down the circular ramp, and dry dust floating over everybody. Fred's stage crew procured their lighting and staging equipment from every theater in Detroit. On the night of the gala, the Pennsylvanians not only played the music for each act but also did a radio broadcast. Everybody concerned took bows, including the new cars—themselves—through an ingenious mechanical arrangement suggested by Fred. It was later reported that he had staged the show without a single error. A sumptuous dinner was served to the thousands of dealers and company executives. The entire event cost Ford a fortune and was a huge success, remembered by the motor car industry as one of the great automobile shows of all time.

The Pennsylvanians recalled the occasion not so happily as "the Dust Bowl Incident." Not only were they covered with grime while rehearsing but the "sumptuous meal" provided for them by the hosts vanished in the general confusion. After fourteen working hours, the Pennsylvanians had the dubious pleasure of observing the dealers and their wives devouring steaks while they sat empty-handed. The sandwiches brought to them after the show didn't quite compensate.

Fred said, "After the affair was over, Jack Davis came back and put his arms around me and said, 'Fred, it was wonderful!' I said, 'Jack, something tells me this is my swan song.' Jack said, 'Over my dead body.' But he was wrong—our contract was terminated."

O'Connor put it succinctly: "I'll tell you why—I got it straight from the horse's mouth in Detroit. The agency didn't like the Lane Sisters, and Waring wouldn't take 'em off—that's all."

Fred's sturdy secretary Helen Helwig told her version: "During the rehearsals at the Ford Rotunda, they handed out cigars to all the dealers right under the bandstand, and naturally they lit them. All the smoke came up. Fred yelled for Johnny O'Connor—Johnny would not tell them to stop smoking. Fred was so furious that he threatened to stop playing unless the smoking stopped." Whatever the reason, the Ford contract was not renewed.

The stress of those Ford years—the long periods of touring and broadcasting plus Fred's enormous vitality and drive, along with his demand for perfection and his quick and seldom explained last-minute changes—triggered many an upset.

"Rosemary was a real musician, and Fred respected that a lot," said her sister Priscilla Lane. "Once in Minneapolis we had train trouble because of extreme cold and a blizzard. We were fourteen hours late and arrived thirty minutes before show time. The show didn't go very well; we were breaking in a completely new one—a rehearsal was called after the first show. Everyone was on edge. 'Ferocious Fuddy' was in a bad mood, and the result was that, one by one, everyone walked out except Rosemary. Fred told her she might as well go, too. She replied, 'I have a job to do here and I intend to do it!' Sheepishly we all came back and finally got the show shipshape. I know he respected her all the more for that. Anyone who worked and trained with Fred left as a real pro."

Another development in 1936 gave rise to a Waring quotation: "You know, Jack, I've spent three years teaching Columbia what a son-of-a-bitch I am, and now I've got to do it all over again for NBC":

> The winter's trip was complicated by decisions of their air sponsor to split patronage between networks resulting in two broadcasts for West Coast benefit.
>
> Here's a typical day: 9 a.m. quick breakfast and a scram for the theater stage for straight music fundamentals until 12:15. Curtain rise is 15 minutes later for an early matinee performance that lasts an hour. Everyone there pelts out for a 20-minute lunch—which is followed by another rehearsal at the hotel, lasting until 3:20. Then a jolting, slamming taxi spree to make the next show at 3:30—followed successively by (1) more rehearsing, (2) 6:30 performance, (3) dinner plus ideas for next week, brewed over the coffee, (4) 8:15 stage show, (5) broadcast at 9:30, (6) their last vaudeville hour starting at 10:15, (7) Pacific coast program at 12 (8) choice of whoopee—or sleep except on Thursday nights when the gang must rush for a railroad rattler.
>
> A Waring tour means a market rise for railroad stocks since the Pennsylvanians hire two Pullmans and a baggage car to house their troupe of 41 humans and a press agent. One gets an idea of the high, wide and handsome way of doing things on the trip when he sees the valuable equipment which includes props, stage settings, special spotlights, 15 file cases of music, a duplicator for stenciling arrangements, etc., loaded aboard.
>
> Trip problems were complicated by fierce weather en route—rain, sleet and snow January 22. The train was stalled in upstate New York, missed connection in Chicago, was 14 hours late getting into Minneapolis in 27 below zero weather. It's remarkable that Fred has lost only six pounds so far.[3]

· · ·

During the thirties Fred Waring, the staunch Republican, disliked Franklin Delano Roosevelt and his New Deal. "Sure," he said. "Help mothers, sick and old people, but hand out money to able-bodied men and not make them work? *No way!*"

The Washington Press Club was always requesting Fred to come and entertain. They not only liked his music, but because of his high visibility in the Lambs, he brought along many famous members. Some of the newsmen learned of Fred's feelings about FDR and decided to play a trick on him.

One day about half an hour before Fred was to go on, he was asked to step into a small anteroom, and was left there alone. In the opposite door two men wheeled in President Roosevelt and then withdrew, quickly shutting the door. There Fred was face to face with his "enemy." In his usual forthright way Fred cleared his throat and said, "Mr. President, I'm truly honored to meet you. But I have to tell you I don't approve of the way you are running the country."

With that, Roosevelt threw back his head, roared with laughter, and said, "Don't worry, Fred, there are millions out there who hate my guts! But I *love* your music!"

The Press Club played another dirty trick on Fred. Vice President John Garner and his wife had asked Fred to entertain his guests at their hotel, the guests being President and Mrs. Roosevelt and two others. Forty-five Pennsylvanians ended up playing to an audience of six. But that was not the dirty trick. The press had led Fred to think that "Home on the Range" was Garner's favorite piece. The Pennsylvanians performed a long, elaborate arrangement, only to find to their embarrassment that it was a piece Garner detested.

15

Hollywood

AFTER the three-year Ford engagement, the Pennsylvanians took to the road for fifteen months. In the midst of this marathon tour, they stopped off in Hollywood to shoot a picture, *Varsity Show,* starring Fred, Priscilla and Rosemary Lane, Dick Powell, and Sterling Holloway. Busby Berkeley was the choreographer. Fred was to conduct a ninety-piece orchestra, which he did with his usual equanimity, much to the surprise of the hard-boiled studio musicians. The movie was filmed on the Pomona College campus, where students doubled as extras. Fred was impressed by a young blond undergraduate who conducted the college glee club with fiery intensity. At the time Robert Shaw was studying to be a minister but changed his vocation when, a year later, Fred invited him to come to New York and help him organize his first glee club.

Making a movie for three months was a pleasant respite from touring. Apartments were rented, and all the wives arrived. Fred and Evalyn rented a palatial home in La Cañada complete with swimming pool, which, in those primitive days, was a status symbol. In the garage—and out—were five cars, including a yellow Cadillac and a Lincoln Zephyr. "I was happier there than anyplace else," Evalyn said. "I was close to my family. It was a beautiful spot. I could relax. It was heaven. Of course Fred was working as hard, and he never spent any time at home without having company. I could never understand it or get over it."

Fred's secretary Helen Helwig mused, "I've always thought Fred was searching and searching for something he couldn't find—that he was a very lonely man. One evening as we finished on location at Pomona, everybody left, and it was just Fred and me, and he asked me to have dinner. We just sat there not saying much, and it was *then* that I realized, once again, that Fred was a very, very lonely man. He was so lonely that night that he felt he didn't have any friends." Fred overloaded his days with activities that helped divert and blot out feelings of emptiness. His favorite source of restoration was the golf course.

Instrumentalist Stinky Davis: "One day FW decided to go out and play a round of golf instead of reporting to the shooting set. About halfway to the golf course, he stopped for gas. The station attendant told him the studio wanted him back for shooting right away. Out there they knew where to find you at all times . . . Fred was always getting arrested for speeding."

Business problems continued to hound Fred. Danny Winkler had cautioned Johnny O'Connor to study his movie contracts carefully. "A movie is not a theater date; the contracts out here are full of pitfalls," he warned. Sure enough, when the picture was over, Winkler noted that "Mr. Waring woke up and found, number one, they had stolen ten of his people, including the Lane Sisters; and number two, they presented him with a bill for arrangements that was staggering—a ninety-piece orchestra."

•   •   •

Fred had spent four years honing and refining the natural talents of Priscilla and Rosemary Lane. There is no better way of doing just that than on one-night stands—especially with a master showman giving out suggestions to try each night. In Fred's contract it was written that Hal Wallis, the producer of *Varsity Show*, was not to lure away his stars—the two brightest and prettiest being the Lane Sisters. But Wallis maneuvered out of the contract by using his sister to outwit everyone. She signed up the leading lights of Fred's group. It was a bitter blow, and Fred left Hollywood with a crippled and ravaged organization. Fred mentioned this Hollywood episode to me just once, saying that Hal Wallis took away his stars in an underhanded way. In later life Fred forgave him, but it took many months to replace so many key people. Even his two top arrangers had been lured away by the bright lights and promises of Hollywood. Fred had experienced many ups and downs in his career, but in that second half of 1937, he hit bedrock. To survive with such a truncated organization, Fred was reduced to accepting a job at the Drake Hotel in Chicago, playing for dancing—something he hadn't done for years and hated. By now the Great Depression was on with a vengeance. It was the nadir of the Pennsylvanians' career.

Fred hired a new arranger, Hawley Ades, the second of the triumvirate of arrangers who, over the years, would help create the unique Waring sound. "The Pennsylvanians had a limited repertoire of music for dancing," Ades said. "Under the circumstances, I assumed that Fred's first priority would be given to getting out as many dance arrangements as possible, without regard for other considerations. I quickly discovered that he did not operate that way. Oh, he wanted new arrangements, all right, but he was not about to sacrifice quality to the exigencies of the moment. He wanted the arrangements to be original, inventive, and distinctive, and he offered specific suggestions as to how this might be achieved. One of these was his repeated admonition to 'avoid the obvious.' He wished, whenever possible, to avoid the use of the trite musical phrase or the hackneyed arranging gimmick, preferring to seek to develop some original approach which would have the Waring stamp. In jazz writing, particularly, he urged the arrangers to avoid using the jazz clichés of the day, since they would inevitably cause the writing to seem dated, a few years hence. His was always the long view.

"He went much further when he recommended experimentation with 'two-tempo' or 'multi-tempo' arrangements which incorporated one or more abrupt changes of tempo and mood within a single arrangement. Actually, these tempo changes may have been quite disconcerting to some of the dancers, but the Boss was not too concerned about that. The experiments in 'two-tempo' arrangements were to prove invaluable later in radio and television, where danceableness was not the vital consideration. Again, he was looking ahead.

"Following the Drake Hotel engagement, the Pennsylvanians were booked in a theater tour for several months," Ades continued. "Since the show was a set production and there was no need for arrangements, I assumed that I would be sent home until such time as a need for arrangements arose. Again, I was mistaken. The Boss suggested that I come along with the group for a few weeks, on full salary, so that I might get a better 'feel' of the organization attending a number of performances and by traveling with the group.

"After a couple of weeks of this, I became restless and again suggested that I may as well go home and wait until something developed which required my services. The Boss readily acceded, but suggested that when I got home I could have access to the Pennsylvanians' library of previous recordings and radio performances so that I might become still more familiar with their way of doing things. He also suggested that I experiment with an idea for combining chorus and orchestra to be called

'Vochestra.' Accordingly, I spent the next weeks, again on full salary, doing nothing but listening to recordings and writing out a few tentative ideas for 'vochestra' treatments. This was still another instance of the 'long range view.' The Boss couldn't care less whether he was paying me to do practically nothing, so long as he felt it was going to make me more valuable to him when he did require my services."

•   •   •

At the Drake Hotel, Tom rejoined the Pennsylvanians to lend a hand, but as Roy Ringwald related, "Fred and Tom got on each other's nerves rather spectacularly."

"Everyone in the orchestra was torn by the clash of personalities because we liked and respected them both," Fred Culley said. "Tom was what I would call a gentle musician. He would have been perfectly happy to go all through his life composing and playing the kind of music he wanted to—intimate, intelligently witty entertainment with subtleties not for the mass audience. Fred's scope was theater—something bigger. Fred knew what he wanted and had to fight and struggle for it. Tom was not in sympathy with it, because he did not have the vision that Fred had. Fred's stuff is not just sitting down and playing the piano or composing a beautiful thing or amusing a hundred people in the salon. What this man wants to do is to put a big spectacular on the stage, produce it, and bring it off the best he can do it."

Fred at this time auditioned four new Pennsylvanians. The first was Donna Dae. "It was in Chicago when I was sixteen," she said. "I was escorted to a small room where I faced Hawley Ades at the piano. Fred sat in a straight chair in a tilted back position, as I later saw him do many times. I was very uncomfortable. He was not like audiences I'd faced before. I felt as though he was seeing through me. Was I faking talent? Was I for real? I had a good job singing and dancing with the Frankie Masters orchestra at the Sherman Hotel, so right in the middle of my song I turned to Hawley and said, 'That's enough!' Fred, with his usual timing, said, 'Ah, temperament!'" He hired her.

Then Fred, with his sure instinct for spotting latent talent, picked up a bouncy teenager in Richmond, Virginia, named Patsy Garrett. Besides her singing talent, she was a natural clown. She and Donna Dae created a liveliness on and offstage that rejuvenated everyone's spirits, but their irrepressible high jinks gave Fred a few mammoth headaches.

The third new member hired was Ray Sax Schroeder. Ray Sax couldn't read a note of music, but he was a superb performer. He played seventeen instruments, danced, sang, and executed an amazing acrobatic feat. While playing two clarinets, he'd bend over backwards, touch the floor with his head and come back up, never missing a beat.

Ray: "When I joined the Pennsylvanians in 1937, I was handed the second alto book and Mr. Waring said, 'You have five or six days now to look over the music, to become familiar with it, memorize as much as you can,' to which I replied, 'I can't read music. I never have, it hasn't been necessary for me in vaudeville,' and he said, 'Well, listen to it and relate the sounds you hear to what you see on the page.' So four or five shows a day I would stand in back of the stage while the Pennsylvanians were performing—with the music stand and my horn (without a reed), and I would finger all the notes. I'd make the sound with my voice. I became familiar with what the notes were, where they were in relation to the keys on the horn. I had taught myself to read."

It was in Chicago that Fred happened upon the fourth new Pennsylvanian. Jane Wilson, a pretty young college girl, came backstage armed with notebook and pencil, requesting an interview for the Northwestern University paper. Fred asked his usual question of any pretty girl—could she sing? He was delighted to hear her true clear soprano untainted by voice training artificialities. After graduation that June, she, too, became a Pennsylvanian. Her distinctive lyric soprano was heard on the air for twelve years.

Johnny O'Connor finally managed to get the Pennsylvanians back on radio in October, 1937, for the Groves company, selling Bromo-Quinine, a long-established laxative cold remedy. "We did thirteen weeks and then the government took the show off," Fred Culley said. "One of the commercials said that Groves Bromo-Quinine would cure your headache. The government told them to cut it out, and they didn't cut it out, and the government said if you do it once more, the program's off the air. They did it once more, and by God the program's off the air. We got no notice—nothing. That was the FDA."

"I really don't know what happened," Fred said. "We were just getting started when bang—the product was pulled off the air. The only time I took the stuff, I got violently ill. The cure was worse than the flu."

• • •

The positive impact of *Varsity Show,* although not a blockbuster, was felt once the Pennsylvanians resumed touring. They broke house records—even some of their own. In January of 1938 they broke the biggest house record of all—the Paramount Theater in New York.

But Fred was concerned about the future. He decided to give up the road for the summer—to rest, play golf, and reflect. What better place than the village of Shawnee-on-Delaware, Pennsylvania. Shawnee Inn and the golf course had been built by the Worthington family around 1909 as an exclusive rich men's club—for the likes of the Vanderbilts and the Du Ponts. In the 1910s and 1920s, Shawnee Inn was in the news as host of one of the five most important annual golf tournaments in the United States. In 1924 Fred, the newly born golfer, was delighted when he and his first wife, Dot, were invited for a visit. But he thought the decor was pretty tacky for a millionaires' hangout: "Our room had a concrete floor, a dirty old rug, some very dirty old wallpaper and a not too nice bath. It cost $28 a day." Soon after, Fred took his song-plugger friend Danny Winkler with him to Shawnee one weekend and had to bootleg Danny in because he was Jewish. He then decided that not only did the wallpaper and the bathroom taps need repair but also the club policy had to go. But Fred fell in love with everything else about Shawnee-on-Delaware—the village, the two summer mansions the Worthingtons had built for themselves, the golf course, and the hotel, which had one hundred and twenty rooms.

For his 1938 summer of rest, Fred, typically *le patron*, bought not only a home for his family but also a large lodge across the street where he housed all the Pennsylvanians—kit and caboodle—wives and children. This was known in Pennsylvanian lore as "the unemployed summer."

But that was not quite true. As the inn had fallen on hard times and was in a stage of receivership, the man running the place was, as Fred described it, "*no fool!* He had us entertaining and, for the great PGA golf tournament—probably the most important competition of the Professional Golfers' Association year in 1938—we did everything but caddie. I did the marshaling of the crowds. Yes, we had quite a *wing-ding* in 1938!" Fred, "Mr. Take Charge," was in his element organizing and producing. Shawnee received an enormous amount of publicity for that event from the fact that a sensational young man named Paul Runyan beat the great Sam Snead, 8 and 7.

But Evalyn, as usual, was not happy. "Fred already had his heart set on Shawnee, so we went there to live part of the time. At first I enjoyed living at Shawnee, but Fred never came home without people. The next thing—he had everybody in the band living in that lodge across the street. Even though I liked all of them, it was just too close. My gosh, we had a steady stream of people going in and out of the house. Sometimes, even when he wasn't there, Fred would send up people to stay at our house—

they were having breakdowns or were sick. It was terrible. I couldn't stand it." One is mindful of Fred's father, Frank Waring. Only Fred brought home, instead of drunks and visiting ministers, his Pennsylvanians.

The fall tour resumed, and Fred arrived in New York in December for the birth of William Griffith Waring, the third and last of Fred and Evalyn's children. He was named after his great-great-grandfather, the horticulturist of Penn State. The family had moved to a spacious Park Avenue apartment where there was room for children, toys, and a pet dachshund, "Coffee." (One of its offspring was named "Demitasse.") Entertaining, which Evalyn more and more disliked, again was high on Fred's priority list. "The place was always full of people," Dixie recalled. "And, even when I was very little, I can remember drying what seemed like hundreds of dishes. Mother thought it was good training—and Mother was the disciplinarian of the family."

•   •   •

In late 1938, Johnny O'Connor learned that the famous comedy team of Amos and Andy was leaving NBC for CBS. They had occupied a priceless spot from 7 to 7:15 P.M. across the board on weeknights for more than ten years and had probably the largest cumulative per-week audience of all time. Johnny immediately got in touch with John Royal, vice president in charge of programs at NBC, reminding him of how much he loved Fred Waring and suggesting they both talk to the people at the Liggett & Myers Tobacco Company and tell them that Waring would be perfect for the fifteen-minute spot selling Chesterfield cigarettes.

When contacted, Liggett & Myers said, "What can Waring do in fifteen minutes?"

Johnny said, "If you'll come over to the office tomorrow, we'll show you," knowing the resourceful Fred Waring would not let him down. He called Fred immediately, and by 2 P.M. the next day, when the agency and sponsor executives arrived, Fred had lined up a wide variety of fifteen-minute programs. Fred played show after show for them all afternoon. O'Connor related, "When they went out, as those gentlemen generally did, they urinated ice water."

Still, the combination of O'Connor and Fred won a five-year contract. The entertainment industry and trade press were greatly puzzled by Fred's ability to cook up and perform so many shows overnight. Their contract started June 19, 1939, over eighty-two stations, five times a week, with a weekly investment of more money than had ever before been spent for combined radio time and talent. *Time* magazine reported the amount at 2.5 million annually—$37,000 a week for the network with $12,000 for Waring.[1]

Johnny O'Connor went before the executive board of the Local 802 of the musicians union to clear up two remaining problems. The union was demanding $12 a man extra for the repeat show at 11 P.M. for the West Coast. The agency had said the additional cost was too much, and threatened to call off the deal. O'Connor talked to the union men for thirty minutes: "I told them that here is the first time in the history of radio that a musical show has been presented across the board, and if we do well, it's going to mean twenty-four musicians are working, as well as others, and it might start a trend of music shows instead of soap opera or comedy combinations. They didn't like the idea of knocking that twelve dollars off. I said it was a silly argument, since Fred always paid way over scale, and I also said, 'If you say no, that's all right—but let me tell you something about Waring. He never held down two jobs in his life. He spreads the work. So, for Christ's sake, don't you think you ought to bend backwards? He is the one guy who not only put up his reputation but his bankroll to knock off recordings against live music, and you fellows know it.'

"The union spokesman said, 'Step outside the room.' So I stepped outside. Waring was with me, but he didn't have anything to say. We were called back into the room, and they said, 'Well, we've agreed to allow it in your case because everything you said is true.'

"I said, 'There's one extra thing. We've got to give a warmup show of about fifteen minutes—either before or afterwards. We have demanded a theater for this show, and you can't recruit a live audience for fifteen minutes to hear good music and then stop. So after the show we'd like to entertain the audience for fifteen minutes.' They agreed but I said, 'I want that included in the minutes of this meeting, because next year there may be a new board here, and this is a five-year contract.' So I dictated the resolution that became part of the minutes. And it's a goddamned good thing I did, because when Rosenberg was knocked off, they tried to knock Waring off."

· The show, taking its cue from Chesterfield's theme of smoking pleasure, would be called "Pleasure Time," and its theme song, "A Cigarette, Sweet Music, and You" would fill the air every night. The program would start in June of 1939, and end in June of 1944. Once again, Fred was set with a nationally famous sponsor and a most desirable prime time spot. Five shows a week meant that, for the first time in twenty years, the Pennsylvanians would not have to tour. For the first time, they could lead a somewhat normal life—although theirs was not exactly a nine-to-five job. They wouldn't get home until around midnight—because of the "after show"—but at least it was home, not a Pullman car or hotel.

Fred's first move was to set in motion the realization of his dream—a glee club of twenty-four men separate from the orchestra. He called in the young man he had seen conducting on the Pomona College campus two years before, Robert Shaw. Fred Culley would rehearse the orchestra and continue to play violin. Bob Shaw recalled, "I put a three-line ad in the *New York Times* in August, 1938, and got seven hundred applicants."

Fred's second move was to reorganize the tenth floor of the Hammer-stein Building. A large working space was needed for his fifty-plus Pennsylvanians, as well as his business staff and secretaries. The tenth floor was divided into two parts: business and music. As the organization grew and became more complex, the psychological division between the two became more pronounced—an invisible wall. A visitor stepping off the elevator would see all business personnel—the manager, publicity department, accountants, and publishing division—at one end, and the rest of the space at the other end devoted to music.

There were two rehearsal rooms—one for separate glee club rehearsals, plus a huge, soundproofed room big enough for all half-hundred Pennsylvanians. The glee club room boasted a Ping-Pong table. When the singers weren't seated around it rehearsing, they were playing table tennis on it. Before and after rehearsals and during breaks, the Ping-Pong table was going full blast. Almost everybody played, and the rivalry was intense. Some of the marathon tournaments went on for years. A complete system of handicaps was devised that was under constant debate—a euphemism for all the yelling that went on. Table tennis pros stopped by often to challenge the better players. Fred was no slouch himself. Ping-Pong was practically his only exercise those busy years.

The arrangers occupied three small rooms, each with an upright piano. The music library, where several busy copyists worked, was equipped with a hand duplicating device—no photocopying machines, yet—and was presided over by a handsome woman, Kay Parker.

Fred's secretary, Helen Helwig, sat at the entrance to his office. Like Cerberus, she protected Fred, screening him from intruders. One had to pass the red-headed guardian to get into the inner sanctum—Fred's office—where he spent long hours of the day and night. Helen's space was like the old-time drugstore: a place to hang out, exchange gossipy tidbits, put in a bid to see Fred, or register complaints.

Fred's office was a comfortably cluttered room with a large desk, and a conversational area with couch, chairs, and coffee table. Each year it became more and more cluttered with mementos brought by fans and ex-Pennsylvanians. John Royal had watched the growth: "This was a part of Waring—the snowshoes, skis, artillery shells, part of a propeller, a bomb remnant," a bust of Sibelius given him by the composer, who admired Fred's interpretation of his *Finlandia,* and a lamp with a glass cylinder base containing two goldfish who were always swimming happily around. I had heard that the collection included a long curved bone—a piece of intimate equipment of a walrus—the only creature, it is said, possessed of such a bone. It disappeared in the move to Pennsylvania.

Nearly every night two or three Pennsylvanians were invited to Fred's office to share a home-cooked meal. Most considered it a special treat to be included. An adjacent kitchen was presided over by a cook/valet whose name also was Fred—Fred Lewis, a most congenial man who held long two-way conversations with himself about what delicious dish he would serve his boss. Between the kitchen and large rehearsal room was a tiny control booth where recording technician Lou Metz presided. This office setting would be the scene of Fred's life for the next five years, and much of it for the next fifteen.

The three Waring children were quite young when the Chesterfield engagement started. Dixie, the oldest, was five. They all remember spending many happy hours through the years at the office—but always without their mother. They loved being there—free to wander about, watch rehearsals, hang around Helen Helwig's desk, and play with the Pennsylvanians. Billy remembers a special drawer in his father's office where fascinating gadgets were kept for them to play with. The aroma of Fred Lewis's delicious food permeated all their reminiscences. The penny arcade across the street was the highlight of their frequent visits, as it was for the two who came after them, Paul and Malcolm.

The Vanderbilt Theater, about five blocks down Broadway from the Waring offices, on Forty-eighth Street, was leased for the Chesterfield "Pleasure Time" show. Fred had a line installed from the Vanderbilt control room to a two-way speaker behind his desk, and another line from his desk into the large rehearsal room. This setup not only permitted him to record the show on his own equipment, but also allowed him to hear the rehearsal sessions at the Vanderbilt before he went down for the broadcasts. Some of the Pennsylvanians resented being monitored—someone listening in—but in truth, it saved Fred hours of rehearsal. Being a man who could do six things at once, he could accomplish much in his office. At the same time, he was getting the "music in his ear." Rarely would Fred interfere unless he heard a conductor expressing his own musical ideas. He would admonish his conductors to "just get the notes and words, but don't interpret. Let me do that." But interpretations were apt to creep in when the Pennsylvanians were in the theater, from 5:30 to 6:45 P.M., and that was when, I'm sure, some blasts came over the speaker from the office at 1697 Broadway, such as "I can't hear the chimes!" or, "Repeat those last four bars a half tone higher!"

"It did drive a few people out of the organization," quipped Ray Sax.

At the beginning of the Chesterfield hour engagement, the third imaginative and creative arranger arrived to take up professional residence at 1697 Broadway. His name was Harry Simeone. From the combination of Roy Ringwald, Hawley Ades, Harry Simeone, and Fred evolved the famous Waring sound. Ades explained that "Fred was blessed with a remarkable faculty for judging which pieces of musical material would be best suited to the talents of the various arrangers. The Boss knew his people, their strengths and limitations."

Hal Kanner, a fourth arranger/performer, was hired as well. He seems to be the *only* arranger who occasionally felt slighted because he was never given the "better" things to arrange. I quizzed Fred about this in the eighties, and he was surprised that Hal felt that way, and said it was because Hal treated the cute pop tunes so cleverly and humorously—necessary pace changes for his show.

Since the shy, introverted Roy Ringwald had given up performing, which he detested, and had become a full-fledged arranger, he decided to leave noisy New York and the constant pressure of a daily radio show. He removed himself as far away as possible—California—and sent in all arrangements by mail from then on, his music always accompanied by pages and pages of handwritten, detailed explanations. Fred was as placidly amicable about this new setup as he was about all other personal quirks of his talented stable of composers/arrangers who were hired only for their *creative* abilities. These men didn't have to fit anywhere; it was Fred who bent and worked around their idiosyncrasies. In the eighties, I once asked him why he became so angry with and demanding of his Pennsylvanians, while his track record with the arrangers was one of gentleness, understanding, and patience. He said, "Pennsylvanians are hired by me to perform as my instrument. If a bass or soprano or instrumentalist performs badly by singing too loud or not playing cleanly or musically, it destroys the effect of the whole. The arrangers are *creative*."

Creativity received the utmost respect from Fred. He appreciated and applauded his close friend Fred Allen's retort after a radio show when someone criticized Allen's material. Allen said, "Where were you when the paper was white?"[2]

Roy Ringwald, for the first time, started composing complete orchestral scores. "When you are learning to score for an orchestra, it's pretty much trial and error," he said. "Mine was done on the air three thousand miles away. I heard my first mistakes over national hook-up; I learned quickly." He further explained how the arrangers achieved the distinctive Waring sound. "It was standard choral procedure to use counterpoint, words going against one another. Fred wanted the words understood, and the chorus had to sing the words at the same time, with a few minor exceptions here and there. The traditional choral style uses a great deal of counterpoint just to get variety. The choral instrument is basically monochromatic, and getting color requires every possible device. We have gotten color. Fred's arrangers created a choral technique for Fred. I don't mean just the tricks with the girls oohing and aahing. I mean things within the actual harmonization—technical things and voice-leading harmonization.

"It was an actual contribution to choral singing, and it advanced choral techniques, although the method is limited in some ways. I think that 'Smoke Gets in Your Eyes' is a beautiful song, but I would not recommend anyone to try to arrange it for chorus. If someone used the traditional methods of arranging and harmonizing, he would get a very static sounding affair; whereas we have an arrangement that flows and goes all over the place, and it is one of the most difficult arrangements I have ever made. It is difficult to sing, too, but it does sing, and Jerome Kern recognized that. I am amazed that no one duplicates this technique. Take the Norman Luboff Chorus. They sing in a very static, colorless way—but we do not.

"You have to remember it is ten times as hard to achieve that with a male chorus as with a mixed chorus—technically, I mean. It's a question of range. Popular music uses a great deal of things like the eleventh chord, and if the composer has an eleventh chord in one of the low spots of the melody, it would take you into real mud in male voices. We worked these things out. They haven't been duplicated because they are so difficult to arrange."

Bob Shaw noted later that "Fred guided the development of a choral arranging style which had two handsome qualities. The first was a richness of harmonic texture, using male voices through enormously wide ranges; and the second was the superiority of the principal melodic voice by very careful and calculated octave doublings. Others certainly made contributions to this—principal among them Roy Ringwald and Hawley Ades. But I think they would agree that they also were trying to create sounds which they felt Fred had already heard in his imagination." All the arrangers had high praise for Fred Waring even though they took the brunt of a hectic daily schedule. Harry Simeone found Fred "an easy man to work for, always imaginatively wide open. He never dictated, never said, 'I want it this way or that way.' He let you use your head, although he might suggest."

Hawley Ades added, "During all our years on radio and television, the Boss was consistently generous in giving credit to arrangers. At a time when *no one* else in the business ever lifted a finger to acknowledge the arranger, Fred invariably, on every show, mentioned and gave credit to one or more of the arrangers. Sometimes he would devote entire programs to the works of single arrangers."

When asked if he did any arranging, Fred replied, "No, I simply request and lay out and dictate some ideas. I do not do any scoring whatsoever." But he was always involved—always!

Robert Shaw was a busy young man when he first arrived. The World's Fair opened in April, 1939, and Billy Rose wanted his water ballet to be accompanied by a Waring glee club—a far cry, indeed, from the attitude of show business six years before, when choral singing was not considered entertainment. The *New York Sun* reported that "the aquacade starred swimming champion Johnny Weismuller and Eleanor Holm. Paul Whiteman's orchestra played under one diving tower and the Waring Glee Club sang from under the other."[3]

Bob had everyone doing calisthenics for weeks before going on the air—the orchestra, as well. At first Fred said that the orchestra had to help sing, and they did until the arrangements became so complicated that they couldn't play and sing too. Sometimes it was difficult for Fred to get the professionally trained singers to sing the way he wanted them to. Their approach was too vocal and their style too stiff for his taste. In frustration, he would call upon the instrumentalists to sing part of an arrangement in order to demonstrate to the glee club how he wanted it to sound. But gradually the glee club was becoming an integrated and special unit of the Pennsylvanians.

As erudite singer/conductor Jack Best recalled, "It's hard to get a true perspective from here—at a point where there is so much choral work—but it seemed like unbelievably good fortune in 1939 and in the 1940s. Most of us were trained for serious music and had looked forward to a church job, some solo work, and, of course, choral parts in oratorios or smaller choirs. The idea that steady—and, believe me, exacting—choral work would come along in the entertainment field, where singing males had usually been in a chorus line, was unheard of. That first year we commuted from the Fair Grounds to the Waring shows, we worked hard, and we discovered, to our great delight, that we were becoming a choral group worthy of the finest." Fred generally won over the classically trained singers by his unrelenting artistic demands. "*Good enough*" was not part of his vocabulary. Even 100 percent was not enough most of the time. Since he put 150 percent of himself into a performance, he expected everyone else to do likewise.

Donna Dae remembered a "for instance" during a Decca recording of "Blues in the Night." "Jane Wilson couldn't make it. I had a freak voice. Fred asked me to switch from low fourth voice to high first voice. I told him I would try once with no rehearsal. One try and it was good. I would have liked to have had a picture of my eyeballs when I hit E flat above high C and the high C's on the ending. So, you see, anything was possible with the 'Great White Father.'"

One of the first singers hired for the glee club was a young man of Romanian heritage with a voice like Mario Lanza. (He did some advance recorded bits for Lanza, whose pitch was not always exact.) His name was Sammy Gallu, and he later became a playwright and producer. "I was a smart-assed kid making a hundred bucks a week as a Pennsylvanian in New York, so after a year Fred fired me and sent me to college," he said. "Paid my way for four years."

In 1939 the Les Paul Trio—Les on lead guitar, Jimmy Atkins playing chorded guitar and singing in a warm baritone, and Ernie Newton on bass—brought an exciting intensity of sound to the Waring setup. Highstrung Paul, with only ten fingers and a mind full of ideas, built a studio in New Jersey and multiplied himself into a full orchestra with his clever and innovative recording devices. Fred told me that when Paul broke his arm, he was given a choice of having it fused straight or bent—joint surgery was in its infancy. He naturally chose the latter—the position he needed for playing his guitar.

• • •

It was during this time that Fred became Shepherd (president) of the Lambs, which was considered an honor. Fred did not take his duties lightly. One can see he would have even less time for his family, since no woman ever had been permitted in the Fold—the clubhouse—of the Lambs. He couldn't dine there with Evalyn or share many of its festivities with her.

"I knew I was incapable of handling the whole thing myself, so I appointed what I called a Shepherd's committee," Fred said. "I got this idea from my fraternity days—the rushing committee where the boys with the best personalities handled the activities. Our committees had regular meetings, and members practiced a 'keep everybody in good spirits attitude' around the club by greeting everyone, making them feel at home and wanting to come back.

"Then if I needed any special errands, or some little problem had to be solved, I called on the committee, and they would solve it . . . such as delinquents—members who weren't paying their dues, who ran up bar tabs, and so forth. The committee would work on them in a nice way and straighten them out. I had little pins made for my Shepherd's committee, a little gold shepherd's crook, which they wore in their lapels proudly. They, in turn, had one made for me in diamonds.

"My regular board was a wonderful group of men, and all were behind me 100 percent. They included Sam Forrest, who is acknowledged as one of the greatest producers Broadway ever had—superior to Ziegfeld—and who did all of George Cohan's shows; plus Hiram Bloomingdale, David Warfield, George Cohan, John Barrymore, Fred Astaire, Ray Bolger, producer John Golden, Conrad Nagel, Russell Crouse, Otis Skinner, Jimmy Walker, and others.

"The club was $350,000 in debt when I became Shepherd. With the help of these man and all of the talented playwrights, actors, comics and performers in the Lambs, we raised enough money with our gambols [extravaganzas] to reduce the debt to nothing. These were big years for me, 1939 through 1944. We'd been in radio for a decade and were really on top of the heap. They called me Mr. Shepherd, even after I was out of office."

· · ·

In the thirties, Tom and Fred saw very little of their father. "He was ensconced in Harrisburg, almost a hermit," Fred said. "He had isolated himself. Much as he hated smoking and drinking—the Blendor was a shock to him because it was in all the bars—he nevertheless was proud of his sons. I can remember once when he came in while we were having a quiet cocktail party with a few friends. He tried so hard to be gracious and pleasant—but his lifetime aversion to liquor and smoking wouldn't let him stay."

In the files I saw a photograph of Frank Waring, posed in front of a huge Chesterfield poster of his son Fred, apparently pointing with pride at the figure. The father looked old, ill, and defeated. Frank Waring died in 1939.

"When Father died, we had a meeting in Mother's apartment in Tyrone: Tom, Fred, Mother, Dolly, and myself," remembered Helen. "I said to them, 'What are we going to do with the golf courses?' [One was in Harrisburg, the other in York, Pennsylvania.]

"Fred looked at me and said, 'Do you want to run them?'

"I said, 'Yes, I do.'

"He said, 'Then go run them.' This was the shortest business meeting I ever went to."

Yes, a five-minute meeting was the only kind Fred liked. Helen ran those two courses for seventeen years, until she was sixty. When a highway was designated to be built through the course in Harrisburg, the family sold it, and Helen continued running the York golf course, always adhering to the liberal membership standards set by her father. No one was excluded from the club except in the sixties, when hippies and longhairs emerged on the scene. Helen could not stomach the sight of shoulder-length tresses on young men, and barred them from her golf course. Her announcement made the news, but the club members stood behind her. She had brightened all their lives with her infectious laugh and great Pennsylvania Dutch meals. Helen retired in her late eighties. She was ninety-five when she died in 1991.

16

"A Cigarette, Sweet Music, and You"

ON A typical day during the five-year Chesterfield era, rehearsals would start in the afternoon, since the second broadcast and "after show" ended around midnight, and many Pennsylvanians lived on Long Island or in New Jersey. The glee club and orchestra rehearsed separately most of the time. Fred relied upon his able conductors Bob Shaw and Fred Culley to *woodshed*—to get the notes or clear up mistakenly copied parts—while he remained in his office handling business matters and planning programs. He would write the titles of numbers he was considering on small color-coded cards. He then spread the cards on his desk, changing their order until he "heard" a show with variety and pace.

After the office rehearsal, everyone except Fred and the recording technician reconvened at 5:30 P.M. at the Vanderbilt Theater for a final run-through. At this time a few hackles were raised if Fred heard interpretations creeping in on his line to the office.

· · ·

The tiny control room, between Fred's office and the big rehearsal room, had a wire recording system installed by the imaginative genius Bill Lear. Fred had met Bill through his wife, Moya Olsen Lear, daughter of Fred's longtime friend Ole Olsen (Olsen and Johnson of *Hellzapoppin* fame). They became fast friends—Bill dropping by at intervals to show off the latest of his brainstorms. The shows were recorded on sixteen-inch acetate paper discs—this was before tape. "During the war, the metal used in the acetate recordings of the show was impossible to get, and we worked with fragile discs of glass," Jack Dolph said. "I recall the floor of the little recording room next to Fred's office being constantly strewn with the broken stuff. I recall, too, that Muriel Stevens, the tall, slim girl who had done much of the 'off the line' recording from the Vanderbilt, got so pregnant that she couldn't get through the little door, and had to quit."

For the record, a homing device for airplanes invented by Bill Lear saved many lives at sea during World War II. Pilots could tune into the radio station of any designated city and follow that wavelength to its source. Pro golfer Tommy Goodwin, who had served in the Merchant Marines, brought his crew to Fred's broadcast and said, "I just want you to know, Fred, that Bill Lear's homing device saved our lives."[1]

Backstage at the Vanderbilt, one of the dressing rooms was set aside for Helen Helwig, her large typewriter, a telephone, reams of manuscript paper, plus constant panic-stricken traffic. Fred would arrive for the seven P.M. broadcast any time from 6:30 to 7:02:16. Every so often, he would turn up at 6:54, throw his coat and hat to anyone standing nearby, wave the script (which he'd already approved at 4:30) at Jack Dolph, and say, "See if you can fix up that opening, will you? It doesn't sound right." By 7:00:30 it would be rewritten, typed in triplicate, distributed to the control room—because of cues—to Chesterfield announcer Paul Douglas, who was never much astounded by anything, and to Fred, who'd read it "cold" with complete unconcern.

Everyone had traumatic memories of that 7 P.M. deadline. "I'm conducting the theme song and Fred isn't in the theater," Fred Culley said. "I get to 'Sleep' and Fred would walk out from the wings. *Nerve-racking!*"

An aide recalled a special broadcast in Studio 8-H in the RCA Building when Fred and scriptwriter Jay Johnson kept revising the script until air time: "While the show was on the air, Jay was typing the script in Toscanini's office at the back of the auditorium, and I was running with it page by page to Fred while the musical numbers were being broadcast. I don't know about Jay but I surely aged a little more rapidly that night."

I'm certain Fred enjoyed every minute of it—living on the edge. "We never missed an announcement but there were some close ones; my heart pounded many of those nights," Helen said. "I was a *wreck!*"

Before he went into movies, Paul Douglas was hired as an announcer for the Chesterfield show. Paul was a gruff, warm man with an alert mind and an easy, natural talent with scripts. But he took an instant dislike to Fred. On the first night of the job, Paul confronted Helen Helwig with his beetle-browed glare and said, "How can you stand to work for that bastard?" Helen was quite taken back. Evidently Paul Douglas had heard all sorts of stories about Fred Waring before coming on the show, that he was a hard man to work for, and that Paul's friends knew that he'd never get along with Fred.

"Fred isn't a perfect person by any means," Helen told Paul. "But I'll tell you what! I'll bet that if you are around a few months, you'll have a different opinion of Fred."

"All right," Paul said. "I'll make a bet with you right now—for six months. If you're right, I'll buy you a couple of drinks."

"In less than six months, Paul invited me for a drink," recounted Helen. "'Do you recall a discussion we had when I first came on the show? Well, I've changed my mind.' He grinned. 'You know, I love the little son-of-a-bitch.'"

Paul Douglas was to prove an unexpected blessing for Fred, as well. He became the first genuine "foil" Fred could ad-lib with or swap prepared dialogue—both forms requiring expert showmanship. They had fun—and provided much enjoyment for the listener—announcing baseball and football scores. Paul's personality was unique among the radio announcers of the day. "When Paul first started with us, he was a blustery, big know-it-all," Culley said. "But later every time he saw me, he'd say, 'Fred, goddamn it, how are you? How's Nelson? How's Poley? Oh boy, I miss the old gang.' Real soft."

• • •

Fred's propensity for last-minute changes also included music selections. To the end of his life, Fred would not print programs for the audience. This could be hard on the performers, but was a key reason his shows were always alive and vital, even after months on the road. His Chesterfield show was never frozen until minutes before air time. Maybe a piece sounded overrehearsed or didn't follow the preceding number logically, so he would substitute a number in which he foresaw a more spontaneous performance. Sometimes he would try to enhance an arrangement by cutting it or trying it in various keys. With the clock ticking away, the arrangers would rush to their cubicles to rewrite entire passages, push the copyists into a frenzy, rehearse the performers, and somehow manage to get the changes ready before the show went on the air. The Chesterfield program was perfectly timed, including commercials, to fifteen minutes; it was a taut frame and a tight show; it never seemed hurried, and neither did Fred—but everyone else was in a frenzy.

Once signed with Chesterfield, Fred, the eternal entrepreneur, let it be known that he would compose a song for any college that would petition for it. By the end of 1940, two hundred and sixty-five colleges had prepared, mailed, and delivered by express their petitions. They ranged from typed lists to voluminous packages that could not go through the office door! This promotion touched almost every state and was most effective in helping establish "Pleasure Time" as a prime collegiate favorite.

The only quiet place Fred could find to compose was in a taxi he commissioned to ply the lanes of Central Park, between rehearsals and radio shows. He wrote ninety-five college songs.

•   •   •

"Once a song was complete in the Boss's mind, he would call in one or another of the arrangers for whom he would sing through the melody in solfège slowly, bar for bar, while the arranger transcribed it onto manuscript paper," Hawley Ades said. "The melody and rhythms were complete and well established in his mind, and the general outlines of the harmonic pattern as well, so that when the arranger played back what seemed the natural harmonization, the Boss would know at once whether this was or was not the harmony as he had mentally conceived it."

Fred heard and sang everything in solfège (do, re, mi, fa, sol . . .), which he had learned as a boy in Tyrone. Fred Culley said it was a great thing for Fred because, "If he heard something wrong in the orchestra, he'd sing the note he wanted to hear, in solfège." This bit of trivia amazed me. Solfège in Tyrone, Pennsylvania? I never heard the term until I arrived at Mills College.

The sole college song that was refused was a spirited number called "Nebraska U." The administration sent a formal message of regret with the terse admonition and reminder that it was The *University* of Nebraska, *not* Nebraska *U.* In later years not only was it known as Nebraska U. but in 1984 the university administration bestowed an honorary doctorate upon Fred, the very man who had, in the minds of their predecessors, disparaged their school forty-five years before.

Early in our marriage, Fred and I were on a television show where two celebrity couples vie with each other in a game where the more you know about your spouse, the more points you make. I was aware that Fred had written some college songs but had not the vaguest idea of the number. So when I was asked, given a leeway of five, how many college songs Fred had written, I made what I believed to be an extravagant guess of thirty-five. With that, Fred picked up my hand and kissed it. The emcee Lyle Waggoner, knowing I was sixty songs short, asked Fred why he had kissed my hand. "That's better than a punch in the nose, don't you think?" Fred replied. The audience guffawed. I later heard Michelle Lee on that same show guess the length of the inner pant seam of her then-husband James Farantino as forty-four inches, which would have made him as tall as Kareem Abdul-Jabbar. We busy wives can't be perfect, you know.

Timing on any radio or television show is critical, and Fred was a master at making it all come out on the second. He always had a legal-sized pad with the full program in order. In one column on the right was the timing of each individual piece, and in the next column, was the cumulative time for the show, including that piece. "During those years of the fifteen-minute 'Pleasure Time' broadcasts, one became enormously sensitive to the possibility of making up fifteen seconds here or spreading thirty seconds there," Bob Shaw said. Fred would drive to their wits' end people in the control room desperately wig-wagging that he was too slow. He would pay absolutely no attention to these harried producers, finish the show right on the dot, and then turn around and grin at them.

The seed of Fred's exquisitely precise inner clock that he developed over the years must have been planted when he was a little boy. "I remember—before I would go to sleep—I learned to count seconds by the ticking of the alarm clock, and I would see how long I could hold my breath," Fred said. "I would do that every night, finally falling asleep holding my breath." Later in his television years, Fred had a clock built into the conductor's podium. One Sunday night the clock gained eight seconds during the show. Fred was unaware of it and took the program off the air eight seconds early. During the last number the orchestra had not played to his liking. Thus not only did the Pennsylvanians hear his reprimand, but so did all of America—for eight seconds!

• • •

Fred's business was located on Tin Pan Alley, that section of Broadway containing numerous music-publishing offices from which a cacophony of sound resembling the tinkle of tin pans emanated from badly tuned upright pianos played all day long. Every singing star or bandleader was bombarded daily by "song pluggers" who were paid by music publishers to persuade high-profile musicians to sing and play their tunes. The job of song plugger was a thankless one because performers were busy and temperamental, and scarcely any of the song pluggers could sing a note worthy of attention at an Elks clambake or play more than a set of chords on the piano. One wonders how any song survived.

Accepting such favors as theater tickets, admission to sports events, and suits of clothing was done. The biggest inducement to a bandleader, however, was to offer him a piece of a song, a financial stake in future sales and royalties—the old payola. "If you accepted gifts, you had to play many songs that were dogs," Guy Lombardo said. "Some leaders jumped at the opportunity of airing songs under their own names, hoping to add to their incomes but never succeeding. All they did was establish reputations for playing bad music.

"Abe Lyman probably would have become a giant in the band business if he had just played his fine music and stopped looking for those pieces of songs. He had his name on almost as many titles as Irving Berlin, but the difference was that few of them became hits. Phil Spitalny was another," Lombardo added.[2]

"The most coveted spot for a new song," an observant reporter noted, "is a place in a Lombardo, Vallee, Waring or Whiteman program. Some song writers take manuscripts to bandleaders before trying a publisher. If Fred Waring, for example, agrees to play a song a few times, any publisher is glad to get it. The Waring judgement is respected."[3]

Since the song pluggers' calls and demonstrations in his office were time consuming, Fred devised a nifty scheme whereby he would meet with them once a week for lunch at his favorite restaurant—Horn and Hardarts—to see them en masse. The Horn and Hardarts cafeteria chain, "The Automat" for short, was a unique institution—an embryonic fast-food idea. Along one wall of the cafeterias were little windowed cubicles big enough to hold a piece of pie, cake, or sandwich. There one could insert a nickel or dime, and the little door would pop open to dispense the item. At the height of its popularity, forty automats were located in Manhattan. Their perfectly cooked vegetables were extolled in the pages of *Time* magazine.

Each week gin rummy, trade talk, and full access to Fred were concentrated into a couple of hours. The song pluggers saved up jokes to tell Fred, who was a real Americana lover. These boys were the genuine article that Damon Runyan and Ring Lardner wrote about. This luncheon became a Broadway ritual and lasted for years. According to *Radio Mirror*, "Waring pays for everything, sometimes the gang does. A guest bandleader is now invited each week—only one standing rule—song pluggers can talk business to Fred but *never* bother the visiting maestro."[4]

When Fred bought Shawnee Inn in the forties, he invited the song pluggers up each year for an outing. He hired several buses and they came—more than one hundred and fifty men. They played golf, tennis, swam, played cards, drank, ate, and had a marvelous time, all "on the house."

They, in turn, presented him with their first annual Apollo Award in 1960—twenty years after their initial meetings at Horn and Hardarts. "I guess," he admitted, "I felt guilty at having treated so many of them so badly in the early years."

·   ·   ·

Fred's new separate glee club with its solid foundation of good voices, individual musicianship, and innovative arrangements, produced a new concept of choral singing. He had pioneered group singing with his instrumentalists, creating wonderfully effective music. But now that all the glee club members were superior soloists, and the arrangers had increased latitude to experiment, Fred at last had something he'd always dreamed about—a *choral instrument.* It was the beginning of the "great Waring sound." Robert Shaw stated in 1991 at the Kennedy Center Honors that "the Fred Waring glee club contained the best voices ever assembled in the history of man."

When Robert Shaw was first starting out with the collegiate choral group Fred had built for him, "the Metropolitan Opera people asked me to organize and train a chorus for an Easter presentation of some Bach chorales," Fred recalled. "It would be for Leopold Stokowski, who was doing it at the Metropolitan. I had known Stokowski and his wife, Olga Samaroff, for many, many years. His personality was well known; he was unusual.

"I studied the idea carefully. Did I or didn't I want to? And I realized this might be good experience for Bob Shaw. We held many auditions and built an exceptionally fine chorus of about thirty-five voices—all singers with experience. We trained them so well for three weeks that the singers were excited and said that for the first time in their careers they knew what they were singing. Then came the time for Stokowski to hear them and I tried to warn them:

"'You may be in for a letdown. I can only say that what you have done for me has been all that I would ever hope for, but you're about to meet someone for whom this may mean nothing. I will give you a picture. He will come in the room. He will wear a blue shirt with cuffs that have been worn, frayed. He'll probably have a white tie. He'll carry a walking stick and he'll wear dirty white gloves. And he will, in some very grandiose gesture, tell us to start and we won't get very far, and he will stop it to say one of two things: it is fine or it is wrong.'

"In ten seconds he was announced. I said, 'Be ready. But no matter what his reaction, make up your minds that you have done a wonderful job. It would be great for our classics if we all performed them as you have to-day.' So they applauded like hell.

"In walked Stokowski with the homburg hat, the blue shirt, the frayed cuffs, and the dirty gloves. He sat down, didn't even shake hands with me.

"He said, 'Start!'

"So we started. We got perhaps thirty seconds sung and he said, 'Stop! Stop!' He walked up to the podium and said, 'This is *not* vat I vant! I *don't* vant to hear the words. I *vant* to hear the music.'

"So I said, 'Thank you, Maestro. My work is done. Mr. Shaw, if you care, you may take over, and again thanks to all of you,' and I left the room. Of course Bob was a sucker. He didn't want to lose this opportunity, so he stuck with him. Stokowski, of course, was a brilliant musician. No question about it."

In a 1980 radio interview, columnist Jack O'Brian said to Fred, "Last night I thought of you while I was listening to the Westminster Choir with Zubin Mehta and the New York Philharmonic doing Verdi's *Requiem,* which is one of the most powerful single—. . . "

Fred (interrupting): "Did you understand the words?"

Dead silence, then O'Brian finally saying: "Uh, no, *no,* I did not understand the words." Fred had made his point, and the interview moved on.[5]

• • •

Two old friends from the New York theater, Cornelia Otis Skinner and Dorothy Stickney, approached Fred one time during the war. They felt that Julia Ward Howe's great old hymn, "Battle Hymn of the Republic," inspired by a visit near the lines during the Civil War, was worthy of revived interest as one of the great war songs of all times. Roy Ringwald was given the opportunity to arrange it. "It was the words that decided me," he recalled. "The tune [written by William Steffe] had fallen into disuse, in part because the extra syllables Mrs. Howe added gave it a jiggle that was hard to sing. I kept the old march time but doubled the value of the melody notes in the verse, making them twice as broad, thereby giving the wonderful words a chance to express themselves. It was this device that unlocked the 'Battle Hymn' for good."

"Battle Hymn of the Republic" was broadcast for the first time by the Pennsylvanians on June 22, 1943. There was an immediate reaction from listeners—a mountain of mail. Maud Howe Elliot, daughter of Julia Ward Howe, wrote of the performance: "As the last living child of the author, it might interest you to know that your performance was the finest and most moving rendering of the hymn I have heard in my long life of eighty-nine years."[6] Fred's recording of the hymn for Decca hit astronomical sales and soon became a gold record. Shawnee Press, to date, has sold more than twenty million printed copies to schools, churches, and independent choirs. Roy Ringwald had written a part for the audience to sing the last chorus with the Pennsylvanians. On all of Fred's concerts thereafter, he closed with the audience standing and singing the final triumphant stanzas. "It would be impossible to estimate how many millions or billions of people have sung it with us," Ray Sax said. "Even on television Waring would turn to unseen singers and lead them, saying, 'I know you're out there singing with us.'" In later years Fred, the constant modifier, did substitute one word: "Let us *live* to make men free . . ." instead of "*die*."

• • •

At this time, *Oklahoma!*, Rodgers and Hammerstein's new show, was ready to open, and they called Fred. "They wanted to make certain that I'd hear the score and get on the music as soon as possible, so they invited me to opening night," Fred said. "We did an album almost immediately and used the score on our radio show. They were so delighted with the arrangements by Ringwald, Simeone, and Ades that they invited me to present their next musical, *Carousel*, and then *South Pacific*. For *South Pacific*, I had the great honor of being invited to what they called a dress rehearsal. I discovered I was the only person in the audience. They did a complete run-through of the show on the stage with no costumes. The only props were some orange crates or boxes to sit on. An upright piano was in the pit—all of the orchestra they had—but they ran through that show with such tremendous zeal and earnestness that it was perhaps the most moving experience I had in the theater. To see Mary Martin, the way she worked; Pinza, the way he sang. It was breathtaking. The result was that we immediately did an album and introduced that score on the radio."

• • •

When World War II began, Fred had realized that thousands of men and women would be placed in camps, stations, and training areas far away from home. He devised a scheme called "Victory Tunes." Part of each program would be devoted to ten or twenty thousand servicemen in a camp and their families throughout a large geographical area. Thousands of request forms were printed and distributed throughout the military installations and the men filled in the names of their song requests.

At the same time, millions of penny postcards were printed with the name of the camp to be saluted, the date of the show, and the invitation to listen. These were made available to the boys and needed only to be addressed and mailed home. With five programs a week, the show reached a great many people. The military brass were delighted, for Fred's efforts contributed immeasurably to the morale of the troops and their families at home.

People in the armed services were also aware of Fred's ability to write specialized, catchy college songs, and requests began to come in from the various branches. Fred ended up writing more than fifty tunes as well as innumerable pep songs to help speed up production for the war effort. (Those taxi drivers must have enjoyed cruising around Central Park with Fred, since his generous tipping habits were well known.)

Henry Kaiser, Jr., telephoned Fred and said that their shipyards were turning out one ship a day, and they needed a song to boost morale.

"Do you have any mottos?" Fred asked.

"Dad's rule has always been that if you can't go straight to it, go around it; if you can't go around it, go under or over it," Kaiser responded.

"I had my song," Fred said. "All I had to do was put it together."

Kaiser wanted it for a broadcast in two days. Fred, his mind busy composing, left the office and rode around Central Park. Finally the lyrics and the tune jelled. It began, "We'll do it, we'll do it." Fred returned to the office and sang it to Hawley Ades to be arranged. It was printed overnight, and a thousand copies were put in the mail.

Another time Fred was composing a song for Kaiser while driving to Shawnee. With the words, "faster, we'll go faster" his foot involuntarily began to press heavily on the accelerator. Soon a cop pulled him over and, with great glee, gave him a whopping fine. Nabbing Fred Waring as he traversed the eighty-five miles across New Jersey from New York to Pennsylvania on old route 46 every Friday or Monday was the most fun the officers had all week. Unlike Fred, a speeding Pennsylvanian was never fined. Livingston and I were caught three times rushing in from Orange, New Jersey, for broadcasts, and the magic words were "the Fred Waring show." I was puzzled when I learned the state police never let Fred off. I suppose it's like the fisherman who throws back the little ones but brags over the big one he reels in—the trophy fish.

The toughest song Fred wrote, he admitted, was "Sky Anchors Aweigh" for Navy pilots. "I drove around Central Park seven times for that one."

Fred naturally made the Pennsylvanians available for entertainment at Norfolk, Annapolis, and other reachable bases, but he was limited with his five-day Chesterfield show. It was then that the idea of entertaining the servicemen and women at 1697 Broadway after the "after show" came to be.

In 1942 Fred rented the entire unused and dusty eleventh floor and called it the Tom Waring Canteen. Tom, who had been leading an aimless sort of life, caught fire. This was something he could put his teeth into. With broom in hand, he collared volunteers (including "Himself," as he called Fred) and readied the space for entertainment. Fred did everything, including a bit of carpentry. To get more space for dancing, he designed a means to hinge, fasten, and fold the tables to the walls. The design was faultless except once when a table collapsed and hit one of Fred's secretaries on the head, knocking her out. Fred picked her up and carried her to his office to check for injuries. She soon recovered.

Tom phoned the service organizations, and officers and enlisted men would show up: New Zealanders, Royal Air Force pilots, American GIs, seamen, etc. They went to the 7 o'clock Chesterfield show, then back to 1697 Broadway for a special barbecued meal. Fred would bring gallons and gallons of barbecue sauce each week from a Pennsylvania roadside stand.

Tom decided there would be no rank at his club. Officers who wished to attend (generals and admirals visited on many occasions) were asked to "leave their rank at the door," and they did. Tom also had everyone playing games. It was hard to believe that he could get a group of self-conscious boys in uniform to unbend and play the kind of games he invented for them. But they did, with uproarious results. The Pennsylvanians were expected to show up to talk and dance with the servicemen. Wives, daughters, and girlfriends joined in dishing out food, checking coats, and helping out in general. Mrs. Jimmy Doolittle, wife of the general and a warm, delightful lady, was at the Tom Waring Canteen week after week, year after year. Each Pennsylvanian girl sat at the head of a table, as I did after Livingston and I joined in 1943.

The stage entertainment brought in was always fun, especially the puppets of Bil and Cora Baird. I was still naive then, and when the boys' favorite puppet, an old lecherous "seegar-toting" roué called Nosey Parker, rolled his huge, bulging eyes while making risqué remarks to the well-endowed girl puppets, I would laugh, but usually didn't get the jokes. Fred was always there, everywhere, doing what was needed, playing exhibition table tennis with the world's champion Sol Schiff or with cute Mary Ryan, or holding still for a thousand pictures with a thousand happy young soldiers.

But it was Tom who created the warmth of the evening with his piano, his songs, his inventive games, and his complete and affectionate understanding of the homesick and lonely servicemen. After the radio broadcast, one could see them from a Broadway window—hundreds of them—marching up together, often singing, headed by a devoted Waring friend who led them to the Tom Waring Canteen—1697—eleventh floor. The parties continued for the war's duration, and not one word or photograph about them was allowed to be released from the Waring office. To brag about a good deed was a Boy Scout no-no.

• • •

These were demanding, productive years, and Fred was in top form. The Chesterfield show was "the best quarter hour in radio" according to the *World-Telegram* editors' poll—the toughest national survey to win—for the second time.[7] More people heard "Pleasure Time" each week than had ever listened to a musical show.

During those war years, many of the Pennsylvanians joined the service, either enlisting or meeting their draft calls. Fred was proud of their records. Combined with the people from the front office, a total of forty-five answered the call. But this constant turnover of personnel was hard on Fred the precisionist, as he called himself. Integrating new singers and instrumentalists into his method of performance put extra demands on an already overloaded Fred Waring. It was frustrating to try and maintain his rigorous standards. One afternoon Fred heard Fred Culley conducting a new production number. Dissatisfied with what he'd heard, Fred walked in from his office and took over. He started conducting vigorously. Thirty minutes later, most of the oxygen and all of the occupants of the room had been exhausted. Neckties were loosened and hair mussed, as fifty pairs of eyes stared glassily at their conductor. They had finally played the number to his satisfaction. Fred drooped into a chair. After a moment of complete silence in the room, he spoke. "Now," he said plaintively, "look what you've done to my arm!"

Amazingly few mistakes crept on the air during the Chesterfield years, considering the amount of new material learned and the constant last-minute changes. If a crisis did arise, Fred, with his musical ear and quick mind, usually was able to circumvent it. "One time I left out the bridge of a solo," said baritone Leonard Kranendonk. "Fred cut off the orchestra, yelled, '*Coda!*' and we all finished together."

The only real disaster anyone could recall was a new number that called for the glee club to sing the first sixteen bars a cappella, after which the orchestra would join in for the remainder of the score. The starting note of any a cappella number was always played softly by one of the pianists while Fred was making his introduction. This night the piano sounded just as Fred turned to give the downbeat, but for some inexplicable reason, the pianist played an E instead of the F next to it. Everyone knew immediately they were singing in the wrong key. Frantic inter–glee club and inter-orchestra signals began! At the end of the sixteen bars, the orchestra came in with a self-righteous, "We saved the day" smugness, transposing down to the key of E, while the glee club moved flawlessly up to the key of F. The ensuing pandemonium was finally brought to a halt by Fred, who turned to his mike and sadly announced, "So sorry. Excuse us while we make a fresh start."[8]

By 1942, when the "after show" of fifteen minutes stretched to an hour, some of the Pennsylvanians began to grumble and crab, threatening to go to the union. So Fred Culley beat them to it and went to Local 802 and told them Fred was doing a longer show. Jimmy Petrillo's assistant asked, "How much do they make a week?"

When Culley told him more than two hundred and fifty dollars, the union man said, "Tell the men that if they were making sixty dollars, they'd get some sympathy from here, but not with that salary."

"It never pays to try and outwit Fred," Culley said. "One time we had to play a benefit. Fred was not taking anything himself, but the union said we had to get paid because the abuse of not paying for benefits was so bad. We were getting our regular salary on the Ford show and then we were to get union scale for the benefit. One Charlie B., who loved the buck, made a big issue with Fred. He wanted to make sure he was going to get enough, so he went in to make his complaint—in his rich Southern accent.

"Fred said, 'Well, Charlie, what do you expect to get for this job?' Charlie said he expected to get $50 or $60. Fred said, 'OK, Charlie, that's what you are going to get.' Come payday, Charlie got $60 extra and everybody else got a hundred."

· · ·

In those days, publicity gags and stunts were de rigueur in show business. Fred and Paul Douglas were always teasing each other on the air. One night they made a bet on the outcome of a baseball game. Whoever lost was to lead a bull through a china shop—literally! Fred lost, and his publicity gal, Hilda Cole, jumped at the chance to write about something besides Fred and the Boy Scout fife and drum corps in Tyrone, Pennsylvania.

The china shop chosen was the elegant Plummers, Ltd., on Fifth Avenue, complete with aisles of expensive merchandise on glass shelves. The bull was a blue ribbon, thousand-pound two-year-old named Dandy. Hilda was at the scene early, pacing up and down. Her original enthusiasm had turned into apprehension and anxiety, especially when the gargantuan trailer arrived with the bull, and the handlers told her that the floor at Plummers was too slippery, and Dandy might slip and fall down. So Hilda rushed around to such neighboring stores as Saks Fifth Avenue and Bonwit Teller to borrow their doormats.

Suddenly the media appeared—reporters, photographers, and radio announcers with microphones—plus Paul Douglas and a cold and shivering Fred. The huge bull stepped cautiously from the ramp. Fred took the lead rope and guided him into the shop. The flashbulbs went off, Dandy tossed his head and rolled his eyes apprehensively but, to quote Hilda, "the bull was a hundred percent more cautious than I had been in planning the event." Stepping carefully between tables with Limoges teapots, the bull managed to get his massive body down one aisle and up another without knocking over anything. Paul broke a plate and teacup in the hope of arousing Dandy to anger and action, but the bull just switched his tail and moved on out the door—as glad the visit was over as the worried Fred was.

The United Press report, picked up by every newspaper in the United States, began: "A bull, 'Royalist Dandy Victor,' was led through a china shop by Fred Waring, orchestra leader. Both nearly died of fright, especially the bull." The episode at least squelched forever the notion that a bull in a china shop meant destruction and devastation. Dandy proved them wrong.

Another promotion stunt was Sammy Gallu's idea. He wanted to arrange a national glee club contest, and Fred told him to go ahead. Sammy went to the Chesterfield people, they looked over the plans, were satisfied, and laid out $90,000 in cash. When the contest was announced over the air, more than one hundred and fifty entries came in from campuses of every size and degree of prestige. The work and judging took several months. The last stage of the competition was a trip to New York for the entire personnel of the eight sectional winners to attend the final championship judging in Carnegie Hall. It was a big night for the college students. The University of Rochester won the "Best All Around," Purdue was second, Oklahoma took the "Best Choral Quality" award, and Dartmouth won the "Special Award for Showmanship."

When it was over, six thousand members of one hundred and forty-nine glee clubs had competed; choral singing had advanced in popularity; Fred was brought in closer contact to the music education world; and several talented participants later became Pennsylvanians—notably Lara Hoggard, who had conducted the award-winning Oklahoma choir, and Bob Lang, manager of the Dartmouth contingent. The Waring organization returned $48,000 of the original $90,000 outlay. Chesterfield never questioned the entire operation. One exhausted Pennsylvanian, a preliminary judge, said, "Remember those hundred and fifty-five recordings we had to listen to afternoon after afternoon? Oh, Christ!"

·   ·   ·

As shown throughout the years, any nonmusician who had enough chutzpah could get him- or herself hired by Fred Waring, whether qualified or not. Fred liked spunk. A good example was a sturdy, bright-eyed young man, Lou Metz. "As a teenager, I had a part-time job in a drugstore in the CBS building," Metz recalled. "Since I was a rabid Waring fan, I established an instrument carrying service from the Vanderbilt Theater back to the office building. I started off with Marvin's horn and Fred Culley's fiddle. I used to love to come to the theater every night, go to the office at midnight, and leave the instruments. It gave me a chance to watch the show. I was on the inside instead of out front. I had a scrapbook, I had autographed pictures of Fred. I had once met Fred after a broadcast at NBC. I asked him if I could come up to the office and listen to the records. He said, sure. I spent all afternoon playing Waring records. I continued my instrument service and wound up with fifteen or twenty, using a cab. I usually ran into Fred when he came back after the late show, and he would invite me in for cookies and milk or a sandwich. One night he asked me what I was doing, and I said, 'Nothing. I'm looking for a job.' He said, 'Come to work tomorrow morning.' Marv, the librarian, put me to work cataloguing some of the old orchestrations that we had in a storage room on the eleventh floor. I was sort of a general factotum [today called a gofer].

"One night I started down to the theater to help with the script, and Fred said, 'You're not going down.'

"I said, 'Why not?'

"He said, 'You're recording the show. Scotty's joined the Navy, and somebody's got to do the show . . .'—from the line in Fred's office. I did the first show, not knowing much of anything and got four beautiful sides of nothing. In the meantime, I was still lugging instruments. Everybody had gotten used to it, and I couldn't quit. I had friends and cousins coming in to help me. This lasted until July, 1943, when I went into the service. I came back in February of '46 and the next day I was back in the office working."

• • •

Because a large percentage of the seats at the Vanderbilt Theater were filled with servicemen and women, Fred tried to keep the "after show" light and fun. This segment of time each night proved to be not only a good experimental laboratory for Fred to develop his impromptu laughs but also a free and easy relief from the stringently paced radio shows.

The "after show" was always enlivened by the unexpected antics of the mischievous teenagers Donna Dae and Patsy Garrett. One night Jack Smart, the star of a popular radio program called "The Fat Man," came backstage to say hello to Fred. The "after show" had just started, and Fred was onstage. The two girls asked the enormous man if they could borrow his pants for their duet. Jack Smart obligingly went into Fred's dressing room and handed his pants to the girls through the door. They both got into them—one in front, one behind, two left legs and two right legs in each of his, and started out onstage, managing to get halfway to the mike before tripping and falling flat, face down. The audience was in hysterics. Fred was laughing, too, but he just left them there—helpless, like an overturned turtle. Is it any wonder he referred to them as the Katzenjammer Kids—two bratty comic strip characters.

Another time, the vocal range of the sweet-voiced but rather solemn tenor Stu Churchill was unexpectedly extended an octave, when he was given the hot foot during his solo. A hot foot, according to Patsy Garrett, occurs when someone sticks a lighted match into the space between the sole and upper part of a performer's shoe. The sudden, intense heat causes the recipient to jump high and the voice to rise.

And singer-comedienne Daisy Bernier, who was absolutely terrified of mice, encountered one in the middle of *her* act, to the utter delight of everyone. Daisy always performed with four men in an act called Daisy and the Dandelions. One of them pulled a concealed wound-up toy mouse out of his pocket during their number. When it ran across the floor in front of her, she picked up her skirts and ran shrieking off into the wings.

Fred had observed Lumpy struggling down a Pullman aisle on a "sleeper jump," wrestling with his huge bass fiddle and emitting exasperated sounds. He then had Lumpy fighting his way down an even more cramped aisle from the top of the bandstand. Lumpy would arrive at the center stage microphone for his monologue in such a state of hatred for his unwieldy instrument that he would get a laugh before he opened his mouth.

But the one song remembered by all at the "after show" was a stage bit called the Giggle Opera. For years, the irrepressible Patsy giggled continuously at lunch, at rehearsals, and during breaks. Finally, in self-defense, Fred worked up a number built around Patsy, who sang a spectacularly ornate coloratura solo (which in itself was a surprise because Jane Wilson was the clear true soprano), using only the words "ha ha." Bits and pieces were added—a flute obbligato and a mass of wound-up paper butterflies floating around the theater, and finally the audience ended up singing and laughing as well.

At times, Patsy was able to constrain her youthful exuberance. "Shortly after I joined, Fred had to attend a huge Boy Scout rally on Long Island, and made sure all the Pennsylvanians had left the rehearsal halls before he dressed in his Scout uniform, only to face *me* as I stepped off the elevator!" Patsy said. She was returning to pick up some forgotten music. "I started to roar with laughter—seeing my Boss decked out in short pants, with frying pans and knives in his belt—but straightened up fast when I saw the glare in those blue eyes from under his shaggy eyebrows. I knew, without a word being said, that I was not to mention the incident . . . and I haven't, until today."

"Patsy and I were young and had a way of getting in trouble with Fred," Donna Dae said. "Once Patsy and I had a big sack of popcorn in the rehearsal room. Fred walked in, went to his podium, tapped his baton, and started rehearsing an instrumental number. Patsy and I were not singing, so we continued eating our popcorn. Fred got angry. He took his baton and flipped both sacks of popcorn in the air. The popcorn landed all over the musicians and their stands. Fred stormed out of the rehearsal hall. The musicians had a good laugh. Fred needed no words; his emotions were easily read."

The two continued their antics and eventually became so enamored of their own importance that, exasperated, Fred was driven to the extreme measure (for him) of writing them a letter of reprimand after they had misbehaved on a trip to Penn State:

> Since it was utterly impossible for me to do any talking and since it seems you'll never be willing to hear me without discourteously interrupting, I've decided to write a few things for your careful (and I advise—*careful*) digestion.
>
> Most of them you've been told before—but haven't taken to heart. Please consider them individually, if you will.

I want to remind you both that my apology last week concerned my loss of temper and subsequent bad manners. However, lest you have decided the case is closed and you are vindicated, may I point out that you are still in my employ and expected to perform all duties willingly and to the best of your ability.

There may have been in your minds the assumption that because Penn State is not Chesterfield, I should have had little or no interest or authority, for such was indicated . . . but don't be disillusioned. Your trip to Penn State, while under the guise of publicity and honor, was still *your job* . . . and the fact that I didn't "tell you longer in advance" doesn't relieve you of its import nor of your responsibility to me. You should have remembered that I'd like to see what you had prepared.

True, I have been very loose in discipline . . . because of my genuine fondness for you. That laxity in discipline has proven a big mistake and resulted in your habitually forgetting me as your employer, entitled first to your respect as an employer, and surely during business, your considerate behavior. Frankly, I've tried in every way to impress you with the danger of your constant childish horseplay at serious times—during rehearsals, shows, before strangers, etc.—but to no avail. You insist on belittling . . . laughing . . . making cracks . . . *anything* to attract attention or to show the rest you can control the boss' disposition. You've gradually lost cast with the serious workers and finally convinced me through your impudence that a change in setup is the only solution. . . .

Never before, in my employ, has anyone been treated with more consideration. Never has opportunity within my organization been so advantageous to hard-working young people. Individually, you both have what it takes . . . in slightly varied portions. And, whether or not you agree, there is *no conflict in your talents.* As Swingerettes, your work is usually superb—sparkling and most beneficial. You should be cooperative . . . not competitive.

So far as my policy is concerned, there's room for *anybody who wants to put in more than he expects to get out.* That's what makes stars. . . .

Don't let me do it all . . . that's avoiding responsibility, *and nobody* will *believe* your *alibi.* I'm here to *guide* you . . . and God knows I'm always sincerely trying. *Most* employers are interested more selfishly in a good show—to hell with individuals. I'm just as anxious to avoid mistakes that will impair the futures of you kids.

It's better to put all you've got into a poor song than to coast with a hit. But it's still better to wait for one that fits than to make so many appearances per week just for the sake of appearing. They'll remember you longer *for a good thing.* But they'll forget you because of a "not-so-good" one.

I believe I have proven beyond all doubt my sincere fondness for you both, that I couldn't intentionally do anything to harm you, and that I have your professional interest at heart. . . .

I promise you that I'll be darned strict with you in your deportment and behavior at rehearsals and during all actual performances. Don't give me a growl if you are suddenly told to leave the room or stage . . . you've earned the exit and it's for the good of the morale of everybody who likes his job. . . .

As your friend, I ask only that you treat me as such. Don't attempt to take advantage of my moods, and remember this . . . I mean everything I say. There's no need for further upheaval—only sincere effort and understanding.

F.W.[9]

The two teenagers settled down and became reliable professionals. Patsy thereafter always addressed Fred as "Mr. Waring," even when she became a senior citizen and he was in his eighties.

• • •

Many felt that one of Fred's greatest assets was his ability to see the potential in those who could be of value in his organization. He gave everyone a splendid opportunity to try their wings in any area. "I came as a singer but, under Fred's guidance, I soon was conducting, writing script, acting in skits, narrating occasionally, and sometimes emceeing!" conductor/singer Don Craig said. "Not all discoveries became famous, but many latent talents flowered under his leadership. Poley was never more than an adequate drummer, but what a winning comedian he became— a shy, guileless, lovable comic. Joanne Wheatley was a soprano when she became a Pennsylvanian, and Fred persuaded her to sing contralto songs because her voice was warm and rich in that register." Joanne, a Phi Beta Kappa who came from a strictly academic musical background, did put up some resistance at first, thinking the whole show biz arena was a bit on the shoddy side.

Fred recognized Linda Wheeler's potential when he and I happened to witness her unobserved mimicry of some Miss America talent winners in the days when their bodies had a higher priority than their abilities. "He showed me and taught me how to be a comedienne," she said. "I never had that talent before and it has been the forte of my career."

Lumpy Brannum joined the Pennsylvanians as a bass fiddle player. Then Fred coaxed him out to do comedic monologues. But it was Lumpy's "Little Orley" stories that brought the most fan mail later on the morning radio shows, little five-minute fables set to music. All the Pennsylvanians were involved as background animals or trains or whatever. Fred excelled at being an oinking pig. "I am not and never was a great bass player nor a great writer nor a great comedian," Lumpy said. "But Fred provided me with a platform on which I could strut in any capacity. He is great on taking advantage of everyone's capacities—everyone does everything! Everybody rake! Everybody paint! Or [in Blendortime] drink frozen daiquiris—or *not* drink. He had always given people the opportunity to display whatever talents they might have—to showcase them with expensive arrangements and that sort of thing. He gave me leave to work on a children's show—no hooks or anything. It was a flop. When I'd fallen on my face, he welcomed me back. That was Fred's part—and a big part it was! I'm sure he would do it today or tomorrow—or as long as he lived." After years of experimentation, Lumpy was well prepared to become the legendary Mr. Green Jeans on the Captain Kangaroo show. He added, "There's one thing about Fred: an office boy could submit an arrangement, and it would get serious attention."

Fred: "During the radio days, we had an auditioning committee that got a little too ambitious. They wanted to make certain that everybody could read music, so they were not bringing to my attention those that could sing well but couldn't read—they just turned them down—like Gordon McRae and Frankie Lane. The Gordon McRae thing really made me angry, because Gordon's father was an executive of G.E., and we were on the G.E. Hour when he was turned down. The first five or six girls we ever had couldn't read a note. My theory is that everybody can sing. All they have to learn is *how* to sing."

Later, as producer of the Waring show in the sixties and seventies, Ray Sax was responsible for auditioning a steady stream of applicants. "If we heard someone with a fairly good voice and [he or she] was personable, then they would be introduced to Fred," he said. "His first words would be ones to put him or her at ease, like, 'You look very nice,' or, 'Do you have a boyfriend?' 'What do you like to do?' etc., and then, 'Why do you want to be a Pennsylvanian?' If someone said, 'Because you look like a family,' that person would probably get the job even though the voice might not be as good as another. Fred could tell by the way people handled themselves in an audition or interview whether they would fit."

Fred also used "home talent" whenever he could. Wives, husbands, and parents of regular members often filled in for special programs. Livingston's mother appeared several times on television vignettes of the Victorian days in Tyrone, Pennsylvania. When a Pennsylvanian married outside the group, it often meant it was time to welcome a new member, as, for example, when violinist Lou Ely married violinist Jean Ryden, and she was given a chair next to Lou's in the orchestra's violin section.

· · ·

Odd as it may seem, at the height of their success, the "old team" was feeling even more hurt and resentful that Fred no longer was one of them. Their presence wasn't the core as it once was in the twenties and thirties. No one was indispensable, new people were coming in, there were no real stage shows, they didn't live together or sing together or just *be* together. There was no closeness anymore.

As a newcomer I didn't sense this at all. Everyone was warm and friendly to Livingston and me. Those who joined in the thirties were true blue Pennsylvanians, who enjoyed being a part of such a unique organization, and basked in the ambience created by Fred's concern for their welfare. But a few veterans were disenchanted and started to leave, one by one. Even Nelson Keller, who had joined in 1922, felt left out. He later admitted it was a jolt to face the real world after twenty years with the Pennsylvanians. The warm security was missing.

17

My Debut

IT WAS in 1943 that I entered the picture as a part-time Pennsylvanian. My arrival was circuitous. I was born and raised in the long, flat San Joaquin Valley of California, framed on the east by the rugged Sierra Nevada range—which my great-grandmother came over as a pioneer—and the coastal range to the west. The town I grew up in, Dinuba, sits about thirty miles southeast of Fresno in the midst of the Sun Maid raisin country. Dinuba, population around five thousand, is the kind of place where old-timers still show up for high school reunions fifty years after they cheered for the Green 'n' White of Dinuba High.

My friends never changed from kindergarten through high school. Prejudice was unknown. I had no idea that my classmate Robert Seligman or his violinist cousin Anne, whom I accompanied on the piano, were Jewish. We all attended the same Presbyterian Sunday school as did two other friends whose mothers were Catholic.

My father died when I was sixteen. These were the depression years, and I felt lucky to receive a scholarship to Mills College, a women's college in Oakland, California. The fact that the president, Dr. Aurelia Reinhardt, was Mother's first cousin probably didn't hurt. When I was a freshman at Mills, one of my courses was European history. On the third day of class, the young professor, Dean Rusk, said in his soft southern accent, "Miss Clotfelter [my maiden name], would you please remain after class." I was mildly apprehensive, wondering why he singled me out. When the room cleared, he said, "Tell me about your name. I am asking because my mother's maiden name is Clotfelter." I told him that two brothers came over from Switzerland. The original name was Glattfelden, and so on. Years later when Dean Rusk became secretary of state, I was tempted to send a letter of congratulations from his "kissin' cousin." He married a Mills girl, Virginia Foisie—one of his students.

When a few of the trustees saw that I possessed some pianistic ability, they provided financial aid for music lessons and summer master classes with such renowned international pianists as Harold Bauer and Belgian artist Marcel Maas. It was at Mills that I was first exposed to an enriched environment. During my senior year, the Fleischmann Yeast heiress Mrs. Christian Holmes heard me play and arranged a scholarship for me to study in France with the eminent pianist Robert Casadesus. The night I graduated, I left California for the first time in my life to embrace the unknown.

The summer school of art and music I was to attend was in the château of Fontainebleau. The school had been established after World War I as a center where American musicians, artists, and architects could study under famous French professionals. It was at Fontainebleau that I met Livingston Gearhart. He was on scholarship to study composition with Nadia Boulanger, the great musical pedagogue. The students were housed either in hotels or in homes, but it was mandatory that we all dine together in a large pavilion-type structure not far from the château. The tables were of various sizes, and service was withheld until all seats were filled. The first day, I stood in the doorway feeling a little shy. Five young men were seated at a table for six. One of them poked Liv and said, "Go get that girl so we can eat!" He complied, and that is where I stayed for the rest of the summer.

Livingston was unlike any boy I had ever known—with his intensity, musicality, wit, looks. It was an instant mutual attraction. We became inseparable. Our scholarships were extended, and that fall I shared an apartment on the Left Bank of Paris with a Mills College chum who was attending the Sorbonne. Livingston lived some blocks away with an aged and impoverished relative of the poet Paul Valéry. My apartment contained an old dilapidated upright piano, so I rented a slightly better one. Livingston brought over some two-piano pieces he had played with his mother, a piano teacher, and I began to learn the parts she had played. By our second year Liv and I had become sufficiently proficient to perform for various American clubs and churches in Paris, and finally decided to rent the Salle Chopin and give our debut. The critics fortunately gave us glowing reviews—the career of Morley and Gearhart was launched. The name Clotfelter not being compatible with Gearhart, we decided to use Merritt, my mother's maiden name. That, too, was not euphonious, but we kept rolling Merritt around on our tongues until finally the name Morley evolved—a more harmonious duet.

After two and a half unforgettable student years in France, we returned to the United States, married, and began the challenging task of establishing ourselves professionally. In order to survive until we found a good manager, we accepted a job playing twice a night for ten or fifteen minutes at a supper club in the old Hotel Brevoort on lower Fifth Avenue (long since demolished) run by a tall, lanky Frenchman called Jacoby. He paid us a pittance, and that, most reluctantly. Sometimes we appeared at his other club, the Blue Angel, in upper Manhattan. We were allowed to play classical pieces if they weren't longer than three or four minutes. To round out our repertoire, Livingston wrote some elegant, sophisticated two-piano arrangements of Gershwin, Rodgers, Berlin, and other popular favorites.

After a year of playing in a smoke-filled classy nightclub we, like Fred on his first trip to Chicago with a single night's engagement in his pocket, went to California with the promise of one concert at Mills College. I now wonder what made the two eminent music critics of San Francisco, Alfred Frankenstein and Alexander Fried, travel more than an hour to hear a totally unknown two-piano team—we had not even made our New York debut. What luck! Their rave reviews inspired the active Mills College alumnae clubs to present us in concerts in the five great cities on the Pacific coast. It benefited us both—publicity and scholarships for Mills, and important reviews and needed cash for us. Just as Balaban & Katz, the large booking agency, caught Fred's act in Chicago and signed them on, so did the prestigious booking firm of Columbia Artists, Inc., hear us and sign us to a long-term contract. We were set for a busy schedule of yearly concert tours.

One evening we were invited to a dinner party at a friend's apartment in New York City. Our friend had two pianos, and it was there that Bob Shaw heard us play and suggested an audition with Fred Waring at the Vanderbilt Theater. And it was at the Vanderbilt a few evenings later, when we played for Fred while he leaned on the piano listening intently, that the course of our lives was changed, just as Fred's presence on the Pomona Campus had changed the life of Bob Shaw from the ministry to music. In the thirties, Fred had frequently used two piano teams—Jacques Frey and Mario Braggiotti, who were later replaced by Vera Brodsky and Harold Triggs. No wonder he immediately saw potential in our team of Morley and Gearhart.

Livingston and I became the fifty-ninth and sixtieth Pennsylvanians. I distinctly remember my first rehearsal. We had been sitting on a bench for hours just outside the big rehearsal room at 1697 Broadway waiting to run through our one piece with all the Pennsylvanians. Suddenly I heard Fred yell, "Where's that two-piano team? God damn it!"

I was furious. I jumped up, stood in the doorway, and swore back at him, saying we had been waiting at least two hours. Everyone turned white. I can still see their mouths hanging open. Absolute dead silence. Then Fred burst out laughing. He never could really understand why people were afraid of him. I've told him it was his quick tongue. He's admitted he wished he could cut it off sometimes. Fred never raised his voice to me again, although after we were married, he didn't always think it was so funny when I stood up to him in defense of someone. I did try to be a little more diplomatic, however.

Since Livingston and I were only part-time Pennsylvanians, we didn't spend all our waking hours at 1697 Broadway and at the Vanderbilt as everyone else did. Our pieces were already prepared, and unless we were playing with the orchestra or the glee club, we didn't need much ensemble rehearsal time. However, on the days we performed, we had to hang around in the afternoon in case they needed us and then, of course, all evening for the two shows at 7 and 11 P.M. Between the first and second shows, everyone usually spent the time eating, resting, rehearsing, chatting, or playing Ping-Pong. Liv and I were forever polishing our concert repertoire. Sometimes on the nights we played on the show, we'd be invited to join Fred and others after the 7 P.M. broadcast for a home-cooked dinner. It was a nice break and always a little exciting. Fred Lewis was a superb cook.

In fact, the entire atmosphere at 1697 Broadway was far removed from anything I'd ever known. It was like a beehive. The frenetic activity that went into producing those daily fifteen-minute shows on radio resulted in a continuous pandemonium of sounds and movement. Often all rooms were going at once—the orchestra room, the glee club room, the three cubicles with arrangers or small groups at the pianos, the two librarians working like mad, the scriptwriters rushing to and fro, and the distinctive click of the Ping-Pong balls at rest intervals. But through it all, an electricity emanated from Fred's inner office that reached even the CPAs out in the front offices. It was fascinating, to say the least.

Because Liv and I were so disengaged from the daily grind, we weren't always aware of the undercurrents that flowed throughout the organization—gripes about the lateness of the "after show," who was doing what to whom—all the scuttlebutt. At first, because I was still so unsophisticated, I was only dimly aware of the vibrations radiating from that inner sanctum—Fred's office. It took a few months before I realized that sometimes more was going on in there than rehearsal discussions.

Since Livingston created all of our two-piano arrangements, it was logical that Fred would suggest he write for the whole group. Fred, quick to appreciate Liv's imaginative and fertile mind, and knowing anything he brought would add color to the Waring show, gave Liv the freedom to arrange whatever he wished, and those pieces were always performed, even though the orchestral backgrounds were sometimes slightly esoteric. I can still see him going around the house, hitting pots and doorknobs and various objects to get the proper sounds for his choral arrangement of "Dry Bones."

When Livingston and I were not booked on serious concert tours for Columbia Artists, we played a two- to four-minute piece once or twice a week on the radio show. For the "after show," the girls were expected to change into long, pretty gowns to look more glamorous for our men in uniform. We wore street clothes for the broadcasts. One night at the "after show," Fred announced us, as usual. We came onstage, bowed, and seated ourselves at the keyboards, facing each other across the long strings of the two Steinway grands. I was gazing placidly out at the audience. After all, the hard part—playing an encore-type piece over the air to millions with no warmup—was over, and now I was waiting for Fred at the front center mike to announce the name of our next number. Instead, he suddenly turned to me and asked, "What are you going to play, Virginia?"

That old cliché is true. I was struck dumb with terror because I had never opened my mouth onstage. Livingston had announced the encores at our concerts. The same brain that enabled my fingers to play lickety-split all over the black and white keys and, at the same time, create musical emotions—that brain closed down. I could not remember anything. I finally named another piece, which Livingston obligingly started with me. My lip was trembling, I was skittering around on the keyboard, and I was furious with Fred.

Undaunted, each time we appeared, Fred turned to me with an impish grin and asked the same question! I was still mad, but there was something about my honestly innocent defiance and his dialogue that made the audience laugh, and so he had another "find laugh." He never let up on me, and our repartee worked because of my genuine resistance to talking onstage!

In the long run, Fred's perseverance paid off for Livingston and me on our concert tours. In those days, an audience seldom heard the sound of a performer's voice. No serious artists would dream of selling their art in such a fashion, but people hunger to know what they are really like. An announced encore at the end is all they get—a crumb. We decided to talk a little from the stage. Livingston had an engaging manner and would elicit laughter from the audience before we played a note—a rapport was set up between the listeners and us that lasted throughout the evening. The stiffness was gone, our nerves were assuaged, we played better, our fee went up 500 percent, and everyone wanted us back. We had learned one key to Fred Waring's success—music was written to be enjoyed. We made our audience feel good. And the reviews verified this: "It was one of those rare concerts from which you emerge warmed and fed," and "Morley and Gearhart mixed a measure of good looks with a little subtle humor, a lot of stage presence and a heaping of two-piano artistry."[1]

· · ·

When Livingston and I first started our career, I needed stage dresses. Don Loper, later to become a well-known Hollywood dress designer, was a ballroom dancer appearing with his partner in New York nightclubs and hotels. He had designed ballerina length dresses for her. When he went west, I bought some of them and found, to my delight, they solved a nagging problem I had endured with long evening dresses. Sometimes my floor-length gown would catch between my right foot and the sustaining pedal of the piano. When pressed down, the pedal would pull on the garment, a highly disconcerting annoyance. The full ballerina skirt with its numerous petticoats underneath just barely touched the floor as I sat—and thus it became my unofficial trade logo. One time as I was walking offstage, all my petticoats loosened and fell around my ankles.

In the beginning, Liv and I had an attractive, tiny penthouse on West Fifty-fifth Street within walking distance of 1697 Broadway. In those days, I could make the trek safely at night. In a 1978 radio interview Fred stated: "I cannot recall *any* time prior to 1960 when it was dangerous to be on the New York streets after dark. I used to take short cuts through Central Park at night or walk all around town—that's when it was interesting."[2] It hadn't been easy to find a place where two pianos were allowed, but we did. Our landlord, in contrast to many, was not persnickety about the inclusion of music in his building. The occupant of the other penthouse was a singing teacher whose pupils emitted hideously gruesome sounds that sent Livingston and me into hysterics. A few interesting guests dropped in now and then. One was composer and critic Virgil Thomson, who wanted to hear us play Stravinsky's *Concerto for Two Pianos Alone.* (We had played it for Stravinsky himself in Steinway's basement on Fifty-seventh Street. At the time, I'd treated the episode blithely, but in retrospect, I'm quite impressed that we actually performed that monumentally difficult work for the maestro. I can picture the scene—the huge basement filled with silent concert grands, Livingston and I in the middle, and Stravinsky, a most dour man, seated at my elbow. Stravinsky seemed very pleased with our performance. He actually smiled and congratulated us, and afterwards invited us for tea at the Russian Tea Room across the street.)

Whenever we played for special musicians, they *always* placed themselves next to me, which was disconcerting. Isador Philipp did it in Paris, making little complimentary quips in French that made me blush and distracted me no end. I was only twenty and he was an old man!

John Cage came by a couple of times to "prepare" our pianos for one of his experimental creations. He put small metal objects such as pennies, paper clips, and screws between the strings, which produced strange sounds when the keys were struck.

Later, when our son Paul was born, we moved to Orange, New Jersey, and commuted to New York for the radio shows. Our final move was to a little farmhouse about a mile out of the village of Shawnee. It had an adjacent red barn that we turned into a studio to house our two nine-foot Steinways. We kept another piano in the house since most of our practicing was alone—necessary to perfect the notes. I resisted the move to Shawnee, but Livingston longed for a more pastoral milieu. I think my resistance came from not wanting to be part of any "Waring compound" possibility, as already a nucleus of Pennsylvanian families had settled in and around Shawnee.

18

For the Sake of One Singer

IN JUNE, 1944, the five-year Chesterfield contract came to an abrupt end. "I went into Fred's office to ask about something, and evidently he'd just been on the phone, because his face . . . you know how he gets, you can always tell when something happens . . . and he looked up and said, 'We're through!'" Fred Culley said. "'We're through, we're finished with Chesterfield.'"

Jack Dolph told John Royal that they lost the Chesterfield show "because of one singer. The five-times-a-week strip we lost because of *one singer.*" It was Donna Dae. From a swing singer complete with gestures, she was to become, as Fred introduced her on the radio shows, "GI's Joy, the girl with a song in her heart, and her heart in a love song."

"They didn't like her?" Royal asked.

"They did *not* like her, and Fred would *not* fire her. The girl, five years later, would have been very successful. Her style was a little ahead of her time."

"Well, you have to admire Fred's integrity in standing up for his show," Royal said. "He never compromised if he thought he was right." As a memory and a confirmation of Fred's integrity, we have in our home a beautiful silver tray given to Fred in 1944 by the Liggett & Myers Tobacco Company, with one hundred and seven names engraved on it—all directly connected with the successful five-year Chesterfield show (including eighty-six performers and eight arrangers).

As soon as the Chesterfield program ended, Fred hauled everyone to Pennsylvania for the summer to help run *that* show at Shawnee Inn. Shawnee-on-Delaware was the one place where Fred could be with his children on a daily basis, especially during the summer months even after he and Evalyn were separated. Pennsylvanians served as swimming pool life-guards, assigned caddies to players, announced tee-off times, worked in the gift and golf shops, and handled refreshments at the halfway house. Meanwhile, the hotel manager was gnashing his teeth, for besides paying them, he had to feed and house them. The poor soul had one bonus— free entertainment.

Even an unwary houseguest was set to work on various projects. Admiral Edwin Dexter, newly retired at age forty-two, whom Fred had met during the war years when the Pennsylvanians entertained at Annapolis, arrived at Shawnee. Without ceremony Fred said, "Dex, put on some old clothes. We're going over to the Inn; there's a job to be done there."

"I was impressed by the great spirit of the Pennsylvanians and their friendliness," remembered Admiral Dexter. "For the next two or three days we spent most of our time at the Inn painting tables and walls of the Totem Pole Room while Fred Waring was plying back and forth from his house with sandwiches and drinks, acting as a real quarterback."

One can imagine the hotel manager's sigh of relief when he heard that the Pennsylvanians had a new job—half an hour on Thursdays on NBC in New York for Johnson's Wax. This meant at least four days a week in New York for Fred, but Evalyn chose to stay in Shawnee. Bored and at loose ends, she decided it would be a good idea to offer ballroom danc-ing instruction for the guests at Shawnee Inn. She called someone she knew who ran a dancing school in New York. "I want you to send me a gentleman." she said. "Don't send me one of those crazy Latins." Of course, the school director sent the most Latino of all, Romero Santiago, the man Evalyn later would marry.

"Romero asked me if I would dance with him at a show at the Inn," Evalyn recalled. "I said sure. So we started learning all these routines, and it was a lot of fun, and, gee, it just changed everything. People were com-ing from everywhere. In a small place like that, it goes all over that Mrs. Fred Waring was *dancing* at the Inn."

Johnny O'Connor produced a job for the Pennsylvanians, an engage-ment in the Roxy Theater with the movie *Woodrow Wilson* in August for six weeks, seven days a week. Walter Winchell reported that the Wilson picture and Fred Waring had brought in $155,000 in the first week, and added, "That's a record for any theater anywhere, anytime!" Trade papers reported that Fred was earning, between the Roxy and the NBC broadcast,

$43,500 a week.[1] This was good news for the Pennsylvanians' exchequer but bad news for Fred's marriage—six weeks in New York with no days off.

Evalyn said, "Fred was at the Roxy and couldn't get home, and I was having a wonderful time getting all this attention. When he finally got home, he couldn't stand it." Evalyn seemed to think Fred was jealous, but the others felt he was embarrassed. Fred was at the height of his career, and it was obvious to everyone but Evalyn that her sexy dancing with Romero was tabloid news.

Undeterred, Evalyn continued dancing. "Drigo [her nickname for Romero] and I accepted some engagements. We went to a nightclub in Baltimore, and then we got a job in Florida. We never did too much with it. It was more fun to rehearse and dream up all these wonderful ideas, but when it came to the actual work—I couldn't stand it again, I hated it. Then I was told by my lawyer that I shouldn't dance in public, so I forgot about it for a while."

· · ·

Fred soon had six radio shows a week. NBC had come up with an innovative idea, that since no evening musical show of any consequence had ever been broadcast in the morning hours, the proposed program would be aimed at the housewife and aired at 10 A.M., five mornings a week. The sponsor was Owens-Illinois Glass Company. As usual, Fred wrote the theme song—all parts of the lyric referring to something suggesting glass, for instance, crystal memories, sparkling songs of love, reflections bring words. It was called "I Hear Music," and he retained it as his theme song along with "Sleep" for the rest of his career. The Thursday night weekly broadcast continued contiguously with the morning shows.

Once the Pennsylvanians were conditioned to rising early, and even with twice as many numbers to prepare, the show itself was not too stressful on them—the backlog of repertoire and trained personnel from the "Pleasure Time" years paid off. However, the decision was made to broadcast and play concerts in different cities, and the long grueling cross-country tours began once again in earnest. More than seventy people would be on the road. The logistics were staggering, entailing transportation to and within the city; housing, sometimes on the train and sometimes in hotels; theater bookings, with all the promotion involved: brochures, advance men, tickets; and finally, most difficult of all, securing broadcasting facilities in each city with microphones, a control booth for balancing voices and instrumentalists, and a room large enough for everyone.

"We were doing so many shows, we didn't know what year it was," quipped Fred Culley.

At first the Pennsylvanians lived in three Pullman cars numbered FWI, FWII, and FWIII, plus baggage cars. These were hooked up to a train, transported to the designated city, and then shunted to a sidetrack while the Pennsylvanians performed a concert that night and a broadcast the next morning. Sometimes they traveled all night on the train, arriving before dawn. Sleep was impossible, as the Pullman cars were jolted and shoved from one track to another. It was a brutal schedule, especially for vocalists, who as a rule never open their mouths before noon, let alone sing at such a ghastly hour. Rest is required for a singer to be "in voice," and there was precious little of that. Gordon Goodman, known as G. G., with his clear tenor voice, was the exception. He could reach his high notes anytime without a warm-up, and drink, smoke, and play cards, to boot. The instrumentalists, as a rule, never worried about such petty things as rest and health. Their idea of heaven was to be attached to a dining car where they could eat, drink, smoke, and play poker all night in comparative comfort.

When Lou Metz, the enterprising gofer, returned to the Pennsylvanian fold after three years in the U.S. Army, he immediately was assigned the position of stage manager. "My duty as stage manager was a matter of seeing that everything got on and off the train, to the theater, set up onstage . . . and then start all over again," Lou said. "At no time did we ever spend more than one night in any town. We never missed getting on the air on time, and there were a number of times when I think Fred welcomed a crisis—practically a catastrophe!"

Every Pennsylvanian would concur with that statement. As Jack Dolph recollected: "Once in Washington, things were going very dully. We were rehearsing a broadcast in the National Press Club auditorium. Waring was hanging over the stand, complaining. There was a guy setting up metal chairs who had annoyed Fred very much, and Fred drove him out. I hired the guy for ten bucks to go ahead with a whole armload of chairs and drop them. You should have seen that rehearsal pick up. Have you noticed with Fred that he lives by crises? Unless the world is about to cave in, nothing goes on."

•   •   •

As Livingston and I traveled on our own concert tours, I wasn't aware of these problems. But one time during an unscheduled week, we joined the Pennsylvanians in Ohio. There sat the three legendary Pullman cars with the large numerals on the side of each. Fred had the single compartment in the first car, star soprano Jane Wilson and her violinist husband Johnny Richardson, the same in the second car, and Liv and I were assigned the compartment in the third car.

On one tour, in order to cover the long distances between cities in the west, the Pennsylvanians traveled royally for several weeks on their own United Airlines plane, complete with pilots and stewardesses, who became attached to the warm, friendly group. Liv and I never flew with them, but at least we knew their trips weren't always milk train runs and derailed baggage cars.

The broadcast schedule was the same regardless of the time zone: a run-through of the show from 8:30 to 9:30 A.M., broadcast from 10 to 10:30 A.M., rehearsal of the next day's show from 11 A.M. to perhaps 2 P.M., and the concert at night. Sometimes there were two concerts, at 7 and 9:30 P.M., and then back on the Pullmans for a jolting ride to the next city. The Pennsylvanians were one sorry sight of exhaustion as they emerged each cold morning from the train.

Livingston and I performed twice on the air the week we toured with the Pennsylvanians, and we also played each evening for the stage performance. Sometimes the concerts were held in colossal arenas because the crowds were so big. I remember looking out at ten, twenty, thirty, even forty thousand people. It was difficult to play for several reasons. First, we never had a chance to practice or even try the pianos, which could be of varying sizes, such as a nine-foot concert grand cuddled up to a baby five-footer. And the action of the keys varied. Some were stiff, like driving a Mack truck, some tended to stick, and some were just fine. Usually the spotlights were so strong that the keyboard was a blur of black and white shadows, always unnerving for me.

One night, somewhere in the Midwest, we all wearily climbed back on board the train. No dining or parlor cars were attached, and all the seats had been made into berths, so several of us ended up in the ladies' lounge, the only available place to congregate. We were perched around the crowded room, but Lumpy had the seat of honor—the lidded toilet seat. I can still see him laughing and talking animatedly, his foot propping the door open, as we rocketed through the night. This was the first and last time I ever drank a boilermaker. I do remember a phrase: "Beer-whiskey, very risky; whiskey-beer, never fear." I also remember hearing the life story of an inebriated Pennsylvanian that night who soon after reembraced his basic Christian Science teachings and never touched a drop thereafter. Luckily, Livingston and I weren't on call for the early morning radio broadcast. While the crew and performers were forced to rise and sparkle, we were able to luxuriate in a few extra hours of sleep. We were accustomed to a more monastic lifestyle.

It was on this same tour that all the girls were ready to liquidate the one female violinist (not Ferne, who had retired). I sympathized with the violinist because we classically trained instrumentalists are not, as a rule, schooled in show business etiquette. Backstage, where dressing space is usually limited, strong unspoken territorial rights prevail, just as in the animal kingdom. You don't spread your paraphernalia all around, monopolize the mirror or invade anyone's bailiwick. The dear girl would come in the stage door and rummage through the communal shoe boxes, leaving everything in a mess; or barge into the dressing room, accidentally knocking the elbow of someone putting on eye makeup. Since she was completely unaware of the havoc she was causing, the girls decided someone had to speak to her and, because I was the one most neutral, they picked me. Well, I did, and the young violinist was overcome with remorse. She cried all night, bought presents for everyone the next day and, within a week, reverted to her old habits. After this hectic week, Livingston and I continued on our Columbia Concerts tour which, although rigorous by some standards, seemed rather peaceful in contrast.

•   •   •

By now, the Pennsylvanians were performing two-hour shows in concert halls and gymnasiums instead of fifteen-minute shows in movie theaters sandwiched between a picture and a newsreel. And Fred was finally kindling a little interest among the so-called longhair music critics. In 1946, Claudia Cassidy, one of the most widely read and fear-inspiring critics, wrote an amazingly benign tribute in the *Chicago Tribune,* which started out: "There are all kinds of musical mousetraps and Fred Waring must have built one of the most alluring, for the world undeniably beats a path to his door. He not only filled the capacious Civic Opera House, but the overflow filled every available nook of the cavernous stage and peered in wistfully from the wings." She went on to praise the show, but registered a complaint against the arrangers: "When some of these so-called wizards get through with a good tune it reminds you of Mr. Waring's Ray Sax who not only plays two instruments, dances, juggles and stands on his head, but does them all at the same time."[2]

The *Chicago Daily News* stated emphatically, "Waring, with his suave and wholly likeable way, is one of the master showmen of this era."[3]

The threads of Fred's and Evalyn's marriage slowly continued to unravel. They did not understand their mutual needs. The long separations added to the pressures. "I was getting to the breaking point," Evalyn said. "I used to put a couple of martinis in a pitcher and fill it up with ice and go into my room."

Cora Ballard, Evalyn's best friend, who became Fred's secretary after Helen Helwig's departure, noted: "During the years 1945 and 1946, Evalyn was a bitch. I told her so. She said she knew it, but that it was an accumulation of aggravations over the years." In later conversations, Evalyn did not acknowledge the rift with Fred. She told Jack Dolph she was surprised when Fred asked for a divorce: "I didn't have a divorce in mind because I kept thinking that sooner or later something would work out—that because of the children we should straighten it out." In the mid-forties, they separated. Evalyn lived in New York, and Fred's home base was Shawnee, with a small apartment on East Sixty-eighth Street in New York during the workweek.

While Evalyn had been off dancing with Romero Santiago, Fred became involved with a Pennsylvanian whom everybody loved but pitied. Her name was Daisy Bernier. She was completely mesmerized by and in love with Fred, but also a little afraid of him. She seemed so lost and insecure, and was frequently in tears. I felt great pity for her. Even back then as an observer, I sensed her biggest mistake was to aggravate her delicate position by residing in Shawnee during the absence of the Pennsylvanians. In those days no one noticed these things in New York, but a small village like Shawnee found it a bit indigestible, and Fred never realized until later how painful this affair was for his children.

About Fred's apparent discontent with everything that went on all his life, including the women he married and those he didn't, Fred's cousin Tot Fisher gave a derisive laugh: "I hate to tell you, that is the background of the Warings! The whole outfit: uncles, cousins and aunts. Fred's Grandfather Waring was married twice—had two sets of children. Fred's father Frank had an uncle who was married and had a son. The uncle left his son and wife Mary in Tyrone, and went west taking his *wife's sister* with him. They lived together and when Mary died [probably of a broken heart], he finally married his sister-in-law, and then his son went out to live with them. They didn't seem to have any *family feeling*. As for Frank, Fred's father, he neither smoked nor drank, but was hell for the women!"

Ray Sax said about Fred's romancing over the years, "There wasn't any cheapness. The thing that frightened me more than anything is this—the warmth and emotion he can feel for not necessarily a beautiful girl in appearance but a beautiful girl inside. I know they are not always bowled over by the name of Fred Waring, but this is a man who really is very warm, has a great deal of emotion, and he gets deep behind you and encircles you. I have seen this man—the demands made upon him—the speed of his work, and this pedestal business of thousands of people around him who say, 'Fred,' and 'this great, great . . . Mr. Waring.' I think he gets so sick sometimes of knowing, of being aware of what he is or what people believe he is, that he wants to find a closet with somebody somewhere. Now, a man is a lousy companion unless you have a deck of cards or a fishing rod, so what's the alternative—a beautiful girl with bosoms, and he's a grapefruit man, let's face it!"

Fred and Evalyn's three children were the ones who suffered the most and were emotionally scarred by the coolness and strain that existed in the marriage. In 1946, twelve-year-old Dixie asked to be sent to a boarding school. "My escape was reading," she said. "I used to read constantly. I wanted friends so badly. I wanted to be accepted." Evalyn insisted on sending the two little boys to a New England boarding school. They were ten and eight years old. Fred told me years later how heartsick he was over that decision, but with his marriage crumbling plus his relentless schedules, he felt helpless. Fred spent more and more time in his office, and he depended more and more on the Pennsylvanians for his emotional life.

· · ·

Fred and Leopold Stokowski had known and respected each other since the twenties. Although not a close relationship, theirs was a congenial one punctuated by a pattern of mutual bantering. An unfortunate misunderstanding brought it to a sudden end. Fred was deeply hurt and disappointed to lose one whom he considered a friendly colleague. He described the incident: "Stokowski, of course, was unique, no question about it, and he was very interested in youth. He felt he had a great idea for youth orchestras. He transcribed some of the classics so they would be playable by high school orchestras. He was anxious for a publisher, particularly Shawnee Press, because we had a link to the high schools. So Stokowski brought his work to us, and we studied it, and all of our staff concurred that some of the brass requirements were too difficult for kids. He could either change a couple of notes or change the key. He very stubbornly insisted that to do either would be a desecration, unforgivable.

"I tried to reason with him: 'You've already made alterations. Why don't you just go a step further and fix it so that nobody on the high school level would be called upon to play any notes more difficult than his capabilities?' He argued and claimed we were wrong. So we volunteered to make up an orchestra of the best musicians from the high schools of Long Island, of which there were many. He volunteered to come and conduct, which was, of course, what we wanted. The result was a fiasco. The poor kids just couldn't, as they say, cut the mustard. It was just impossible for them to freely play some of the most important passages. Mr. Stokowski stalked out angry and withdrew his offer to let us publish his work. There's no questioning his incomparable ability as a conductor, but his judgment as far as kids were concerned was quite lacking.

"I think he gave up the publishing project but he must have kept that in his craw, because later on I was invited to guest conduct the Houston Symphony when he was then its conductor. It was a benefit. Naturally, I assumed Stokowski would be there, at least for the rehearsal. But he was not. Not only was he not there, but he had locked his dressing room, which is the dressing room I had always used in our appearances in Houston, so that I had no place to change. I never saw him again."

•   •   •

For a highly visible performer, the ever-present threat of plagiarism charges is a constant menace. Thus, Fred always returned unsolicited registered manuscripts unopened: "Desirable as is new material, one can rarely afford to take the risk involved. There is always somebody ready to recognize his own melody in the work of another if there is the slightest peg on which to hang a plagiarism suit. As a result, songs and instrumental numbers are usually returned without even being opened. We average twenty-five to thirty a week among which there might be some masterpieces if it were possible to separate them from the chaff."[4]

Although Fred had several lawsuits filed against him, he refused to settle because it would have suggested that he had pirated someone's idea. One time he spent $10,000 when he could have settled for $500. Since he had never accepted payola of any kind and stayed on the right side of the law (except for speeding tickets), Fred always won his cases. However, I do remember a long and expensive lawsuit in the forties when Fred was sued by a Pennsylvanian in spite of the fact that Fred had previously paid the young man's salary and hospital bill when he was ill with pneumonia. The musician claimed that Fred owed him $24,900 for extra "work" done between May and October, 1945—$2,000 a week above his salary. Fred never assigned work he didn't pay for. The fact that almost everybody contributed because they wished to—a tradition as old as the organization itself—was the simple and successful defense. He also claimed Fred had purloined some lines of his script for a show, an original script by manager/writer Ed Lee. Ed's original script in his own peculiar scrawl on his oft-used yellow pad was produced to refute a claim that it had been stolen. That cinched it for Fred, but it cost him a vast amount of money, not to speak of aggravation and energy. Fred had spent days and countless hours in court with various Pennsylvanians as witnesses. Is it any wonder Fred Waring used only music that had been copyrighted and published by reputable houses?

• • •

In 1938 Ed Lee, Dolly Waring's husband, had been brought in to help market the Blendor, but he was not sold on the new mixing device. Because he felt it was a limited product with no future, he took over the publishing end of the business—Words and Music—Johnny O'Connor's baby. An immediate divergence of opinion arose between the two on the stability of an enterprise depending on hits for its success. For Johnny, a gamble on a horse or a song was a matter of favorable odds and the ability to select the winners, whereas Ed heartily disapproved of O'Connor's style of business and living. The rift between Ed and Johnny became apparent by 1945. Since there wasn't room for two managers, Johnny left at the end of the year. But he held no resentment against Fred, and stated, "Fred has earned every honor and every dollar that he got. He worked!"

Ed Lee found himself responsible for more and more of the other enterprises: Shawnee Press (the former Words and Music), the magazine *Music Journal* (published by Fred), Shawnee Inn, and the Pennsylvanians, but he, too, became frustrated by his undefined responsibilities. "I was never officially appointed general manager," Ed said. "Somebody asked Fred what I did around there. He said, 'General manager,' and that was it." Unfortunately, Ed Lee never had the rapport with Fred that O'Connor had. Johnny had procured the bookings and money, and never interfered as to how it should be spent. Fred regarded Ed and Jake Cohen of the front office as necessary but troublesome elements who were constantly complicating his life.

"I was never Fred Waring's manager, in the Johnny O'Connor sense, and had no desire to be," Ed said and then added rather wistfully, "I was never considered one of the Pennsylvanians." We, the Pennsylvanians who found Ed Lee to be rather cold, unapproachable, and not always given to the indirect or more tactful response, would have been greatly surprised to know that he longed to be one of us and not one of *them* in the front office.

Fred's erratic working habits were the bane of his organization. The specific one that literally drove everyone to the bottle—Fred had more than his fair share of alcoholics—was his procrastination. He delayed decisions, he did not answer his mail, and his staff was sometimes mired in a state of non compos mentis. Everyone at times, except Fred's loving and adoring sister Helen, became irritated and annoyed with him. Jack Dolph thought a book about Fred could be entitled *The Beloved Bastard*.

In the twenties, the Pennsylvanians would have had no jobs if Fred hadn't been on the ball, but by the thirties, his nascent exasperating traits began to surface. "When Fred returned from lunch or from anywhere else, numerous persons (often including me) would be lurking behind doors near the elevator, waiting to pounce on him," Hilda Espy said. "'Fred, *Fred!*' we would all yelp. He might stroll by, wearing an 'I don't see you and I don't see you' expression, or he might unexpectedly respond, 'Yup?' And somebody might be invited to follow him into his office and reveal what was on his mind."

Lumpy added, "After Fred walked past me a few times, I got a memo book and I submitted every idea, plot, and suggestion on paper—a habit I continued to this day."

Public relations man Howard Everitt recalled a Sunday afternoon at Shawnee when Fred Waring was inspecting the employees' quarters during renovation. "Well, he hit the ceiling and this, added to other mistakes in the renovation, nearly caused us to be late for the G.E. show in New York where Ronald Reagan was emceeing, and the director wanted to know which of the five scenes should be used for one of the sets of the almost to go on G.E. show. Fred Waring was always this way, more so than any other person I've known. Always a deadline before making a decision."

Admiral Dexter, brought in as Fred's PR man after Everitt left, was possibly the most frustrated of the lot. After all, he had been in charge of four ships—a highly disciplined chain of command in an organization that went by the book. Dex remembered an instance when he had tried to get Fred's attention and accomplished it only by arriving next morning in full uniform. "But Fred didn't like to be pressed or cornered into giving answers. He avoided that. Every time I put on my sailor suit to get a response, I knew my usefulness was decreasing just a little. I left Fred exactly two years after I joined him—as friends." Dex admitted that decisions were forthcoming when necessary. "Fred would usually assemble all the facts and then he would decide very shortly before a deadline," he said.

And the under-the-blotter problem—all those unanswered letters! His secretary Cora said it had been going on forever. "He'd make notes on letters he'd received—congratulatory or condolences, etc.—and I would write the letters," she said. "He'd sit down with a bunch of mail—and maybe spend two hours. He'd go through it fairly fast and mark things, but he did it so seldom, and it was so frustrating, that I had a stamp made to mark his mail years ago with 'Yes!' 'No!'—or what to say. He did it for a week or two and then stopped using it."

Fred's last secretary, Ruth Sibley, worked with him at night in our home whenever she could pin him down. "One time," she said, "Fred opened a suitcase full of unanswered mail, stared at it and said, '*Gawd-a-mighty*,' then shut it. Sometimes there were four suitcases—months and years old." I think Fred felt as overwhelmed as Dukas's Sorcerer's Apprentice in Disney's *Fantasia*. No matter how fast he ran, the buckets kept filling up with water. Only this time it was letters.

· · ·

On April 12, 1945, at 4:49 P.M., the news was flashed on the air of the death of President Franklin Delano Roosevelt. Everyone was stunned. The media and radio people were unprepared, yet at 10 o'clock that evening, the Pennsylvanians, with a beautifully delivered eulogy by Orson Welles, performed on Fred's weekly NBC show, a magnificent tribute to the man who had, throughout his entire administration, been an outspoken admirer of Fred's music.

· · ·

Each summer Fred returned with the Pennsylvanians to broadcast his shows at Shawnee-on-Delaware. Keeping the group intact was his main priority—practicality be damned! In the long run, it was that one trait of single-minded fanaticism (so infuriating to his business associates) that sustained his institution of Pennsylvanians for nearly seventy years.

When I was one of the Pennsylvanians, we all took Fred's paternal care of us quite for granted. At least I did. It never occurred to me even to wonder how he managed to keep that huge organization together and functioning. Everybody leaned on him. Everything was arranged for us—summer and winter.

Fred's paternal tradition produced many of the advantages of family life but, unfortunately, its disadvantages as well. Unlike a baseball club where a player may be released, traded, or sold with a minimum of emotion in order to maintain a winning combination, Fred simply couldn't fire anyone—especially a Pennsylvanian. That was tantamount to kicking out a relative—*unthinkable!* As a result, he ended up supporting a goodly amount of deadwood over the years.

I remember one particularly happy and fun-filled summer of 1947. Fred had moved all of us to Shawnee from where he would broadcast his daily live morning radio show. He had an ulterior motive: he could work in the morning and play golf afternoons. The hotel manager, as usual, was responsible for our room and board—not a joyful thought for his bottom line. But Fred maintained that the Pennsylvanians made the purchase of the Inn possible, and thus were entitled to its perks and privileges. We were housed in various buildings throughout the village with the luxury of eating our meals not in the "zoo" with the employees or in the side room with the executives, but in the hotel's main dining room where the guests dined. As usual, first class only, for the Pennsylvanians.

That summer of 1947 three families shared a sprawling unrenovated carriage house, which Fred later remodeled into our unique home, the Gatehouse. Choral director Don Craig and his wife occupied the caretakers' quarters, choral director Lara Hoggard and his family lived upstairs in the hayloft, which occupied the length of the barn, and Livingston and I, our one-and-a-half-year-old Paul, and his "Nana" shared two airy sections formerly populated by horses and cows. This setting was perfect for us with its arty bohemian atmosphere and plenty of room for our two nine-foot concert grands that Steinway lent us year-round.

The daily radio programs were rehearsed and broadcast in a small playhouse established by the Worthingtons when they built the Inn in 1909. The theater seated one hundred and fifty people who came from all over the United States to observe rehearsals and airings. The local volunteer fire department was located in the rear of the building, and needed equipment badly. After each broadcast Fred would ask the audience if they enjoyed the show. When they clapped enthusiastically, he would pass the hat. Most were ashamed not to give generously to such a worthy cause after such an interesting morning.

Once the program was aired and the next day's show was rehearsed, the Pennsylvanians were free to use the recreational facilities—to swim, play tennis, canoe on the river, enjoy the golf course—having your cake and eating it too. Liv and I spent many of these afternoon hours at the pianos preparing for our next year's concert tour. Pianist/composer Charlie Naylor expressed the prevailing mood of the summering Pennsylvanians: "I remember driving to Shawnee from New York the first time. I remember stopping along the river road with the two Pennsylvanians I was with. It was so beautiful we laughed; we were very young and we were happy with this great place we could visit."

Veteran Pennsylvanian Tommy Cullen, who had a home in Shawnee, coined a nickname for Fred: Old Owl Eyes. We all swore he had eyes in the back of his head, plus his well-known ESP, as he'd suddenly appear when least expected, sometimes to the delight but often to the dismay of those present. He was never vicious or threatening. He always just seemed to know what was going on.

As a Pennsylvanian, I experienced Fred's seemingly ubiquitous presence. One summer when we Pennsylvanians were housed at Shawnee doing morning radio shows, Fred thought up a way to bring in some money for a local charity. He placed an umbrella table on the grass between the Inn and the pool. For a dollar, anyone could hit three balls and win a prize if a certain marker were reached. The Pennsylvanians, of course, were conned into donating two hours a week manning the stand. Jane Wilson and I had drawn Fridays from 5 to 7 p.m. No one ever came by at that hour, as I suppose Inn guests were having cocktails or dressing for dinner. So after a couple of weeks, Jane—who had just been introduced to martinis—decided to go into what then was called the Grill Room nearby in the Inn and bought us each one cocktail, which we sipped leisurely. We enjoyed it, so we did it again the next week. At 7 p.m. each week Livingston and Jane's husband Johnny would arrive to take us into the hotel dining room.

After a few weeks of that Jane said, "Why don't we bring our own martinis?" The next Friday Livingston very obligingly filled a thermos, and we settled ourselves comfortably in the two directors' chairs, the sun gently warm on our backs, and chatted and sipped. Near the end of our session, Fred suddenly appeared. Now, in all the previous weeks, he'd never once shown up at our two-hour sessions, but there he was saying brightly, "You two have had a long session out here. Let me buy you a drink in the club room." I looked at Jane. Her smile was frozen, and as I stood up, I realized Livingston had been overly generous. Fred, the wicked devil, could see what bad shape we were in, and knowing we seldom had a drink, was enjoying the little *tableau vivant* he was witnessing. Imbibing on duty was frowned upon, so Jane and I, thinking we had fooled Fred completely, clung together, focusing on getting to the end of what seemed an endlessly lengthened corridor. Fred was chatting amiably alongside, laughing quietly at our concentrated efforts at nonchalance. Fortunately, Livingston and Johnny came to our rescue. Ever since, alcohol has been low on my priority list.

Again, in the seventies, Fred showed he had not lost his touch. Early one summer morning at 3 A.M., he rose from bed, got in his car, and drove across the grass to a concrete shuffleboard where a car was suspended—all four wheels off the ground. The driver, a Pennsylvanian obviously under the influence, was futilely attempting to get the car unhooked—racing the engine forward and backward.

The driver's version: "Someone rapped on the car. I looked up, and there was Old Owl Eyes peering through the window at me. I cut off the engine and rolled down the window, and he said, 'The keys, Ray, the keys.' [Not Ray Sax.]

"And I said, 'The keys?'

"And he said, 'The keys!'

"I handed him the keys, and he said, 'Now, get home,' and then he drove off. When I asked for the keys the next day, he gave them back and never said a word." This was a prime example of Fred's deathly fear of anyone drinking and driving.

That same night while he was up, Fred drove over to the Inn and passed our fifteen-year-old (who was ostensibly camping out), driving a Volkswagen that belonged to a cute Pennsylvanian. The very sight of his father appearing in the middle of the night only reinforced the Old Owl Eyes legend. Actually, Fred never said a word to him.

Fred was also affectionately referred to as Old Elephant Mind because of his phenomenal memory. He could rattle off all the names of children and grownups he knew as a child of four. We all could relate some incident of his almost total recall. I remember one that had to do with his special yearly golf tournament at Shawnee. On Friday at the end of the week we would have a cocktail party, and Fred would stand at the gate of our indoor court and introduce me to all three hundred and fifty guests. He not only knew the wives' first names but most of their children as well. "In Toronto my Aunt Emmy, who was eighty-three and dressed up like Mrs. Astor, comes backstage, and she says, 'Where's Fred?'" Fred Culley said. "I'm sensitive because I've got a million relatives. She says, 'He'll remember me! He'll call me Katie.' We turn around and there's Fred, and he says, 'Hi, ya, Katie,' and kisses her. He knew her name was Emmy."

"Fred had a memory like a computer," recalled Mickey Dugdale. "Back in New York he astonished me one day, sitting on a stool in the coffee shop at 1697 Broadway, when I realized he remembered the name of every person who had attended each workshop session."

In later years Fred, tired of that same inconsiderate question—"You don't remember me, do you?"—would sometimes retort, "Should I?"

One beautiful fall day in the forties a couple of bus loads of Pennsylvanians were driven to York, Pennsylvania, where Fred's sister Helen lived, for an evening concert. We were in Amish territory, and she had arranged for us to taste the seven sweet and seven sour dishes of the Amish cuisine. Our hosts had never heard of Fred Waring since they didn't have "electric," but they graciously invited us into a farmhouse with a dining room ample enough for all of us. It was my first intimate view of that singular sect—the scrubbed-faced little girls in their quaint dresses, and the boys and men in their flat-brimmed hats. We all ate heartily of the Pennsylvania Dutch dishes—the shoo-fly pie and the apple pan dowdy. To express his appreciation, Fred decided the Pennsylvanians should sing a few songs and hymns. We went out onto the wide wooden veranda where a lush green pasture sloped up to a distant and fairly high ridge.

Soprano Jane Wilson remembered that Fred's back was toward the view as he conducted the impromptu concert: "Across the road was a rail fence where we could see grazing cattle silhouetted across the sky. As soon as we started to sing, we could see the cows one by one starting to stroll down the hill toward the fence. Some of us had a hard time trying not to break up as the cows gathered, and a look of displeasure was growing on Fred's face. After the final chord, everyone broke into laughter. Fred turned to look behind him and was surprised to see a long row of cows lined up side by side, heads over the fence, listening with rapt attention. He laughed as hard as anyone."

19

Music Workshops

FRED'S entry into the music education arena came in a roundabout way. Ennis Davis, a portly, genial man who had spent his life working for a firm that published music textbooks, Ginn and Company, and personally knew most of the leading music pedagogues in the country, decided academia could learn a thing or two from Fred Waring. He cajoled Fred into attending a music education conference in Boston. Fred was leery: "I had not only never attended such a meeting, I'd never even heard of one!"

Davis hoped, like some devious Santa Claus, to get Fred into an argument with the group of distinguished educators. "They put me on a dais with a fellow named [A.] Walter Kramer and Lillabelle Pitts, director of music at Columbia University, and various other people whom I had never met, and had us facing a hall of others," recalled Fred. "They looked like a very tough audience, indeed! Ennis had brought along some 'off the air' recordings of a number of our songs which he felt would be suitable for schools, and a welcome change from the unimaginative materials routinely in use."

By the time Fred had advanced his theories about school music and the method of tone syllables by which he achieved such clarity of articulation in choral music, the hall was in an uproar of debate. Fred was surprised and pleased that Lillabelle sided with him sympathetically. The meeting finally settled down because Fred spoke well, not only with force and conviction but with a background of broad accomplishment in choral music no one had ever before achieved.

What is the tone syllables method? A brief explanation is in order. Fred would study and analyze a song carefully, and then base his musical interpretation on the meaning of the text, not just the musical notes. And that is how, little by little, over the years, he developed what, for want of any better term, he called tone syllables: to sing all of the beauty of all of the sounds of all of the syllables of all of the words. Most of the great songwriters of Fred's era—Rodgers, Berlin, Kern, Carmichael, Whiting, and others—often asked Fred to be the first to perform their new songs because his treatment was so satisfying to their inner artistic needs. Fred fervently believed that a beautiful song, beautifully sung, was the epitome of musical expression—the exquisite meld of words and music. He said, "You can whistle the melody or read the lyrics, but the only thing you can do with a song is sing it."[1]

Learning tone syllables is a rather complicated process, akin to learning a foreign language. It is not a set of rules but rather a concept whose application grew out of each phrase of a song. I won't go into all the details but will simply highlight a few, since so many have asked me about the distinctive Waring way of singing. To begin with, many letters represent diphthongs—that is, they have more than one sound. The single letter *a* has two sounds (ay-ee); *i* (ah-ee); *o* (oh-oo), and *u* (ee-oo). Even single-syllable words contain more than one sound. The word *we* is (oo-ee); *our* (ah-oo-r). And as I mentioned, Fred was serious in his search for all of the beauty of all of the sounds of all of the syllables of all of the words.

Fred sang a phrase of a song as you would speak the words. Eventually he de-emphasized the articles *the* (thuh) and *a* (uh) (as in "in a song"), and often hooked the last part of a word onto the next one for clarity. For example, the folksong "Black Is the Color of My True Love's Hair" is printed:

Fred would look at what is being said—it's a love song. Then by speaking it—*the* would be shortened; *black* and *true love* would receive a warm, caressing tone. And, as in spoken French, the last syllable is hooked onto the next word. The phrase would sound more like this:[2]

Fred might linger ever-so-slightly on *true love,* but would make up the time in the next bar. That's why his music never got out of shape. He was always feeling an inner pulse. Very few laymen realize the blood, sweat, and tears it takes to achieve his subtle nuances.

Harsh consonants like *k* (cuh) and *d* (duh) are de-emphasized. An entire chorus singing a sibilant *s* set his teeth on edge. As a demonstration, Fred would ask a class of two hundred or more singers to sing a word like *history,* leaving out the *s* sound. After the entire group had mastered the challenge, they would suddenly clearly hear the *s*—sounded quietly by Fred alone—in the middle of the word. To counteract this disparity, Fred asked for less vocal energy in singing the sounds *s* and *sh.* The accepted written division of the word *history* is *his-tory,* which places undue emphasis on the letter *s.* So Fred transposed the sibilant *s* sound to the second syllable—*HI-story.* This emphasizes the vowel and diminishes the volume of the *s.* Mystery becomes MI-stir-ree.

The consonant sounds should be articulated *before* the beat and the vowel sounds should fall *on* the beat, that is, *my* is sung *m|mah-ee.* The *ah* falls precisely on the beat and the *m* precedes it. Thus "America" as printed

A - mer - i - ca, A - mer - i - ca,

becomes

Uhm - meh - ri - cuh Uhm meh - ri - cuh

and "Havah Nagilah" as printed

Ha - vah na - gi - lah,

becomes

Hav - vah n nah - gi - lah

This principle of emphasis of closing to an *m* or *v* before the next downbeat gives energy and makes the music flow.[3] Fred was doing it instinctively, but years before I met Fred, as a student in France, I had attended classes of the great musical pedagogue, Nadia Boulanger. She often stressed this means of making music come alive and move forward. This is not applied to all music, of course, but when this method is viable, music becomes exhilarating, instead of leaden and static.

Fred had his detractors, especially during his early years of experimentation when he overstressed the *m*'s and *n*'s. But the creators of the great songs of his day were not offended or upset by all the liberties Fred took; rather, they were enthralled with the results of his distinctive distillation of their words and music, and they never failed to call or write and tell him so. Fred put his unique stamp on choral singing because, as Robert Shaw noted: "Fred Waring not only was an exceptional 'natural' musician, he also had an intuitive sense of the emotional content and melodic contour of the American popular song. He said to me one time—quite free of egotism—that, 'It is difficult for me to make a mistake in the interpretation of a popular song.' That seems to me right."

As Gary Giddens said it succinctly about Louis Armstrong, "Interpreting a phrase in a way that makes it personal is the mark of a master."[4]

Fred often posed the question, "Why do we sing?" and then answered it, "We sing to make what we say more beautiful, more poignant, and more meaningful. It's that simple." With that as his creed, one can understand his constant emphasis on the equal value of the words and the melodic line. He must have won a few converts after the Boston music education conference, because he began to receive many letters from music educators asking if they could spend their Christmas holidays observing the Pennsylvanians at work, especially in rehearsals. Fred wasn't too sure about that idea, not keen on having one of his blowups witnessed by a group of music professors. However, figuring that not many would show up at the NBC studio, he agreed. More than three hundred and fifty choir directors from all over the country accepted the invitation, and he had to move the entire operation to the Astor Hotel ballroom. "We were swamped," Fred said. "We had to build up some clinics. I persuaded Irving Berlin and Richard Rodgers to come and talk, which pleased everyone."

From that session came the idea of a summer workshop. The Waring Music Workshop would teach teachers—an idea regarded with suspicion by Fred. But Ennis had it all planned. Fred would explain new concepts and ideas these people could get nowhere else. By working firsthand with stage and radio professionals, they would learn Fred's techniques of tone syllables, methods of rehearsing and preparing a program worked out under deadline pressure, program selections—what comes after what, and new and improved arrangements for all school levels.

The choir directors and others who attended the workshops were eager to get the published versions of the arrangements they had heard. And through the years, their avid interest and strong response provided the real boost that made Shawnee Press such a thriving enterprise.

The first six weeks of workshops started in the summer of 1947 at Shawnee, in addition to the six radio shows per week. Workshoppers came for one week and stayed busy day and night. They attended radio rehearsals in the morning and were taught in the afternoon by Lara Hoggard and Don Craig. Fred taught in the evenings. With two production staffs, full arranging staffs, the orchestra, glee club, soloists, and small vocal units, there was always someone to whom a workshopper could address a question. One exhausted attendant sat down one evening in the back after a hard day's work running here and there, music in hand, trying to look attentive, when Fred walked in. "He sat down beside me," Mickey Dugdale remembered, "and after a quiet greeting, reached over, took 'All the Things You Are' out of my hand, turned it right side up, and handed it back to me. Touché."

Over the years there were always a few academic diehards. Ennis took great delight in throwing Fred in among them and, as Fred said, "watching them knock my head off." The most derisive were the music director at St. Olaf College in Northfield, Minnesota, and John Finley Williamson at Westminster Choir College in Princeton, New Jersey. The others, however, paid no heed and came in droves, but Fred was not really happy teaching teachers. He found them too rigid, too inflexible. In the fifties after we were married, Fred would come home night after night, more exhausted than if he had conducted ten concerts. "How can they teach?" he'd complain. "They can't keep time, they can't read, they don't follow me."

When the youth workshops were started, Fred finally began to enjoy teaching. Two hundred youngsters would arrive for two weeks and perform a full concert at the end. The students were like sponges, able to absorb. By demanding every last bit of their time, energy, and concentration, Fred taught them what it takes to be a pro. He changed their lives, and in later years, his work with those eager young people was to be one of his greatest rewards. How does one judge the life of a person? Is it by his or her accomplishments or by the impact the person has on the lives of others? There is no doubt that Fred influenced innumerable lives—the many Pennsylvanians, the thousands of students who attended his music workshops, and those involved in his various enterprises.

In 1978, a reporter caught their intense dedication:

> Graduation night for 200 youngsters from a Fred Waring Music Workshop. One of the workshoppers is Cathie Matson, 18, of Kansas City, Missouri, a sophomore at Tulsa University. She is weeping.
>
> "Telling Mr. Waring goodbye is one of the most difficult things I've ever done," Cathie says.
>
> "But you've known him only two weeks."
>
> "Yes, but in that time he did more to motivate me than anyone else I've known. He makes you want to give 100 percent of yourself in anything you do."
>
> "For an old guy, he's got a lot of spirit, right?"
>
> "*Old* guy? Listen, at heart, Mr. Waring's as young as any 28-year-old I've ever known." [Fred was 78.][5]

· · ·

During the Chesterfield years, Fred developed a style of singing and presentation that was the precursor of the now well established show choir. Donna Dae and Patsy Garrett, the Swingerettes, sang arrangements with a fresh, youthful, lively, up-to-date feeling. A dusty, plain old song such as "Annie Laurie" or "Comin' through the Rye" in a Harry Simeone arrangement in Swingerette style was gay and not too difficult for a couple of energetic teenagers. This was fun music—the basic precept of all show choirs. That's why they're so popular today, more than fifty years after their inception.

In the forties, the workshoppers were housed at Shawnee, but later the school was transferred to Delaware Water Gap, three miles from Shawnee, when Fred bought the old summer resort, Castle Inn, in 1952. The U-shaped building served many needs. One wing was turned over to his large choral publishing company. The other wing contained a theater on the first floor and two stories of rooms above. In the early 1900s both Enrico Caruso and John Philip Sousa had performed in the theater. For Fred it was perfect as a setup for his summer workshops and later as a place for his Pennsylvanians to prepare for the road tours. The center of the U held an ample kitchen and the prettiest dining room in the Poconos.

One summer in 1955 Leo Arnaud was brought in to head an orchestra workshop. "At one concert, completely unrehearsed, I asked Fred to take over, and he did," Arnaud said. "He conducted an overture—one done at the Roxy twenty-five years before and never since. The score was on the stand but he never bothered to turn the pages. He was as comfortable doing it as he always was conducting anything."

A few summer sessions were spent on college campuses as far away as California, but no matter where he taught, Fred always insisted his Pennsylvanians be "in residence." During the last four summers of his life, the host was Penn State, his alma mater. I know much agonizing went on behind closed doors to justify a housing fund for Fred's group. The university didn't want to disappoint their famous alumnus, so once again he had his way. In all, Fred's summer workshops continued for thirty-seven years, ending with his death in 1984.

●   ●   ●

Fred was very fond of Fabien Sevitzky, conductor of the Indianapolis Symphony. They enjoyed each other's company, and when Fred was asked to perform with the orchestra, he quickly acquiesced. He was to conduct Debussy and Ravel, while Sevitsky would conduct a few Pennsylvanian arrangements.

Fred, the showman, utilizing Sevitzky's quick wit and heavy Russian accent, turned the evening into what the *Indianapolis News* announced as "a hilarious show. The audience was rolling in the aisles." At one point, I'm told, Fred grabbed Sevitzky's hand and the two gentlemen waltzed together in their white ties and tails while the orchestra played on. The critics were impressed with Fred's musicianship and his command of the "serious" numbers. It's too bad Fred didn't conduct more of the philharmonics around the country. He would have brought a breath of fresh air into an oftentimes static arena. His ability to make a few musicologists squirm only brought a gleam to his eye—keeping the music alive, fresh, and, above all, palatable was his raison d'être.

●   ●   ●

Whether Fred was conducting symphony orchestras or his own Pennsylvanians, practically everyone found him funny (most of the time). "Besides being a musician of no mean accomplishment," one newspaper observed, "Waring is a comedian, too. More than one face in the audience was wet with tears—the kind that results from uncontrollable laughter."[6]

The only one who disapproved of Fred's humor was his good friend John Royal: "Fred's not funny! When he puts his stick down on the stool and starts to clown with his people or the audience, he's a pain in the neck! Two people with great talent were disappointed comedians; one was Fred

Astaire and the other was Fred Waring." In the end, though, it was Fred's love affair with his "singing machine," as he called his Pennsylvanians later in life, that always drew him back to conducting choral music. Unlike symphony players whose eyes are glued most of the time on their music, his singers gave Fred their full attention, which was the only way he could "play" his "instrument."

. . .

In the forties, Fred's boyhood friend Poley McClintock contracted tuberculosis. Serious complications developed, and in 1947, after many, many months, he was released from the hospital and sent home to die. Even though the Pennsylvanians were performing five radio shows a week, Fred drove from Manhattan to Jackson Heights in Long Island many times each week, month after month, to see his friend, according to Poley's wife Yvette. But Poley became more and more depressed, because all the Pennsylvanians were moving to Shawnee for the summer.

One night Fred said, "You're going to be up there with us. You're going up in the station wagon, a hospital bed is coming with you, and you are going to have one of the cottages. Donna will come over every day with a menu, and you will order what you want." So instead of spending a lonely summer separated from his buddies, Poley joined the gang. His spirits were lifted by the daily visits of not only Fred but the Pennsylvanians, who took turns calling on him. For three more years Poley was bedridden. Fred continued to see him nearly every night. Slowly Poley recovered, returned to the show, and toured for thirty-eight more years. He was seventy-nine when he died.

As most Pennsylvanians have admitted (yes, they may have bitched about *Fred, the Adamant Boss*), no one ever complained about *Fred, the Loyal Friend and Concerned Father Figure.* Almost all have some private incident to relate.

Soprano Jane Wilson: "Fred called me into his office before I left for Ohio at the time of my father's death. 'Now remember,' he said. 'You must forget your own feelings. You are going to help your mother through this difficult time. This must be your first and foremost thought.'"

Sydney Johnson offered: "In New York one day, some family misfortune had fallen on one of the Pennsylvanians. Fred asked me to go talk to the person about it.

"'But I've already done that, Fred.'

"'Go again,' he said quietly, and I went."[7]

In 1942 a faithful trombonist was inducted into the Air Force. Marv Long recalled, "The Boss called me into the office the day I left, wished me good luck, promised me my job upon my return, and added a promise that I should not worry about my parents, should anything happen to me. He would take care of them."[8]

One talented singer had a breakdown and spent time in a mental institution: "When I got out still not feeling too well, I went on tour. The kindness of some of the veteran Pennsylvanians and the *will* of Fred for me to get out and *do it* finally worked. One day I called him from Phoenix and said, 'Guess what? The pain is gone.' He said, 'I know.'"[9]

In the fall of 1947, Fred was at the height of his musical activities. He aired his show one evening a week for General Electric with Bob Considine as commentator, as well as his regular five morning broadcasts a week and his nightly concerts. It was at this period that Evalyn Waring applied for legal separation. The papers were served on Fred during a broadcast.

• • •

Fred was nearing fifty. The year was 1948. For the last ten years he had aired a sparkling, fresh radio show five times a week in addition to his constant touring. He had expended an enormous amount of energy and was now showing signs of fatigue and confusion. Two of the Canadians who joined him in the twenties, Bill Townsend and Curly Cockerill, had both died, his personal life was empty, his children were in boarding schools, and then his mother died in August of 1948. He said to Jack Dolph, "Sometimes I wish I couldn't feel anything anymore."

Fred's mother, Jesse, had suffered a series of small strokes, and, Tot said, "the family doctor, who was very, very fond of her, told Dolly, 'Dolly, you are all to blame for your mother's health.' He said, 'Your father started it, then Bud went to war, came home, got married, was divorced, got married, was killed. Fred was married and divorced. You were married a year before you told your mother. Every one of you has contributed to it.' Jesse had a tragic life—I'll tell ya." But Fred admitted, "Mother was not always as ill as she thought. She got to like all the attention and pampering she received in the Phillipsburg hospital. Tom was far more devoted from the standpoint of being near her all the time, but every so often she would create a crisis to get us all there. One time we were gathered around her bed. She was almost comatose. She finally opened her eyes, stared up at a big flask of glycerine, her eyes followed the tube down to where it was attached to her arm—then she looks around the room, sees Doll, Tom,

Helen, and me and says, 'Well! This is better than a chicken dinner!' Just that spry: we laughed."

Fred had installed her in a room at Shawnee Inn that summer. Interestingly, my brother, who managed the inn at the Rancho Santa Fe in California, did likewise for my mother, who also had a weak heart. A resort hotel is a most pleasant atmosphere where friends and relatives can easily drop by and help pass the time, especially in the era of no TV. I, as a Pennsylvanian, found Fred's mother to be a rather formidable old lady. My piano playing pleased her, which put me on the plus side, but her bitterness dismayed me, and I vowed I would never be like that in my old age, no matter what life dished out.

The day after her death, the Pennsylvanians sang her favorite song, "You'll Never Walk Alone," on the morning broadcast, and then about sixty-five members were loaded into two buses and driven to Tyrone, some two hundred miles away. There, after more music and eulogies, Jesse was placed to rest among the Calderwoods and the Warings, finally at peace.

After his mother's death, Fred decided to take a six-week vacation in Mexico—his first in more than ten years. He left Jack Dolph and Fred Culley in charge of the show and took off, leaving instructions that no one was to bother him about anything. Dolph set up some thirty-five shows. All of Fred's professional friends rallied round—Paul Whiteman, Eddie Duchin, Rodgers and Hammerstein, Deems Taylor, Jimmy Stewart, Tex and Jinx McCrary—to name a few. Some morning shows were centered around featured Pennsylvanians who would perform music of their own choosing. A few boo-boos popped out, of course. On an evening show for General Electric, Deems Taylor became confused and announced "Carioca," a very fast and complicated arrangement. "We had no music but we played it," Fred Culley reported.

While Fred was in Mexico City, his main occupation was golf. He was particularly exhilarated by the colorful flower beds throughout the courses and wanted to do the same at Shawnee, but for years was hampered by the usual catch—lack of funds. Fred's other solace was the comic strips sent to him daily by his secretary. His addiction to them had started in the Victorian household before he could read.

His Mexican friends invited him to some elegant parties. The one scene that etched itself on his mind was a dazzling ballroom filled with decorations, lights, and beautifully gowned *señoras* who, as was revealed when they raised their arms to dance, had not shaved under them. Still, he was lonely and upset that no one wrote him except his secretary, Cora Ballard, who sent him the comics. He typically forgot that he had left "Do Not Disturb" orders.

In spite of himself, Fred returned rested, looking well, and feeling fit. The morning shows now had three sponsors: Johnson's Wax on Monday and Wednesday, American Meat Institute on Tuesday and Thursday, and the Minnesota Canning Company (famed for the Jolly Green Giant, which the Pennsylvanians were the first to Ho-Ho-Ho), plus the G.E. evening show.

The touring began again, but by December the cost of "night time" quality in the morning had become too expensive for NBC, and Fred, with only one evening show a week, was faced with the problem of finding more work. During all his radio years, according to Johnny O'Connor, "Waring was generous to a fault—but secretly. Thousands and thousands of dollars went to down-on-their-luck bandleaders, former managers, etc., plus weekly paychecks to a few Lamb members. Fred couldn't say no to people who needed a job—one reason he was always getting inadequate help."

As the music end of his operation expanded, Fred had less and less time to attend to the mass of day-to-day business details. The front office began to sneak in more conventional business procedures, and that is when Fred's frustration really began. According to his secretary Helen Helwig, everyone who came in wanted to change Fred's way of operating—first Jake Cohen, then Ed Lee (Fred's brother-in-law), then Admiral Dexter, etc. They were always trying to cut down on his expenses. Fred was taking an allowance each week, and Helen was putting it away for him. "If he wanted a new car or something and Ed and Jake would say no—that he couldn't afford it [this was in Fred's heyday, his peak of earning power]—then Fred would go into his account and buy the car anyway," Helen said. "Fred paid my salary for a year after I left."

Shawnee Inn golf pro Harry Obitz said, "We had a siege when Fred's whole business was so *tremendous* that everybody was running it. Ed Lee had assistants who had assistants. And one would say, 'Well, Fred wants this done.' If you were a half-wit, you might go ahead and do it, and then Fred would come in and say, 'Who the hell did this?' So then Fred would say, 'Unless you hear from me personally, don't do it.' You wouldn't do it, and Fred would blow his stack—'Nobody will do anything I want done!' And that's the way it went for five or six years. And then we got into a period when it was run strictly by what we called the New York executives."

Fred felt he had already proven his business acumen by his track record in the twenties when he singlehandedly steered his band to the top. Since worrying about money was his least favorite occupation, Fred gradually left the business end more and more in the hands of others. Their negative response to some of his ideas was tantamount to a red flag in front of *el toro*. Whether the scheme was feasible or not, Fred would often charge ahead just to prove them wrong. They gradually wore him down—being a farsighted man in a nearsighted world is enervating. They thought he was foolhardy, headstrong, and unrealistic. Fred felt they couldn't see the forest for the trees. They never seemed to grasp the overall picture of Fred's intent—keeping the Pennsylvanians intact, no matter the cost.

I didn't get involved in the financial picture until Fred's stroke in 1980. Not that he kept it from me—it's just that I really wasn't interested, and we seemed to be living comfortably. Anyway, I couldn't make head nor tail out of the financial reports I would see lying around and which, I'm told, he seldom reviewed either. Nevertheless, his business instincts were good. In the fifties and sixties, several properties in the Shawnee area were for sale, but his CPA's wouldn't allow him to buy them! Later, the Poconos became a bedroom community of New York and New Jersey. Had he bought in the fifties and sold in the eighties, he would have made a handsome profit. At the time, I remember him storming around saying, "If those accountants know so G.D. much, why aren't they rich?" Well, the sad truth of the matter is that many of them did get rich.

In the eighties, Fred once said to me, "If I'd cared more about money, I could have been very wealthy." For him, wealth was simply the means to do something better—to perfect artistic ideas.

"I always had a lot of ideas, but when they were put into other people's hands, they made up their own modus operandi," he said. "To carry out my ideas their way. I was a great organizer of new ideas and projects if I could be the boss."

Few ever mastered one of the secrets of *how* to deal with Fred. Bill Flick, a maintenance man at Shawnee Inn and an engineering genius, had the key. He never said *no* to any seemingly harebrained idea Fred produced. He never said yes, either, but he would study the idea carefully for possibilities. As Bill said, "Once you agreed, you'd better be well prepared with financing and know how." Fred didn't want a yes man who couldn't follow through.

Bill remembers an incident when he brought Fred an idea for an entertainment platform at the end of the Shawnee Inn dining room. Fred, the showman, became enthusiastic. But in the end, after much time and energy spent, they weren't able to pull it off. In frustration, Fred said, "God damn it, Bill, why'd you bring it up in the first place!"

Fred Waring, Donna Dae,
and the Les Paul Trio (Les
Paul, guitar; Jimmy Atkins,
guitar, and Ernie Nevins,
bass) on the Chesterfield
Pleasure Time Show, 1940.

Robert Shaw rehearsing the glee club at 1697 Broadway, New York City, 1940.

Left to right: Rudy Vallee, Fred Waring, Donna Dae, in New York City, 1941.

The Chesterfield radio show during the war years, 1944.

Waiting to broadcast on NBC, August, 1945. Front row, left to right: Leo Bernach, Ruth Cottingham, Louise Sechler, Joanne Wheatley, Eleanor Ohms, Jane Wilson.

Morley and Gearhart, 1945.

Fred snacking on a late-night apple, 1940s.

Fred Waring and the Pennsylvanians at the Roxy Theater, New York City, 1946.

Pennsylvanians relaxing at Shawnee, 1947. Left to right: Louise Sechler, Daisy Bernier, Dave Glissman, Jane and Jack Wilson, Joanne Wheatley, Gloria Nudell, and Bob Bolinger.

Fred Waring and Bing Crosby, taken while rehearsing the "Whiffenpoof Song," June, 1947.

Left to right: Oscar Hammerstein, Jane Wilson, Richard Rodgers, Jack Dolph. Rodgers & Hammerstein were guest hosting the Fred Waring Radio Show while Fred was away on March 29, 1948.

Fred Waring conducts a rehearsal of an NBC radio broadcast, New York, 1949.

Ike and Mamie Eisenhower with Fred Waring at the inaugural reception for Dr. Milton Eisenhower as president of Pennsylvania State University, October 5, 1950.

Shooting a CBS television in New York City, 1952. Pat McBride is the cameraman with Fred Waring.

Left to right: Harold Lloyd, Bill Lear, Moya Lear, and Fred Waring.

All the Pennsylvanians, traveling during their five television years (1950-54). The entire plane was taken over by the Pennsylvanians, crew and all.

Left to right: Ed Sullivan, Fred Waring, Harry Obitz (golf pro at Shawnee), Eddie Fisher, and Perry Como, at Shawnee, June, 1953. Fred annually gave a "Song Pluggers" outing, for members of the music profession; many of the same celebrities came each year.

Fred Waring and his Chrysler Imperial, at Shawnee, 1953.

Ronald Reagan and Fred Waring on "The General Electric Theatre," 1954. The Pennsylvanians were only on a couple of times each month. Reagan was the host for the show and credited as "Program Supervisor."

Center to right: Fred Waring, and Arnie Palmer, in 1954, when Arnie came to Shawnee, won this trophy, and met Winnie Walzer, his future wife.

At the Little White House, Augusta, Ga., for Christmas, 1954. Left to right: Fred Waring, Mamie and Ike Eisenhower, unidentified man, and Virginia Waring.

Ike at Shawnee-on-Delaware, on the Green Terrace with Fred, mid-1950s.

At the Alfred Vanderbilt home, Long Island, N.Y. Left to right: Tony Martin, Virginia Waring, and Fred Waring, 1956.

20

Television

IN APRIL, 1939, Fred and the Pennsylvanians were featured on the first televised program from the New York World's Fair. It was reported that, for the broadcast, the Pennsylvanians were arranged in four rows across a narrow studio, facing three cameras and a blackboard with the show routine out of camera shot. The scene was illuminated by a system of movable lights that was invented by Clarence Birdseye, who also originated the frozen-food process.

Fred's second appearance on television was in 1941 during the Chesterfield years. The NBC brass had asked him to come to one of their studios. He brought ten glee club men, Poley, a pianist, and instrumentalist Ray Sax. They were asked to do a fifteen-minute experimental show in front of one TV camera on a pedestal. Ray was to do a specialty stage act where he would tap dance, play a saxophone, and spin a lariat at the same time. That number included Fred. As Ray said, "Once I got the lariat going, Fred would jump in." The room was tiny, filled with so many hot lights that no one could breathe, and the performers were drenched in fifteen minutes. When it was over, the group assembled in the coffee shop to evaluate their experience. Ray remembered almost word for word what Fred said: "I *hate* it but I know I'll be drawn into it."

"In 1949 I was not ready for television," Fred said. "Throughout my career, I had always sat back and studied anything new before venturing into it. But Charles Wilson, president of General Electric, and Bob Pear, vice president, persuaded me to go on for G.E. We had a handshake, an agreement that if I would go into television, they would see to it that I would never regret it. They were a thousand percent in my corner. Even so, it was against my better judgment."

It would be the first weekly one-hour musical show on television. In this day of million-dollar extravaganzas all carefully pretaped and prerecorded, wide-angle camera lenses, zooms and booms, it's hard to imagine the tremendous effort it took to put on a spectacular every week—live on television. Live meant just that—one chance was all you got. The trade papers heralded it as "the costliest ever—a $25,000 production over 27 stations, the time alone to cost $8,000."[1]

Fred's thirty-year battle with stagehands, radio engineers, advertising agencies, and sponsors to uphold his artistic standards was multiplied twofold in the new medium. Television programs are produced by a team of people bearing such names as producer, director, audio engineer, floor manager, and company manager—usually with assistants to each—plus set designers, costume designers, and lighting engineers. It is easy to see that Fred's passion for changing things for the better and his need for flexibility in programming would be seriously hampered by these "production by committee" methods.

The General Electric shows to be aired each Sunday evening on CBS began April 1, 1949. General Electric is known as G.E., so naturally, Fred's theme song for that show was built around those two notes. During the first eight-day period, Fred put on six radio shows, two television shows, and a concert at Madison Square Garden. After that, it was just the television Sunday night performance. Fred considered it "a monster, voracious in its appetite for time, money and patience. The entertainer is at the mercy of the technician."

Fred said in 1960, "I think the youngsters who are brought in fresh out of college with *no* experience and are trusted with responsibilities where they have authority over veterans of show business is a horrible thing. It belittles the artist. The other glaring fault with television today is the shackles which bind it in the form of control by unions. They are always fighting for jurisdiction—the disputes and cross-purposes make it unbearable. A Perry Como can laugh it off because he's a great singer but not a creator of his own show—consequently it would never occur to him to resent any shackles. I have an organization. I'm not only the head of it but the producer, director thereof. Television is not made for that kind of thing. Jackie Gleason finally got himself knocked out by being exactly what I've been! He was producer, director, idea man, and master of ceremonies all rolled into one, and Milton Berle was another. I have always been committed to fine performances, but how can one do that without adequate rehearsal? Television was the most draining, enervating work I have ever done. It just put me up a wall. We were involved with twenty-three unions for one show. We had a budget which you didn't dare go over. The budget was $25,000 a week, and I paid all expenses."

The first General Electric television shows took place in the Ed Sullivan Theater, which was located in the same Hammerstein Building at Fifty-third and Broadway where Fred's offices and studios were located. Since there was an audience, all the performers, cameras, and technicians were crowded on a most inadequate stage. The show ran from 9 to 10 P.M. on Sunday, and was rehearsed five days. The glee club had to memorize everything because the show was live—no tape, no film. Having just finished five years of the Chesterfield radio show, which was all music, the Pennsylvanians were green on choreography. They were not accustomed to seeing themselves as the camera saw them. And they were camera shy.

Dancer Nadine Gae Schroeder originally joined the production staff to "help out," but wound up creating choreography, developing material, and dancing with a partner. Nadine would point out that someone made too many gestures or seemed stiff, or there was need for more makeup or a new hairdo, but a few people would fight it. However, the kinescope—precursor of tape—was the best teacher of all. When they saw themselves, there were quite a few instant reforms. (Jane Wilson had fought reducing her eyebrows prior to seeing a few kinescopes.) Mirrors were installed in the glee club room at 1697 Broadway, which enabled the Pennsylvanians to check their own gestures and steps as they rehearsed. Nadine could see some of the men dancing near the door and then ducking out—the two regulars easing out being two Pennsylvanian vets Gordon Goodman and Leonard Kranendonk.

"The first year was completely experimental," Ray Sax said. "We did impossible things that were devised for cameramen who in later years said, 'I don't know what I would ever have done without those first couple of years with Waring. I've never seen such imagination.'"

Then a new more flexible camera was brought in by CBS. As *Newsweek* reported, "A Hollywood-like device, the crane, allows the mounted cameraman to be swung from a height of 1 to 12 feet. This enormous traveling boom camera affectionately called 'The Monster' enabled technicians to come up with startling visual effects."[2]

"The stage door of the Ed Sullivan Theater was about one hundred fifty feet from our office entrance on Fifty-Third Street," Fred said. "I had designed the stage platforms which CBS built, but when we got there to rehearse, there were no music stands. CBS was supposed to supply them.

We couldn't rehearse without them. So I said, 'Boys, go get your music stands.'

"The union said, 'No, don't touch them. We'll do it.' Our music stands at the time cost maybe $10 apiece, and we needed twenty-five of them. So they sent the stagehands over, and they carried them a hundred and fifty feet.

"At the end of the rehearsal, I said, 'OK, boys, back to our studios and we'll rehearse. You better take your own music stands.'

"'Oh, don't touch them. We'll handle them!'

"So we waited for the stagehands to bring them to us, which they did. During the week, the stage manager inquired if we would like to continue using our music stands, to which I replied, 'Well, if CBS doesn't wish to supply any, it's all right with me. They are very convenient to the studio, so let's go ahead.' I said, 'We'll bring them with us.'

"They said, 'No, don't. We'll take care of it.'

"A half-hour before our rehearsal, I notice this large truck outside the street door, and two big guys get off and said, 'Where's the Fred Waring studio?' and I said, 'the tenth floor,' so they went up and got the music stands, brought them down and put them on the truck! Drove the truck a hundred and fifty feet to the stage door. The two guys unloaded them. The stagehands came out and carried the stands onto the stage.

"After ten weeks of this, I got a bill for fifteen hundred dollars for moving my two hundred and fifty dollars worth of music stands. About four unions were involved. CBS would not pay the bill. I had to pay it. As things went on, there were twenty-three unions in our one little show— even in those early days."

And then there was the rocking chair the stagehands gave Fred because he had to stand around so much while they were setting the lights or changing the film. "I needed a chair. I said, 'Gawd a'mighty, can't I have a chair?' So they bought me this very nice hickory rocking chair. They made a big thing over presenting it to me one day. 'That's great,' I thought. And they placed it where I wanted to sit. One day the damn chair wasn't exactly in the right place, so I grabbed it, and one of them said, '*Don't touch that chair!*'

"I said, 'What do you mean, "*don't* touch that chair?" It belongs to me, if you remember.'

"He said, 'That's all right. We have someone to move that chair for you.' That was the gimmick. They'd hired a chair mover, a union man, whose job was to keep putting that chair where it was comfortable for me, but I had to pay his salary."

An obstreperous cameraman knew Fred hated cigars. He sometimes smoked a cigar just to be cantankerous. He would then put it under the camera, a little place where it was attached to the tripod. It would still be smoking. Whenever he would do that, he would go moving in right toward Fred, and Fred would say, "There's a *cigar* in here somewhere," and the cameraman would play innocent.[3]

The first year was filled with many gaffes, mostly because everyone was squeezed onto such a small stage. Fred had devised a round revolving platform to hold the two pianos because in such cramped quarters the cameras could not move around us as we played. The device operated rather jerkily anyway, but it was really unnerving to have it stop unexpectedly in the middle of a piece and then lurch forward again—no Rolls-Royce, that one.

One night we were playing Chopin's "Minute Waltz" at a breakneck speed, and the platform stopped suddenly, nearly throwing us off our benches. It was stuck, so while we were playing madly away, the TV viewer saw nothing but a portion of each piano. Finally, as we neared the end, holding our breath, the turntable started up again with a momentous jolt that nearly finished us both off. I'm sure I sprouted a few gray hairs that night. Lumpy Brannum added, "The band was on moving platforms, too, and one night one of them went amok and chased Fred to the footlights, and I nearly fell off." For a South Seas number, Nadine and her partner Marc Breaux were allocated a narrow pie-shaped wedge. At the rear of this space, a G.E. refrigerator had been stored for a commercial. The two dancers got so carried away in their enthusiastic interpretation that they ended up in front of a refrigerator instead of a palm tree.

In 1949 when there was an audience and the Fred Waring show was the most expensive hour on network television, free tickets to it were scarce and very much in demand. General Electric allowed the Pennsylvanians seventy-five tickets each week, and it was one secretary's unenviable task to try and distribute them fairly among one hundred and twenty Pennsylvanians working on the show in front of and behind the cameras. At first only the secretary knew that number. To celebrate the first anniversary of the show, the G.E. company asked her for a list and was very surprised at how many people it took to put their show on the air. The G.E. people generously gave each of them an alarm clock. As Mickey Dugdale, the secretary, recalled, "Someone asked Fred if we could get discounts on G.E. products because of the show. His answer? 'Since I don't ever want G.E. to ask me to give them a discount for my product, I can't ask them to give us one.'"

"One year during the TV shows, Ronald Reagan delivered the sponsor's message," Harry Simeone said. "If somebody had asked me which of these men would be president of the United States, I would have said Fred Waring. Fred was the brightest man I ever met."

. . .

In 1950, the second year, the show was transferred to a theater on Ninth Avenue. All the seats were removed, leaving none for an audience, a devastating blow for Fred, the showman. The theaters during his radio days had always been filled with receptive auditeurs. Now he had no foil, just the cold, unresponsive eye of the camera.

Television production was so new at the time that directors with successful practical experience in the medium were almost nonexistent. Couple this with Fred, the perfectionist, who knew how he wanted his show to look on the air, and conflict was rampant. At least three CBS network directors came and tried, without success, to do the job to Fred's satisfaction. Fred finally sent his business manager to Chicago with a warning: "Don't come back unless you bring the director of the [Dave] Garroway-at-Large Show with you . . . that young Bob Banner!"

Banner was teaching at Northwestern University, married with one child, in 1950. "Television seemed so precarious that when Fred asked me to come to New York, I didn't feel I could take the job," he said. "Fred then asked me to meet him in Kansas City, where he had a concert. I arrived and found the city was having a water problem—a shortage and loss of suction. The next morning the newspapers headlined the cause.

"There was only one television station, and it carried whatever program came over. One Tuesday night during the Milton Berle Show, so many people watched it that when the first commercial came on and they all went to the bathroom at the same time, it made the city water supply lose suction. I thought, 'An industry that can change the bathroom habits of Kansas City will eventually change the bathroom habits of the nation.' I called Fred up and told him I would come to New York. When I asked Fred what my salary might be, he replied airily, 'Oh, don't worry about that. We'll discuss it when you get here.' And so I uprooted my family and moved to New York on a mere phone call. I sometimes wonder what made me do it.

"When I joined the Pennsylvanians, there was such a feeling of family camaraderie. I was suddenly thrust in the middle of it. Fred Waring had the Pennsylvanians as a working machine. Because they knew the music and how to perform the music, they were flexible and could do some of the things that we asked for. I watch our staff today [in the 1990s]. They shoot one number and then another—it's all edited and then put together. It may look and sound better today, but it doesn't have as much spirit.

"On the second day of the job three Pennsylvanians—Jane Wilson, Joanne Wheatley, and Bob Bolinger—said, 'We're taking you to dinner tonight. We have to prepare you for Fred.' I later thought, 'What a loving gesture.' I hardly knew them. "They said, 'There are certain things that are going to seem very harsh to you. Here's the way to ease into things, here's the way Fred works, here's what you'll find, here's what to expect.' They said, 'Lots of times Fred is the last one to rehearse the show, and because of that, he sometimes becomes very edgy at the rehearsal if he feels ill prepared and out of control. Television sometimes takes over— the cameras come between him and the glee club. That's when he might lash out at people, and if you understand, you won't feel as harshly toward him. Remember, he's a perfectionist. Be prepared. *It may be you!*'

"Sure enough, in the next rehearsal, Jane was singing 'Indian Love Call' with the glee club and orchestra. I remember the number because it was the first time *I got it.* I directed the camera to move in among the performers, and apparently some of the equipment obstructed Fred's view, and things got distracted in his mind. Jane was to sing two choruses—the first ending was soft, and the second ending big. Fred thought it was the second ending and gave a big downbeat, which no one expected, thus resulting in a pathetic sound.

"Fred turned and said, 'Bob! How can I do this show with these goddamned cameras . . .' and he went on and on. I remembered they had said I must be prepared with my answer. When he finished what had seemed like a ten-minute tirade, I quietly opened the talk back and I said, 'Pardon me, Fred, were you saying something to me? We had the microphones closed.' He simply walked out of the studio, and I never ever had another cross word with him."

Nadine Gae spoke of cameraman Pat McBride as being extraordinary and innovative. "In one number, *Capriccio espagnol,* this fabulous Pat was in top form," she said. "His camera was dancing in arcs of rhythm!"

Pat recalled how they all felt about each other: "Fred was involved in getting one of the singers to express her solo better—it was her debut— Fred was working on her. Unless you've been around doing the show— particularly when we would have technicians there just for the day, they would look and watch Fred the way he would talk and be out there trying to get her to perform, and they would say, 'Oh, what a son of a bitch he is!' Frank Davis was doing 'Old Man River.' Fred was really giving him the business—he was unmerciful. I was watching Davis, feeling at any moment he was either going to walk out or punch Fred in the nose. That night on the air, my skin tightened up and I was shaking because the rendition that Davis came out was . . . if there had been an audience, they would have torn down the house. All the people in the studio were hugging and praising Fred. We of the immediate family knew what it was all about. We knew there was no hatred there. He was doing it for them because he cared. We felt that he loved us for what we did, and that he knew we loved him. We all felt we had accomplished something when we left the show. Now you don't get that feeling. It was the fastest hour I ever experienced on television, and I've been doing it for over forty years."

In 1981 a cameraman from that same G.E. show came to our home in the California desert. He had searched Fred out thirty years later to tell him how much the training he received on those shows meant to him for the rest of his career. He held no animosity toward Fred. He, too, understood what Fred was striving for.

But those who didn't understand went out and sowed seeds of hatred that, I'm afraid, permeated the whole media industry. In 1972 our son Paul, who was Fred's manager for a few years, went with the publicity director to see a man in charge of special programming at NBC. He was friendly to Paul at first, but suddenly all of his old grudges against Fred came to the fore. He, too, had been a cameraman in those early days. He started ranting, "I saw that SOB destroy people. As long as I sit in this chair, he'll *never* be on NBC—guaranteed!"[4] My own observation is that those with low or shaky self-esteem were the ones who couldn't see what Fred was trying to accomplish.

Ray Sax recounted a week's routine: "Immediately after the show on Sunday night, we would have a meeting—on what we would or would not do again in future shows. Usually Fred was in on these meetings. The production staff, the director, and all the way down the line, would begin to kick around ideas. Let's say that we have gotten the nucleus of an idea some three or four weeks previously, and everyone had gone off to find out the costs, the yeses, and the nos. Almost 50 percent of the show then is decided on that night—Sunday night before we go home. We would know whether a guest will be on the show; what will be required of Mr. Waring and the writers, what equipment the cameramen will need, etc. In other words, the foundations were laid Sunday night, and this was within three hours of the finish of the final show."

Bob Banner added, "Fred would say, 'I like this number, I don't like that one,' not much else—just that you knew how to blend with his taste—what he was wanting to do on the show. He never came in and said, 'I think the camera should do this.' Musically we would start with an idea, and then Fred would work around it. It was a give and take. He had to get used to the television part of planning. Many times he would plan numbers because they were in contrasting keys or because of certain rhythms, and suddenly you had a visual relation—like a winter setting of snow. Fred absorbed things. His mind was like a sponge. He would worry with all of us about the show, and I could talk to him about anything—ways it could be done—even about various artists on the show, i.e., do you really think you should put that one first because it's a little too special? And he would listen. He wouldn't always agree, but he would always listen."

Mondays through Fridays the days were filled. The arrangers worked on music, costumes were ordered, guests were interviewed, scenery was planned, and meetings and rehearsals were constant. By Saturday at 9 A.M. the scenery was delivered to the studio. "It was set up and we would pace through it, and have a dry run without cameras; the costumes would come in at 6 P.M.," Ray Sax said. "Any changes that had to be made—costume, lights, etc.—were all done before 9 P.M. Saturday so that Sunday at 9 A.M. they were ready to go. Sunday morning we started with smaller groups. At first we were using tapes of the band to help the sound engineer, but the union made us stop—said it was depriving people of income. They allowed us to have a rehearsal pianist, which was not as good, obviously, because the sound engineer never knew quite what to expect until three hours before the show."

With rehearsals starting at 9 A.M. Sunday, it was one long grueling day until the show went on the air for CBS at 9 P.M. Last-minute adjustments of costumes, scenery, and music were constant. Ernie the hairdresser spent all day Sunday in the girls' dressing room and kept it in an uproar. He was *très gai,* had high and low moods, but *loved* his work. With a different theme each week, he could expend his creative talents endlessly on all the eight or nine girls. Fred spent all his time worrying about the most perfect rendition of the music he could muster out of everybody and spent *no* time at all on what he was supposed to say. As a result, he sometimes came across ill prepared or nervous, and certainly not funny at all. Later, when he got back out on the road, his audiences were amazed that he could be so witty onstage. Bob Banner, who had had theater experience, begged Fred to let him help prepare him, but Fred never took up the offer.

If Livingston and I were playing alone on the show, our call was usually for Sunday morning, since the small groups were staged then. I had absolutely no idea of the amount of work that went into producing that show. If ours was a number with the orchestra and glee club, we might have run through it with them at 1697 one afternoon during the week. If it was a big production number with dancers, we rehearsed on Saturday, too. Otherwise, all we had to do was appear Sunday at the designated time. In looking back at those Sunday evening programs, I am amazed at the classical compositions Livingston and I performed on a weekly commercial show—all short, of course—Bach, Brahms, Ravel, Stravinsky, Fauré, Rachmaninoff, Bartók, Milhaud, and so on—Fred catering to the small percentage out there hoping to hear something special. Still, it was almost impossible to perform anything reasonably well. On a four-minute production number, let's say, of our two-piano arrangement of the *Rosenkavalier* waltzes, we at our pianos would be in the middle with dancers swirling around, but Fred, the glee club, and the orchestra might be fifty feet away partially hidden by scenery . . . Fred is watching us like a hawk keeping singers and orchestra together and following us as we play faster and faster. There are no retakes, it's *live!*—we all finish together! Whew!!

"We were doing spectaculars every week with not enough money to do it," Ray Sax said. "We were without enough people. We should have had swing groups—a week on and a week off. Also, several Pennsylvanians were not photogenic or capable of moving well, but Fred guarded and maintained them to the detriment of the whole."

One advantage Fred had gained from the precise pacing of his fifteen radio years was the ability to finish a live television show on the exact last second of the hour. "Fred's uncanny way of timing was all in his head," cameraman Pat McBride said. "Many a time when the commercial went too long or, for some reason, somebody couldn't make a scene right away with changes of clothing or scenery—Fred would be able to hold up but also he would be able to relay to the control room, 'Don't worry, we'll be able to get off.' Banner would know that with that clock in his head, Fred would finish on the second. If directors today could time a show as Fred did, there would be no problems.

"He gave me an opportunity to use some film I had shot in Paris during the war for a scene around April in Paris. I sweated bullets trying to edit the damn thing. I had made it too short. I was so unhappy. I hadn't slept for two nights working on it. I thought, 'Oh God—this is all in vain—he'll throw it out in the garbage.' But no, Fred played the film and wove the glee club in and out and made it work. I couldn't believe it. The minute he said, 'Don't worry about it,' somehow I didn't. Only he could have done it."

Jack Dolph said, "Fred Waring and the Pennsylvanians were asked to participate in Jackie Gleason's show featuring Charlton Heston in a reading from *The Ten Commandments*. Jack Philbin was producing the show, and at dress rehearsal the show was two minutes too long. To the uninitiated, two minutes doesn't seem like much, but Philbin had to find those minutes, and nobody seemed willing to cut any of his material.

"He finally went to Fred Waring and said, 'What can I do?'

"Fred said, 'Forget it. I'll find it for you.'

"No material was cut, no routine changed. The show seemed exactly the same, yet it came off on the button. Fred Waring, the greatest clock-in-the-head timer in the business, simply picked up in tempo where he could do it appropriately. I have always been convinced he enjoys that sort of thing."

•   •   •

One year special guests were invited each Sunday to perform with Fred. Victor Borge played the piano, Rudy Vallee sang a duet. Raymond Massey, better known for his portrayal of Abraham Lincoln, danced a soft shoe routine, and one time Fred dedicated an entire show to Richard Rodgers. The famed songwriter came and played the piano while the Pennsylvanians gathered around him, singing short excerpts from his great repertoire. Livingston and I played a two-piano version of "With a Song in My Heart," and we felt highly complimented that he wanted our recording of it. I had been told he was a bit of a roué, but one would never have guessed it from his shy and almost diffident manner.

"When you look at variety shows today, I don't think there's been a show on in years that was as complicated as the Fred Waring show," Bob Banner said. "The glee club dancing and singing, Nadine creating and dancing something new every week, the musicians performing individually, in ensembles and all together. It really was a *large* revue. Most of the people spent seven days preparing for that. During the year, I just never thought of taking a day off. We simply tried to get ready for the next week's performance.

"One Christmas interim, I had a chance to get to my hometown in Texas for about a day and a half to see my father. With television being new, Dad still thought I was going to come back and go in with him in his insurance business. When I asked him if he saw the shows, he said, 'Yes, we see the shows, but are you getting along OK?' I said, 'Yes.'

"Then he said, 'Are you getting enough work?'

"I said, 'Why sure, Dad . . . I'm doing the Fred Waring show.'

"He said, 'Well, I *see* that, but are you getting any other jobs? That's only one hour.' He was so distressed that I worked only one hour a week. I was furious. I thought, 'How stupid can he be?' It was not until years later that I realized that it was a huge compliment. We tried to make the shows easy and fun.

"We were given three cameras. It didn't seem to occur to any of us to ask for more. I wish we had thought to have another camera system just watching the Fred Waring show being done. It would be a wonderful, wonderful record. I remember looking out on the floor so many times. There was Joanne Wheatley, the star of the number, and maybe two men or two dancers with her, but then you looked over there where most of the glee club was standing singing oohs and aahs, and what was happening? Ernie Adler would be combing their hair while they were singing, Fred would be conducting, and they would be oblivious to the fact that they were being groomed. One would have on a hoop skirt, another would be in a slip. Half the glee club would be dressed, the other half literally undressed. While they were singing, they would be slipping on jackets, tying scarfs, touching up their makeup. People were crawling under cameras, moving in with cue cards. They were so beautifully trained in the way they adapted to the confusion. It was a tremendous education for all of us—including me."

Prerecording wasn't the fad then, and Fred was adamant about spontaneous performance. "I want to be able to use and make my instrument perform as I want it to at that particular moment," he said. "In a studio at nine in the morning, I would have an entirely different interpretation as opposed to nine at night on the air."[5] And so the sound often was poor because half the group would be performing and dancing, and half would be singing. Unfortunately, there were no wide angle mikes in those days to pick up the sound of those moving about. The overhead mike picked up only what was beneath it.

Fred was much too progressive and demanding when it came to production. He wouldn't moderate his requests even when it was shown that it was technologically or almost physically impossible to do a sequence well.

Fred's old friend Danny Winkler went over to see a television rehearsal and told him, "I've never seen such confusion in my life. Look, Fred, I've seen some million dollar pictures where I thought confusion was rampant, like at Metro in their big shows, and other big major studios. But, my God! This is terrible!" Danny remembered that day well: "First of all, there wasn't room for half the equipment and the cast and the lighting and everything. And I asked Fred, 'Incidentally, how did you ever get into the directing of this?'

"Fred said, 'I'm not directing this. The director's up there in that little booth, and I want you to meet him.' So I went upstairs with him to meet the director. It was a young fella; I know he was under thirty years old. He couldn't possibly have had over ten or fifteen days' experience in show business.

"'Well', I told Fred, 'another thing I can't quite understand is these young cameramen.' Fred said, 'They're not cameramen, they're technicians.' On television, Fred became an employee instead of the employer. Instead of being a dictator, he was dictated to."

Fred often wasn't available to make spot decisions. "There were many times when the production couldn't wait for Fred to get off the golf course, so they would go ahead," Ray Sax said. "And it would build—every piece of costume or scenery or choice of number or length of time, and soon it became more of Mr. Producer's show rather than Fred Waring's."

Fred wasn't the only one who hid out on the golf course. In the sixties, Jackie Gleason used to spend five months of the year at Shawnee Inn. His producers and directors were getting ready to put together the Gleason show and had to see him. Jackie wouldn't go to New York, so they came to Shawnee. One time seventeen golf carts went out to meet him on the golf course where he was playing a round with Fred. They were forced to wait to talk to him between shots.

"If Fred thought the show was not his show, if we weren't following his memos to the letter for various reasons, he wouldn't appear for rehearsal; he would sulk," continued Ray Sax. "Consequently, it would cause him to work twice as hard, and many times our shows were complete flops. The only good things in them were the things he was sure of. He always made sure that there were certain Waring numbers in the show that nobody else could touch—lights couldn't hamper, sound couldn't destroy. Everybody stood still and were just photographed so that the music had a chance to be heard."

In spite of all this, the General Electric show was considered one of the best on the air and won several awards as well as complimentary press reviews. But the financial burden was overwhelming: unregulated waste in scenery and costumes, demanding union rules and salaries. In order to survive, Fred had to tour whenever possible.

In today's media market, the bottom line controls creativity—whether it's books, movies, or TV. Those in control of the money, for the most part, dictate content. But in the early fifties, "CBS and General Electric didn't get involved in any production number," Bob Banner said. "It was a general overall policy. They would talk with Fred and occasionally with me. Whatever they did was about one-tenth of what is done these days. Today network control is *absolute.* If they don't want a number on, it's just cut. It's network control, not the sponsor. The network today is total—casting, script, and concept of a show as it gets on the air—and they doodle and fedoodle every single week on every single show. It drove us so crazy that we now do more syndicated shows [bypassing the networks] because we have more freedom."

We the performers heard from the brass only if we strayed from our goody two-shoes, apple-pie American image, for example, a girl sitting on a piano singing a torch song with too much of her leg showing. They were forever putting tulle in the front of my concert dresses to hide any possibility of a cleavage from the overhead boom camera. (MTV, take note!)

· · ·

In the early fifties, Bill Lear won the Collier Trophy, which is given "in recognition for greatest achievement in aeronautics or astronautics in America." The trophy people called Fred and said, "Would you like to have Mr. Lear receive the trophy on your program?"

As Fred related to me much later: "'I sure would,' and I arranged it. I didn't speak to G.E. about it and they were sore as hell."

"Why?" I asked.

Fred: "Because they make a robot pilot too, you know."

"You didn't realize it or you didn't care?"

Fred: "I never even thought about it. They didn't win the award. Bill did."

One summer Fred invited all the G.E. executives for an outing at Shawnee Inn. All the Pennsylvanians were included, too, of course. The party was on the "green terrace," a grassy area overlooking the golf course, covered with tables and colorful umbrellas. Fred had seated the VIPs at different tables, introduced us to them, and then asked each Pennsylvanian to move around and become acquainted.

As soon as I sat down at the table of Charles Wilson, president of G.E., he asked to see my hands. It seems that his wife was a pianist and that they had had discussions about how long my fingers were (fairly long). Incidentally, long fingers are not always the criterion for great pianistic ability—it's the flexibility, breadth, and strength of the hands that count.

Some splendid pianists have had rather stubby fingers. One in particular was Josef Hofmann, whose hands were so small he had a special piano with keys slightly narrower so he could play octaves with more ease.

· · ·

Fred had known Irving Berlin for many years. "In the early fifties during our television years, Berlin called and said he would like me to hear a new score he'd written for a show called *Miss Liberty*," Fred remembered. "I said, 'I'm so tied up with rehearsals, I don't know when I can get to your apartment.' He said, 'No problem. I'll come to your studio.' He came on a Saturday and brought his own piano to 1697, a special piano with which he could change a key by shifting a gear and pulling a lever."

Admiral Dexter said, "There was Mr. Berlin sitting at this little upright piano, singing in his wonderful croaky voice the entire score of *Miss Liberty*. After each song he'd turn and say, 'Fred?! How did you like it?' Fred would sort of nod his head but didn't say much. Here was this magnificent and successful man doing a song-plugging job."

At the end, as an afterthought, Berlin said almost apologetically to Fred, "There's one other song to which I did not write the words. In the search for inspiration for *Miss Liberty*, I went to see the statue and I read the beautiful inscription. It is a poem by Emma Lazarus which was Miss Liberty's greetings for those who come from other nations to find peace and comfort and freedom here. I wrote a melody in fifteen minutes and called it, 'Give Me Your Tired, Your Poor.'"

"Irving, it's magnificent!" Fred said after hearing it.

Berlin said, "It's yours. You publish it and record it"—which they did.

Arturo Toscanini also had evidently become a Fred Waring fan and watched the Sunday night television shows. One day a call came into the office that Toscanini wished to meet Fred and hoped it was possible for him to come to NBC following his concert. Fred went over to the NBC studios, where one of the public relations men met him and took him up to Toscanini's quarters.

"There was a line—there must have been two or three hundred people—which is customary following a symphony concert—they all congregate and pay respect to the conductor," Fred said. "Toscanini was there. I recall very vividly he had taken his shirt off and was greeting everyone. He was soaking wet. The man took me directly into the small reception room where the maestro just happened to see me, and he dropped the hand of whomever he was greeting and, with a very loud flourish, said, 'Ahhh . . . my favorite director,' or something like that, and came over and threw his arms around me and kissed me on each cheek. It was a little bit embarrassing to me—number one, that he would recognize me, and, number two, that he would break off with this line of people who were devoted to him and, number three, that he kissed me and was so—of course, these gestures I understand—I kind of felt guilty—and then he began telling me how very, very greatly he admired my work and the work of my organization. He did make most of it personally—he made no attempt to withhold his enthusiasm, and included everybody in the room when he complimented me on phrasing and good taste and richness."

"Soon after, the office got a call from Eugene Ormandy in Philadelphia," Admiral Dexter said. "He said, 'I would very much like to have Mr. Waring come to Philadelphia to lead my orchestra. I have heard from my friend, Mr. Toscanini, that Fred is a wonderful conductor.'"

During those years Fred's longtime friend John Royal was vice president in charge of programming at NBC and was totally involved with all of Toscanini's radio programs, which emanated from Studio 8H in the NBC building in New York. At that time, Toscanini (whom Royal always referred to as Toscuhninny) was held in high esteem by everyone, and he was as relentless in his demands for perfection as Fred was. Like Fred, Toscanini could never fire anyone either, although he could be a tyrant in rehearsals.

Don Gillis, a composer and educator, had worked intimately with Toscanini in the production of his regular symphony broadcasts: "I remember Maestro asking me several times if I had heard Fred Waring's broadcasts. He was particularly struck by the beautiful sound of the orchestra, the orchestration of music like the lovely ballads of Jerome Kern. But he was always amazed at the diction of the choir—'Every word and every syllable can be understood!' He was a champion of perfection, as you know, so his feeling toward the Waring music was that it was the best. Many times in the dressing room he would comment on it."

But the ax was soon to fall on Fred Waring and the Pennsylvanians. "When Bob Pear and Charles Wilson and I had our handshake agreements, they did not reckon that Bob would die and Charles, the president of G.E., would be retired," Fred said about the drastic changes in 1954. "And when Mr. [Ralph J.] Cordiner became president, there was absolutely no warmth whatsoever. His team went in and eased us out in a very, very uncouth manner. I shall never forget it . . . *never get over it.*

"Mr. Cordiner had been my guest at Shawnee a number of times. He had tried to buy the Waring Blendor setup, when he was with Schick Razor. I refused to sell it to him, and I wouldn't be surprised at all if that had something to do with it. Mr. Cordiner ignored me in Florida one time when I was only a mile from him for a vacation. Gene Sarazen called him and said, 'Fred is here. Would you like to say hello, or can we have lunch together?' And he not only didn't want to say hello, but he wouldn't even have lunch with me, and that, to me, was pulling the curtain right in my face.

"Also, we were so friendly with all the sponsors—G.E., Ford, Old Gold, etc.—that we again built up resentments in agencies, and they just left no stone unturned to get rid of me."

Walter Socolow, Fred's New York lawyer: "Fred had integrity. He never mixed social and business life. He never cultivated the friendships of the network and sponsor representatives. He was arrogant in those days. Music is tough to perform on TV, and he was no Mr. Nice Guy. He gave producers and agency representatives as little comfort as possible—and they carried a grudge."

Sammy Gallu: "Later, Kraft was interested in Waring, but ABC was against it—the president of the network didn't like Fred. I had an idea for a show for Fred. All the chairmen of the boards of the companies wanted him, but not the agencies. No way! When it comes to agencies and networks, you run into a hidden wall. Fred didn't play the game. He was not represented by MCA or William Morris. He had Johnny O'Connor and Fred Waring. That was it. And you know those goddamned agents are pretty vicious. If they can't represent you, they'll misrepresent you. It exists today. I hear it all the time."

Except for a couple of shows in the sixties, Fred was never invited back on network television. The young people of America didn't know who he was when he died in 1984, except those who had attended his summer workshops or his yearly concerts throughout the United States. There was nothing on the air quite like the Waring sound. Fred never said anything, but I know it made him sad to be so completely ignored by the media.

21

The Anti-Semitic Rumor

FOR fifty years an anti-Semitic rumor dogged Fred. It was subtle, persistent, painful, and completely unfounded. Anyone who has been the victim of a malicious accusation knows how impossible it is to reinstate the truth. The innuendo metastasizes like a malignant tumor and can never be put to rest. Throughout this period, Fred was deeply troubled by the rumor's persistence.

Walter Socolow, a devout Orthodox Jew, saw Fred's dilemma and wrote to him in 1983: "As your friend and lawyer since 1934, I personally have been intimately aware of your professional and personal life for fifty years. I know that you and your brother Tom grew up as children in Tyrone, Pennsylvania, with friends consisting of Jewish children as well as Catholic and Protestant Christians, and that your banker father actually loaned money to a black man, without collateral, to enable him to open a barbershop. I am convinced that you were not reared in a home in which anti-Semitism and other prejudices were taught you. In fact, my knowledge of you confirms that you were taught to attain high standards and that your entire professional life in music was driven by your motivation for perfection.

"My investigation reveals that the anti-Semitic accusation arose more than forty years ago from Abe Lyman, a bandleader who vainly sought to make a profit from your booking in the Club Forrest in New Orleans [in 1931]. Lyman exploited this incident by blaming his frustration on you personally and referring to you as an anti-Semite wherever he found the opportunity to do so. I also recall Lyman's attitude when he was not included with you, Paul Whiteman, Guy Lombardo and Jack Benny in our joint music publishing enterprise known as Words and Music, Inc. Obviously, Lyman continued to believe that you caused his displeasure only because he was Jewish, and he disregarded the merits of the business decision."[1]

Fred, by the early thirties, had been touring for nearly fifteen years, and never before had such slur been cast at him. "In 1922 on our first visit to Los Angeles when Sid Grauman arranged for me to meet all the important movie people, two or three of them joined me in my love of golf in organizing what we called the Divot Diggers, a group of people in the theater and movie world who loved to play golf but had no particular club affiliations," he said. "We had a group of twenty-eight people including Sam Goldwyn, Al Jolson, Jack Warner, Al Kaufman, and many others who met every Sunday at a different course (which opened its tees and greens for us) and had a wonderful day. The group went along for several years and we enjoyed great camaraderie and friendship. Al Kaufman was the son-in-law of Adolph Zukor and was one of the best friends I had at the time.

"During my tenure of office as Shepherd of the Lambs club (1939–41), George Jessel had applied for membership and was turned down by the admissions committee as being not of the right character for the club.

"Later, the board agreed to reconsider George Jessel's application. He was admitted but it turned out to be a big mistake. Within a few months he had run up a bill of $2,500, which he refused to pay, and he had offended nearly everyone with his rude behavior and remarks. So, at a subsequent meeting of the board of directors, a motion by Sam Forrest, seconded by Hiram Bloomingdale, carried unanimously that Mr. Jessel be dropped from membership. *I, as Shepherd, did not vote.*

"Several weeks after the incident, I was in my barbershop, Seventh Avenue and Fifty-second Street, where I had been a customer for many years. The barber had shaved me and a hot towel was covering my face as George burst into the shop and demanded his barber, who was also mine. The manager of the shop apologetically said, 'Very sorry, Mr. Jessel, but your barber is still busy with a customer.' Jessel said, 'Who?' The manager replied, 'Mr. Fred Waring.'

"Jessel, in a very loud, ugly tone, said, 'You mean to tell me I have to wait for that Jew-hating son-of-a-bitch?'

"Everybody in the shop was shocked by his uncalled-for remarks. He strode out of the shop and swore he would never come back."

Fred's long-term Jewish business associates also decried the vicious rumor. Danny Winkler, a close friend from 1925 to his death in late 1960, said, "From time to time I'll always find that one guy would pop up and say, 'I can't understand you and your friendship for Waring when you *know* he doesn't like the Jews.' I would always say, 'You show me *one act* of his that proves your contention that he's anti-Semitic, and I'll apologize to you because you *can't.*'"

Jake Cohen, who joined the Pennsylvanians as CPA in 1938 and stayed forty years, said, "From time to time throughout the many years of my association with Fred Waring, the 'Jewish' issue has been thrust at me; sometimes a mere raised eyebrow of a friend on learning that I worked for the Waring organization; at other times a blunt accusation of anti-Semitism. I cannot point a critical finger at a single incident that should cause Fred Waring to be thus labeled or libeled. He's had Jewish performers, Jewish agents, Jewish lawyers, and Jewish accountants. This gossip is persistent, unfair, and unfounded."

Murray Luth, Waring Company manager from 1953 until his death in 1974, said, "In the forties I was one of about six hundred and fifty song pluggers [predominantly Jewish] who knew Fred and loved him because he was so considerate in many, many ways. Fred always tried to concern himself with any song plugger in distress or with any problem." Each year while he owned the Inn, Fred chartered several buses to bring the song pluggers to Shawnee for a day of golf, swimming, tennis, boating, cards, eating, and drinking. It was his party for them and he loved doing it. Fred also treasured a beautiful Haggadah emblazoned in rich jewel colors made especially for him in appreciation for the years he had produced shows at Madison Square Garden in New York for the American Israel Cultural Foundation.

Fred Culley (a Gentile), when quizzed by Jack Dolph: "Oh, well, I tell you, Jack, Fred has bawled out everybody, not just Jews, for Christ's sake! He's anti-you, anti-me. He's been anti-everybody, *if they are performing sloppily.* From the thirties on, I hired almost all the musicians, and never once has Fred asked me a man's religion. All he asked was, 'Can he do the job?'"

The smoldering coals of the anti-Semitic rumor were fanned when Fred bought Shawnee Inn. It had been built in 1909 by the Worthington family as a rich man's private club. Jack Dolph said Fred was concerned about its reputation, and he went to Philadelphia to a rabbi and said, "I don't want to run a Jewish hotel and I don't want to be anti-Semitic. How do I work it?"

The rabbi said, "I think you should choose your guests as you see them and not deny admission to anyone because of his name. If you choose everyone alike on the same basis, you will find enough Irish that you don't want and enough Jewish that you don't want, so that you will, in the end, accept the same number of Jewish applicants as there are proportion of Jewish people in the United States." Actually, Fred's criterion for acceptance was anyone who dressed and acted like a lady or gentleman.

During the sixties, the rumor would flare up and affect Fred's concert engagements. One was a prestigious event at the Brooklyn Academy of Music and another at the Philadelphia Academy of Music. Both had to be canceled because of telephone campaigns to discredit Fred. He was bewildered and hurt.

As late as 1980 I encountered this maliciousness myself. I was in the small appliance department of Bloomingdale's in New York. When I handed my credit card to the pleasant, middle-aged saleswoman, her face lit up and she engaged in the usual small talk of fans. Suddenly her expression changed. She glanced around to see if anyone was near and then asked me if I knew one particular highly visible Jewish comedian. I said, "Yes, I certainly know of him but I have never met him."

She hesitated and then said, "He was in here not long ago, and when he saw the Waring Blendor and other Waring appliances, he pointed to them and said in a rather loud manner, 'Well! I'll *never* buy any of those products! Fred Waring is a Jew hater—he has never hired any Jews in his organization, and he . . .'"

The clerk couldn't remember his exact words after that, but to tell the truth, it made me feel a little sick. I merely said, "It's obvious he doesn't know Mr. Waring very well." The clerk looked as sad as I felt.

Stephen Birmingham stated in his book, *The Rest of Us,* that the boardrooms of the three major networks became largely populated by descendants of Russian Jews.[2] Sammy Gallu said, "I have run into the Jewish thing myself a number of times and I go to Fred's defense. In the TV business it's a very closed business. You've got three networks—only three networks. I've always said they've got the greatest monopoly that man created. What business do you know where you go to three people and they turn you down and you're out of business? Does that mean your product is bad? Hardly!"

A few years ago the great investigative reporter, author, and attorney Sidney Zion became interested in the anti-Semitic slur on Fred and wanted to write an article about it for the Sunday magazine section of the *New York Times.* The *Times* refused to print it. Zion then wrote the following "To Whom It May Concern" letter:

Sidney Zion
Attorney At Law

Fred Waring has been a virtual synonym for anti-Semitism for many years. As a Jew, I grew up "knowing" this, and since it had all the power of a received opinion, it never occurred to me to question its validity. One night somebody asked my wife what she thought of Fred Waring and she said, "Oh, he's anti-Semitic." I asked her how she knew and she said she had always heard it—and she comes from a small town in upstate New York with a zero Jewish population.

A couple of years ago, I met Mr. Waring. He surprised me by being very anxious to discuss this subject. It turns out that it's been plaguing him all these years, causing him great mental anguish. I found it rather endearing that he wanted to clear his name. So I began to challenge those who said he was anti-Semitic and in every case found they had nothing to support the charge, it was hearsay on hearsay ad infinitum. This discovery, plus the many hours I spent with Fred Waring, convinced me that the label pinned on him is false.

I hope there is some way to put this old slander away for all time.

Very truly yours,
Sidney Zion[3]

22

Life with Fred

DURING the late forties and early fifties, I was having trouble keeping a balance in my marriage with Livingston. On the surface we looked to be the ideal couple, and in some ways we were. I was crazy about Livingston. He had many of the same qualities as Fred: brilliant, handsome, affectionate, sensitive, possessed of a great sense of humor, and a fabulous musician. Nadia Boulanger, the great French pedagogue, thought so highly of Liv's creative talent that she gave him a house to live in just outside of Paris.

But he was brought up by a cruel and demanding mother. By today's standards this exceptionally gifted and sensitive human being would be considered an abused child. He in turn could wound me with words, and I, coming from a gentle, soft-spoken family, had no verbal weapons. I found it more and more difficult to cope with his sudden moods and withdrawals, and so in 1953 I decided for our child's sanity and my own that I would have to leave. I told no one of my decision except my own family.

Fred, with his strong ESP, must have known. I had no idea that he had already made up his mind that I was to be Wife Number Three. He had done nothing to plant such a thought in my head. I knew only that he liked me, as he did several of the other young women. He told me years later of an incident that occurred several months before I actually left Livingston. He named the date, which was engraved on my mind because it was a turning point for me as well.

It seems that Fred was asleep in his newly renovated Gatehouse when he awakened at 3 A.M. and felt impelled to put on a coat over his pajamas, get in his car, and drive up the road where Livingston and I lived in a small farmhouse. The house up on a hill was dark except for the third floor—an attic used sometimes for quiet sleeping space.

Over the years Livingston had used this attic as a refuge, and sometimes would withdraw from us—me, our little boy Paul, and his Nana—and remain up there for several days when he was not able to cope with the world. Liv's inexplicable moods were getting more and more difficult for me to deal with, especially now that Paul was becoming anxious and worried. I adored Livingston, but that night at 3 A.M. as I stood before him, I made an unspoken sudden decision that in order to survive I must leave him and return to California. It was that visceral agonizing thought process that traveled the unknown airwaves and wakened F.W.

I did not tell Livingston or anyone else of my decision to leave him because of the extra emotional burden in fulfilling our concert obligations. But just after our final appearance, which happened to be in the Hollywood Bowl with Arthur Fiedler and the Los Angeles Symphony, I began to make plans. It was the summer period of rest when I usually took Paul and spent time in California with my family. Livingston always remained in Pennsylvania. This time I told him I was leaving permanently. He obviously didn't take it seriously, because when I left, he was quite nonchalant, as though it were for a few weeks. When it sank in months later, he fell apart.

I stayed with my sister Helen, who was living near San Francisco. We talked over and deliberated everything, and I finally, reluctantly, decided to get a divorce. The whole process was terribly painful and sorrowful. It took six weeks in Nevada to obtain a divorce in those days. Helen and her two little boys arrived from the Bay Area to stay with Paul and me at a lodge on Lake Tahoe.

When Fred heard I was in Nevada, he called and asked to drop by and see us. I said, "Certainly, why not?" But when he came and revealed his desire to marry me, I was stunned. Such a thought had never occurred to me. The decision of divorce was extremely troubling to me. I was suffused with conflicting emotions. I needed time to grieve and to remain in neutral before shifting gears in a new direction. But Fred stayed true to form—he was an impetuous man and he was fearful I would weaken and return to Livingston. In retrospect, he was probably right. Liv and I were so bonded by our music and years together that it was difficult to fathom a radically different lifestyle. My brain and heart were at odds. My decision to leave surprised everyone, and some assumed Fred had a hand in it, but he absolutely did not. Leaving Livingston made my heart ache. Everybody loves him, but no one can live with him—not even his second wife.

Jack Dolph wrote in 1960, "In the early summer of 1954, I had spent some time with Fred and found him restless and seriously concerned with both his personal problems and the future of the Pennsylvanians. Evalyn's long-deferred divorce action had come to the attention of the public, and was causing him some embarrassment. As always with such actions, he had been the target of criticism—often spiteful—and of careless gossip among his neighbors in the Shawnee area. He was unhappy about the effect on his children of the talk and, it seemed to me, his attitude was uncharacteristically subdued. I would have expected him to be defensive and a bit defiant. It would be several weeks before I would learn why."

Jack went on, "It was later in the summer that I was suddenly informed of the reason for Fred Waring's earlier subdued and thoughtful manner. We had been talking in the office one afternoon when nobody else was around. The conversation had been casual, largely about business matters, then, without preface, Fred said that he had fallen in love and, when his divorce was final, would marry. While I was recovering from the unexpected news and wondering why I had not heard something or other to suggest it, he said, 'You know who it is, of course.'

"When I told him I hadn't the slightest idea, he got up and walked from the office out into the hall where photographs of The Pennsylvanians traditionally covered the walls. He took my arm and walked me along the hall until we had reached a picture of Morley and Gearhart at the piano. He turned me squarely to it and stopped. He said nothing.

"I had heard nothing of any trouble between the Gearharts—no gossip which might have suggested that Fred had been paying special attention to Virginia Morley. Given a dozen guesses, I could not have arrived at her. My admiration and affection for both Virginia and Livingston would not let me say that I thought it was just fine.

"What I did say was, 'You're not serious!'

"'I have never been more serious in my life.'

"We walked slowly back into the office, Fred still holding my arm. When we sat down again, he talked. I have never known him to be more earnest—or more gentle and without defenses."

When Fred asked me to marry him, I wasn't sure that I wanted to. I was fascinated and intrigued by him but wary of that terrible reputation of his unstable relationship with women. We talked at length about it. As

I look back over his history, no wife stood a chance in those hectic days of the twenties, thirties, and forties. Now, however, because he was fifty-four and seemed to be getting his priorities in focus and I knew he respected and admired me, I felt our union stood a good chance.

I heard later that mine was the only autograph that he ever wanted, and that, once married to me, "Fred seemed like a man who had arrived in a safe harbor out of a storm."[1] Actually, at the time I didn't sit and analyze it in a cold and calculating way. I live and act, in large part, intuitively, and my gut feeling was that it would work mainly because I understood him better than anyone else did.

Fred's divorce became final after eight years of separation, and, on December 2, 1954, we were wed in a Methodist church in Indianapolis. It was the Pennsylvanians' day off during the fall tour. Not knowing Fred's marital history at the time, I didn't realize that our marriage fit his pattern of getting married between shows. Why didn't he wait for the Christmas break? Simple—his beloved Pennsylvanians would not have been present.

The wedding party in Indianapolis included four friends who made all the arrangements; Fred's brother and sister, Tom and Helen; my sister Helen; and all the Pennsylvanians. The lavishness of the ceremony impressed Fred, who remembered the Spartan atmosphere in the Tyrone Methodist Church. Afterwards, we congregated at a country club for food, drink, and gaiety. Tom was in rare form. He kept us laughing. On the next day, the tour resumed.

We celebrated our delayed honeymoon a couple of weeks later at the country club of Augusta, Georgia. At that time the "Little White House" was on the grounds of the famous club. Ike and Mamie were in residence for the festive Christmas and New Year's holidays and warmly included us in some of their social activities. Mamie had planned a special New Year's Eve dinner at the club and had a run-in with a powerful club member of the old school whom I likened to a tsar or small-time Hitler—in retrospect I realize that he must have been a misogynist, wishing it were like a British club where women were not allowed. Anyway, Mamie merely wanted to decorate the long table with some charming fat cupids, and this man, who seemed to intimidate everyone, said "no." I'm happy to say Mamie won, and I do believe this man's stranglehold lessened after that.

Mamie possessed a most endearing trait of trying to put everyone at ease. She would sit and chat with me about various homey topics. I had said one day that Fred had taken me out on the golf course for some beginning pointers. Mamie said, "Oh, no! It doesn't work. Ike tried to teach me how to play bridge, and I cried and cried."

"I certainly had my doubts about this new marriage—Fred even at fifty-four still continued to be explosive, dynamic, and rushing headlong in his planning and living," Jack Dolph said. "Virginia would have had few illusions about this man with whom she had worked for many years. The tendency of most of us who were fond of them both was to shrug it off, trying to avoid a sneaking suspicion that she had thrown herself to the lion.

"Then, during the summer, a story came to me that delighted my heart and caused me to take another look at this gentle and normally rather shy woman. Fred, Virginia, and a friend were having lunch. Before the food was served, Fred had some disagreement with the waiter—he is a bit fussy about his food and such an encounter is not unusual. He is not one to call attention to the fact that he is famous or to be unusually demanding. But, in an argument with a waiter, as in all things, he is persistent. The friend reports that Virginia, after having remained completely quiet during as much of the conversation as she wished to hear, smiled sweetly, picked up her bag, announced that it had been most pleasant to be able to spend a few moments with them, waved goodbye and went across the street and had her lunch! I decided then that, if anybody could do it, Virginia could."

Even though we were married a little ahead of my time schedule, it was Fred's determination to make me happy that brought it all into focus. I grew to love him profoundly and deeply, and I must have made him happy because he told me so hundreds of times a year.

Since I was one-half of a two-piano team, the dissolution of my first marriage meant the end of my piano career, but I did not mind at all. I really wasn't physically strong enough to endure those arduous tours. I think it was Jascha Heifetz who said, "To be a performing artist, you need the constitution of an ox and the digestion of a peasant," and unfortunately I had neither. I was content to sit back and bask in the warmth that now surrounded me. Tom came over often for his favorite breakfast—Elsie's chipped beef on toast. He evidently had been observing me closely and said, "I certainly hope you don't start playing second fiddle to '*himself*,'" meaning, of course, he didn't want me to start giving in to Fred as everyone else did. Mainly with Fred, it was knowing how and when to deal with him. Most of the things I did were intuitive. From the first—even when Livingston and I worked for him—I knew if we had a problem, that only one of us should talk with him alone—otherwise he would be "on" with two of us there.

One strong point Fred and I had in common—we were both optimists. We never considered negative options—just plowed ahead, assuming that we would manage and succeed. It irritated Fred to have some idea of his rejected before it was seen or heard or made or whatever. He wasn't foolhardy in that area—all he wanted was a chance. At first when he threw what I thought was a hopeless idea at me, I reacted immediately and said, "Oh, no!" That not only dampened his fun but it was counterproductive. Instead, I found that if I listened carefully to his thoughts, he, in turn, would give any of my feelings and attitudes full attention, and out of it would come a totally new, but often better, concept.

. . .

In 1954 Fred was still on top of the media heap. His five-year weekly TV musical spectacular with G.E. was ending, but television specials seemed to be lining up for the future, so I assumed that his present tour of two busloads of Pennsylvanians was an interim one. It never occurred to me that he would spend the next thirty years crisscrossing the country in a bus.

After the first year I decided not to go on one-night stands. I joined Fred here and there throughout the country, when he stopped for more than one night: three weeks' stay in Nevada, ten days in Los Angeles playing in all surrounding cities, and so on. I had several reasons, especially after our youngest was born in 1957. Leaving my first son at home while I toured as a pianist had torn my heart out, and I couldn't imagine anything more stultifying than riding on a bus every day and listening to the same show every night. Excruciating boredom! My instinct must have told me I would be nothing but a gofer, for during our thirty years together I noticed that conductors' wives who follow their husbands faithfully end up doing all their chores and nitty-gritty jobs and are, for the most part, treated very badly by their famous maestros. The husbands are often rude and inconsiderate, and the wives become doormats.

So what did I have going for me that Fred's other wives didn't have? With the added years, Fred had finally straightened a few of his priorities. First, he wanted and was willing to strive for happiness. Secondly, as I had been a part-time Pennsylvanian for ten years, he knew what I was made of. He not only loved me, he trusted me and had a great deal of respect for me, as I did him. He told Jack that I was devoid of resentments, jealousies, and envies, which I guess was true.

Of course, I've always known that, to Fred, flirting was as normal as breathing. A pretty face or a child made him light up instantly. One time we were watching a TV program called Tattle Tales—three celebrity couples are asked questions about each other. The question to the wives was,

"If your famous husband were sitting on the aisle seat of a plane and the stewardess was fawning and fussing over him, would you make him change seats with you?" I remember turning to Fred laughing and saying, "If I made you move every time that happened, you'd never be able to sit down."

I unwittingly made a request at the beginning of our marriage that won me a few brownie points. I said, "I don't care a whit about jewels and furs; all I want is plenty of help in the house." Because of my career, I was never obliged to do housework or cook, and I wasn't about to begin. That, of course, suited Fred fine. At the end of a busy day we could sit down to a quiet dinner and talk, or enjoy the teenagers that filled the house or our youngest, who would come toddling in to entertain us while we had a cocktail.

Since Fred granted my wish for plenty of household help, it seemed only fair that I become involved in some of his pet projects, the three most important being his yearly invitational golf tournament, the song pluggers' outing, and one that I haven't mentioned until now, the cartoonists' party.

Over the years, Fred maintained an enduring friendship with the creative visual scribes of his generation—the men and women whose fertile minds illustrated day after day, week after week, year after year, the adventures of their individual characters in the newspapers—the "funnies." And it began almost by accident. In the forties, the cartoonists of America banded together to form the National Cartoonists Society. The group decided to meet once a year for an outing, and by chance, Shawnee Inn in the Poconos was chosen to be the place. Little did they know that the owner was the numero uno aficionado of American cartoon strips. Fred was so thrilled that he invited them to be his guests every year to celebrate his birthday on June 9. The event became a tradition.

The outing was a day and night of fun and frolic for those clever creators—a few moments stolen from the pressures of daily deadlines. The average person has no idea how confining a cartoonist's life can be. I had gained some insight a few years earlier when Chester Gould, creator of Dick Tracy, was given an award on Fred's Sunday television show on CBS. Mr. and Mrs. Gould and their daughter had flown in from their home in Chicago just for the one night. His daughter told me that it was her first trip to New York, but unfortunately they had to return home the next day because of the demands of her father's daily strip.

Milt Caniff, dean of the cartoonists: "Each year the annual freebie for the dirty fingernail set and their spouses took place on schedule. We would arrive, have a stunning luncheon, play golf or tennis, swim, play cards, make love, lie to each other about how many papers carried our cartoons, have cocktails, dinner, and then a floor show such as was never seen anywhere else. The Pennsylvanians would entertain us, and then we would do a certain show for them. The other hotel guests would sit in on this one-shot gala and wonder why it had not been mentioned in the Shawnee Inn brochure. The catch was that some of our people would lean to the blue side in their 'chalk talk' patter, and Fred's distress flag would go up."

Cartoonists' minds seem to run on a different track than yours or mine. It's when you are surrounded by this special tribe at close quarters that you see it happening—their unorthodox and outlandish visions of everyday events. And how unique in appearance they all were! A few looked like their characters. Otto Soglow was diminutive like his Little King but Mell Lazarus, creator of short, squat Momma, was surprisingly tall and lean, with eyebrows that went up in the middle, and a perpetual small smile that gave him an endearing quizzical expression. I once asked him what his mother thought about the unflattering mama he painted in his daily strip, and he said she told everyone it was her sister he was portraying. Rube Goldberg was a big, rough, warmhearted man who smoked large black cigars and sometimes told off-color jokes after a few drinks. His elegant, devoted wife, Irma, said she often would hear him laughing all by himself when he was concocting a new Goldbergism in his studio in their New York apartment.

Milton Caniff ("Terry and the Pirates" and Steve Canyon) was dean of the cartoonists for many, many years. I considered him one of the kindest, most thoughtful of men. He and his wife, Bunny, never had children. Their lives were entirely devoted to each other. When he died in his eighties, Bunny could not face life without him, and she died within a few weeks.

Every year for twenty-five years until the Inn was sold, the members of the National Cartoonists Society arrived with pens, crayons, paper, and ink. Thus, our collection of personalized cartoons grew. One year we received fifty tabletops. Each cartoonist had drawn on a thirty-by-thirty special paper, which was then laminated. It was a difficult process in those days. The delicate paper could tolerate no erasures or revisions. Most of the ideas were centered around Fred or me or the Inn or golf. The aggregate probably constitutes one of the largest personal collections of cartoons focused on one man not in politics. It is often assumed by some of the stuffy elite that anyone who is a comic strip buff has to be lacking in

"LET'S TUNE OUT THESE BUMS AND GET THE FRED WARING SHOW."

Hazel © 1950, Ted Key. Reprinted with permission.

GREETINGS TO
FRED WARING
WHOSE GENIUS HAS BROUGHT
SO MUCH JOY TO SO MANY FOLKS
OVER SO LONG A
PERIOD OF TIME....

THE BUMSTEADS
AND
CHIC YOUNG

SEND
THEIR
BEST

Blondie reprinted with special permission of King Features Syndicate and Dean Young.

Dick Tracy reprinted with permission of Tribune Media Services.

Henry reprinted with special permission of King Features Syndicate.

Beetle Bailey reprinted with special permission of King Features Syndicate and Mort Walker.

gray matter. I have known some dull intellectuals but I have never known a dull cartoonist.

Fred's invitational golf tournament was no trivial affair either. All rooms in the hotel were filled with his personally invited players and their wives—some three hundred and fifty people. The Pennsylvanians, in residence, entertained for the weeklong event. I have to admit it was hard on me at first. I was still rather shy and they were all Fred's friends. As hostess, I was obliged to greet all three hundred and fifty participants at lunches and dinners. I usually ended up sick in bed.

One time I became really quite ill, and I finally analyzed my problem, working out a perfect solution. Each year I would greet everyone at the opening cocktail party, which usually took place outside on the Green Terrace at the Inn. Then, when everyone went upstairs into the dining room, the guests—by then all slightly sloshed and happy—probably assumed I was in another part of the spacious dining room. I would go home and have a quiet peaceful dinner. In this fashion I paced myself the rest of the week. Fred thought that was fine. He never quibbled or complained about anything I chose to do. In fact, he was a women's libber's dream. He helped in any way he could on any of my projects.

.   .   .

Concert pianists of necessity lead solitary, rather restricted lives—like existing with blinders on—always practicing or performing. Fred's support and encouragement helped me to grow and develop in other areas. The one project for which he hugged and kissed me and thanked me constantly was my effort to pull his estranged children back into the fold. I knew I was a bit clumsy at first, mainly from ignorance and lack of experience. I was the youngest of my family and had never been around teenagers as an adult. When Fred and I were married, I inherited three adolescents who all half-hated their father. Unfortunately, their mother had expressed only negative thoughts about their father to them during those delicate and formative years. Fred loved them deeply but felt really quite helpless. I'm not saying a self-made man is the best father in the world, but he did truly love and care about them. He often spoke about all the charming and interesting things they did and made when they were little, and how he agonized over Evalyn's adamant demand that the two little boys be sent away to school.

The summer after we married, Dixie was home from college and sitting with us having a cocktail, and out of the blue she said, "Daddy, I really have to admire you. All those years when Mother was saying such terrible things about you, you never said a word against her." That was the beginning of her acceptance of Fred—to see him as he was—warts and all.

Billy, Fred's second son, had to leave the East and live in the California desert and see how adored his father was there before he could admit, "Dad, it has taken me forty years to say, 'I love you.'" What a wonderful present that was.

Fred loved my son Paul, who was eight when we married. Paul asked to be called Paul Waring because he wanted his last name to match the others. Fred adopted Paul when he was sixteen and could make his own decision.

Fortunately, even though we were rather old to be parents, we had a son whom we called Malcolm, which was Fred's middle name. This was like a second chance for Fred, and how he did enjoy and laugh at that little boy as he grew up.

• • •

Fred retained an abiding enthusiasm for colorful clothes. When I first knew him, he always wore a shirt and tie (usually a bow tie) during his working hours. But then he discovered the turtleneck long before it became popular with men, and that constituted his daily apparel. The color range for men was limited, so I bought him large-size ladies' turtlenecks that came in a spectrum of pinks, yellows, and shades of blue. It bothered him not a whit that they zipped up the back of the neck. His slacks came in every color and every weight, plus, of course, endless interesting jackets. None of your nine-to-five look for him. But he was careful and never looked garish. Fred was comfortable with his own taste; he even wore a flamboyant Pucci velvet jacket with aplomb and flair. Because he was a showman he could make his own rules—perhaps offbeat sometimes, but always in good taste. These colorful clothes suited our Pennsylvania country and Palm Springs desert life. Still, Fred could look as well turned out as any in his city suits.

Fred made one sartorial request of me. Please! No jeans! It was easy for me to dress to please him, because it was my taste, too—no sloppy, blousy, waistless outfits. How he loved to buy clothes for me. Each time he arrived in Dallas on tour, the buyers in Neiman Marcus would gather round him. Fred knew exactly what looked smashing on me—color, style, and all. He was always good for a designer dress or two. I once said, "If you had put all that money into great paintings, we would have a fabulous collection by now." He replied simply, "You are my painting." I guess, in a way, his enjoyment came from looking at what he had created rather than something inanimate hanging on a wall. The first year he bought me three coats. I finally persuaded him I could wear only so many coats. When we were dressing to go out, he would ask what I was wearing in order to choose a proper tie or jacket that wouldn't clash.

Fred always observed certain niceties of etiquette such as walking on the curb side when on the street, taking my arm up and down steps, standing behind me on an escalator going up, and in front when going down (in case I fell), and always opening doors for me. He liked doing it. In his last years when he was so frail, I had to restrain an impulse to open the door myself, thinking I was saving him. I quickly realized that by doing so I was diminishing his already weakened male role—so demoralizing for a once powerful, take-charge man.

Fred was afraid of only two things—horses and the dentist. He loved all other animals (never shot or killed any). He enjoyed watching horses and thought they were exciting and beautiful. But in his youth, horses had sharply nipped him several times, which made him forever wary. I had occasion to see this firsthand, when Fred was in his seventies. We were in the California desert driving home in a blinding sandstorm. While we were creeping along, I thought I saw a horse in the middle of the road a few feet ahead. Fred pulled over, and I jumped out. Although I knew nothing about horses, I coaxed it toward a nearby corral. I could see the poor animal wanted to get in the corral and was whinnying and stamping its feet while I was below him on my knees, trying to get the gate open—hoping the frightened animal wouldn't step on me. I finally turned around, and there was Fred a few feet away, frozen to the spot. My Fearless Freddy (as he was called by the cartoonists) was afraid of a poor old horse. He accepted my teasing and admitted openly that even proximity to a horse terrified him.

Fred's phobia about dentists I understand, because in my childhood any session in the dentist's chair was sheer agony. Science had not yet invented novocaine or deadening devices of any kind or high speed drills with water coolant—just a bore that rotated very slowly, made a horrible noise in one's head, and became unbearably hot. When it hit a nerve, well . . . In spite of some neglect in the early years, at eighty-four Fred's teeth were still intact.

But standing up to bullies was another matter. We were waiting in a crowded foyer at Trader Vic's in San Francisco, when a powerfully built man pushed rudely past us, nearly knocking Fred down. The man turned his head slightly and said, "Sorry," in an insincere, brisk way.

Fred looked up, arms akimbo, and said, "Are you?" The giant glared at this small upstart and was about to hit Fred but thought better of it. Later he found out he was Fred Waring and came over to our table bowing and scraping like Uriah Heep. Fred had no time for people like that.

He always remained calm and supportive of others in some very scary situations, such as being aboard a plane in serious trouble. Ruth Sibley, who was at his right hand for forty years, remembered a trip in a bucket-seated Navy plane that was taking the Pennsylvanians to a special performance during World War II and passed through a severe storm. Everyone was white-knuckled. Ruth recalled that "Fred got us playing some crazy game he invented which involved passing oranges."

She reported that when our house burned down and she called him up weeping, he said, "Well, honey, when you get to be my age, you can expect anything."

Fred's shyness did not end with his boyhood. "He was shy almost to the point you thought it was a pose," said agent and music publisher Danny Winkler. "He was brash only when he wanted to overcome it. Then you'd wonder, 'Now, why did he say that?'"

Fred Culley said, "He hates himself for being shy and fights it like hell, which gives the opposite impression." This talk of shyness might strike some of the more recent generation of young Pennsylvanians, who viewed him as a domineering boss, as utterly hilarious. Nevertheless, I have to agree. He never, ever, was shy onstage, but don't ask him to walk in late down a theater aisle when the lights are still up and everyone is seated. In his later years when he was asked to accept awards and honors, Fred's unfeigned humbleness and reluctance seemed strange to me. He never lacked confidence in what he was doing, so why not reap the rewards and enjoy a little praise here and there?

Admiral Dexter said in 1960, "You never get close to Fred Waring. Nobody I know is actually close to Fred. I spent the better part of a year and a half being with Fred from ten to twelve hours and seeing him under all kinds of occasions in many, many cities, and have gotten to know Fred pretty well. He's actually three or four different people!"

"Mr. Waring can teach you to sing a love song from depths in your heart you never knew were there, yet he finds it hard to say, 'I love you,'" Patsy Garrett said. "Perhaps, because over the years he's had to put a protective shelter around himself to avoid the hazards of vulnerability that are occupational problems for people who are in charge of others." Most could not get it through their heads that, for Fred, expressing love verbally was not his style. He was a doer, and his acts of friendship and love were more profound than mere words. In his later years, I saw him put himself out for many who weren't worthy of his limited physical capabilities. It was never with a feeling that it was a chore—it was a real giving, a generosity of spirit and self that few of us can match.

． ． ．

Fred had allergic reactions after eating raw onions or garlic, and he was not fond of the aroma or breath of one who had partaken heavily thereof. Onstage he had a fast repartee with soprano/comedienne Lette Rehnolds. They would stand face to face at center mike, so she was careful of what she ate before the show. I happened to be in the audience one night when Lette unwittingly had ingested a substantial amount of garlic. On her first explosive phrase right in Fred's face, he reeled back as though he had been given a whiff of cyanide. The Pennsylvanians almost fell off their risers laughing. Fred quickly ad-libbed an aside, so the audience laughed too, but it definitely was an "in" joke.

Fred was allergic to a musk that Estee Lauder used as a base for many of her colognes and perfumes. He'd start coughing immediately if anyone walked in with it on. He let Miss Lauder know his feelings in a more direct way.

Fred and I almost always ate at "21" when we were in New York. One night we dined fairly early because we were going to the theater. We were seated along the wall next to an elegant woman and her escort. And when we arrived at the theater, we sat next to the same couple. So Fred leaned over me and introduced himself and me to the lady, who turned out to be Estee Lauder. In his most charming manner Fred said, "Miss Lauder, you are a beautiful, elegant, and successful lady, but I just can't stand your perfume. It makes me cough." She laughed. She was amused, not put off by his frankness.

Allen Funt's former wife wrote a book with the sad but quizzical title, *Are You Anybody?* It seems she was standing amidst a group of celebrities when an autograph hound turned to her and queried, "Are you anybody?" She subsequently interviewed about twenty-five wives asking what it was like to be the wife of someone famous.

At first I was quite surprised by people's reactions to me when I was introduced. While shaking my hand, they would be looking not at me, but at Fred. It could be hard on a wife with a shaky self-esteem, and one could easily discern in Mrs. Funt's book the marriages that were headed for trouble. Fred was keenly aware of the eyes focused on him and kept me close, with his arm around me, as though to make it clear to all that, in his mind, I definitely was a somebody.

• • •

In May of 1957, when we had been married for two and a half years, Fred was asked to be a summer substitute for Gary Moore's television show. It was to take place at Shawnee, five mornings a week. Fred asked me if I would play a song Tom had written for glee club and piano called, "I'll Wait for My Love." My fingers were rusty but I said I would try, since it would be performed in our living room with my own Steinway. The piece was not your everyday love song—no catchy tune. We rehearsed it once, and then the moment arrived. I sat down at the piano, glanced at Fred who was smiling broadly at me, played a lengthy solo introduction and, when I didn't hear the glee club come in, I looked up, and there was Fred totally absorbed in watching me play, completely oblivious to his surroundings. He finally came to. We started again, but precious seconds had been lost, and we finished off the air. I couldn't be angry, seeing that beatific smile on his face, but I also decided life was too short to be tied to an instrument. And so I quit playing for twenty-three years.

• • •

For thirty years Fred called me at least once, sometimes two or three times every day that he was away. As a result, I don't have too many letters from him (nor does anyone else), but our daily contact created a strong bond. We discussed family news or problems and worked them out immediately. Little unimportant things were mentioned that might seem trivial a day later. I would often leave a party or dinner early so as not to miss his call.

We began leaving notes for each other from the start. If he would be coming in late after a show or a tour, I would leave a welcoming note propped up in the kitchen that he would see as soon as he opened the door. He in turn would leave a billet doux on the floor of my dressing room to brighten my day when I got up. One of my favorite exchanges occurred when I left Fred a note explaining that I was going to bed early because I was "under the weather." His response was "Dear *Ma*—Maybe you are *under* the weather but you are *above everything else.* I love you—Pa."

The influx of the numerous newspapers to Fred's doorstep continued unabated. The *New York Times* was not on the list because it carried no comic strips. However, *USA Today* made it because of its thorough sports coverage. All editorial pages were absorbed and digested. The number of papers tapered off somewhat in his later years, but at the beginning, cleaning six or seven newspapers out of our home each day was a minor housekeeping nightmare.

Dear Pa
I'm still sort
of under the
weather so am
retiring early
xx
my love
ma

Happy Birthday –
"My Beautiful One"
And Welcome To A New
World Of Wisdom!!
At Least You bring to us
a great abundance of love
and compassion and Under-
standing — Be patient —
we're slower – but mean
well — Welcome-Welcome,
My Very best Friend —
My Love–My Love – My Love
— Papa —

Notes exchanged between
Virginia and Fred.

Fred would often leave a particular columnist's write-up at my place at the kitchen table, where we ate breakfast and snacks. It was always something he thought would interest me. I did the same with him, and for quite a while after his death, I caught myself starting to set aside something for him. Fred read constantly but was not a bookworm. However, he was a grammar fanatic. He could parse a sentence to a fare-thee-well. When a Pennsylvanian would say, "between you and I," Fred would shudder, as if he heard the proverbial fingernail running across the blackboard.

One trait Fred and I had in common was a shunning of confrontation. "Letting it all hang out" was simply not our style. In this day and age, however, when everyone feels such a compulsion to agonize verbally over every nuance of a problem, I thought perhaps we were a little out of step. Early in our marriage, I hit on the idea of writing a letter that Fred could digest in private. Over the years, not too often, to be sure, when something unsettled me, I put it all down: pro and con. Since it didn't seem to be the au courant or ideal way of communication, I never mentioned it to anyone, until by chance I told our dear friend Moya Lear. She laughed because that is exactly what she did throughout her long marriage to that brilliant but difficult genius Bill Lear. I remember her reply: "They know we're not dummies! When we have something to say—they listen!"

Fred, the sentimentalist, never forgot a birthday, Mother's Day, Valentine's Day—flowers and presents would appear. I'm the one who goes to the foot of the class—even forgot our youngest son's birthday the first year he was married. For years the St. Francis Hotel was our oasis when we stayed in San Francisco. Until it was enlarged, we were greeted effusively by the same burly doorman, and our bags were carried by the same porters. It was Old Home Week for us. Fred's sentimental traditional gift for me at the St. Francis was a gardenia. It was his first act when we arrived. I would often take Malcolm, our youngest, with me when I joined Fred on tour. Mal must have been observing the gardenia ritual, because I was told indirectly that when he brought his bride to San Francisco for her first visit, he bought her a gardenia.

Fred brought new meaning to the word "meticulous." When he dressed each morning, he always placed his folded paper money (no wallet), keys, handkerchief, and 1900 silver dollar—the only superstition I knew him to have—in the back pockets of his trousers. He never carried change. Each night any coins he had garnered during the day were dropped into a receptacle on his dresser. He was very selective about who cut his hair. He traveled to New York just to see his barber until he found someone in nearby Stroudsburg in whom he could place his trust. No clippers were used—feathering with scissors was required, a skill not everyone possesses. (I suppose curly hair does present problems.)

Fred was the only human being I know whose feet didn't smell. He could have worn the same socks every day for a month if he had wished. Having brought up so many boys, I found this an amazing phenomenon. He said it was because he didn't eat garlic or onions. We've all heard the old saying "Cleanliness is next to godliness." If this is true, then I guess, if for no other reason, Fred is up there in heaven occupying a number-one seat. And I am not the only one to attest to this special trait of Fred Waring.

His sister Helen said, "From a little boy on, Fred had his face scrubbed and spotless, and so was the front part of his hair. But in the back it was a mess." Typical of the old Victorian code—so long as it didn't show or no one knew about it, it was just fine.

John Royal added, "Fred and his men had dignity and were clean looking. It was a natural thing for him—he couldn't do anything else."

"In restaurants, Fred would sometimes embarrass you," Johnny O'Connor said. "He'd pick up the glass and clean it out with his napkin, and clean the knives and forks. I remember one time a headwaiter came over, scooped up all the things in front of him, brought back a new set, and said, 'These have been sterilized!' and gave Waring a three-dollar look."

The world seems to be divided into those who save everything and those who clean everything out. Fred was the former, a graduated magna cum laude pack rat. Most human pack rats seem to have a well-established rationale and justification for their saving. The basic reason seems to be a variation on the theme "I may need this someday."

Fred never bought just one gadget, one tie, one pair of shoes or whatever—he would buy three, five, or ten—"just in case." Many times he would give the excess away, but too often it lay forgotten in our large basement.

Elsie, our German housekeeper and cook who had already been with the family eighteen years when I came on the scene and remained another twenty until incapacitated by age, was also a dedicated collector. The difference between the two was that Fred saved mainly new things or those in good condition, whereas Elsie hung onto old worn-out objects—pieces of string, boxes, chipped dishes, and bent spoons. She was the quintessential pack rat whose oversized nest is an incredible conglomeration of junk—truly an amazing sight.

Fred, who disliked being surrounded by Elsie's hoarded castoffs, would bring her unblemished dishes, shiny balls of string, and scissors that actually cut. But the habits of that pair were too deeply ingrained. Neither ever changed. From time to time, when it all became a bit much, I would wait until Fred went on tour and Elsie visited her cousins in New York, and then I would call in the Salvation Army.

Once I had a huge barrel stuffed to the top, ready to go, but unfortunately it didn't get picked up in time. I was caught—and little by little those two removed some of their precious cargo. When our nine-year-old Malcolm started hauling some of his things out of that barrel, it made me wonder if pack-rat genes are inherited.

The entrance hall of our home encompasses a large walk-in closet called the "gift" closet, replete with leftover presents from the latter half of Fred's life. In his waning years, after a dinner with special friends, Fred loved to bring out gifts for everyone—always good for a laugh or two—a silver bracelet from a vacation in Mexico in 1948, a brass tray from Korea, ties (some made especially for him by "Countess Mara" in the forties); wallets (which he never used—one still contained the enclosed birthday card), and so on.

In the eighties, Fred donated his sixty-five years of memorabilia to his alma mater, Penn State. The VIPs who came to the old Castle Inn at Delaware Water Gap expecting to see some awards and photos were stunned to see room after room, warehouse after warehouse, of material: 60 filing cabinets filled with vocal and instrumental arrangements of more than 6,400 songs; 7,500 pages of scrapbooks dating back to 1922; 8,524 phonograph disks holding 1,160 hours of radio broadcasts from 1933 to 1949; 1,092 commercial recordings; 6,000 photographs, and much, much more. The Penn State officials agreed that it was one of the most promising archival collections they had seen in years—a reflection of America's tastes from the 1920s to the 1980s.

Well, I guess Fred had the last laugh on all of us. His seemingly odd quirk paid off!

• • •

Fred was most tolerant of my foibles. I could emerge from my dressing room all clean, neat, and tidy, and leave a horrendous mess behind me, and he, who actually folded his dirty clothes when he was little, did not complain. I never realized I left drawers open until, after an early rushed departure for a day in New York, I returned home to find all the drawers in my dressing room pulled open (and there are many). But that was the end of it—Fred had made his statement and never referred to it again.

Evidently I used to treat recalcitrant cupboards and doors in a rather ruthless fashion. If they stuck and wouldn't behave, I would sometimes become exasperated and slam or kick them shut. I was completely unaware of this inelegant habit until Fred said with a one-sided grin on his face—"Remember! I'm not inanimate!"

I never hit anyone in my entire life except once when Fred and I were in the study. He was reclining in his favorite lounge chair, and I was standing across the room. I had asked him how to get some new curtain equipment to work. He had explained it twice, and since I'm pretty slow at grasping technical solutions, I asked for it "once more," to which he replied in an offhand way, "Oh, skip it." There was something about the tone that so exasperated me that for the only time in our married life I wanted to hit him. The first thing I grabbed was my purse—it happened to be a little soft purse with only tissues in it. I gave a huge swing, missed him completely, lost my balance, and fell right on top of him. How we laughed over that one!

Except for his bout with rheumatic fever, Fred enjoyed exceptionally good health due, in large part, to moderation in living habits. He didn't smoke. Our number-three son was caught smoking at a prep school, which at that time was a serious infraction, and I overheard Fred on the phone tell him, "Paul, I gave up smoking in 1907." Fred was seven at the time.

Fred didn't drink until he was forty. Even then he indulged only rarely, having one or two drinks at the most.

His secretary Cora said Fred missed only two shows during his seventeen years of radio. Fred Waring was the iron man, usually the healthiest Pennsylvanian at the end of a tour. That's not to say he didn't perform when he was quite ill. In the fifties during a week's engagement in Atlantic City, he was extremely sick with the flu. Nevertheless, he did two one-hour shows a night—never said a word about how he felt. We were newly married and I was astonished by his stoicism, knowing how truly ill he was. It never occurred to him not to perform.

In 1979 during the last week of the spring tour, Fred mentioned over the phone that he was feeling some inexplicable pain in his groin. When I joined him for the final concert in Hershey, Pennsylvania, to be televised by PBS, he admitted it was worse, but said no more. He was on his feet all day for the camera shot rehearsals and two and a half hours for his show. The next morning the doctor was aghast. Fred had such a badly infected testicle that the doctor could not imagine how he bore the excruciating pain—especially the final torturous day. And yet he said not a word to anyone but me.

Fred was precise about being on time for a concert, but his daily life was a different story. If we were leaving for a day or two somewhere (except by plane), we might start one or even two hours after our stated departure time. My stepdaughter Dixie, who keeps a rigid daily schedule, was sitting in our kitchen during a delayed takeoff. "Doesn't Daddy drive you crazy when he leaves so late?" I figured it was a deep-rooted habit, so I always readied myself by the appointed time and then did other things.

One of the secrets of Fred's success on radio was his ability to do six things at once—watch the clock, conduct, announce, give cues, fill in when someone missed a signal, etc. He told of a time Tom failed to come in on cue during the Old Gold Show. Fred automatically sang his part—not a fraction of a beat was missed. Sometimes at home, though, trying to talk to this animated dynamo was disconcerting. I once had to tell him about a little girl whose mother was baking, moving about the kitchen half listening, while the child was trying to tell her about her day. In exasperation the child said, "Mommy! Listen to me with your face!" I always had his full attention the hour before dinner. That was one of our favorite tête-à-tête times—no distractions.

·   ·   ·

A word about our home, the Gatehouse. When the two Worthington brothers built Shawnee Inn in 1909, they also constructed two summer homes for themselves. One of the houses boasted a large carriage house that contained not only carriages but horses and cows and a three-room apartment for the caretaker, and above all of that was a hayloft—some six thousand square feet of space. For two years before we were married, Fred, the frustrated architect, worked with architect John Muller, an elegant, lovely man, and converted the sprawled-out building into a stunning and unique home where we lived for thirty years.

The living room, formerly the garage for the carriages, is fifty feet long and twenty-four feet wide. Fred installed Vermont slate on the floor with radiant heating pipes underneath—a toasty warm place in winter. My Steinway piano and the fireplace are at the far end, and the large lazy Susan dining table at the other end. Comfortable yellow and white sofas with coffee tables fill the space. With the sun streaming in and its variety of furniture, the living room exudes an air of friendly welcome. High up on one long wall in front of the original half-round windows, an extensive collection of antique bottles sits on a shelf. They glow like stained glass when lit from below. (Passersby used to think we ran a bar.)

The opposite long wall has floor-to-ceiling double paneled windows that look out on a courtyard and a round icehouse. The icehouse, twenty-four feet in diameter, has thick double walls filled with sawdust, which keeps the room very cool. In the early 1900s, there were no iceboxes or refrigerators, so in the middle of winter when the Delaware River froze over, workmen cut the ice and filled the icehouse to the ceiling, where the ice would remain to be used throughout the summer.

For the kitchen, Fred knocked out the walls of the caretaker's apartment and made one big L-shaped room. It includes three sinks and plenty of cupboards and counter space. With carpet on the floor (except for the work area), hanging copper pans over an island, and antique copper pots, pitchers, kettles, and large pottery bowls on a ledge around the room, it too has a warm feeling. In fact everyone came in the kitchen door unless I was having a special party and insisted guests enter the front door.

The seventeen-by-twenty-feet entrance room has two walk-in closets and a vestibule. Above the closets is a balcony where the original drum with Waring's Banjo Orchestra painted on its face sat center stage. Fred grew up with Victorian furniture and had a goodly amount of it scattered throughout the house before we were married. Sensing that I wasn't too all fired up about that style of furniture, he suggested I put a sticker on the pieces I liked, figuring that would simplify matters. Most of it ended up in the entrance hall with a grandfather clock and a square Steinway piano.

The rear of the house, where the horses were stabled, became a study full of trophies, awards, albums, tapes, and two walls of books. It was always a mess because the TV and sound equipment were there, and it was our favorite place to relax. One summer evening Arnold Palmer came over to watch a sports show that wasn't available on his in-laws' TV channels (they lived up the road). I had just removed all the books from the shelves to reorganize them. When I gave Arnie my excuse as he stepped over the piles to find a chair, he grinned and said, "That's the perfect reply when people come into my messy den." Although the rest of the house is decorated in light, sunny colors, the study is restfully brown—wood paneling and leather.

Our bedroom and two separate baths are where the cow stanchions used to be. I always had an affinity for Oriental things, and when we married, brought a couple of antique Japanese tables with me that I treasured. When asked if he would mind if the bedroom had a Far Eastern feel, Fred replied, "No, as long as I don't have to sit on the floor."

Fred inserted dormer windows in the entire hayloft upstairs and devised three bedrooms with baths, a large play/sewing room with a pool table in the middle, and a six-bed boys' dorm over the entire living room. Sometimes in the summer when the dorm was full of our boys and their cousins, I felt like the old woman who lived in a shoe—especially when Dixie graduated from Penn State and took off for her first job in Denver. That left me the lone female at dinner seated at our round table next to Fred, completely surrounded by young boys.

Fred enjoyed those dinners during the summer. He loved to tease the youngsters and make them laugh. Even though later as teenagers they were all working at the Inn (mostly on the golf course) to earn money for cars or stereos, nevertheless Fred couldn't resist reminding them he was given a nickel a week's allowance. This refrain would pop out regularly when one of them would complain about something he didn't have. After a while, they began to anticipate Fred's response and would roll up their eyes, sigh loudly, and wait. Finally they would groan loudly and say it before Fred could get it out of his mouth.

As a punster par excellence Fred relished nothing better than practicing his craft on his captive audience around the table. Not one of us could have matched him, but that didn't stop us from making loud noises of disdain (it's so easy to be a critic). I finally decided, in deference to Fred's feelings, to have a "Be Kind to Father" week every so often. We had to laugh at his jokes and all his puns, no matter how corny.

After we were married, when the boys were quite small they loved to pitch a tent and camp out all night. The darkness was a little scary, and they made sure the house was within sight. At the first clap of thunder, Fred would jump out of bed and rescue them—describing to me later "the little white faces peering out of the tent flap." He would bed them down in the living room in their sleeping bags. It was he, not I, who waited up for them at night when they started to drive. I never worried, figuring it was a waste of time for both of us to lose sleep.

Two rooms of the huge basement were filled with every power tool imaginable, workbenches, racks for tools, and bins containing all sizes of screws and nails. It was a skilled woodworker's dream. One time Fred was giving a concert at the Philadelphia Academy of Music for the wives of members of President Eisenhower's cabinet. I was seated in a box with some of them, and as Fred was introducing them, he spontaneously included me as the wife of a cabinetmaker, much to my chagrin.

For the first twenty years of our life together, when Fred was still actively engaged in business and music affairs, on most weekday mornings the table in the kitchen would be filled with people waiting to see him.

They knew they could trap him because he always kept his tour hours even when at home—late to bed and late to rise. Since Elsie was in the kitchen, I could be present or not, as I wished.

We did get away together sometimes. For years after we were married, Elsie would pack us a lunch, and quite often we would drive up some unused back road, pull off in a secluded area, and talk, eat, and "make out," as the kids say. Come to think of it, we were pretty old to be carrying on like that . . . but it was fun.

The stories about Fred's father bringing home, housing, and feeding not only all visiting ministers and preachers but also every drunk and homeless creature in Tyrone were known to me. Since Fred had cut his teeth on this family behavior, it seemed natural to him that he should continue this open-house tradition with his beloved Pennsylvanians. Still, what wife wants hordes of people traipsing in and out of her home? I don't think Fred ever thought of it in those terms, because when it looked as though I were facing an incipient problem, I expressed my concern and feelings about the privacy of our home. Fred was surprised. The look on his face told me that he never realized it could be a thorn. He acknowledged my apprehension gracefully and without resentment, and the problem ceased to exist. We entertained guests frequently, which I was happy to do—it was just that I liked to know when they were coming.

Fred was strongly visual. He often sat with one eye closed while someone was talking to him—he was sizing up vertical and perpendicular lines. He could tell if something was off a tiny fraction. He once walked into the back of the music hall and said, "Pete! The movie screen is about three inches off-center and too far back."

Tom bought a house in Shawnee after his mother died, and became a cherished member of the Stroudsburg community. He ran the Shawnee Inn gift shop and used his artistic talents making a variety of fine gift items to sell to hotel guests. Being the lesser of the two Warings in the public eye was galling, prompting Tom to form an "Other Brother's Club." He recruited Edgar Eisenhower and Carmen Lombardo as charter members. Tom used to fashion bow ties for sale. The label read: "Fred's brother makes ties."

Now, it's quite true that during the last years of his life Tom had probably acquired more friends locally than Fred, but Tom was never burdened with responsibilities. He was always cared for by others. Fred, on the other hand, took care of everybody. For example, he paid alimony for more than twenty years to his second wife despite a handsome divorce settlement, and even though she married her dance partner the same year we were married. Naturally curious, I asked Fred about it one day. He said, "We..ll, she's the mother of my children and I figure her husband won't make much of a living, so . . ." Fred was forced to tour eight and nine months each year just to keep his head above water.

In Fred's later years, he and Tom were more at peace with one another. At the summer choral workshop nearby at Delaware Water Gap, Tom would entertain one night a week. He still referred to Fred as "Himself," and made up amusing, sometimes biting, songs about Fred's weekly activities that kept the audience laughing—but the edge was gone and the long hidden profound love the two brothers had for each other began to shine through.

I grew to love Tom dearly—he was so witty and such fun to be with. Sadly, he never gained satisfactory self-expression from his singing, playing, and composing. He even tried his hand at painting and design, but never realized any great success—a big disappointment. In the last twenty years of his life, however, his greatest talent came to fruition—his ability to create an atmosphere of warm repose, goodwill, and love among people wherever he went. He had attained recognition less for what he did—and he did so much—than for what he was. He gave whatever he could, whenever he could, asking nothing in return.

When Tom became terminally ill and was admitted to our local hospital, Fred and his sister Helen organized a vigil of family members to surround him with constant loving vibrations. Later, the chief surgeon said that he and his staff never had seen any patient so embraced by round-the-clock love and compassion such as Tom had received. Tom would talk and reflect, and then doze off. He was not in pain. The only blemish was the rigid heart specialist who wouldn't let Tom reminisce on the phone with any of his old Hollywood buddies. Tom died on December 29, 1960. He was fifty-eight.

•   •   •

Around eleven o'clock on the evening of August 16, 1955, Fred and I were driving home from a song pluggers' golf outing in New Jersey. We'd been married eight months. On the golf course it had drizzled a little, although we'd heard the rain had been coming down in sheets in Pennsylvania for several days.

To reach Shawnee-on-Delaware in those days, one drove west through New Jersey on two-lane Route 46, crossed the Delaware River about ten miles downstream on a charming wooden covered bridge, and wound north along the river through the historic Delaware Water Gap. The last bridge to cross, about two miles from Shawnee Village, was an ancient iron structure that spanned Brodhead's Creek. A creek to a Californian such as myself is a small rivulet or stream. Brodhead's Creek would be halfway between a creek and a river—but by August a mere six or so inches deep, far below the bridge.

On this particular evening, I looked down through the rain as we were crossing, amazed to see glistening water lapping the edge of the bridge. At the same time, we heard a deafening roar—a horrible screeching sound. Hundreds of bloated creeks up the mountain had poured water, trees, and debris into the Brodhead, transforming it into a swollen, thundering channel, wiping out everything in its path. A dam and a paper mill just an eighth of a mile above us had given way, and within minutes the bridge we had just traversed was three hundred yards downstream. Hurricane Diane had just struck and we were driving through it.

Fred drove us home without incident, and I went to sleep—I never worried about anything when he was in charge. He changed his clothes, drove down to the little bridge that connects the mainland to the golf course (on an island in the middle of the Delaware River), and planted a stick to take a sounding. "The river was coming up visibly, five feet in one hour, a tremendous rise," he said. "What fascinated me was that the river was not flowing down, but up. The Brodhead's Creek below had dammed the Delaware River. It had knocked out thirty-five bridges and taken ninety-six lives—many were children at a camp. For years I had been taking soundings and watching the river, and I knew we were in for trouble."

Fred alerted the Shawnee Inn management, the greenskeeper, and the local volunteer fire department. "Get ready, boys," he said. "It isn't here yet, but prepare for a big flood, an emergency. Get all boats off the piers and up on high land!"

Many key Inn personnel—the manager, assistant chef, baker, bell captain, and top kitchen staff—had gone to the movies six miles away in Stroudsburg and were cut off, leaving 185 hotel guests plus 160 employees—maids, waitresses, and kitchen help. Fred did not awaken the guests since there was no place for them to go. He was certain the solid concrete hotel would hold. He ordered the parking attendants to move all cars up on a nearby hill for safety. Fred then drove along the river road to warn cottage residents close to the water's edge. "I literally had to pull them out of their homes," he said. Some were angry, thinking Fred was unnecessarily apprehensive. But by 5:30 A.M. the water had trickled over the bank's edge. The sun rose to a brilliant clear day, while the water level increased relentlessly, hour after hour.

When the Inn guests awakened and saw they were completely surrounded by water, and all roads were blocked, naturally they were alarmed and apprehensive. But when they observed Fred running around, smiling, cheerfully giving orders, doing this and that, they didn't panic. He asked everyone to fill their bathtubs with water to use sparingly because the water supply could become contaminated. By early afternoon the hotel was an island in the middle of the river, cut off from the main road. Fred had plied back and forth in every imaginable conveyance—canoe, flatboat, motorboat—from the entrance gates. As all phone lines were down, the telephone operators organized games for the children. Meals were served for everyone. After lunch, the guests stood on the porch watching the gruesome spectacle passing by faster, now on a reversed-again river: outhouses, dead animals, docks, furniture, trees, and nearby cottages. Even a human body was sighted. While the river was rising all day, our house—half a mile from and slightly higher than the Inn—had quickly filled up with about forty of the homeless, including children and dogs.

Fred had been checking the water level all day. It had already risen above the 1906 flood level and the all-time record high in 1936. But by late afternoon, the water had risen only thirteen inches in an hour instead of the earlier fourteen. Now Fred could begin to calculate its demise. Each time he returned to the Inn, everyone asked, "When is it going to stop?"

The water had reached the top step of the Inn, just about to go over the porch, over the second floor, when Fred drew a pencil line several inches above the water mark and announced: "At quarter to seven, the water will reach that point and stop. I shall return." He left.

"About half past six, I rowed back to the Inn," he recalled. "As I splashed across the porch, I looked at the water level—it was within a quarter inch of my mark." They all waited. The water rose no further. By 7:15 it had dropped an inch. People cheered, trooped into the dining room, stood up when Fred came in, and sang a blessing. It was a touching moment.

The lovely Delaware is ordinarily serene, barely seeming to move—not a dimple on its surface. It is the color of Victorian green, with a little yellow in it, and it mirrors the ancient trees along either bank. But overnight it had become a monster. It had risen thirty-nine feet.

For me, a westerner, where water is treasured and portioned out, this was truly a horrifying experience. When I was ten, our family had driven through an out-of-control forest fire in the High Sierras to the safety of the valley below. The heat of those flames on both sides of the car was a different kind of nightmare.

Once the water began to recede, it went down quickly, displaying the vast devastation it had wreaked. The entire golf course was covered with slime, muck, mud, and much of the debris seen floating by. The stench was nauseating. A lake had formed in a field next to our home and emitted an unbearable odor.

Three days after the flood, intrepid Fred, with characteristic bravado, called his staff together and said he planned to stage his annual golf tournament—just forty days away. Bulldozers, shovels, and scrapers were brought in. After forty days the golf course was still a muddy mess, but all the contestants showed up, out of friendship and respect for Fred's courage in such a crisis—an unforgettable experience in human relations and golf.

Hurricane Diane also partially destroyed the factory in Connecticut where the Waring Blendors were made. From that year on, his financial position worsened. He was never able to pull together enough money to replace the destroyed cottages or to rebuild the golf course properly. Fred never once complained. He forged ahead, did everything in his power to make the Inn a success, ran his choral workshops, toured in the winter and played golf in the summer, enjoyed his life in the Gatehouse, and told himself that all would be well.

23

Golf

FRED adored Shawnee Inn and its golf course, and he created the same kind of ambience at Shawnee as he did at his performances. Just as everyone would crowd into his concert auditorium because it was a happy, enjoyable place to be, he likewise strove for the same atmosphere at his resort in the Poconos. He enhanced the natural beauty that surrounded him by adding good food, cheerful, reliable employees who returned year after year, and, of course, spectacular golf. A *New York World-Telegram* columnist wrote in 1958: "Serene Shawnee Inn is like living in the home of a millionaire friend."[1]

These were the days when bell captain Jack Courtney would greet you by name, adding a few Hail Marys and God luv ya's while attending your luggage; when jackets were worn for lunch and dinner in the dining room, the glassware and silver shone, and chef Buckel created dishes he'd learned at Escoffier. Yet it was never stiff or formal—due to Fred himself and his department heads, who greeted longtime returnees with genuine warmth. It was a summer resort, after all, and even its decor with its white painted Victorian wicker furniture surrounded by fresh cheerful colors emitted an intangible exhilaration that matched the mood conceived by the owner. But the number-one priority—the heart and soul of Shawnee Inn—was the golf course: the country club that Fred founded, the game itself. We often debated which was more important to Fred—music or golf. It was fairly close most of the time.

The long history of Shawnee is almost the total history of golf in the United States. Even in the first days of Fred's ownership, the maintenance men of the greens and fairways were, in many cases, sons of fathers who had done the same work before them. Fred's best friend at Shawnee was the greens superintendent, John Dimmick, whom he loved and respected. John had been on the course since its inception in early 1900. Shortly after we were married, I was riding with Fred in a golf cart on the course, and an ancient wizened workman yelled out, "Hi ya, Freddy!!" It surprised me—only Fred's sister Helen and I called him that. He reminded me of the chummy stagehands who gave Fred a first-night "goose" in the early movie theater days.

Golf pro Harry Obitz said, "When I first started at Shawnee, I told Fred I would hire one extra man so that, no matter how busy we were, I'd always have a wheel man to send out to play with him. Before I hired a fellow, that is one of the things I told him—'When you play with the old man [Fred], you'd better go your best. He will give you a hard time and try to rip you out of it, he will cough and sneeze, saying allergy and the haze and the sun, and the green tilted, and he will talk (which you must not do). But you better not let him beat you if you can help it. Don't come in and tell me he was lucky, because I know better.'

"There were days when Fred played like a pro, particularly on his own golf course, because he knew every blade of grass on it," Obitz continued. "When I came, in '45, Fred was playing pretty good golf, but because he was doing all those radio shows, he got a little shaky with the irons, and his game got worse during those years of television. Then he developed the worst fault in the game, which is shanking—hitting it right off the heel of the club. His game really went to pieces. He quit using irons. I give Fred full credit for conceiving the idea of playing all the shots with the wooden club, because it had no heel on it. He got the manufacturers to build, seven, eight, nine, and eventually ten up to fifteen, sixteen, seventeen, in the woods. The use now of that many woods in the game of golf can be attributed to Fred's influence—being a celebrity and playing in a lot of those tournaments. He started shooting in the seventies again.

"Then he came up with another innovation—a forty-eight-inch driver. When I started the game, the driver was forty-two inches long. Then forty-four inches was considered to be real long, and Fred came out with a forty-eight-inch one, and he hit the ball better than he hit it back in 1945. I have seen this sixty-year-old man hit the ball up alongside par five greens in two shots."

Bob Intrieri, manager of the Penn State golf courses, never met Fred but studied his clubs in the memorabilia residing there.

Fred Waring was a perfect example of what golfers should be doing with their equipment through their golfing career. When first learning to play in his younger days, Mr. Waring would shorten the club shafts, evidently to get closer to his work, so to speak. As his golfing years progressed, the shafts got longer; the grips became thicker, quite oversized, in response to the developing arthritis in Waring's hands. The flex of his clubs graduated from a firm hickory shaft in his younger days to a more flexible A shaft. Then he put aside his irons and used all woods to eliminate shanking. He had a white or clear face inserted on the face of the clubs to help align the angle enabling him to aim the ball properly.[2]

"Fred had a lot of dexterity and timing," Harry Obitz observed. "He was a great Ping-Pong player. I did a show at Madison Square Garden the other day for *Sports Illustrated*, and Fred Perry, the world's championship Ping-Pong player, was there. He told me to remind Fred about the time he and Fred had played Ping-Pong and Fred had come pretty close to beating him.

"Fred does another unusual thing in golf. His right hand is wrapped around his left. He has only one or two fingers, excluding the thumb, on the golf club. He does not have the Sarazen Interlock or the Vardere Overlap; he has the Waring hand-over-hand, which has a lot of merit because it is impossible to snatch the club with the right hand—a great fault of many players. The other day I remarked he was playing exceptionally well and he said, 'Today I feel good using the one finger grip.' He was playing with his right forefinger on the club.

"People blow shots for different reasons. Fred does not blow because of fear. He blows because of things that distract him. Somebody three fairways away will holler, 'It's your shot, Joe!' and Fred's mind goes completely off what he's doing; or he'll find a divot turned over or a sand trap not raked—and he'll steam and rant a bit."

When Fred first bought Shawnee Inn, he decided to have a yearly golf tournament based on the slogan "Good Friends, Good Sportsmanship, Good Fellowship, Good Golf." He invited club people and friends nationwide who enjoyed the game—not necessarily professionals. His became a nationally prominent tournament and was a spawning ground for such great players as Dick Maier, Art Wall, Gene Littler, Willie Turnesa, Julius Boros, and Arnie Palmer, who all played there in their formative years.

For many years at his tournament, Fred inveigled senior players to sponsor promising young golfers. They were billed as the Young Masters. He also persuaded Dixie and her confrères to dine and dance with them at the evening parties. When Arnie Palmer arrived, in September, 1954, he was a fledgling pro not yet in the limelight—just an engaging young man. The first evening he met Dixie's best friend Winnie Walzer, an enchantingly pretty girl, and for the rest of the week they were inseparable. Winnie and Arnie decided to get married, but her parents—like the McAteers of the twenties—were horrified at the thought of their beautiful daughter marrying a nobody golf pro. They had visions of her walking down the aisle in a beautiful gown. The two young lovers thought otherwise and eloped three months later. Her father didn't speak to her for a year.

When we were first married, I, not being a golfer and never having attended a golf tournament, assumed all tournaments were like Fred's— six days filled with pleasurable competition for the men and the women who played golf; card games, antiquing, fashion shows, and other events for the ladies; nightly entertainment by the Pennsylvanians; a variety of dinners: Pennsylvania Dutch, picnic by the pool, Hawaiian luau, Mexican night, cocktails and dinner at our house; and black tie awards night. Fred called them golf parties, not tournaments.

It was then that I began to appreciate Fred's focus on every minute detail of his favorite golf project. Just the pairings took hours of his time. He would place everyone's name and handicaps on cut-up index cards, and shift them around on his desk (the same method he used to plan his musical programs). He would balance compatibility, handicaps, and even the sound of their names. Fred wanted everyone to feel personally welcome and happy. He greeted them as they arrived; he mingled and was in evidence every day and every night, even though playing competitive golf himself; we both stood at the entrance gate of our home to greet them again on Friday night; and finally, as they left the dining room Saturday night, we stood at the door and said good-bye to all three hundred and fifty as they filed out single file. It was a slow process and I'm sure there were a few who would have welcomed a chance to skip out a back door—if one had been available. But that was Fred the entrepreneur; no detail was overlooked. Most players realized such a tiny annoyance was a small penance to pay for a superbly run golf tournament. In the seventies the "Waring" was listed each year in *Golf Digest* as one of the top ten amateur tournaments in the country. Fred put on that tournament at Shawnee for twenty-eight years, and in the California desert for another thirteen.

Everyone agreed Fred was a fiery competitor, and he enjoyed playing tournaments with professional and amateur champions. Jim Miller said, "Once we were very close to not qualifying. Toward the end of the round on a par three hole, I put my ball in the water. With all the pressure on him, Fred put his shot straight on the flag for a hole in one." It was his sole hole in one in sixty-two years of golf.

Another favorite amateur partner, Howard Everitt, said, "We had one match we won as underdogs. Our opponents were top senior golfers, and Fred wanted to win very badly. We were one down coming to the eighteenth hole and both of us are on the green about twenty feet from the cup. I putted first and missed. Then, in front of the big gallery, which he loved, Fred put his ball right in the middle of the cup. You should have heard the demonstration he got from the crowd."

.   .   .

In the sixties, Fred needed a new public relations person and decided to interview a personable young golf amateur fresh out of the University of Oklahoma. His name was Fred Scrutchfield, but everyone called him "Scrutch," and he pronounced *pin, pan,* and *pen* all the same way—*pa-yun.* The following account by Fred Scrutchfield is a typical example of Fred's playing the business side "by ear." The fact that Scrutch obviously knew nothing of the art of PR was unimportant. It was his skill in golf that mattered.

"An old friend of Fred's put me on a plane in Florida for my first trip to New York," he said. "It was a cold, snowy winter night. I had on a seersucker suit. I met Fred at his office with his hotel manager and the Pennsylvanians' manager. Fred asked me about myself first, then they spent about an hour explaining the different enterprises and that he needed a young man to handle public relations for all the entities. He kept emphasizing golf—the golf!—and never mentioned much about music, which I thought strange. After the session he said, 'OK, why don't you spend the week looking over everything, and if you like it, you've got the job. Meet me in California.' Well, I about fainted right there on the elevator. Fred looked at my light suit and light raincoat and said, 'Is that all you have to wear?'

"I said 'Yes.'

"So he took off his beautiful cashmere coat and said, 'Try this on.' Sure enough, it fit like a glove. That was my first overcoat, and the Boss has been supplying me with coats ever since.

"I joined Fred in California and went out on tour with them. I didn't know what to do—I'm just hangin' around—no job description. Fred just threw me in the water. Later, I usually learned the direction he wanted to go. About the only job description I got was how to run the Fred Waring Four Ball Golf Tournament. He would take the time and effort to do that.

Fred had two rules: '*Never* overlook the smallest detail, and *never* assume that someone will do an assigned job. Always check to be sure.'"

Years later Scrutch admitted to me, "Fred paid me for six years, but I should have paid him because of all I learned from him."

The Waring way of impromptu hiring extended to former song plugger Murray Luth, who was hired as the Pennsylvanians' company road manager and sent out on the road with no instructions. "I get to the show—green—and am told to count the tickets and do a box office check. What can you absorb in an hour? I say, 'Which one of you women is going to do the box office?'

"They all say, 'We don't know nothing. We'd hoped you'd do it.' It's like throwing a kid in the water—he swims. I learned in six hours to check a box office correctly."

In the fifties when Fred was fifty-five and had to get back on the road, his golf clubs went on the bus and, with his boundless energy, he could easily play eighteen holes during the day and perform two and a half hours at night. In the sixties, Fred bought a plane (a Navion). The pilot was a Pennsylvanian who, besides playing trombone, was a good golfer. "I'd go with them on the plane, and we'd play three or four times a week. One of my jobs was to set up games—we had governors, golf pros, and senators, etc.," Scrutch said. "Fred was a lot of fun to play with. He completely got his mind off everything when he played—which is the secret."

Fred's bag full of woods was attracting attention. An *Evansville (Illinois) Courier* reporter noted: "Fred Waring can cut some pretty hot licks on the fairways with 10 woods and 3 irons and a putter—fired a two over par 73." The *St. Louis Dispatch* ran a two-column feature with a photo headlined "WARING USES WOODS TO IRON OUT PROBLEMS."[3]

A reporter once asked Fred his opinion of the golf prowess of some of his stage peers. "Bing Crosby was my favorite golf partner," Fred replied. "He was such a gentleman—we had mutual respect for one another, both as persons and as golfers. We were pretty close in ability, although he had the edge on me. Bing and I had some really lovely matches, but he hated to lose. Once, in the fifties, we were playing at the Thunderbird Country Club where he was club champion. I beat him for six dollars. He said, 'Let's play a couple of extra holes, so we can even this out'—we played ten and eighteen which are parallel—over and over until it was almost dark—(seven times)—and he finally got his money back.

"Once or twice Bob Hope would join Bing and me, but Bob had trouble playing an entire eighteen holes. If he were winning, he usually had another engagement or he came late—nine holes late."

"Como: an excellent golfer, but doesn't keep his appointments.

"Gleason? Well, we taught [Fred always pronounced 'taught' and 'daughter' as 'tot' and 'dotter'] him to play at Shawnee. He was the worst golf addict I've ever known. He wanted always to be the first on the golf course, first to cross the bridge in spring, last to come back over the bridge in fall [the maintenance crew had to put up the bridge, piece by piece, in the spring and dismantle it in the fall], and first to finish a round. He finally was able to shoot even par at 72 and, not only that, he shot seventy-two holes in one day.

"President Eisenhower played at Shawnee. Was he a good golfer? Well, he wasn't a great golfer. Over the years, I played a lot with him. His brother Edgar was a champion senior golfer."[4]

I was sitting with Ike at Shawnee when he had just finished an evidently frustrating round of golf with Fred. One of the fingers of his left hand was extremely swollen and stiff from arthritis, and it was ruining his game. He said he had suggested to the doctors that they cut it off. He was serious!

Fred had one trick on the golf course that made me extremely uncomfortable. It is called "the needle." He did it only once when I was around because I said I wouldn't go out with him again. As explained by a golfing Pennsylvanian: "What is the needle?—Very dry and subtle, and Fred's good at it. For instance, Fred was playing with a country club member. When they got to the sixteenth hole [where you hit across the river to get back on the mainland to play the last three holes], Fred said, 'The water has come up; there's a lot of water down there.' The man hit it right in the water, and he lost his composure for the rest of the day."[5]

Another idiosyncrasy that sometimes nettled a few was Fred's impulse to change certain things, and not just on a golf course. He always had to straighten a picture on the wall; to change rhythms of musical notation; to change the words of a song; to change the color of something; to change the position of a sand trap or a tee; to change the yardages on a score-card; to change the handicap system. Trombonist Chuck Evans, after wearing out many an eraser making changes on his trombone part and getting in many a sand trap that hadn't been there before, said, "I hope I die before Fred, 'cause I want to get to heaven and see it before Fred changes it."[6] Unfortunately, he received his wish.

Our son Bill had majored in hotel management at Cornell University, and after he had spent a few years with the Sheratons and Hiltons, Fred had given him the opportunity of running Shawnee Inn. It was a mixed blessing because the bottom line is of great importance to a good manager, but for Fred it was the lowest of his priorities. Every change of a golf hole meant money down the drain.

Bill was standing at the halfway house watching his father in the distance measure and mark off the dimensions of something he was going to alter and improve, and he groaned, "God! I can see it all now! Dad will be buried on the third tee and he'll have it in his will that every year he has to be moved from one place to another."

Fred's son-in-law Al Wilson, the golf superintendent at Shawnee, said, "Fred and I were standing quietly in front of some bushes, when suddenly we overheard an old guy on the work crew say in loud disgruntled tones to his buddy, 'Why in the hell doesn't Mr. Waring just put the greens on wheels, then we can move them wherever he wants!' Fred wasn't too pleased with that remark.

"Another time Fred was out driving stakes for another change. It was interfering with the golf play, and a conventioneer—a big guy—rode up to him and said, 'Why the hell don't you do this at night?' to which Fred retorted, 'I own this golf course and I'll change it around any God damned time I want to!'"

In the fifties, Fred, with the help of golf architect Bill Diddel, designed and laid out nine new holes at the end of the golf island. Between changing tees, putting in lakes, and overseeing the new nine, he was in seventh heaven—striding off yardage, driving in stakes, using his measuring wheel, and so on. Malcolm, born in 1957, frequently accompanied him. When he was about five, someone asked him what his father did. He looked off thoughtfully for a minute and then said, "Oh . . . he works on a golf course."

Dixie said, "As a child, I didn't realize that my father was famous. We lived in a community and my father played golf and went out to make a living like all the others. In prep school and college I became conscious that he was famous."

It takes immense imagination and love of the game to be a top golf architect. A specialist who had worked with Pete Dye, one of the greatest, said Fred reminded him of Pete. Fred viewed any and all topography in terms of a potential golf course. I never really understood that passion of his; in fact, I considered it a wacky aberration. He fell in love with some land next to the Salton Sea in California and bought it. He already had the slogan for a golf complex: "In the mountains, on the desert, by the sea." Unfortunately, he didn't have the time, energy, or money to push it through, but he never gave up hope.

When he was sixty-nine, Fred bought a dune buggy for two reasons—to drive around on the sand dunes (it was still allowed then) with his twelve-year-old son, and to drive pell-mell over the steep, sandy slopes of his Salton Sea property, usually with some petrified captive visitor clutching the safety bar with white knuckles.

In the early sixties, Jackie Gleason decided to visit Shawnee Inn for the first time. Many performers are inherently shy people, and Gleason was no exception. As a rule, when he and his entourage went to a hotel, he would remain holed up in his room for a few days, and then leave. On the lovely summer day when Jackie arrived at the Inn, he prepared to do the same. But this time Fred and our golf pro Harry Obitz lured Jackie out on the golf course, and he fell in love with the sport. He decided to stay and learn the game. He took a few lessons and then braved the course. All but three of the twenty-seven golf holes are on a large island in the middle of the Delaware River. On the sixteenth hole—a par three—the ball must soar over a narrow section of the river to reach the green. Jackie hit thirty-eight balls before he made it. What a bonanza for the scavengers who combed the river at the end of the day! A caddie called Dusty was assigned to Jackie, and one of his jobs was to tee up his ball.

New York Columnist Nick Kenney: "The caddie tees up each ball for Jackie so he doesn't even have to bend over. Waring is trying to invent an extension for a golf club which will enable Gleason to hit the golf ball without even getting out of the cart."[7]

Jackie played thirty-six holes many days, and it wasn't long before he could boast a most respectable handicap. He was able to relax and enjoy himself because Fred had put out a directive to all employees that Mr. Gleason was a most special guest and needed their protection. As a result, no one bothered him—not even the guests. It was amazing how well it worked. In Gleason's own words: "My hideaway is in Shawnee—Fred Waring's country club—and in the early hours I'm the only one on the course, and I love it. I revel in being alone and I revel in being with good companions."[8]

There is no doubt in my mind that the reason Jackie Gleason came back year after year was this comforting feeling of being surrounded by people who really cared. He didn't have to hide his shyness with his blustering facade. He stayed in residence six consecutive years. Jackie was all braggadocio with a group, but on a one-on-one basis he was gentlemanly, quiet, attentive, and just plain nice. He had a brilliant mind. He said there were three times when he wouldn't touch booze: when he played golf, shot pool, or worked before an audience.

Sometimes at night in the Cartoon Room, Jackie would decide to walk onstage and improvise with the surprised entertainer who happened to be performing. Fred was often in the back of the room acting as straight man with his quick wit. I'll never forget one hapless harpist who became inextricably enmeshed in the middle of their fast repartee. The locals still reminisce about that hilarious evening.

The first summer after Jackie had been at the Inn about a month, someone asked him about his unusually long visit. He said, "What a way to relax. Before this, the longest walk I'd take was from the bar to the men's room at Toots Shor's. I'd get no sunshine except from Toots' smile."[9]

Jackie eventually moved to Florida, where he could satisfy his golf addiction year round. Many years later he returned to Shawnee with his wife, Marilynne, for an *auld lang syne* visit. We had sold the Inn but we took the precaution to warn the new owner and his employees to leave Jackie alone. Fred and I joined him for dinner in the dining room, but Jackie was unable to enjoy his meal. Every employee—including the head of the dining room—asked for his autograph. At 6 A.M. the next day, the condominium residents were pounding on his door, wanting to meet him. They literally drove him out, which made us all very sad.

Shortly after we were married, I decided I should take some golf lessons. At the fifth lesson the pro said, "You know—you must practice." I said, "*Practice?* I've been practicing the piano since I was six years old—I'm not about to start something new" and I put the clubs away. But after a few years I decided to try again. Fred was delighted. He enjoyed playing in the late afternoon and would take me along with two other men. That's how I learned golf etiquette. I had three clubs: my five iron, my nine iron, and my putter. I would hit my five down to the fairway (I was always straight down the middle—just like Fred), and then my nine to pitch on, and then putt. I didn't hold up their game, didn't talk, didn't stand in their putting line, didn't move when they putted—almost didn't breathe. As Jack Best said, "Fred knew the rules; was stern about the protocols, the courtesies and the unwritten laws. To stand quietly—in the correct place—and to be silent when a playing partner was making a shot was considered a part of the 'bill of rights' of the game, and this applied to the group on the next tee or the adjacent green, and any sound when Fred was addressing a shot or putt was a direct affront, whether from his own foursome or a group on another part of the course."

After I spent a year tagging along with the men, a lady asked me to go out for nine holes with her. She talked incessantly, took five minutes to get her tee back in her shoe, another five minutes to fix her skirt each time in the cart, parked the cart on the wrong side, and made shadows when I putted. I was a wreck. I came home and said to Fred, "There's no place for me on the golf course! I'm not good enough for the men and I can't stand the women." I found later, of course, that she was an exception.

Years before anyone else had thought of it, Fred redesigned the inside of his golf bag. He took out the partitions and glued hollow tubes around the inside edge. Each tube held a club upright so it didn't fall over and tangle with all the other clubs. In the center rested his ball retriever, putter, and nine iron. He used the nine iron for all approach shots—no five, seven, eight, or pitching wedge—always the nine. More often than not he chipped in, and everyone agreed he was a fantastic putter. One time we were standing in front of our condominium in California, which lay on the first fairway of the Bermuda Dunes Country Club. The celebrities of the Bob Hope Classic were passing by, and suddenly Jack Nicklaus stopped to say hello. Lawrence Welk came up and, pointing to Fred, said in his Scandinavian lilt, "Here's the best putter in the world, and that includes you, Jack!"

In a radio interview in 1978, Fred said, "I can hardly name an old-time pro with whom I have not played golf—Walter Hagen, Bobby Jones, Gene Sarazen. I went to the British Open with Tommy Armour as a companion. Sam Snead was a pro at my course at Shawnee. Ben Hogan, Byron Nelson—you name all the greats."[10]

Fred disliked being hustled on the golf course by anyone claiming a high handicap—a twelve, say—when really he was an eight and thus would get a four-stroke edge on his opponent. He felt players should compete head to head. "I began to reason—everybody loses yardage when they get older," Fred said. "It's a natural thing as you age—so I would go out every day with the pros and we'd experiment. After years of trials with hundreds and hundreds of people, we figured that if you get one percent of the yardage of the hole for every stroke of your handicap, you're all just about even with one another. The 'A' tee would be farthest from the hole—'E' the closest. And then," he beamed, "we'd all play from scratch! No handicaps, you see."[11]

Golf pro Glenn McGihon wrote: "I received my indoctrination of Fred's handicapping system by use of his yardage factor. Instead of giving strokes to the lesser player, let him tee off a certain number of yards closer to the hole. I thought the system would work to my advantage. Alas, I still did not know Fred and his competitive nature.

"Fred gave me grave doubts regarding his ego when on the first tee he announced that we would play even. All he wanted was a little consideration regarding the tees he would use, and that would be all the handicap necessary. Fred was seventy-two years of age at the time, and I, at forty-two, had been playing some of the best golf of my life. Playing for quarter syndicates on birdies, sandies, closest to the pin on par threes, chip-ins, and a match play bet with carryovers, we had a great match. Oh yes, I paid my quarters and bought lunch also.

"My reluctance to acknowledge the merit of the system has long vanished and I welcome the true competition of it. Fred hadn't lost his skills around the greens or his desire to practice those skills and still improve. All Fred wanted was the opportunity to hit the par threes, fours, and fives in regulation. He was just making up the yardage he had lost and could never make up due to Old Man Time—the inevitable."

In 1995, music publisher Howard Richmond stated, "If Fred Waring had lived, I think his 'system' would have been on TV."[12]

24

"On the Road Again"

WHEN Fred's General Electric television contract ended in 1954, he was never again asked to perform on the networks except for a few specials in the fifties and sixties. Throughout the thirties, forties, and early fifties, these radio and TV shows had been the staple of the Pennsylvanians—touring was a bonanza for making extra money and touching base with the American audience. Now, once again, road tours were to be their way of life.

Fred never wavered or hesitated. Adversity was not new to him. He simply set about creating a streamlined show for fifty-five people, put them in two buses accompanied by a huge trailer truck and a car with stage crew, and hit the road the same way he had done twenty-five years before—on one-night stands around the country. I never heard him complain.

At first, I'm sure it was a relief to be out of the straitjacket of a weekly TV spectacular. For some, the road has its advantages. Willie Nelson often said, "I enjoy being on the road. The road, I guess, is the great escape. It's the way out. You get in your car or bus or plane and you take off." For Fred that was true—the mail, his bête noire, could go unanswered without guilt. Likewise, the office didn't bother him with daily business problems unless it was a dire emergency. Besides, no one could reach him anyway—he was either traveling, eating, or performing; car phones had not yet been invented. Escape he relished, yes. But the essence for Fred was the pleasure he gave, and the warmth and love that flowed back up over him from his enthusiastic audiences. No wonder he told me, "The only thing easy for me is actually performing onstage."

Similarly, Dick Cavett referred to the two hours spent onstage each night as "the time you always know you can count on—everything is clear, mapped out, predictable and familiar. There is an order and clarity that everything else in life lacks. For two hours away from the nerve-jangling senselessness of life's random events, the stage is a place, as Yeats put it in another context, 'where all's accustomed, ceremonious.'"[1]

Fred and the Pennsylvanians became the top concert attraction in the country, traveling six and seven months of the year—sometimes performing thirty straight days in thirty different towns, with no days off. The vociferous playwright Sammy Gallu said, "Show me another outfit that does so goddamned many concerts. Fred goes into places you never heard of. He walks into a town in Nebraska, and Christ, these people are happy as a lark. They're never going to see a Sinatra there or a Rudolph Serkin or a Bernstein. Waring plays Kennedy Center and he plays Sheboygan. The most important thing is that the concert in Sheboygan is as good as it is in Kennedy Center. That's the thing. There's no fluff off!"

As Fred put it in later years, "I've been asked many times why I still pursue the concert trail, with its one-night stands, the hazards of travel, the inclemencies of weather, the almost predictable signs of exhaustion, and the frayed nerves that start showing up midway on each tour. But my answer is very simple. I love the concert stage more than any other phase of my musical life. Each concert is, to me, as exciting as if it were my first show, and for a very simple reason. Each performance is a new experience in that every audience in every hall in every town is different than the one before, and these audiences are my instrument. I accept a new and stimulating challenge with each show, for I try to play not only our show to the audience, but in turn also play the audience to the Pennsylvanians, in much the same way a fine organist manipulates the stops and keyboards of his instrument. I, too, have my own stops on my own console—my choice of selections, our staging, lights, costumes, soloists, props, skits, choral and orchestral effects, chorales, dynamics, and so on—and this is the charge I get from concerts. After all these years, I still find a live performance before a live audience the most rewarding of all show business."[2]

Arranger and pianist Charlie Naylor told how Fred reacted to a boycott of his performance set off by cold war issues. "We were on a college tour playing to packed houses. At the University of Michigan they asked for the (then) popular Russian piece, 'Meadowland,' which Fred had played often. However, at that time the United States was having some problems with the Soviet Union. Fred declined to play it, saying, 'It's a fine piece of music but I think it's inappropriate to play it right now.' This was published in the University of Michigan paper and apparently picked up at Berkeley. And the concert [there] was banned. While Fred and I were playing poker on a piano backstage behind the curtain of the auditorium on the Berkeley campus, everyone had assembled onstage ready to perform. He looked out, saw only about two hundred people in the auditorium and said to us, 'We have no quarrel with these people who came. We are going to play the best damned show!' And we did."

Fred went out with the two buses, a truck, and a car with the stage crew. The truck was one of the largest on the road because of the amount of equipment he had to carry—multiple lights on tall stands, a five-by-four-foot switchboard, large speakers, microphones hanging and standing, tall wooden boxes for four costume changes, instruments, platforms (risers), and Fred's trunk.

In the twenties, Fred had played weeklong theater dates in big cities. It was practical to use trains for transportation. But one-night stands means just that—moving to another destination every day. For a large troupe with equipment, buses, trucks, and cars are the only solutions.

The bus driver was one of the most important people in a tour. I had not realized *how* vital he was until I took the group out in 1980 when Fred became ill. In some states, the roads are terrible. The maneuvering around potholes and hairpin turns by the driver is the key to a comfortable ride. He should know all the best routes and be skilled in finding the hotel and theater in each city. A bus driver's life isn't worth two cents if, after a long six-hour drive, he becomes hopelessly lost trying to find the hotel in the center of a town.

"I fell in love with the Pennsylvanians the first time I met them—that was fourteen years and five hundred thousand miles ago," bus driver Lou Benson said. "They managed to make the huge bus look homey. They hung things around. Mr. Waring always had carpet put in. One year a featured singer spent all his spare time getting out a newspaper of social and special events on the bus."

Fred always rode in the back facing the rear. The next-to-the-last seats on each side of the aisle were turned backwards, thus making room for a specially built card table. The toilet in the back was never used except to store stringed instruments—a pit stop was made every two hours, and heaven help the thimble bellies. The card table was in use every day as the Pennsylvanians traveled across the country. Fred said it was the longest running poker game in history. Charlie Naylor, an avid participant, said, "One time we were playing cards after rehearsal at 1697 Broadway. It was about 4 P.M. and we were still playing hours later. Fred drove up to Shaw-nee and called us. He played a couple of hands by telephone."

Ty Cobb reported on another extraordinary game in his *Nevada State Journal* column: "One Pennsylvanian drew a natural royal flush in hearts. Within the same hour he drew a second natural royal flush in hearts. Mr. Albert Morehead, bridge column expert for *The New York Times*, figured, 'The odds against getting these two royal flushes in the same suit are about 938,715,200 to 1. Therefore, it would not be unreasonable to presume that this experience may well be unique among those of all poker players who have ever lived.'"[3]

. . .

The musicians' union used to have a rule that a traveling band had to pay the salary of the local orchestra because supposedly that band was usurping their job. Most people felt it was unfair, but for years Fred paid the salary for an entire orchestra. Finally, one time in Minneapolis, Fred said, "If I'm hiring an orchestra, I want the orchestra to be in the lobby playing as the people come in. If I'm going to hire the musicians, I want to see them."

Lumpy was there and said, "You never saw a more disgruntled, grum-bling, horrible sounding bunch of old broken-down musicians sitting in the lobby playing when the people came in. They hadn't had to perform for anybody else. That's the only time I remember Fred doing it."

When the curtain came down at the end of a performance and before everyone rushed offstage to change and pack their costumes, the com-pany road manager would make an important announcement—the *time* of the next day's departure. If the distance was far, then the departure hour from the hotel was early, which invariably elicited a few groans. The Penn-sylvanians were required to have their bags down by the bus in front of the hotel no later than one-half hour before departure, and to be on the bus ready to go at the scheduled time.

All of our children, at one time or other, worked in and around the Penn-sylvanians. Dixie sang and Freddy played his trombone on a few tours. One year our gentle, soft-spoken Paul went out as company road manager. Fred warned him, "Prepare yourself to be the most hated man on tour."

Fred told me later one singer incensed everyone by showing up late for departures. Finally Paul had enough of this. One morning he got on the bus and told the driver to drive around the block. When they returned, the boy was waiting at the curb—irate. Paul got out and faced him while

Fred was looking on, quietly amused. The singer's face flushed and his voice rose. Paul said, "I can raise my voice just as high as yours." With little more said, they entered the bus, and that was the end of it. Once in a while someone might be a little tardy, and the ritual ribald song would be sung, with its inelegant ending about being a horse's derrière.

On tour, the Pennsylvanians had everything arranged and paid for by Fred except their food. When the bus pulled up in front of the hotel, room keys were handed to them in envelopes—no standing in line to register. The bus would be waiting to take them to the theater in time to dress and make up, and remain there to return them to the hotel. If the kitchen were closed after the concert, the bus driver would take them to a restaurant.

. . .

Sophisticated lighting effects and multiple costume changes weren't considered important when the Pennsylvanians appeared in concert during the radio and television years. The girls each had one pretty dress, and that was it. But reengagements in certain cities year after year (Pasadena; Tempe, Arizona; Washington, D.C.; Milwaukee; Minneapolis, to name a few, for thirty-three consecutive years) necessitated more interesting and more frequent costume changes throughout a two-and-a-half-hour show. An audience is more affronted by a visual repeat than an audio one.

I learned that lesson as a duo pianist. I wore pretty ballerina-length costumes created by a stage designer and sewn by the Brooks Costume Company. Livingston and I were almost always asked back wherever we played, and I inadvertently wore the same dress in one repeat town. The people didn't remember what pieces we played, but they certainly remembered what I wore and consequently felt cheated. After our manager at Columbia Artists informed us of my unfortunate oversight, I always kept a "little black book"—the town and the gown.

Fred's stage light man appeared to be a dancing magician as he stood behind his switchboard manipulating the levers and buttons while the music was performed. He had to have a keen musical ear to keep up with the show's pace—changing lights on certain beats, creating moods and split-second blackouts for a shift of positions onstage. The sound man was just as important, sitting out in the auditorium behind his board, trying to adjust to each hall's acoustics. In today's market, all that equipment would be almost antediluvian, but, as usual, Fred was one of the first to incorporate the totality of high-fidelity quality to the concert stage with a multi-speaker system that produced an all-encompassing sound.

During the television years in the early fifties, Fred had maintained a spot on the show called "Varsity Show Case," featuring each week a special talent selected from colleges and universities throughout the United States. One time a magnificent black singer performed. His name was Frank Davis, and Fred asked him to become a Pennsylvanian. Frank's father and his brothers were all Southern ministers, and a move into the wicked, licentious world of show business, in their minds, was only a step from the devil and his evil ways. Fortunately, the Pennsylvanians' clean-cut American image plus Fred's persuasive arguments soothed the family fears. Frank joined the Pennsylvanians and was soon loved by all. What a performer! We all watched him from backstage, onstage, wherever, with amazement and awe. When the television contract ended in the fifties and the long, long road tours became a way of life, problems of housing and restaurants surfaced for Frank.

"In Kansas we had two bus loads of Pennsylvanians," Fred said. "For a lunch stop, one bus would pull up and then, of course, the other one. One time we stopped at a roadside place and the first bus unloaded. Frank, his roommate Lumpy, and I were the last off the second bus. We walked into this large roadside restaurant. There were only three open seats, at the fountain. The rest of the Pennsylvanians were seated and had given their orders. Lumpy, Frank, and I walked to the empty seats at the counter. A very rude man approached us and said, 'We don't serve niggers here.' Of course, I bristled and yelled out, 'Everybody out! We're not welcome here!' And fifty-five Pennsylvanians rose and left. We boarded our buses and went to where we were welcome."

The South was still in the dark ages of segregation. Once the Mason-Dixon line was crossed, Frank was not permitted to room with the Pennsylvanians. He was forced to sleep in private homes and sometimes terrible motels. After the incident with the lunch bus stop, seven or eight of the Pennsylvanians decided to form a club—the TOTCTM (Too Old to Cut the Mustard) Club.

"We had it all organized so that we would take turns being shoppers," Lumpy said. "We'd buy bread, cheese, ham, mayonnaise, mustard, and maybe a couple of bottles of beer. We made out the menu before each tour. Lou Bode was the Magic Chef—that was his title. He'd put on an apron, butter the bread, and slap on ham or baloney. By the time everybody got back, we had our crumbs all cleaned up—the rinds of the baloney and everything out in garbage cans on the streets. Anyone could join in if they wanted from time to time."

The spirit of the "lunch bunch" was invariably upbeat, with its repertoire of marching songs and old hymns with new lyrics, such as:

BLESS THIS BUS

Bless this bus, the driver too,
Bless the air so stale and blue.
Bless the aisle all smeared with beer,
Bless the bridge game in the rear.
Bless the roads and railroad tracks,
Bless our poor old aching backs.
Bless our Captain brave and bold,
The Magic Chef so fat and old.
Bless us all that soon we'll be
In New York, My City, 'Tis of thee.

But the threat to Frank's well-being outside the bus was ever present. "We were giving a concert in Ruston [Louisiana], and the local big shots wanted to have dinner for us at this very prominent restaurant," Fred said. "And I always had a rule that I would never go out to dinner unless they invited everybody. It was made explicit. The mayor had assured me that we were all invited, and I reminded him that we had a black singer, Frank Davis, with us. He said, 'That's all right. Don't worry about that.' I said, 'Now, we have been denied the privilege of eating at various places because of Frank, and I don't want anything to happen.' He assured me that everything was taken care of, and I said, 'Well, I will come with him to make certain there is no problem.'

"The dinner was across the street from the hotel, so I stayed back with Frank and Daisy, one of our singers, and we walked across together. All the Pennsylvanians had been admitted and were seated. We walked to the door and somebody at the door said, 'Oh, there's been some mistake.' I said, 'No, there's no mistake at all. I'm Mr. Waring.' 'Oh, we are expecting you, Mr. Waring, but . . . ah . . .'

"He looked at Frank and then our host came over and very effusively tried to beg off. He said, 'I did my best and everything was all set, but I got here and they were afraid they would lose their license, but I have arranged for Frank to eat with the employees.' I said, 'Well, that's fine. That's where Daisy and I will eat.' He said, 'Oh, no, you don't have to.' I said, 'I know I don't have to. I don't have to come in at all. But I was invited, so I'm coming in, and if that's where one of my people has to go, then I will go there.' We went out and sat in the help's dining room and had a very pleasant dinner. But my heart was bleeding for Frank.

"It so happened that his cousin was president of Grambling State University, which adjoins Ruston. We were appearing there the following day. Of course, we were naturally all welcome there, and we saw a great demonstration of how people can rise above such problems. The best dressed students I had ever seen were on that campus. Every boy wore a suit, shirt, and tie, and every girl wore a pretty dress and had her hair fashioned. It was really a thrilling sight to see this audience, to see these attractive people, and to watch their fine behavior.

"We arrived in Memphis, where we had played many times and established records there in several theaters. Frank had been the star of our show and it was well advertised. We featured him in the twenty-minute Creation number called 'God's Trombones' as well as several solos. In the afternoon while my crew was setting up for us in the evening, the local stage manager came over to me and very apologetically said, 'Fred, I have some bad news.'

"'What is it?' I asked.

"'Well, the mayor's office called and said that we were not to raise the curtain tonight if I insisted on using the black singer.'

"I replied instantly, 'Well, that's fine with me. You don't need to raise the curtain. We'll do the show in back of the curtain. Our contract is to do the show, and they knew that we had a black performer before they signed the contract. You just tell the mayor that it is OK with me—fine—they don't need to raise the curtain. We'll do the show behind the curtain.' Evidently the ruse worked because the stage manager came back to me very apologetically and said, 'I gave them your message, and they fell for it and I'm awfully glad. I apologize for their bad manners.'"

Company manager Murray Luth said, "Early in the show when Fred came offstage I said, 'Fred, be careful. This is the first time these people have seen a black man perform with whites in a city-owned auditorium.' Fred reached into his pocket and pulled out a dollar bill—put it down on a property crate. 'Cover it!'

"I said, 'What am I betting on?' Waring glanced across the stage, ready to go on again. 'I'm betting that Frank stops the show!' He did."

The concert at Jackson, Mississippi, the next night brought with it a repeat of what they had encountered in Memphis. And Fred had his own solution. After the performance he left Jackson and never went back with his beloved Pennsylvanians.

· · ·

Every Pennsylvanian has some anecdote about the horrendously long bus tours during the thirty years they spent on the road after the radio and television era. Soprano soloist Lette Rehnolds: "On tour there are only three things discussed. First, what's the Boss's mood today? Second, who had a crush on whom? And third, what's the best restaurant in town? The first is always discussed at length and is the most important and *fun!*"

Stage manager Lou Metz recalled a fifteen-hour trip from Rochester, Minnesota, to Omaha, Nebraska, in a blizzard in the dead of winter. The bus door had blown off and the troupe was one sorry lot, but the show went on for the few hundred brave fans.

Poley's wife, Yvette, said, "People associated Poley with clowning. One day he missed his chair and fell ten feet from the set to the stage. The audience laughed. They thought he was playing pranks, as usual. Fred walked to the footlights and called out, 'Is there a doctor in the house?' The audience laughed again. Poley was taken to the hospital and they wanted to amputate his thumb. His bones were so smashed and the flesh so torn and bruised. Poley said, 'You can't do it.' Fortunately, the man who set his hand was a New York Yankee specialist." Poley was soon back onstage and continued to clown and improvise the rest of his and Fred's professional life together, from 1916 to 1980—sixty-four years.

Fred Culley mentioned that Fred would sometimes get annoyed and take it out on somebody else, often the first person who was handy. "One night after an altercation with the local theater stage manager, he introduced baritone Joe Marine, and then abruptly walked offstage," he said. "I got up and conducted for Joe, who was furious with Fred. Joe went to his hotel and started packing. Finally the phone rang. Joe picked it up and said, 'Who is it?' The other end said, 'Fred.' Joe said, 'Fred who?' Fred said, 'I want to talk to you,' and went to Joe's room, but Joe was so stiff and reluctant to remain on tour that Fred got mad all over again, yanked open a door and walked into a closet. That broke the ice."

On long tours the length of each show was of great concern to the Pennsylvanians, especially the girls, who sometimes stood onstage in their high heels five hours a night performing two shows back to back. Bob Harris tells of such a tour:

"As usual we didn't have an absolutely set program. Fred would change things around or add things. We had a shortened version of the 'Song of America' which I guess ran about twenty-two minutes or so. Occasionally in the second half of the show he would insert the piece. It was rather long, and everybody would be tired at that point. There was some grumbling and shaking of heads about that insertion. I decided to start an insurance business. I would insure any member of the orchestra or the glee club against 'Song of America,' and the premium on my policy was ten cents. If we performed 'Song of America' in the concert, I paid fifty cents. I was doing pretty well. I was several dollars ahead.

"Then we went to Purdue and did two concerts in the huge auditorium there on one night. On both concerts, Fred did 'Song of America.' I had several double indemnity policies that night (people would pay twenty cents), so I really lost my shirt—economically—and my business went on the rocks. When I got on the train the next day, I put a black arm band around my jacket sleeve. Someone said Fred saw me in the diner and asked if there was a death in my family, and they said, 'No, he just lost his shirt on his insurance business.'"

Bob Harris had another anecdote about "Song of America." In those days, recording was harrowing and nerve-wracking. There was no splicing or dubbing in corrections, and a take had to be flawless from beginning to end. "We had been recording 'Song of America' for almost three hours and were all very tired," he said. "Our last segment was the 'Midnight Ride of Paul Revere.' It had a lot of lyrics and was complicated and difficult. We started out and everything was going great, looked like it might be a take; we come to the finale—*The people who waken and listen to hear, the midnight ride of P-a-u-l R-e-v-e-r-e*'—the piano finished didly, didly, didly, *bong!* On the *bong*, Hawley hit the wrong chord. There was stark silence. Fred slowly took off his granny glasses, put down the pencil he was conducting with, and said, '*Hawley, Hawley, Hawley . . . Lord God almighty.*'"

Ray Sax spoke of the logistical problems of providing meals for such a large troupe in remote geographical areas: "We were in the Snake River Canyon and everyone was starving—we hadn't found an eating place. Suddenly we see a very small diner. Fifty-five of us pour in. The owner is overwhelmed. He said, 'You are most welcome but I have no help.' Fred said, 'We'd be happy to help.' Fred cooked, the girls waited on tables, and the boys cleaned up and washed dishes, and a delightful time was had by all."

I joined Fred in Palm Beach one year when he decided to give the Pennsylvanians a break in the middle of a long tour. He booked a week at the charming Poinciana Theater, which holds about eight hundred people. The Pennsylvanians could rest and go to the beach each day. It was common knowledge that the opening night crowd was a pretentious one—dressed to the hilt in their furs and jewels—and much more interested in themselves than what was transpiring onstage.

On Fred's first night, true to form, they arrived late, and at intermission stayed at the bar, returning long after the final bell. As was his custom, Fred was in front of the curtain, having a field day teasing one and all as they straggled down the aisles. Some of them were amused, and some were flustered and embarrassed. At one point a bug flew up slowly from a front row seat, clearly visible to all in the spotlight. Fred studied it thoughtfully as it went up, and then looked down at the audience and said seriously, "That was a chinchilla moth." Later in a TV interview in the lobby he expressed succinctly his opinion of the audience's rude behavior. He wasn't asked back. But then he was in good company. Helen Hayes was also persona non grata for speaking her mind.

It was at the Poinciana that I decided to sharpen my skills as a gin rummy player. Fred, a champion contestant, had taken me on a few times and had defeated me. I asked our company road manager, Murray Luth, to meet me backstage each night to give me some pointers after he had counted the front box office. Murray had bested Fred on many occasions. And so we played every night for two hours while the gang performed onstage. On the fifth night the show ended, and the fans trooped backstage amidst the hustle and bustle of the stagehands' activities and Pennsylvanians changing into street clothes. Suddenly the theater was dark and quiet. Everyone had left except Fred and me. We were in his dressing room. He took the deck of cards and said with his impish grin, "Shut up and deal," quoting the famous Judy Holliday line. We played until 3 A.M. and I beat him cold. What a satisfying evening! I haven't played since.

I always joined Fred in Los Angeles for his annual concerts in the area. One time he took me to meet the spectacled daredevil/comedian Harold Lloyd, a loyal and devoted friend of both Fred and Tom since the 1925 movie *The Freshman*. We drove into his huge estate in Beverly Hills, and there was the Spanish type house as it is pictured in magazines and books, the enormous pool far below, the fully equipped child's playhouse, the formal cypress trees. Harold Lloyd came to the door in his bathrobe (it was three in the afternoon), and greeted Fred like his long-lost brother— kissing and hugging him over and over. After I was introduced, he took us into a room where a Christmas tree stood ceiling-high, covered with ornaments. A few years before, at Tom's request, I had sent some of my hand-decorated Christmas balls to Mr. Lloyd. I was amazed and touched that among the hundreds and hundreds, he was able to point out mine, randomly hung around the tree, which remained in place year-round.

• • •

For the Pennsylvanians, 1960 was not their happiest season. This was the year Tom Waring died. It also marked the unforeseen and tragic death of Gordon Goodman, the veteran performer with the high tenor voice. Everyone was devastated, especially Fred.

Gordon's death followed a series of tragic events, one leading to another, and finally the mysterious death. Fred told me about it. "In New Orleans, an enormous house detective broke into Gordon's room," he said. "Gordon had a girl with him. The detective became very abusive and beat him up. I didn't know about it—only noticed that Gordon lost a lot of weight (he was skinny to begin with). He became run-down. He was able to sing, but was frail. I remember walking up the street with him one night and grabbing him by the arm. His arm was so small—I couldn't believe it. He had been a truck driver. He had been very tough and muscular."

Two weeks after the incident, everyone was backstage getting ready for the show. Gordon, for the first time, said he wasn't feeling well, requesting they start without him. Fred, accustomed to emergencies, shifted solos and selections during the first half, but at intermission when they all trooped down into the large dressing room, to their horror they found G.G., as he was affectionately called, lying on a table curled into a fetal position. He was dead. In accordance with the strict rules of show business, the Pennsylvanians had to change into their second act clothes and perform with smiles and jokes. Positive that Gordon's death was caused by the severe beating he had received, Fred requested an autopsy. Nothing was proven by the results.

. . .

During the fifties, sixties, and seventies, Fred was acknowledged to be the King of the Road by music critics, promoters, and colleagues. Andy Williams used to tease Fred, "No matter what town I'm in, you've either just been there or are just coming." What amazed everyone was that throughout this incessant travel, Fred maintained unparalleled standards of performance.

Variety ended a long rave review of a New York concert with these words: "It is difficult to pinpoint the outstanding numbers because of the excellence of them all. All the numbers are show stoppers, and Waring is his usual affable self, and the whole combination adds up to the finest and most wholesome entertainment now on tour."[4] The story was signed, "Lit," which, to the trade, was the signature of Lenny Littman, the most respected show-business critic at that time.

Another critic wrote:

> I went Friday night to hear Fred Waring and his Pennsylvanians perform, thinking my high brow was in for a painful lowering. I found, to my surprise, that Mr. Waring's show and my brow accommodated each other beautifully. Here was the brightest, smoothest, most skillfully organized and executed entertainment that came Winnipeg's way in many seasons.
>
> Mr. Waring, master of ceremonies, conductor and general guiding spirit of the company, is a glamorous old smoothie who works vigorously but unobtrusively covering his trail with a line of terrible gags that somehow inspires affection, mirth and general pleasure. Actually behind the corn there was impeccable taste.[5]

A *San Francisco Chronicle* interview carried the headline: "FRED WARING PERFECTIONIST." "The thing about Fred Waring is his perfectionist attitude. While talking with him, he started to reach for my tie and then thought better of it. I looked in the mirror and realized my tie was askew."[6]

Many others also called Fred a perfectionist, a term that bothered him no end. He said he was a precisionist and stated flatly toward the end of his career that he had the greatest singing machine. That term did not denote anything mechanical in his mind. It simply meant the Pennsylvanians could follow as one any flip or nuance indicated by Fred's graceful and expressive hands and fingers.

In a *Minneapolis Sunday Tribune* interview on August 9, 1959, Fred explained, "I'll go along halfway with the perfectionist label. It's true as far as our efforts in rehearsal go, but I don't mind seeing a few human mistakes in our performances. I can't think of anything duller than to arrive at some sort of perfection or, even worse, having to stay there. I believe in a moving goal, a sort of portable perfection, that I can trust to stay well out in front of me."[7]

Fred couldn't help *but* push on, and what he created through his relentless persistence touched the hearts of the American people. Well into the seventies, the newspaper critics not only continued to extol Fred and his Pennsylvanians but began to widen their view of his impact on the American scene. They described him as a musical chronicler whose lovely medleys represented every facet and thought in our lives.

As one columnist put it,

> So much has been written about the choral conducting genius of Fred Waring that it's become easy to overlook just how good he is right at this moment. *Waring brought to the 20th century choral music the same thing Coco Chanel brought to 20th century dress and Charlie Chaplin brought to*

the movies. He gave choruses a fleet, light, clear sound that perfectly fits this century. There's no sense in going into that old argument about Waring not performing good music, because when you sing the American popular songs, you are singing some of the best music ever written.[8]

25

Ike and the Famous

TO THIS point we can count five presidents of the United States who have touched the life of Fred Waring from the time of his childhood, the first being Teddy Roosevelt. "My father was a Roosevelt man—top to bottom," Fred said. "When Roosevelt was campaigning on the progressive ticket, my father adopted that ticket and ran for county controller of Blair County, Pennsylvania. Teddy Roosevelt, on his campaign, made a whistle-stop in Tyrone and gave Dad the very glad hand. It happened to be noon, so Dad brought him home for lunch.

"The second president was William Howard Taft. The third was Warren Harding, an ardent golfer. The fourth was Calvin Coolidge. President Coolidge seemed to take great pleasure in attending our Sunday night performances when we appeared in Washington at the Metropolitan Theater. There was not nearly as much Secret Service folderol as today. He often requested to meet with me afterwards. Mr. Hoover and I happened to be corecipients of a dinner award (we were seated beside one another) and I found him to be a most congenial gentleman with a special sense of humor. We both had to speak."

It was the sixth, Dwight D. Eisenhower, however, with whom Fred had his closest relationship. He had long held an unreserved and almost boyish attitude of hero worship for General Eisenhower and felt, along with many others, that Ike would make a splendid president. "I knew Eisenhower's two brothers before I knew him," Fred recalled. "I met Ed when he came to our golf tournament, and I met Milton when he was president of Penn State while I served on the board of trustees. Milton made certain that I met Dwight, who by then had become president of Columbia University."

In Eisenhower, Fred saw a true-blue patriot who stood for many principles he believed in, and he decided to go all out and campaign for Ike. Although many people wanted the former general to run for president, Eisenhower, who was in Europe at the time, was rather reluctant about the idea. A political rally was held in Madison Square Garden on February 8, 1952, where an overcapacity crowd roared its approval of Dwight D. Eisenhower as their candidate for president of the United States. Eighty-seven famous and best-loved stars of show business took part under the leadership of Fred, George Murphy, Tex McCrary, and several others. The event was recorded, and renowned aviatrix Jackie Cochran flew the film of the rally to Eisenhower, who then decided to run for office.

Later in the spring Fred selected—from volunteers in the Pennsylvanians—a lively and versatile group of singers who could not only stage a highly entertaining show but who could also hold their own in the bantering and battering of political issues on the campaign trail. They started off in New Hampshire and became known as the New Hampshire Nine. When preparations were being made for General Eisenhower's appearance at Abilene, Kansas, and he was asked if he wanted a delegation of Hollywood stars to take part, the candidate replied that he "just wanted Fred Waring and that little group that did such good work in New Hampshire."[1]

Eisenhower's long and arduous campaign ended with a bang-up rally at the Boston Garden, packed with a solid mass of shouting, singing, and applauding people. This was the night before the election. The general invited Fred and the New Hampshire Nine to ride on his train to New York that night, along with the newspaper people.

Washington correspondent Newman Wright recalled this night a year later in an award-winning piece captioned "Sweetest Music Ever," with the subhead "Years Later . . . and the Power, and the Glory Still Echoes from the Eisenhower Train,"

> Never again—not in this world at least—do I expect to hear music as sweet as the singing I heard just one year ago tonight.
>
> Most of the singers weren't professional—many of them weren't even good singers—and the sounds didn't come from a concert stage or any other place where you might expect to hear good music.
>
> It all happened in the dirty, dimly-lighted malodorous club car of a railroad train that was grunting and grinding through foul weather on its way from Boston to New York.

The train was the "Look Ahead, Neighbor Special" from which Gen. Dwight D. Eisenhower had addressed millions of U.S. citizens in his historic "Crusade" for the presidency. It was making its last run of the campaign.

Back of it, up, down and across the nation, were thousands of hot, cold, wet and dry miles, all of them weary, and nearly all of them incredibly dirty. Back of it, too, were the echoes of scores of good, bad and indifferent political speeches. And the echoes of tens of thousands of "We Like Ike" cheers, campaign songs and 17 gun salutes.

Aboard were Gen. Eisenhower, his beloved Mamie and a host of bright, medium bright and dim political lights.

And some 50 dog-tired, bedraggled, sleep-starved newspaper writers who had been reporting the campaign from its beginning.

And orchestra leader Fred Waring, accompanied by a few of the talented singers from his excellent choir.

The campaign was over.

Earlier that night Gen. Eisenhower had made his last speech to a great throng in the Boston Garden which had nearly torn the roof from the building with its cheers.

He had made good on his promise to return to traditionally Democratic Boston. And he had made good on his promise to do everything he could to bolster up the ill-starred campaign for re-election of U.S. Senator Henry Cabot Lodge.

The rally had been a real dilly. There had been spotlighted "Ike" balloons all over midtown Boston. On the great stage of the Garden, Waring and his artists had contributed to the election eve excitement with a full dress, Hollywood-style production.

We had pulled out of Back Bay Station around midnight, in a driving very-cold, very-wet rain, and were en route to New York, where the Eisenhowers were to vote, rest, and then go to the Hotel Commodore to listen to the election returns.

Fred Waring was exhausted. He needed a shave. His clothes were rumpled, as were those of his entertainers. Mamie, in her own words, was "bushed." The general didn't have to say anything. He looked and acted like a man who had been through an ordeal, and was glad it was over. The appearances of the reporters defied description.

But without any announcement being made, with the heat of the campaign off and with no stories to file, we all gravitated into the club car to sit, chat, or mope.

The general was there wearing a smoking jacket the newspaper photographers had given to him. Mamie was there with her famous bangs a bit askew from the wind and rain. Her eyes glistened with the feverish light of fatigue.

Someone suggested a song and Waring conducted the motley "choir" through such campaign favorites as "Mamie" and "The Sunshine of Your Smile."

The train lurched along. It was getting late. The general looked at his watch, stretched and yawned. He asked for one more song before retiring.

And then it happened.

Waring held up his arms as you have seen him do on television, then gave the downbeat. A couple of professionals seated on the floor at the other end of the crowded car started with:

"Our Father which art in heaven. . . ."

The car creaked a protest, a door opened to let in a mechanical screech from the couplings, and a few of the car lights blinked; but on it went.

Both the general and his wife had started to sing by the time we got to *"Thy kingdom come . . ."* and at *"Give us this day . . ."* we were all in the act.

A train rushing past us to Boston shrieked in disgust. An ash receiver toppled over as we rounded a curve; but not one singer quit.

". . . but deliver us from evil . . ."

The rain and sleet, slapping and swishing out some kind of rhythm against the windows, almost provided an accompaniment.

". . . and the power, and the glory . . ."

The door flew open again, letting in the background of clicking wheels and whistling wind, and someone dropped a glass.

The *"amen"* to which Waring had brought us with smiles of approval and expert direction was the best I have ever heard.

Then there was silence for about ten seconds.

Then the Eisenhowers stood up, smiled in gratitude at Waring and his "choir" and went off to their car.

Everyone else went off to bed, too, with the sound of a great song, well sung, still ringing.

Sometimes at night when it is raining, I imagine I can still hear it; but of course I can't.

And I never shall.

You don't hear things like that twice.[2]

About the only thing that Newman Wright failed to observe from where he sat in the train was the fact that, when the general made his request for "one more song," it was he who had suggested "The Lord's Prayer."

The train arrived in New York in the morning, and Fred flew to Shawnee to vote. "Ike told me, 'You be sure to be back here tonight,'" Fred said. "That was the night of the election *and* my terrible fifteen-minute solo on TV without knowing I was on." Everyone had gathered at the Commodore to await the election returns. When the results came in, the throng in the big ballroom had gone wild. The general had sent Fred to quiet them down until he could make his appearance. Fred was trying to get the obstreperous crowd to learn a simple song for the new president elect's entrance, but they weren't listening. His mike was not on in the hall—just over the air. He sang a solo on nationwide hookup for an endless fifteen minutes pleading, exhorting, cajoling the noisy audience who couldn't hear him.

Afterwards a few friends went upstairs to Ike and Mamie's quarters, and finally everyone left. Fred said, "I was standing in the narrow hall with my back against the wall. Dwight came out and put both hands on my shoulders. I said, 'You look tired. Are you?' He said, 'No, I'm just pooped.'

"Now he was standing there, hands on my shoulders, leaning over, and there was kind of a tunnel between us. A little, stray drunk came along, pushed Ike's hands off my shoulders and said, 'Whersh the General?' Ike said, 'He's right in there.' So the fellow went into the suite, and we walked away."

In 1953, Fred was asked to stage an Eisenhower birthday party. As a tribute to the man he admired and loved, Fred decided to make it a birthday party surpassing all. There would be ten thousand guests to greet the president in a huge arena in Hershey, Pennsylvania. When his plans were completed, he took them to the committee, and they said that several things Fred wanted the president to do would "certainly never be permitted by the Secret Service." Nobody on the committee was willing to ask the White House, so Fred said, "Well, I'll ask him myself!"

"I was going to Denver and I knew the president would be there. I was playing in the Hills Dilly Tournament. After one of our matches, the president was there at the eighteenth hole and said, 'Why don't you come by and have a drink. Mamie and Mim (Mrs. Eisenhower's mother) would love to see you.' They lived about a mile from the club. So I went to Lafayette Street. We went out to the backyard where they had a table and chairs set up. I brought in my blueprints of the Hershey Arena and plans for the production. I said, 'Now, Mr. President, you know about the birthday party. You know I'm the producer and it's a big responsibility and I want to do it well.' He said, 'Well, what can I do?'

"I opened the layout to show him what we were planning. It was done in color. His eyes glowed. The whole arena had a white roadway with white picket fences down the aisles. Hershey gardeners would put in green bushes and flowers. The stage was white with a special red carpet. I said, 'Mr. President, we want you and Mamie to ride in this buggy. Will you ride in the buggy and make your entrance?' '*Will* I? Hell, I'll *drive* the horse,' and

Mamie said, 'Oh, Ike. You know you haven't driven a horse in years.' He said, 'Now Mamie. You *know* I can drive a horse and I certainly will.' And we all laughed and that was settled.

"I showed him the plans of a thousand kids dressed in white singing 'Song of America.' 'We want you to drive around here and then come up the steps where you will be greeted by an honor guard from many organizations including the Red Cross, Salvation Army and Boy Scouts.' He said, 'That's magnificent.' 'At the top of the steps you will be presented the largest birthday cake ever built. It will come up through the floor.'"

Many people were involved during the months it took to plan and coordinate the festival, including those in Fred's organization—some to gather and train the thousand student singers and dancers, some for staging and lighting. A special dinner at a hundred dollars a plate was arranged and also a delicious box supper for the less affluent. The president, after an appearance at the formal affair, ate his fried chicken in the open with the young performers.

Before the president and Mamie made their entrance, driving the horse and buggy, the ten thousand spectators were rehearsed by Fred. Each had been given a miniature birthday cake with a single candle on top. On the bottom of the cake container was a piece of emery and five kitchen matches, lightly glued. Three were for rehearsal, with two to spare for the performance. (Fred, as always, was the stickler for detail.) He first taught them to light their candle on cue, and then he taught them a simple song he and Jack Dolph had written called "Where in the World but in America."

The moment the Eisenhowers drove into the arena, spotlighted against the white path, all other lights were extinguished. The audience was cued to stand up as the president passed, and to start singing. By the time the buggy came full circle at the stage, the whole arena was filled with song. One can imagine the Secret Service downing a few stiff drinks when that evening was over!

While Fred greeted the Eisenhowers, an eight-foot cake rose majestically out of the floor. Eisenhower was given a match which he, with a flourish, struck on the seat of his pants, all the while showing his pleasure with his famous grin. When he lit the candle on the cake, not only did it light up instantaneously but so did those of the ten thousand pre-rehearsed audience. Everything went off smooth as silk, although the crew had been holding its breath because the hoist for the cake had not worked well in the afternoon—tipping the cake sideways and missing the hole completely.

Later, from the presidential box, the Eisenhowers witnessed the tremendous show. I'm told they were deeply touched, and that it was difficult for Ike to control his voice after an awesome finale of the "Battle Hymn of the Republic," his favorite piece. Years later Fred, who was never satisfied completely with anything he did professionally, said, "I think it was one of the greatest things ever done in show business. It was certainly the finest thing I've ever had a part of."

It was not just the performers and pageantry that made the event unique. It was Fred's uncanny ability to reach, touch, and communicate with ten thousand individuals and make each one of them feel an important part of the cast. They were there because they loved the president, but it was Fred who provided them with a way to express it and create a truly spectacular evening. Fred was proud of them. "They did it perfectly! They didn't make a mistake. There never was such an audience!" Hugh Morris of Inter News Service agreed: "Probably nobody in the nation's history ever had a birthday party like Ike's."[3]

President Eisenhower felt a deep rapport with Fred and his Pennsylvanians. True, he liked their music and the way it was performed, but it was more than that. It was their genuineness. Fred was the Real McCoy. He could be faulted for many shortcomings but he never did anything for effect. He *believed* in what he did. He never waved a flag because it was the popular thing. He waved it during the Vietnam War because he felt for and was proud of those serving—the promoters and media be damned. The Pennsylvanians were real, too. They cared about one another, and audiences sensed their sincerity.

Fred Culley once compared the two presidents, FDR and Ike: "Eisenhower personally liked the *people* in the Pennsylvanians—he always remembered the old-timers and would go out of his way to shake hands with Leonard and Poley. With Roosevelt, it was more of a music appreciation. He loved our music and he would sit back and really enjoy it, where Eisenhower would sort of look and beam on everybody and say, 'These are my friends—I *love* these people.'"

Fred, like most people in the United States with personal ties to the presidency, treasured some favorite anecdotes: "I'll never forget one overnight visit in the White House. I stayed in the bedroom right over the main entrance. Eight o'clock in the morning there was a tap on my door. I was shaving. I thought it was probably my breakfast. It wasn't. It was the president.

"He said, 'May I come in? I just finished my first hour of work and I have fifteen minutes and I would like to talk.' I said, 'By all means. Come in. I'm just about finished shaving and then I'll have my breakfast.' He said, 'Yes, I ordered an extra cup of coffee.'

"As I finished shaving, he sat on the toilet seat and talked to me. I've often thought what a wonderful picture that would have been. We talked and when I finished shaving, breakfast was there and we ate together. That was my *most* interesting experience at the White House.

"One time I had occasion to call the White House by telephone. The operator said, 'Unfortunately, neither Mrs. Eisenhower nor the president is in at the moment, but Mrs. Eisenhower's mother is here. Would you like to talk to her? She knows you're on the phone.' I said, 'I would love to talk to her.'

"They put her on. She said, 'Hellooo. Mrs. Lincoln speaking. Who is this?' She was staying in the Lincoln Room and she thought that would be real cute to tell me she was Mrs. Lincoln. She used to be very upset if I'd not call her when I was in Denver or if I did not send her flowers on Mamie's birthday. I think Cora [Fred's secretary] made a mistake and sent them to Mamie instead. Mamie wrote to me and said I had a little patching up to do, that Mim wasn't too happy about being ignored on Mamie's birthday."

Shortly after Eisenhower was elected president, he asked Fred to help organize some of the White House entertainment. In 1953 the Supreme Court was to be entertained at a small state dinner. Since Livingston and I would be touring in the Washington, D.C., area, Fred submitted our names for approval.

We and the music we had selected were accepted. The big night arrived. Unfortunately, in the interim weeks, an enormous brouhaha had erupted among the justices, making front-page news. For several years the Supreme Court had been neither tranquil nor unified due to contentious debates between right- and left-wingers. Outspoken Felix Frankfurter privately referred to Justice Black as Hillbilly Hugo and he also held Chief Justice Vinson in such intellectual contempt that Vinson's sudden death was, to Frankfurter, the strongest proof he had yet seen of the existence of God.

As this was a dinner for nine justices, their wives, and a few others, the small crowd made the animosity even more evident and tangible. All the notables were present—no one stayed away, but no one was smiling, either. It was not a joyous affair. After the elegant dinner when everyone reassembled in the East Room to hear us play, the tension increased. It was an incredibly forbidding atmosphere. Livingston and I sat down, facing each other, at our pianos, and I turned to look at Mamie who was sitting a few feet from us in the front row. She winked and nodded and kept giving us smiling encouragement, as did Ike. But also in the front row were Frankfurter and, next to him, J. Edgar Hoover—both glowering. We were used to love and warmth flowing around us when we played. Performing was not easy that night, but the half-hour passed. No blows or verbal accusations were exchanged during our small concert. At the end they applauded warmly, but everyone departed quickly as though escaping a prison. Under the portico, Livingston and I were waiting for a taxi. Standing next to us were Mr. and Mrs. Sherman Adams. That week's *Time* magazine had carried a lengthy article about them and reported on his testy temper. They wrote that once Mrs. Adams, in retaliation for one of his incendiary remarks, put soap in Mr. Adam's sandwich. As I look back, I can't believe I had the gall to ask her if it was true. Mrs. Adams laughed and said, "I only wish I'd thought of it!" and then they graciously offered to take us to our hotel. And so ended my first invitation to the White House.

• • •

In 1957 Queen Elizabeth and Prince Philip came to the United States on a state visit. Fred and the Pennsylvanians were asked to entertain. It was my birthday, October 18. He and I were invited to the dinner, and after the program the Pennsylvanians were given a buffet supper, during which the president mingled and chatted with them.

This was my second White House dinner, a dazzling affair. There was something quite spine-tingling about walking into the North Entrance foyer to the spirited music of the Marine band, their dashing red uniforms spectacular against the white marble walls. A young, gold-braided serviceman took my arm and led us into the East Room, where ninety-seven guests gathered. No cocktails were served at that time. The ladies were dressed in their prettiest ball gowns, with long white above-the-elbow gloves, and the men wore white tie and tails. Just before dinner, the honored guests and President and Mrs. Eisenhower came in, and we all filed past to be introduced. We proceeded into the dining room, which held a single E-shaped table. The pale green walls and gold draperies were courtesy of the Trumans, who had not liked the handsome dark paneling underneath. The heads of state and those guests next in importance were seated in the center facing the rest of us.

The array of gold cutlery fanning out from each plate probably struck terror in the hearts of a few, while the waiters stifled no small amusement at everyone's faux pas. Today only three courses are served, but at that banquet there were six. Spoons and knives plus a tiny two-tined fork lay on the right side of my plate. On the other side were several forks with a rather odd-looking one on the outside.

The first course was melon with prosciutto ham. Everyone looked around to see what their neighbor was doing. Then came soup. That was easy. Next a fish mousse. Woe to those who had chosen the rather flat fork for their melon, because now they had to eat gelatinous mousse with a two-tined thing that held nothing at all. Wines were served with certain courses—first sherry, then white wine, red wine, and finally champagne. Finger bowls, of course, each with a sprig of sweet geranium, were customary in those days.

The toasts and speeches were short and diplomatically pleasant. After dinner, as was traditional, the men and women separated for half an hour into two smaller reception areas—the ladies to the Red Room for coffee served in demitasse cups. No one smoked. The men convened in the Green Room, over coffee, cigars, and liqueurs. Two hundred additional guests invited for the after-dinner festivities had already been waiting an hour in the now rearranged East Room. It was after 10:30 P.M. when the dinner guests joined the others for the entertainment.

Fred had received strict orders from the White House staff running the affair. First, the program was to be thirty minutes long—that was easy; and second, it had to be approved by the White House—that wasn't so easy. When ten people's opinions are involved, the results are somewhat similar to the camel, which, they say, was formed by a committee.

The Pennsylvanians performed well even though some of them weren't seasoned, since they were new and the tour had just begun. The program ended and everybody was clapping, when the president suddenly stood up, objecting that no Waring program was complete without the "Battle Hymn of the Republic." Fred explained that sixty percent of the Pennsylvanians were new young people, not familiar with the piece—but he would attempt it if everyone would join in. At the final chorus, everyone stood up and sang—Queen Elizabeth, Prince Philip, Mamie—"*Glory, Glory Hallelujah, his truth is marching on!*" Afterwards, a sumptuous buffet supper with champagne was served.

Fred was invited by the queen to visit London and play a command performance, but between concert commitments and prohibitive costs, he had to decline. Most stars take themselves and a few key musicians for those command performances. Fred had more than fifty at the time. One curious fact came to light. The English unions listed Fred Waring's Orchestra as a "dance band" and subject to a different set of regulations than a concert company. Fred hadn't played a dance in twenty years.

Fred was called upon to entertain at the White House again in 1959, when Khrushchev was coming to the United States for the first time for a state visit. The president asked Fred to submit a program for the evening concert. Everyone in the White House was apprehensive and on edge. No one could agree on the music suggested—phone calls and suggestions went back and forth. Finally all was settled, and on the appointed day, Fred and I flew to Washington. We just happened to arrive at the airport shortly before Khrushchev. As we drove into town in a big, black limousine, many curious people lining the streets assumed Fred was Khrushchev. It was eerie. They were just peering; *no one* was smiling or clapping, and men with guns, clearly visible, were on top of every building.

The dinner that night was a sobering affair. The Russian women looked as though they had made every effort to appear as colorless and dowdy as possible. They wore plain drab dresses with ground-gripper Oxford-type shoes. Collars and accessories were a little soiled, and snaps and buttons were missing.

After dinner when Khrushchev rose to give the traditional toast, he started very softly but little by little his voice rose, and soon he started to rant and spill forth threatening words in such a belligerent manner that every American in the room was stunned. He referred to the USSR's recent bloody takeover of Hungary as a mere scratch on the surface of what they planned to do. He hinted at "burying America." Everything had been translated, of course, as he went along. I found it quite frightening and unsettling, and could not fathom how diplomatic relations could be carried on with someone so lacking in tact and out of control of himself. Later on, we all became accustomed to his crude shoe-pounding tactics, but that first night made me very thankful to be an American.

Sol Hurok, the impresario, called Fred's office a week later and said that Khrushchev wanted Fred to perform in Russia. But commitments and logistics also made this tour impossible.

The king and queen of Thailand were quite young when they arrived for a state visit. She was very pretty and elegant, and he scholarly with his glasses. The queen was sheathed in gold—a simple oriental gown of delicate gold threads with a wide band of exquisite gold filigree that encircled her neck, slanted across her bosom and formed a belt around her waist. Most unusual. After dinner, the ladies went into the Red Room for coffee, where Mrs. Nixon was presiding. The queen was seated on a love seat, and Pat Nixon arranged for one of us to sit with her. At one point she asked me. I was surprised and delighted to be included. The queen and I talked about our children.

When Fred entertained the president of Ireland, Eamon De Valera, the program selection was settled immediately. The committee agreed that the Pennsylvanians' Irish choral medley called "Erin Go Bragh" was the right choice. De Valera was beaming throughout. The Pennsylvanians had touched his heart.

Fred was much too middlebrow for the Kennedys, of course, and much too Republican for the Carters. The Pennsylvanians did perform once for Nixon, and that was when I became aware of the round tables in the state dining room and the fewer meal courses. Also, there were many more women, both in the service band and in the dining area.

For many years, Fred had not been invited to the White House, but out of the blue we received an invitation from the Reagans to a dinner honoring the president of Mexico. The date was 1984. As it turned out, it was two months before Fred died. It was the first time in his entire career that the Pennsylvanians had not been invited, too, to entertain after dinner. Fred was *not* about to go without his Pennsylvanians. I didn't say anything right away, but after a few days, I said, "Fred, there are two hundred and thirty million people in the United States, and about a hundred and fifty of them have been invited to this dinner. I really think you should go." The next day I heard him say over the phone, "Yeah, I'm going. Virginia says I have to go." And so we went.

The first person we saw in the East Room where cocktails were being served was a tall, thin, goateed elderly gentleman with a twinkle in his eye. Fred rushed up and said, "Quick, Henry, the flit." It was Dr. Seuss. He and Fred had known each other in the early days of radio, when Ted Geisel dreamed up catchy commercials. The entertainment that night was a talented popular singer, but I couldn't help feeling that Fred's music would have been much more appealing to both presidents.

•   •   •

Fred had met Jacqueline Cochran, the woman pilot, when General Eisenhower's political rally was held in Madison Square Garden. Because Jackie was the one who flew the film of the event to Europe and talked with the general, she laid claim forever after, in her usual forthright way, that it was she who had persuaded him to run for president.

Jackie was married to Floyd Odlum, a wealthy financier. Although the Odlums maintained an apartment in New York, they spent most of the year at their California desert ranch. In the late fifties, Jackie invited us to the Cochran-Odlum ranch, as it was called. It was a working ranch of orange and grapefruit trees interspersed with charming adobe one- and two-bedroom cottages for guests, plus a nine-hole golf course.

Fred and I arrived during a hiatus on the tour circuit. We were housed in a cottage quite removed from the main quarters. The aura of serenity and calm plus the pungent aroma of orange blossoms permeating the air made it a utopia. The cottage had two bedrooms, a living room and a completely stocked kitchen. It was not mandatory that guests appear for meals.

Severely crippled by rheumatoid arthritis, which began when he turned forty, Floyd was able to keep himself somewhat mobile by spending at least forty-five minutes a day in his enormous pool. The temperature was maintained at exactly ninety-two degrees. As the sole nongolfer, I spent many hours supported by an inner tube floating around in the pool with Floyd. He was an extremely gentle and shy man who must have felt comfortable and at ease with me, because at the end of our first visit when Fred was leaving to resume his tour, Jackie asked me to stay on. My visits sometimes lasted weeks, more prolonged than those of "the Man Who Came to Dinner."

Two round dining room tables were set in a corner of the vast living room. I was always seated on Floyd's right, and Fred on Jackie's right at the second table. Fred was not overjoyed about that arrangement because Jackie dominated the conversation and never allowed him a chance to talk. Jackie was often away, however, and then everything took on a different tempo. With fewer guests, we easily fit around Floyd's table. That's when we saw the other side of Floyd Odlum. He was quite funny and outgoing. But when Jackie was around, Floyd would sit back and beam at her. He was her Pygmalion. She was everything he wasn't: brash, outspoken, sometimes rude. She could also be extremely considerate and kind and warm, *but* she had to win, *always.*

One time after dinner we all withdrew into the other sitting room, and I was in a corner playing Scrabble with Jackie. Fred made a bet with Floyd that I would win. Floyd told him to save his money because Jackie made up her own rules, which she did, all right! Jackie loved to play gin rummy, and Fred often ended up in a corner with her. He was just as competitive as she and wouldn't give an inch. You never heard such complaints and screams as when those two played. Jackie was very fond of Fred, mainly, I think, because he stood up to her.

After President Eisenhower left office, he and Mamie spent the winters at the Eldorado Country Club, where he could enjoy his pastime of golf. The Odlums provided an office at the ranch where Ike could work and write.

An old friend, Freeman Gosden (Amos of "Amos & Andy"), used to arrange the president's golf games, and often called on Fred to fill out a foursome. One time Lawrence Welk called Freeman and said he wanted to play with the president. Even though the protocol is that people wait to be asked, his request was accepted, and Fred was called to be the fourth. The day could not be called a complete success. Ike liked to move fast on a golf course—so fast that sometimes the person riding in a cart with him might be left behind, not intentionally, of course. It was just that Ike's concentration was focused completely on his next shot and he'd simply take off. Welk, on the other hand, would take eight to ten practice swings each time he stood up to the ball—not an endearing habit. At one point they arrived at a green to find a group of people waiting for Welk's autograph, as he was at the peak of his television popularity. The president just stood there, completely ignored, while Welk accepted the accolades of his admirers. By the time they reached the clubhouse, Ike was ready to explode.

The next day President Eisenhower called Fred and asked him if he had taken his favorite seven iron by mistake. Fred figured that Welk, who had gone directly back to Los Angeles, must have put it erroneously in his own bag. Lawrence had it, all right, and because he returned it by slow freight, Ike was without his favorite iron for four playing days.

Ike had an interesting trait. His eyes were always focused solely and intently on the person talking to him; his attention never wavered. His brother Edgar inherited the same trait. I was not aware that evidently I honed in like that myself. One time the president and I were deep in conversation. Once again Floyd and Fred were observing, and Fred said, "I bet I can whistle, call, or whatever, and Virginia will never look up." Fred told me about it afterward: the two of us never heard him call our names.

Floyd had spent many years traveling in foreign countries acquiring and reorganizing businesses. In 1932 he formed the Atlas Corporation and also founded the largest independent uranium mining company in the United States. He also saved the U.S. missile program when the Defense Department wanted to drop it, by pouring a lot of money into it through his corporation—which explains the name of the Atlas missile program.[4]

Twenty years later, the government finally gave Floyd an overdue and insignificant token of thanks. Fred and I were invited to the ceremony, which took place one afternoon in a Palm Springs hotel ballroom. There was almost no publicity either about the occasion or Floyd Odlum's heroic deed. The media pains me sometimes, giving hoopla, awards, and kudos to many undeserving individuals, while often neglecting those who have had the vision to make an immeasurable contribution.

• • •

About the second year of our marriage, Fred and his Pennsylvanians were asked to join several celebrities for a concert at the Belmont racetrack to raise money for a charity. It was a two-night affair, put on by socialites. Fred and I were to stay at the Alfred Gwynn Vanderbilt home along with Lena Horne, her musician husband, Lennie Heyton, Tony Martin, and Manny Fox, head of Victor Records.

We arrived at the impressive English-style home about five o'clock in the afternoon and were shown to our room. I remember we both stepped on the threshold of the bathroom, where the tub was filled with invitingly warm water. Fred quickly backed up saying, "I haven't taken a *bawth* in thirty years and I'm not about to start now."

As is customary in such houses, everything in our suitcases was removed for us and put in drawers. Fred was really upset. His suitcase and trunks were *never* completely unpacked. Different portions were replaced or washed or cleaned and then put back in order. I pity wives whose husbands expect them to pack their clothes. When Fred was packing for his tours, I stayed out of his way so he could concentrate. Forgetting black socks or a special bow tie or certain medicines can be a disaster when one is on tour, as there isn't time to go out and search for replacements.

I was designated the dinner hostess because Jeanne Vanderbilt was on the committee and was busy with details for the concert. The table was set exquisitely. However, the gorgeous centerpiece of flowers was so high and wide that I could not see around or over it. The height of my table decorations has been measured to the last inch ever since.

After the first night's event, we all gathered in the kitchen to appease postconcert hunger pangs. Jinx Falkenburg and her husband, Tex Mc-Crary, lived nearby and they joined us. The kitchen was incredibly old and primitive—a sink with pipes for legs, a wooden drain board, and more. It seemed as though Mrs. Vanderbilt was not familiar with the kitchen, because she didn't know where to find anything. Manny Fox finally discovered some food in a walk-in cold room and designated himself chief cook. Tony Martin had been given a set of keys for the wine cellar to fetch some champagne for Miss Horne, her sole drink after a performance. Now we were ready to eat around the huge cutting-board table in the middle of the room, and we had no silverware. Since Tony had been successful on his first venture, he was sent out again for eating utensils and told to hurry, as the eggs were getting cold. He returned shortly with a sack and dumped some knives and forks on the table. The evening was great fun. Everyone was relaxed, as only show people can be after a performance, telling jokes and stories.

The most amazing part to me was the fact that Mrs. Vanderbilt insisted we wash, clean, and put back everything exactly as we found it. She seemed intimidated by the servants.

• • •

Fred enjoyed his friendship with Bill Lear. "Bill and Moya flew to Shawnee in his Beechcraft one time to spend a weekend with me," Fred recalled. "About six o'clock he said, 'Come on, let's go out to dinner.' I said, 'Where?' He said, '21.' I said, '21 is in New York.' He said, 'Sure. Let's go.'

"So we got in his plane and flew to New York. On the way he came out of the cabin and sat down and talked to us. I said, 'Who the hell is flying this plane?' He said, 'My new pilot.' I said, 'I don't see him.' He said, 'Oh, it's just a little black box.' He had built this automatic pilot, and this was his way of showing it.

"Another time we were in Grand Rapids, and Moya came to the hotel and picked me up and said, 'Come with me.' Halfway to the airport she said, 'Bill has a new gag he wants to show you.' A bell rang in the car. She picked it up and said, 'Hello, darling. Do you see us?' And he said, 'I'm right above you.'"

I was present when Bill decided to show Fred his latest toy, the Lear jet. He was like a little kid—eyes dancing, eager. Moya, Fred, and I were on the ground as he took off and soared straight up with that beautiful plane. I could picture him looking down, grinning ecstatically and saying, "Look, Ma! No hands!"

One time when we spent a few nights with the Lears at their home near Reno, Nevada, I asked Bill about his ideas and how he got them. He said, "First of all, I don't invent something and then find a need for it. I see a need and then start thinking about how to solve it." This can be seen in his eight-track tapes, his automatic pilot machine, and his small jet plane for busy executives. At the time of our visit, he was working on an idea for remedying a dead battery in a plane. He would think about a project and then concentrate on his idea before going to sleep. He firmly believed that he was pulling in his solutions from a bank of knowledge out there in the unknown. After all, he was an eighth grade dropout, so where did he get the answers to so many complex and intricate problems?

Just before his death, Bill was building a new jet plane made of material so light as to require only a small amount of fuel. On his deathbed, he asked Moya to finish the plane for him, but without his guiding genius, it was a herculean task. She told me that at one meeting with the engineers shortly after Bill's death, they were deciding to go against Bill's wishes and use heavier material for the wings. Suddenly, a huge black cloud appeared in the sky, emitting a blast of thunder and lightning so strong that everyone jumped two feet out of their chairs. They felt Bill was giving them his two cents' worth on that subject!

26

Crucible of Professionals

FOR twenty-nine years from 1955 until 1984, all Pennsylvanians new and old would migrate to rehearsal quarters in the old Castle Inn at Delaware Water Gap, Pennsylvania, to kick off the yearly tour. The season was early October, when the leaves begin to turn their brilliant shades of red and yellow, and the days vary between the warmth of Indian summer or the crispness of apple cider time. The excitement in the air was tangible. For returnees it was a homecoming; for the newcomers, the beginning of an adventure into the unknown. They were met with a special welcoming dinner served in the big dining room of the old resort. The following day the rehearsals began.

The next three weeks were spent in solid rehearsal—day and night. First the notes of the music would be memorized and then the interpretation began. Singing the Fred Waring way is not easy, and Fred would not be too patient with someone forgetting what was taught the day before. "When we went from the workshop to becoming Pennsylvanians, Fred said, 'Come on, kids, you're pros—you're being paid now,'" Tommy Paterra recalled. "'If you don't like singing, you'd better find a different job.'" There was also much choreography to be learned. Meanwhile, costume fittings were somehow squeezed in. Nadine Gae and I had fallen heir to the job of designing the Pennsylvanians' costumes—no small feat to outfit nearly thirty men and women for four costume changes. Between rehearsals, home-cooked meals were served in the cheerful dining room, and bowls were filled with apples for snacks. After rehearsals, the Pennsylvanians could retire to the Deer Head Inn, another old resort across the street, where Grammy Award-winning jazz artists living in the area jammed on weekends. As departure time loomed, the tension grew. The neophytes were finally perceiving that touring with the Pennsylvanians was not all fun and games—the Big Time that seems so easy to a casual observer requires hard, hard work. A night or two before dress rehearsal Fred and I would throw a farewell party at our Gatehouse to relax the troops. Julia, our housekeeper/cook, always provided enough food for second, third, even fourth helpings. It would be the last home-cooked meal for a long time. A few days before departure, the enormous truck with THE FRED WARING SHOW painted on both sides of the trailer would pull up near the rehearsal room to be loaded with all the equipment— another reminder of the days ahead.

In show business tradition, the dress rehearsal held a couple of days before the start of the tour was usually a shambles. So the final two days were frantic as everyone—performers, department heads, seamstresses— worked around the clock rectifying the musical, choreographic, and costume errors. The only calm one, of course, was Fred. He would be at home packing his trunk, playing a little golf—weather permitting—and exuding a benign air of tranquility.

One of the secrets of Fred's success as director of a yearly touring company was his ability to keep the program fresh and exciting for each performance, month after month, year after year. Hawley Ades, arranger and stage accompanist for thirteen years on tour, offered his thoughts: "During that entire time, every performance was something I could look forward to with the certainty that the Boss would create some thrilling musical experiences. In part, of course, this was due to his great gift as an interpreter of music, but also it arose from his fierce determination to keep the performances fresh and vigorous. The intensity of his own approach to music demanded that others maintain the same level of intensity. He simply would not permit either himself or his performers to sink to the level of a routine, uninspired performance, even though they did the same show night after night. No two shows were ever alike. The Boss would make constant alterations in tempo, dynamics, mood, and other factors, in accordance with the acoustics of a particular hall, the responsiveness of the audience, the degree of rapport with the glee club on a given night, or on his personal feelings at the time. Woe betide the poor glee clubber or instrumentalist who assumed because there was a big ritard in a particular phrase one night, the same thing would happen on the next show."

Sometimes on tour, Fred would get exasperated with the Pennsylvanians when they turned in sloppy performances, and then stay that way for several days. Often they wouldn't know exactly why he was angry. But his behavior, whenever this happened, made me acutely uncomfortable. I could never understand why he never called them together immediately to explain exactly what was wrong and what he wanted. The problem would clear up eventually, and I suppose it was just another way of keeping the performers alert. But it was also another reason I didn't go on one-night stands. I'm a mediator by nature—I seem able to see everybody's side—and I dislike unharmonious surroundings and atmosphere.

At times Fred would show his displeasure in the middle of a concert by letting his hands droop—that was a warning flag—or he might stop conducting altogether or walk off the stage. Then there was the night, I'm told, when he was so furious with their inattention that he conducted the whole evening with one finger. In retrospect, some of the episodes are pretty funny, and the Pennsylvanians, when together, usually reminisce and laugh over Fred's many quirks, but always without rancor. They knew his intentions were pure, that he never got angry without reason. Violinist Pete Buonconsiglio said in 1960, "In the last few years I have played with the largest orchestras in New York. I have played under them all. The best of them. There is no finer, more meticulous or sensitive conductor than Waring." Then he added, "Incidentally, in all my ten years with him, I've never seen him flare up at us when at least one of the group wasn't wrong."

I think all Pennsylvanians would agree that the violent, explosive, and sometimes unreasoned remarks or diatribes were characteristics of Fred the performer, but not characteristics of the man himself. Fred expected professionals he hired to perform as professionals. As Lumpy said, "When Fred got *really* mad, he never said much." We at home never saw that kind of temper—*never!* Nor did Fred ever lay a hand on his children except for one incident that Billy, then age five, remembers. Billy evidently had placed a glob of imitation dog-doo on a beautiful carpet just before some important guests arrived. For some reason, his father didn't find it amusing, and spanked him. Fred had definitely mellowed nearly thirty years later when Malcolm, our youngest, dropped little squares of lucite with flies and bugs encased in them into some of our friends' martinis and cocktails. Fred laughed, too—mainly at the expression on their faces.

Fred never held a grudge for some oversight or mistake. "One time Fred was going up to Shawnee for the Fourth of July weekend," Lou Metz said. "I had moved the station wagon in front of the building so he could get away quickly and then took off, but unfortunately I took the keys with me. When I got back after the weekend, I thought I was gone. The report that I got was that he had raved and ranted and torn my office apart. He found a locksmith somewhere, and went off hours and hours after he had planned, and yet when he saw me Monday morning, I began, 'I suppose there's nothing I can say which will help?' and he said, 'Nothing. Never mention it again.' No repercussions."

• • •

Those not in the performing arts cannot comprehend the demands made on an artist. It's easy to criticize and say that stars are often unresponsive, difficult, or temperamental. But I firmly believe that the extra element that makes them unique is their extreme sensitivity to everything around them. It's a plus and a minus. It makes them more aware of the beauty of the world, which helps them round out and develop their latent talents, but it also makes them unwitting victims of noise, of disturbing emotional auras, whatever. Their only protection is a shield—a detachment—a "no waves, please." It explains why so many stage performers surround themselves with an entourage of faithfuls who create an ambience where they can totally be themselves. The unspoken rules of conduct within the group are set like a delicate minuet or a hierarchy wherein each member knows his role—such as when, whom, and at what level to kid or tease someone. In a way it's like a pecking order. The leader sets the rules, and the rest of the group base their actions on his moods. A Frank Sinatra could put down Sammy Davis about his African-American heritage, which then gave Sammy the license to retort with an Italian dig. A lesser member of the rat pack would be out of line if he attempted anything too forward. Odd as it seems to outsiders, it is their upside-down way of showing love and affection. The insults are like backhanded compliments. Fred once said, "Hello, Ugly," to a new Pennsylvanian, a recently crowned Miss Dakota, and she burst into tears. She didn't realize he would *never* say that to anyone who was *not* pretty. He used to tease his great black singer, Frank Davis, and in feigned disgust, might tell him to go sit in the back of the bus (where Fred always sat anyway), and Frank then, in turn, would dish some innocently barbed insults back to "Whitey."

Creative performers are always on the razor's edge when appearing in public. The critics and audiences judge them every minute. Most of them, with their fragile egos, can't afford to be too introspective. Digging beneath the surface is a fearsome prospect, so in order to maintain an equilibrium, they often deal with people on a surface level. It explains why Bing Crosby was comfortable and content playing golf with Fred. Each knew the unspoken axiom—the game was the relaxing challenge of the day, unsullied by personal problems or confessions. But this so-called lack of depth is merely a façade. There is usually plenty of substance inside. Showmanship is not maintained by talent alone.

. . .

Loneliness seems to be endemic to many show-business people, at least until they find a truly compatible mate. Kirk Douglas refers to his loneliness many times in his autobiography; Nancy Sinatra wrote in her book about her father: "Loneliness is a part of him. It's always there—in his eyes."[1] When Jackie Gleason was finally able to marry his only true love, Marilynne, she made him happy for the first time and his loneliness disappeared.

Loneliness was unknown to me. I had never been lonely in my life. I didn't know what it meant or how painful it must be. As a pianist I had spent two or three hours a day, sometimes more, by myself at the piano—but I was never lonely. I liked to practice—even the boring, repetitious kind one is obliged to do to make a piece sparkle with clarity and precision, and seem so effortless. Even as duo pianists, three-fourths to seven-eighths of our rehearsal time was alone.

Fred, too, had been a lonely man, but since our marriage he seemed changed and more content. The credit doesn't go to me as much as to the atmosphere that now surrounded him. Fred had finally straightened out his priorities. Our home was his focal point. He loved the way I had decorated his "carriage" house. He enjoyed the boys of all ages who lived with us each summer. He relished being with our youngest, experiencing the little daily trivia he had missed when his first three had been small. Also, he and I, among other things, had become very good friends. He had complete trust in me and knew, without my ever saying so, that I would never let him down.

. . .

When on tour, men Pennsylvanians were issued a blue blazer with an embroidered Fred Waring insignia on the left pocket. They could wear any pants except jeans, and they were expected to wear a shirt with tie or a turtleneck. These were to be worn in public areas. The girls were to dress neatly. If a Pennsylvanian got out of line during a long tour, through sloppy singing, nonadherence to the dress code, or too many drinks before a concert, Fred would probably take out his solo (girls, as a rule, didn't present as many problems) or make him sit out in the audience. It was a blow to an overripe ego to see everything running so smoothly onstage without one.

Fred welcomed any Pennsylvanian who felt comfortable sparring with him at the mike. Lette Rehnolds, soprano and comedienne, could do it with aplomb and then sing a moving aria from *Madame Butterfly*. "Fred and I had a unique rapport which we developed every time we got together in front of a mike," she said. "Each night Fred would bring me to the mike and ask my name and a few questions. One night some Pennsylvanians dared me to ad-lib in a nasal Brooklynese accent. When Fred asked my name and I answered, 'Lady Chatterley,' in my funny voice, the audience roared. El Maestro was thunderstruck for an instant and then, seeing the potential, replied, 'Your name, honey, not your ambition.'"

• • •

In the summer of 1966 Fred had a strong premonition of a bus crash. He didn't know when or how, but he was filled with anxiety. He told no one of his fears—not even me. The doctor told me that Fred's blood pressure was up, and I had noticed he wasn't sleeping well, but there were no other signs of distress except on the day of departure. He told me later he didn't know what to do—to cancel the tour or not.

Normally, he was reluctant to leave us—always torn between staying at home and taking off for a new adventure. But this one particular day he kept the entire bus load waiting and waiting, until finally departing with a seemingly heavy heart—most uncharacteristic of Fred Waring.

He told me about it afterwards. They had started out in late October in beautiful fall weather. For two weeks Fred scarcely slept, and then one morning on a crystal clear day, the Pennsylvanians were whizzing along on a turnpike, when the driver ran full speed into the back of a slow-moving truck. The force of the impact buckled the bus in the middle, killing the bus driver. Everyone else had some injuries. The driver was on a cold medication that caused him to fall asleep at the wheel that bright, beautiful morning. Fortunately, none of the injuries was permanent, but there were a few close calls—one girl had put down her sharp steel knitting needles just before the impact. In typical theater tradition, a new bus driver was engaged, and everyone appeared onstage that night sporting patches, bandages, and canes. Fred's knee hurt him for a while.

Along this same vein, about five years before the accident when we were guests at the Cochran-Odlum Ranch, four men came to stay for a few days—Peter Hurkos, a well-known Dutch clairvoyant; a young president of a college in Wisconsin; a car salesman who also had psychic powers;

and a lawyer. These men were endeavoring to fund a chair at the college for research in the field of extrasensory perception, somewhat like the program at Duke University headed by Dr. Jules P. Rhine, and were on a national tour making presentations to potential backers. Peter Hurkos's psychic senses would be set in motion when he touched an object belonging to someone. On the first night after dinner, he left the room, and about ten of us each put a personal possession on a tray. My donation was a simple bracelet given to me by an international banker who had befriended Livingston and me when we were just starting our career. Fred offered a slim, unadorned gold pencil, and one lady put in something that her son had given her.

When Hurkos picked up my bracelet, he described the man who had given it to me—the many languages he spoke, the countries he was associated with, the fact he was extremely musical, and on and on. Fred and I were the only musicians in a room of about fifteen. Fred's gold pencil really stimulated him—much talk of musicians, instruments, he mentioned our son Paul (who later became associated with the Pennsylvanians), but I thought Hurkos had really blown it when he started talking about a bus accident that had not yet occurred!

Having been steeped in psychic lore during my first marriage (I cut my teeth on the tome of Charles Fort, the granddaddy of them all), nothing about the men's visit surprised me. I never learned whether or not they succeeded in their venture. Floyd was not impressed, although Jackie kept an open mind.

In the late forties and early fifties, a horse with alleged psychic abilities was renowned enough to make the pages of *Time* magazine. Her name was Lady Wonder, and she resided in the state of Virginia. One time Livingston and I stopped at the simple cottage, stood in line, feeling a little foolish, and for fifty cents asked two questions of the ancient swaybacked mare, who stood behind a railing in the barn on which lay a crude apparatus of alphabet blocks. I handed my question to a slight, elderly lady who sat nearby on a high stool. My question was, "What will my son be when he grows up?" Lady Wonder then poked two different levers with her nose which raised the letters spelling *DR*. (That son is now a biomedical photographer.) Sometime after Fred and I were married, the name of Lady Wonder was mentioned. He told me then that on his tour with the Pennsylvanians he also had visited the famous animal. It was fortunate, he said, that no one recognized him, because he, too, felt sheepish waiting to ask a question of a horse. His first question: "What state am I associated with?" The answer: *PA*. The second question: "What state will

I be associated with?" The answer, *VA*. Who ever said a horse couldn't say *Virginia!*

• • •

As Fred grew older, he faced the loss of some of his contemporaries of the early decades of his career. Fred and Paul Whiteman had kept tabs on each other through the years. Whiteman and his wife had visited us in the fifties, and it was then I noticed he had lost weight and did not look to be in robust health. In the late fall of 1967, he called Fred from Denver. "We talked and talked—mostly about old times and things." Three weeks later Paul Whiteman died, on December 29, 1967. He was seventy-seven years old. Fred said, "I have lost a dear friend." Ten years later, Irving Berlin sent Fred his annual birthday wire, saying: PLEASE KEEP GOING FRED. THERE AREN'T MANY OF US LEFT. Fred was feeling his mortality.

• • •

During the fall tour of 1970, Fred and the Pennsylvanians were invited to after-concert receptions night after night, city after city. I became concerned because a steady stream of such parties can undermine your health. Small talk with strangers is work when you've given your all onstage. I kept pleading with him and his company manager to please eliminate a few parties—that his friends were killing him with kindness. But he didn't want to disappoint them. Though many faulted Nancy Reagan for protecting her "Ronnie," it is true that it is often difficult for a man to turn down a friend or to say "I can't" or "I'm too tired." For women it's called pacing yourself or being sensible; for men it appears as a weakness or, God forbid, a loss of virility or whatever else goes through their male minds.

To compound the damage, just as the tour finished, Fred's beloved friend Rube Goldberg died, and Fred rose at 5 A.M. to fly to New York to attend his funeral that morning. He finally arrived back at Shawnee in a state of total exhaustion. He was scheduled to conduct thousands of people in a football stadium before coming to California for the holidays. While waiting in the kitchen to be driven to the airport, he had a heart attack and was taken to the local hospital. The doctor called me in California and told me to come immediately. I flew to Pennsylvania, not knowing what to expect, and was disheartened to see Fred lying there so helpless. Fortunately the wild fibrillation of his heart calmed down but his overworked body didn't respond quickly. The doctors, being overly cautious, kept Fred in the hospital for six weeks, which was much too long. The atmosphere undermined his spirit and his will. It was like a candle slowly flickering out. I told the doctor it was imperative that I remove him. Then his dear friend Bill Lear called and offered to fly us in his jet to the California desert, where the warmer climate could hasten Fred's recuperation. It was a wonderful gift of life, and I shall be eternally grateful. While Fred was regaining his strength, his old friends Buddy Rogers, Richard Arlen, and Peter Lind Hayes from the Hollywood days called, offering to help out with his upcoming booked tour—"a friend in need" is what they were.

The most difficult heart-to-heart letter I ever wrote to Fred was during the time he was hospitalized with his heart attack. Our youngest was thirteen—a worrisome and insecure time for a budding young man. I have noticed that many men, especially hard-driving, self-made men, are very critical of their sons as they grow up. That piece of flesh out there is a part of them, and by God, it had better measure up to certain standards. It's seemingly easy to lay down rules and regulations but hard to hug and kiss and praise your children. When we were married, Freddy and Billy were teenagers. They loved their father but also half-hated him. Somehow the profound love Fred felt for them never got through, which might have offset the bitterness implanted in them by their mother. I had brought into the marriage my quiet, introverted eight-year-old, Paul. Fred took him on with total devotion. He felt no inner compulsion to perfect him, and so allowed Paul to develop his own self-image.

From time to time in exasperation I might say—"That Paul! I'm going to—" Fred would put his hand on my arm and say, "Now, now . . ." In other words, let the child be; he's developing nicely. And then along came Malcolm, of his own lineage, eleven years younger than Paul. Fred, for the first time, had the leisure to enjoy him—a luxury he'd never experienced with his first three. When we lived in the California desert, the two would set out at dusk for the evening newspaper, Malcolm toddling along, holding his father's hand. They had a set routine: first the pet shop, and then sometimes a stop for a piece of cherry pie.

Ah, but then Mal entered the delicate teen years. I do believe only a mother can love that pudgy, grubby, embryonic adult—a thirteen-year-old boy. Fred was in the hospital and we visited him every day, but suddenly he reverted to his old pattern: Malcolm wasn't holding the door properly for me or picking up my packages fast enough, his hair was too long, his clothes weren't tidy, and so on. A child has to be taught certain things, but it's how you do it that counts.

Malcolm dearly loved his father but was beginning to dread going to the hospital. So I wrote Fred a loving but very difficult letter. I did not want to upset him, yet I did not want him to destroy the bond he had built over the years with Malcolm.

6 A.M.

My dearest, darling Papa,

This is about Malcolm. You have been so wonderful with him. I can't bear to see you revert to your old procedures that you used on Freddy and Billy.

You were so understanding and patient with Paul because he wasn't a part of you. You were objective about him and let him develop into his own personality.

You are such a perfectionist that when you see a bit of "you" sticking out there, you can't resist hacking and whittling away into what you hope will be a perfect image.

Thirteen to sixteen is a delicate age. The healthy ego is beginning to develop. It needs encouragement and *love, love, love,* not picayune naggings that will drive him right away from your door. He's trying desperately to grow into his own personality. Your thorough belief and joy in him will keep him out of trouble better than any suspicions and accusations. Sure, he needs to be reprimanded sometimes, but do it so very carefully—the psyche is easily bruised during these years. When he needs reprimanding, I beg of you to put your arms around him and do it in private. He is so sensitive and so aware—far beyond his years—that he will respond.

Sure, he didn't clean the basement right away when you asked him to—but every mistake is a lesson to be learned. How the guidance is handled means absolutely everything these next few years. You must remember every thirteen-year-old is ungainly. We don't want him to feel ugly because a good and positive self-image is what develops into solid, happy citizens.

Malcolm truly loves you. I want him to feel, when he walks into your room, the quiet pervading joy in his being there that you feel when Paul walks in.

When Mal and I are alone in the desert, he comes home every evening and does large amounts of homework after a full day of school. At *no* time do I have to remind him. It is his work, and he accepts his responsibility. He doesn't complain—he does it. He is always home on time—never ever a minute late.

Darling Papa, Malcolm needs your firm guidance, but be gentle and guide him on the big issues. Look into that face of his—he has such great potential.

Stress all the good in him, I beg of you. Show him all your love. He's truly thirsting for it. I know he has to be reminded of many things, but it's the *way* it's done that is the key.

All my love and devotion,
Your Virginia

When I called the hospital the next morning Fred said, "Thank you for the letter." After that, he bent over backward to be fair in the treatment of his namesake.

Fred recovered nicely, but his warning attack changed the tenor of future tours. It was imperative that they be less lengthy, the concerts better spaced, and fewer horrendous jumps between cities. Fred also found that the type of singer he could attract was, of necessity, much younger. Established professionals couldn't afford to tour for only two and a half months in the fall and again for the same length of time in spring. So Fred began to draw talent from his summer youth workshops.

The paternalistic second-family feeling became even more pronounced because of the age differences between Fred and his performers. One new Pennsylvanian said, "When I met Mr. Waring, I was sixteen, and he reminded me of my father who had just died. He expected us to always looked groomed and well dressed. At first I resented his running my life but soon realized he was right. He was forever correcting my English, but would always compliment me on my table manners. I knew he was my friend and I could go to him with any problem."

"When we first went out to dinner, Mr. Waring told me where to put my knife and fork—a lot of people would be offended," Fred Scrutchfield said. "I'd never been out of Oklahoma and I took it as a compliment. I'll never forget the first time I lit a cigarette in the car. He said, 'I don't mind if you smoke, but I think you should always ask whomever you are with if it bothers them.' He made some small suggestions about my clothes. Some of the Pennsylvanians couldn't handle it. For my wedding at Fred's house, the Gatehouse, I had bought a new suit but at the last hour realized I didn't have a tie to wear. In a panic I called Fred, and he hurried over with one of his for me. He never wanted to talk about money, but if I needed anything he'd pull out a fifty-dollar bill or, 'Here's the car,' or, 'Do you like that jacket? I'll get you one.'"

Fred gave not just money and advice, he gave of himself. One former Pennsylvanian, Jackie Mayer Townsend, later became Miss America. She married, had two children and, at the age of twenty-eight, this beautiful girl had a stroke that left her paralyzed on her right side and without the ability to speak. She could not utter a sound.

"For a week I felt almost hopeless," Jackie said. "One day I opened my eyes to see an old friend standing at the foot of my bed. It was Fred Waring. Seeing his smile and knowing his love and warmth, just having him there made me know there was hope for me. He said, 'You are going to speak,' and he started me saying the ABCs after him. He would say 'A' and I would try to form the letter. He showed me how to shape my mouth to make sounds and use my voice to pronounce the words. He visited four times and then had to continue his tour. He was fantastic. He called almost every day.

"Months later he would ask what I was wearing—as an exercise so I would have to describe it. He would also give me three words to practice. These were simple words at the beginning, but they got harder and harder, and I would have to practice them until our next phone call. He would say, 'I am with you. You are going to get better and talk again.' This went on for more than a year.

"One day I answered the phone and almost wished I hadn't. 'The word for today,' Fred said, 'is juxtaposition.' It took me three or four years to say that word."

Jackie's mother, Beverly Mayer: "In our time of need, Fred gave of himself, his time, his thoughts, his knowledge and his love. He taught a girl who had known only perfection how to cope with imperfection. He demanded that she try, that she work, that she practice; and he rebuilt her self-confidence and gave her praise for each small accomplishment." Jackie has recovered and now goes on speaking tours in behalf of the American Heart Association.

• • •

Times were when Fred's protectiveness seemed excessive, especially to an outsider like Bill Blackburn, a former record producer for rock musicians, whose favorite words were "hey" and "wow." He had been hired to work on publicity projects and was sharing an office with our son Paul the company manager. Bill had met most of the Pennsylvanians and immediately sensed the family feeling in the outfit.

"It's like Fred was the godfather and Poley was the uncle," Blackburn said. "When I arrived, everyone was saying, 'Betty Ann is coming back!' and, 'Betty Ann this and Betty Ann that.' I said, 'What is this Betty Ann?' I disliked her before I met her.

"I went to a rehearsal and met Betty Ann McCall. She seemed like the sweetest thing I ever met in my life and I said, 'This is the Queen O'Neil of all.' And Fred never treaded upon her and that really irritated me. He was jumping all over everybody and never was treading upon her." Beloved by all the Pennsylvanians, Betty Ann had returned to the fold with her little boy Mark after a disastrous first marriage. She and Mark were staying with Poley and his wife Yvette during the road show rehearsals. [Betty Ann was a fine musician, consistently responsive to Fred's musical directing, never needing his heavy hand. She played an electronic instrument that filled in orchestral sounds.]

"I got together with Betty Ann because of some children's tapes she had made, and the more I talked to her, the more I started to think, 'Wow! She's OK!'" Blackburn recounted. Bill was smitten and had the temerity to fall in love with this paragon of the Pennsylvanians. Almost from the start, he had become aware that his sudden and obvious interest was disapproved of by her "family." "Poley and Yvette walked in and saw me sitting with Betty, and you could *see* the looks on their faces," Blackburn said. "This New York guy was going to take advantage of poor little Betty Ann. That day we spent the whole day together and after that our relationship grew. But because of the negative feelings of Fred, Poley, and Yvette, Betty said, 'I don't like to hide this, but I don't think we should bring it out yet that we are dating each other—at least not just yet.' So we continued to see each other in a submerged way. We were so submerged that we were practically under the Delaware River.

"One day Betty Ann brought Mark over to my office [in nearby Delaware Water Gap] and asked me to babysit Mark while she visited Poley in the hospital—he'd had an eye operation. At the agreed upon time of 3 P.M., I put little Mark in the car and, as I came down the hill by the Shawnee Post Office, here is Fred Waring coming the other way. He says, 'Stop!' so I stop. 'Where are you going?'

"I said, 'I'm going over to Poley and Yvette's.'

"'Who's that in the car with you?'

"'That's Mark.'

"'What the hell are you doing with Mark?'

"'Betty Ann asked me to watch him.'

"Fred said, 'Give him to me.'

"I was livid. 'I'm not giving you Mark. He was left in my charge and he's going to *stay* in my charge.' (Now, mind you, we are blocking the road; cars are beginning to line up behind us.)

"Fred said, 'Who the hell are you working for?'

"'You, but that doesn't make my life yours. Betty Ann asked me to take care of the kid and I'm *taking* care of him! Suppose you take off with him and have an accident?'

"'Are you saying I can't drive?'

"'No, but he was put in my charge and I'm keeping him.'

"'In the first place, why did she ask you and didn't ask me?'

"'Well, my God, you know how busy you are, aren't you busy?' I couldn't believe what I was saying.

"Fred said, 'Give him to me. I'll deliver him.'

"I put Mark in the front seat of Fred's car and returned to the office. I was angry. Some tense days followed. Nobody mentioned the incident. I was shunned by the 'Powers That Be' in the Pennsylvanians. I'm the big outsider. This wise guy, this hustler from New York—that's the way they were treating me.' Anyway, by now we know we love each other and want to get married. Betty Ann asked me, 'Who is going to tell Poley and Yvette?' They had sort of assigned themselves as her guardians. 'And who is going to tell Fred?'

"I had decided to go over and discuss it with my friend Paul and he advised, 'Now play their game, ask permission—of everybody.' I really exploded. 'Ask their permission for a woman over thirty who has been married!' Paul and I went round and round until finally Paul said, 'Look, just go and tell him—now!'

"So I went to the Inn and found Fred heading for the first tee. I said, 'Can I see you?' Fred said, 'I'll see you after golf.' For two days I could not corner that man. In no way, shape, or form could I corner him. [Fred was an absolute genius at evading people he didn't want to see.] Now I was really getting mad.

"One day I knocked on his office door near the golf shop. He opened it and said, 'Oh, hi, Bill—what can I do for you?' I said, 'I want to talk to you,' and he said, 'Go ahead.' I said, 'I've grown to love Betty Ann and I want to marry her.' Fred raised his hand and I thought, *here we go*—it's going to hit the fan.

"He walked over, put his hand on my shoulder and said, 'I'll do anything I can to help you. Now! What are you going to do about Poley and Yvette? Don't let them know I know, that you told me first, because it will hurt their feelings.' I felt like saying—what is this, the CIA? I went to see Poley and he said, 'That's nice, Bill. But you better let me talk to Fred, he might be upset.'"

The wedding took place at our home, and guess who gave the bride away? Fred, of course. And, like all proper Pennsylvanians, Betty Ann and Bill got married between shows. The next night the Pennsylvanians performed for President Nixon at a White House state dinner. (I became an expert at staging weddings at the Gatehouse—two sons and four Pennsylvanians.)

Of the nearly forty couples who met, fell in love on tour, and then married over the past thirty years, only *two* divorces resulted. After spending fatiguing days and weeks on the road when nerves get frazzled and tempers short, you know exactly what you are getting.

Fred's devotion and dedicated interest in his "second family," the Pennsylvanians, was sometimes hard for his wives to comprehend. I knew that we, his immediate family, always came first, yet to be honest, there were a few times when I felt his concerns for those in the organization to be excessive. It wasn't until Fred's stroke in 1980—when I took over his job as conductor, emcee, and matriarch of the Pennsylvanians for thirteen weeks of one-night stands—that I gained deeper insight into that unique relationship. It is not possible to eat, ride, and perform together day after day for months and months and not become involved heart and soul. The feeling Fred fostered in his Pennsylvanians was not just while they were working for him—it was an intangible bloodline that hooked them all together forever—a kind of *mishpokha*. Herman Wouk, in his book *Inside/Outside*, describes a *mishpokha* as a Jewish clan of cousins, aunts, and in-laws—a family connection of individuals. You always belong, no matter how far away you get or how old. Once a Pennsylvanian, always a Pennsylvanian.

When the Pennsylvanians left for other careers, Fred was genuinely proud of their successes. "Eighteen of our 'graduates' have been heads of music departments at one time throughout the country in universities," he reported. "We have seen former Pennsylvanians in nine of the last ten cities we've played."[2]

In turn, they wrote of their deep bond with Fred Waring: "I have never wholly been apart from Fred; his friendly spontaneous warmth did not stop after my detachment from the show." "Fred's most endearing characteristic is his loyalty—his ability to remember all the former Pennsylvanians. Even as an ex-Pennsylvanian, Fred always made you feel very important." "He would be the first person I would call if I needed support."[3]

Lou Metz summed it up: "In looking over the past thirty years, I suddenly realize that working for Fred and the Pennsylvanians was more than a job—it was a way of life. Some old-timer came here a few weeks ago and said, 'Gee, I miss them. I wish I could be back with them.'"

· · ·

During these years, as the dedicated veterans began to retire, one by one, Fred was faced with many indifferent new bandsmen who were there simply for the job—excellence didn't interest them. The music stands had been reinstated some years before, so memorization was no longer required. But the musicians complained about everything. Furious that Fred set his alarm watch and allowed them only ten minutes out of the hour to smoke on the bus, they muttered uncomplimentary remarks behind his back. In the seventies, weary of all the hassling, Fred cut back to just a few musicians, and toured with one bus load of performers.

As early as 1966, when Fred was sixty-six, reporters had begun to quiz him about retiring, and he would get a little testy. It was not his favorite subject. "Sure I'll retire," he snapped, "if I lose both legs and get my head knocked off."[4] As one reporter noted, "Nothing turns normally sunny Fred Waring cold faster than questions presuming his imminent retirement. He says he stays 'young by keeping up with things.'"[5]

In 1979 an interviewer pressed Fred, "After sixty years in the business, do you still get the same charge out of performing?"

Here his reaction was more characteristically upbeat. "You use a fine word there. You take a light bulb out and stick your finger in the socket, and you are going to get a charge—one hundred and ten volts. It feels just the same. When an audience stands and cheers at the end of a show, and gives you a remarkable welcome at the beginning of the show—it feels just the same. We don't just stand up there and look like a bunch of goons playing. We try to please the people, and we succeed."[6]

Sammy Gallu put it in his inimitable way: "Fred's got to use himself to the very end. He's not going to sit around here and putter in the garden—Jesus Christ, the minute he puts a tuxedo on and the goddamn lights go on, you can see that guy walk like a twenty-year-old kid." Most people think that long-term performers are driven solely by their egos. That's a part of it, of course. The sound of cheers and bravos is a reinforcing solace to the inner soul. But the fact remains that the talented and gifted individuals in the performing arts are usually onstage from childhood. Playing, singing, dancing, acting is the very essence of their being—their life force. It is as much a part of their existence as eating and breathing. To quit is tantamount to a kind of death—unthinkable. Happiness is doing something you enjoy doing, and doing it well. After dedicating his life to shaping American choral music and providing a crucible for professional excellence, Fred had no intention of giving up.

Frank Sinatra and Fred Waring, taken while recording the "America I Hear You Singing" album for Reprise, Los Angeles, January, 1964.

Jackie Gleason and Fred Waring cutting up in the Cartoon Room at Shawnee Inn, 1960s. For six years, Jackie spent six months a year at Shawnee. He and Fred frequently did impromptu routines on Saturday nights when the spirit moved them.

Celebrating Irving Berlin's birthday on the "Ed Sullivan Show," May 5, 1968, Ed Sullivan Theatre, New York City. Left to right: Harry James, Ethel Merman, Ed Sullivan, Irving Berlin, Diana Ross, Fred Waring.

The Fred Waring Show on tour, 1974–75. Note the size of the truck and bus it took to transport all the people and equipment. Fred used the same size truck and bus, plus a car, for stage crew, each year until he died in the summer of 1984.

Large crowds gathered to hear the Pennsylvanians sing in Lancaster, Pa., summer of 1978.

A collage of Fred Waring photos, articles, and reviews, put together in a 1979 program book sold at concerts throughout the year.

The Young Pennsylvanians in a TV show for PBS, Hershey, Pa., 1979, performing a fifteen-minute montage of new songs with choreography and costume changes.

Lineup for the Pennsylvanians' farewell, Van Wezel Auditorium, Sarasota, Fla., Feb. 4, 1981.

Fred Waring and Virginia
Waring, after a concert in Sun
City, Arizona, Feb. 17, 1980.

The Waring family, at Penn
State's tribute to Fred Waring,
Sept. 26–27, 1980. Left to right:
Fred Jr., Bill, Virginia, Fred, Paul,
Dixie, Malcolm.

Fred Waring, 1980s.

27

Stroke

FOR almost thirty years of annual concert tours, it was customary for the Pennsylvanians to take a four-week break before and after the Christmas holidays. But when Fred arrived in the desert in mid-December of 1979, he looked exceptionally worried and fatigued. His lifelong friend Poley McClintock had suffered a stroke mid-tour and was hospitalized. Fred didn't seem rejuvenated by the balmy weather and restful days.

One Thursday morning early in January, I had just returned from a tennis game and was half undressed when Fred came into the room with his right arm in one sleeve of a sweater. He asked me to help him with his left arm. I took one look at his face and knew instantly that he was having a stroke. I persuaded him to sit down and I called the only heart specialist I knew—a doctor in Palm Springs who had treated Fred ten years before when he had a heart attack.

While waiting for the doctor to call, I hurriedly tried to get dressed. The phone rang. Fred evidently rose from the chair to answer it, fell on the kitchen floor, and was unable to move. That really frightened me. I called the fire department, which was nearby. They came immediately. Fred could talk—he told them what day it was, the president's name, and so forth, and he could move his limbs. The firemen called the paramedics. They seemed to take forever. Meantime, Fred was on the floor with blankets and pillows over and under him. The paramedics put him through the same tests, and then calmly told me they weren't allowed to go as far as Palm Springs twenty miles away, that I would have to drive him there alone! With Fred slumped against me, it was the longest, scariest trip I hope ever to take.

The doctor was waiting in the Desert Hospital emergency room. Evidently in those days, at least, there wasn't much to be done for a stroke victim. They put him in a cardiac section where a nurse watched over several beds. The next day, Friday, Fred was given a battery of tests and told he had to stay over the weekend for an angiogram the following Monday. Fred, by this time, wanted to go home. He wasn't saying anything but he wanted *out*. Our four boys had flown in and were sitting around his bed. Each day Fred would get dressed and, without uttering a word, would determinedly start walking through the corridors, looking for a way home. The boys took turns trailing him through the hospital, gently steering him away from exit doors. One time he went straight through the busy hospital kitchen. It was difficult getting him back on his bed, because as soon as he recognized his section, he would turn right around and head out again. Fred scarcely spoke, except by Sunday evening he quietly referred to his four sons as his "posse."

In retrospect, I wish I had taken him home that Friday, because on Monday they gave him an angiogram, which consists of a dye injected into the veins to pinpoint the blockage. Fred said later that the heat generated by the dye made the pain excruciating—his ears burned and ached, his teeth felt as though they would break off, his back killed him, and the attendants wouldn't let him move. He was in the room a long time. The angiogram set Fred back months. And the only remedy he was offered was aspirin. Fred had been hiking all around the hospital, yet when he returned home on Tuesday, he could barely make it from bed to couch, and seemed out of touch with us most of the time.

While Fred was in the hospital, Poley McClintock died. I didn't want to burden Fred's already taxed body and mind, but was fearful he might hear the news somehow. When I told him, I think with his strong psychic sense he already knew. Fred didn't speak to any of us about Poley—words weren't adequate. Later that spring when we returned to Shawnee, Poley's wife Yvette said, "Fred came by and sat with me, but he couldn't say anything. It hurt too much."

Our sons flew back to their homes and called Fred every day. One of them said, "This is your deputy calling." I was standing nearby and Fred quickly looked at me with a tiny grin and spoke into the receiver, "Yeah, but you left the *sheriff!*" I knew then he *was* going to get better.

Until his stroke, Fred was the Rock of Gibraltar. He took care of everyone, myself included. We all leaned on him. It was as though he were ten feet tall. I never had to worry about anything. But then our roles changed completely. I had to become "*Mrs.* Take Charge." Having Fred lean on me was not the problem; rather, it was that he was a different person. In a stroke, the brain is deprived of much of its nourishing blood supply, causing personality changes.

The first weeks afterwards were the hardest. He was, as our son Bill said, pretty "wifty." One was never certain what he was going to say or do. He was even more strong-willed and determined than before, so that in many ways, although he was almost childlike, one could not treat him as a child and keep him home away from prying eyes, and possibly rash and embarrassing acts. For example, months before his stroke, Fred had been invited to be one of the speakers at a black tie dinner at the Beverly Wilshire Hotel in Los Angeles, to honor his good friend Arnold Palmer. He had accepted, of course, but the date was two weeks after his stroke. Fred was determined to go. To say I was apprehensive is putting it mildly. Yet what could I do? Never having been around a stroke victim, I didn't know what to expect, and being new in my role as leader I didn't feel comfortable saying no. And so we went to the affair.

Bill drove us to Los Angeles and helped us check in. Fred stood in the lobby and, for a time, didn't seem to know where he was. I was worried about his speech because he had always ad-libbed brilliantly, and I didn't see any evidence of preparation, and, besides, his keen sense of timing was gone. I could only pray that some of the show and sports personalities would be helpful and sympathetic.

Fred, sensing his time clock wasn't working, dressed far ahead of the cocktail hour and lay on the bed waiting. We went down to the reception, which wasn't too painful because Arnie and Winnie Palmer were solicitous and helpful. Later we entered the festive ballroom and wended our way up to the dais. I was at the extreme end and Fred was seated near the podium. Sports announcer Vin Scully was master of ceremonies—a tricky job under the best of circumstances. Several celebrities spoke before Fred, and one of them made a remark about Raquel Welch. When it came Fred's turn, I was amazed to hear him incorporate the Raquel innuendo into his remarks and get a laugh out of the audience. His time allotted was five minutes, but in his dazed state he wasn't aware that he was ruining the sportscaster's evening. It certainly wasn't a dull speech because he kept the audience laughing. Afterwards, in our room, Fred said in a rather aggrieved tone, "Why was Vin Scully pulling on my jacket?"

After dinner many of the celebrities, except Winnie and Arnie, gathered in a pub room. Fred insisted on going in and, I'm sorry to say that as we entered, all those glittering members looked the other way, out of embarrassment. I couldn't believe that there wasn't a single person in the entire room willing to give a little comfort to a sick man who had been in the business longer than any of them.

• • •

Shortly after Fred returned home from the hospital, I began to worry about the Pennsylvanians. Thirteen weeks of bookings were contracted, starting the middle of January. If they were canceled, thirty-three Pennsylvanians would be out of jobs; the booking agent and all the theaters would lose money. There was no one available to head up the show, and so I, who had not set foot on a concert stage in twenty-five years, who had never emceed anything or conducted so much as "Jingle Bells," let alone complicated Ringwald arrangements done à la Fred Waring techniques, timidly proffered my inadequate skills.

The promoters accepted me readily, much to my surprise. Fred's daughter Dixie and my sister Helen planned to take turns staying with Fred to relieve my mind. My pressing priorities were three: learning to conduct, learning the sequence of a fast-moving two and a half hour show, and finding three gowns suitable for the stage.

Conducting: I'm ashamed to say I had never paid the slightest attention as to how Fred produced those wonderful choral sounds. My life had been full of other things—besides, his back was always to me, and I seldom saw the intricate motion of his expressive fingers and hands. I liken it to sitting in the rear seat of a car, being driven around for twenty-five years. The driver, with his back to you, shifts gears and manipulates gadgets while you, the passenger, look out the window, paying no heed, and then, suddenly, you must drive. The music was in my ear—the subtle nuances, ritards, accents, stress of certain vowels, and so on—but how to accomplish it? I asked Fred to show me, but when he didn't seem to comprehend, I knew I had to go it alone.

I packed three bags—clothes for warm weather, clothes for cold, and gowns for the stage—kissed Fred good-bye, and flew east. The first concert was in Norfolk, Virginia. With only one evening and one afternoon of rehearsal, suddenly there I was, standing onstage, facing the Pennsylvanians on the risers. Their eyes, shining with apprehension and love, were fixed on me. We could hear the murmur of twenty-five hundred people on the other side of the curtain, finding their seats and settling down for the show. The downbeat was given for Fred's opening bars of "I Hear Music," which then faded into his sixty-year-old theme song, "Sleep." As the curtain part-ed, I turned and walked to the mike, just as Fred always did, and said, "Hi, I'm *Mrs.* Fred Waring and these are the Pennsylvanians."

At first there was a hushed, stunned silence as though they couldn't believe Fred wasn't there, but then they started to applaud. I hurried on to say that the stars of the show were the young people behind me and this was Fred's show, perfected by him in the fall tour. Despite the warm welcome, I was really behind the eight ball from beginning to end. My fourteen years of touring as a concert pianist had not prepared me for show-business stage presence. The only time a pianist looks at an audience is to bow or announce a number. You are completely focused on the keyboard, on your inner self and, in my case, on my piano partner at the other piano, facing me. You attempt to achieve a state of limbo—shutting out the audience and losing yourself in the music. Yet here I was, impaled by a blinding spotlight that not only took my breath away but made it almost impossible to collect my thoughts. Even though I felt totally exposed and naked, I had to win over that audience. With a day and a half of rehearsal for a two and a half hour show, no conducting skills, and no cue cards, I now look back and wonder how I managed it.

The truth is I had a great deal of help. I shared conducting chores with forty-year veteran Ray Sax Schroeder, Pennsylvanian Rich Taylor, and Fred's choral conductor Lenny Thomas, who remained at the piano and kept everything moving briskly along. In Fred's shows, there were never any stage waits. Ray, working the lights, helped me with timing—entrances, exits, and when to talk: that delicate point in time when the applause has not completely died down and when it's not peaking. The first week on the road I evidently was conducting as if I were playing the piano. One night after I had finished a big number with my hands held high and my fingers spread wide apart, the company stage manager came to me laughing and said, "You looked like you're puttin' a spell on 'em."

Most people assumed I traveled everywhere with Fred and was completely familiar with the show. Actually, during the fall of 1979, I had seen the show only twice and had paid very little attention to its content. When Fred started out with a new show, he was forever "cutting and pasting," as he called it—moving songs around, deleting some, changing a complete sequence until you wouldn't recognize the dress rehearsal show he started with. His shows were incredibly fast paced—never a split second of stage wait—always more and more compelling, right to the end.

My debut in Norfolk received an encouraging ovation, and we slowly moved south, day by day, another concert, another city—all standing ovations. Our warm reception was due to a number of factors—the

American trend to root for the underdog; the show itself, which Fred had polished to near perfection in the fall tour; and first and foremost, the Pennsylvanians whose heartfelt singing shone through and made the audience laugh and cry. Those young people were unbelievably supportive. I felt buoyed by their thoughts and prayers behind me as the curtain opened each night on the sea of faces in the audience. When I turned to conduct them, their glistening eyes focused on me, they would smile, nod, and give tiny winks of encouragement. All of them wrote or spoke words of praise and love for risking my neck for them.

At the beginning I sometimes became confused and mixed up sequences or songs. Benny Hasen, our program salesman for twenty-five years, would grab my hand as I entered the bus after a concert to reassure me with comforting pieces of information he overheard in the lobby at intermission. My occasional faux pas seemed to endear me to the audience.

Conducting was extremely difficult for me in the beginning. In those first weeks, I couldn't look at the faces of the Pennsylvanians while I was directing them. I was saying the words, moving my hands and fingers, and thinking of ritards and crescendos and the musical line. None of it was automatic yet. In order not to be distracted, I would look at only one spot—like someone's stomach right in the middle of the group.

As we arrived in Sarasota, Florida, I was the first to be struck with an intestinal bug. The beautiful Frank Lloyd Wright theater was sold out—three concerts in two days. Before the first show I felt nauseated and light-headed. One of the two Pennsylvanians who looked after me stood in my dressing-room door watching me carefully. The room was not too steady around me, but I managed to get onstage. While I was conducting, concentrating, and just hanging in, there was a rustling, hurried movement among the singers. A fainting girl was being dragged off the riser by the boy next to her. In my next piece, the same thing happened on the other side of the chorus. It was a real hazard for me to encounter unexpected happenings. That's why I didn't even look to see what was going on when those poor girls were fainting! The little flurry onstage didn't prevent the local newspaper critic from saying kindly in his column, "The flowers were for Virginia, but the standing ovation was for Fred Waring."[1]

Staying well on the road is one of the constant perils of show business, what with the daily changes of climate, arduous bus journeys, irregular hours, lack of rest, and bad food. One time in the sixties, half of the Pennsylvanians were mowed down by the flu, and Fred had to perform with a shrunken group. Illness is endemic to those who tour. But you have to be exceedingly sick not to perform. Once I tried to play a concert with Livingston when my temperature was a hundred and two, because it was too late to cancel. I was unable to continue up to intermission. Therefore, we had to return the next year and play for free.

Illness wasn't our only problem on the tour, however. Keeping the show intact and in shape was not easy. When you are performing almost every night, sloppiness and imprecision tend to creep in. If I made a ritard two nights in a row, the Pennsylvanians would begin to anticipate it, losing the pulse and slowing up. I felt like I was literally dragging the entire state of Pennsylvania, trying to get them moving again. When playing the piano, your fingers and arms bring instant response as the keys are struck. A chorus reaction is less defined. I later complained to Fred, and he said, "Change your tempi. Make variations every night. They will follow you." I did, and they did.

While Fred was present, his word was law. With me, a complete novice at the helm, it wasn't long before everyone was getting in the act, trying to be helpful. I suddenly had to become the Boss—a role I had never desired or needed, so I called a meeting of the three leaders and laid out the lines of procedure. All musical problems were to go through Lenny Thomas, our choral director; and all choreographic and stage problems were the concern of Ray Sax, producer and company stage manager. I would handle personnel problems. A meeting was called about every two weeks in order to keep the show running smoothly. The only personnel problem I had was enforcing the dress code upon a couple of rebels. On my first day, one boy was standing in the lobby with jeans on. When I asked him if jeans were allowed, he said, "No," and went and changed. He tested me from time to time, but his heart wasn't really in it.

Just as Fred called me every night while on tour, now I, for the first time in twenty-six years, was calling him. A close friend who often invited Fred for dinner told me Fred would leave before the others, to be home for my call after the concert. I used to do that, too.

After about six weeks, we had worked our way west. Fred had decided to join us in Arizona. What could I say? I knew he wasn't strong enough for the rigors of the road, but I certainly wasn't going to say no. I flew ahead to Phoenix to meet his plane. I was so happy to see him, but he looked extremely thin and frail. I was worried because now I had a double load and I wasn't sure I could hold up.

The Pennsylvanians were to perform on a Sunday afternoon at Sun City for seven thousand people. It was decided that Fred would watch the concert—the first time in more than sixty years he had observed his own show. It was my first outdoor performance, and I sorely missed Ray's subtle cues with lights, which didn't show up in the daylight. I could see Fred wandering about. He had bought a new camera and was snapping pictures of everything and everybody. At the end of the show I asked him to come up and conduct his favorite encore, Cole Porter's "Every Time We Say Goodbye." He came onstage, walked over to me, took my face in his hands and kissed me, then turned to conduct. Tears were streaming down the faces of the Pennsylvanians. I don't know how they managed to get through it. Afterwards, Fred complimented me and then added, with a slight grin, "If I were the Pennsylvanians, I would be scared as hell to see those piano hands coming at me." Even so, he didn't show me how to conduct, and he didn't want Lenny helping me either. He wanted me to find my own method, which is what has happened since then. I still refer to myself as the "poor man's Fred Waring."

And so we continued the tour with Fred on board. But it was scary for all of us, especially me, because I was never sure of what he was going to do. He was out there on his will alone. Physically, the strain was too much. He was conducting most of the show, although I spelled him here and there. He wasn't always able to remember his stage patter, but he was in total command when conducting. However, I noticed he was getting more and more glassy-eyed onstage. After California, we started back east, hitting favorite midwestern cities like Milwaukee, Minneapolis, and Indianapolis. Finally, with three weeks to go, we landed in the town of Punxsatawny, Pennsylvania—of groundhog fame.

In the first act of the show, Fred started behaving very strangely. He had brought onstage a rolled-up paper gadget that unrolls in a straight line, with a flick of the wrist, and then quickly rolls back up. It wasn't at all unusual for Fred, from time to time, to bring out a diversion to tease the Pennsylvanians. He'd do it only to a spunky Pennsylvanian who could react and make the audience laugh as well.

That night he'd announced a tenor's solo, and while the Pennsylvanian was walking to the mike, Fred directed the paper gizmo at him. It was a playful gesture and got Fred a laugh. But he kept doing it over and over, and it wasn't funny anymore. Fred was oblivious—he was probably having a small stroke onstage. Lenny, at the piano, kept turning around to me where I was watching in the wings, his eyes begging me to do something. I felt helpless. I was afraid to confront Fred onstage, not knowing what he might do. I did know it was time for him to terminate his road tour. At intermission, I told him gently that he shouldn't continue and that the bus driver would take him back to the hotel. He stubbornly continued to change into his second-act evening jacket. With the help of some of the closer Pennsylvanians, who naturally were timid about telling their boss what to do, we finally persuaded him to put on his street clothes. In the meantime, I had to don my second-act outfit and finish out the show alone. When we all arrived back at the hotel, Fred was sitting in the bar. He wasn't about to go to bed.

I called one of our sons to come the next morning and take his father home to Shawnee while I finished the tour alone. We weren't sure what Fred's reaction would be. Fortunately, he was amenable and, as he got into the car, he turned to me and said guilelessly, "Aren't you coming with me?" obviously unaware that I had to complete the final weeks of the tour.

. . .

Fred improved mentally and physically over the next few months, and by the fall of 1980 was ready to embark on his "Farewell Tour." The promoters and booking agents were enthusiastic, but only if I were part of the package as insurance. They also wanted me to play the piano. My fingers seemed to be all thumbs after twenty-five years of neglect, but Charlie Naylor dashed off an arrangement of "The Man I Love" with choral obbligato that wasn't too taxing. I learned some new pieces to conduct, and so I went along to keep Fred happy and busy, to spell him onstage, and to calm the bookers.

Fred was determined to live and work as he always had, though it took every bit of willpower he could muster to tour and to conduct with his weakened faculties. The auditoriums overflowed with his fans, and he satisfied them with his wit and musicianship. I garnered a few kudos along the way for my conducting and piano playing, but I abhorred the road. However, I never complained. Neither Fred nor I were whiners.

Everyone was concerned about Fred's health, and it was hard on him to be watched over to save his strength. As Ray Sax said: "He has always been Mr. 'You Do What I Say.' Now he is being told what he can and cannot do. I think he realizes that they're all trying to save his life and he has made a tremendous adjustment, but it isn't easy for him. He doesn't like situations where he isn't in control."

The stroke affected his left side and, when he was tired, his left foot would drag a little and his diction would be somewhat slurred. Toward the end, his vocal cords weakened. Of all his frailties, *that* seemed to fret him the most. I tried to treat him compassionately so as never to embarrass him or make him feel inadequate. And patience! I needed infinitely more patience than with any child. He was slow in dressing, slow in making simple decisions. Unfortunately, as patience is not one of my minimal virtues, I failed a few times in the beginning, because we had been so responsive to each other's moods and thoughts. I learned to temper my reactions. The one trait I sorely missed was his spontaneous laughter. We used to constantly chuckle at something—an "in" joke, a gesture, a remark on television, a double entendre, one of my clichés, whatever. But now his finely tuned senses were dulled. He had almost become a stranger.

Toward the end of his life, Fred was carrying extra baggage on the bus to make his life more comfortable. He was fragile, and the unyielding hotel beds were intolerable, so a bedroll (a canvas-covered rubber mattress used by campers) and two suitcases of soft down pillows went along, plus one suitcase with clothes and two small hard cover cases, one of which we called his commissary. It contained cereal, honey, bowl, spoons, crackers, and a peeling knife. The other held vitamins, toiletries, aspirin, and so on. Everything in those two suitcases had its own container and place. The cereal tin had once held cigars (perish the thought) but was chosen for its size and shape.

Any Pennsylvanian who wished could receive extra pay for certain offstage duties. Upon arrival at the hotel, one young man brought in Fred's bedroll and placed it under the bottom sheet of the bed. Another was responsible for setting a carton of milk in an ice bucket for Fred's bowl of cereal in case no restaurant was open after the concert, and for setting out a bowl of apples—*only* Golden Delicious. Procuring tolerable food on the road was one of the biggest problems for Fred. In a 1982 interview, he observed, "Eating is the only facet of our career which has deteriorated."[2] Even if a tasty meal were available, we never had time to savor it except on a day off, when Fred would take a crowd of Pennsylvanians to a favorite restaurant.

Each morning on the road, Fred made himself a cup of tea and munched on a few crackers. The problems always arose in the coffee shops when he went down for breakfast. He insisted the waitress warm his cup first before filling it with coffee. Usually that elicited a blank stare and then, "How do I do that?" He would point to the carafe of hot water, tell her to pour the water in and then pour it out. Cholesterol or no, Fred always had scrambled eggs for breakfast. Until a few years ago, eggs were available any time of the day. But suddenly the chefs of America united and decided never to serve an egg after 11 A.M. It was frustrating. Once we were in a restaurant whose menu read eggs "anyway, anytime." It was 1 P.M. We had slept late because we had a short bus ride in the afternoon. I ordered poached eggs. The waitress came back and said the cook had just thrown out the water. I pointed to the menu and its large printed statement. She yawned, looked at her watch and said, "Dearie, it *is* late, you know." That was the end of it.

After his stroke, Fred craved food he had enjoyed as a child. Milk toast was something no waitress had ever heard of. Fred would tell her to put a cup of milk in the microwave oven, toast two pieces of bread, butter them, put them in a bowl, and pour the hot milk over it.

Backstage dressing rooms can vary from A to Z. If it was Kennedy Center, Carnegie Hall, or any of the beautiful new auditoriums, then Fred and I each had our own dressing room. Unfortunately, in many of the performance centers, the dressing rooms are not easily accessible to the stage—too far away or up and down flights of stairs. That's when the crew concocted a cubicle backstage for Fred to dress in. It consisted of Fred's trunk, his folding chair and a naked light bulb suspended overhead—all surrounded by three propped-up baffles.

The large arenas and gymnasiums usually had offbeat dressing rooms that often added another dimension to our hectic lives. In an amphitheater in West Palm Beach, Florida, our dressing rooms were improvised spaces under the bleachers. And in some high school gyms (the auditoriums were usually too small for Fred's crowd), men and women sometimes shared a locker room separated by a temporary curtain. Mirrors, hooks for clothes, and adequate lighting were often lacking in these makeshift quarters. The backstage dressing rooms of some of the oldest theaters are drafty and cold with dirty uncarpeted floors.

Fred's trunk was unloaded and set up each night in his allotted dressing space. It was stocked with everything one might need in an emergency. Any Pennsylvanian who had a toothache, hangnail, stomachache, diarrhea, cold, or any other common ailment knew that trunk probably held a panacea. The trunk stood upright almost shoulder high and opened in the middle, clothes hanging on left side and drawers on the right. The top two drawers held comb, brush, accessories, Band Aids, and cups in special compartments. Fred cut a slit in one drawer to extract tissues easily. The middle drawers held clean underwear, socks, and shirts. He would stuff his used clothing in a pillowcase, which was then put under the bus with the luggage. In the bottom drawer he had drawn an outline of each shoe so all would fit. Sometimes in the summer on a short mini-tour, the trunk was left behind. Fred and I were sharing a dressing room one night, and as Fred leaned down to put on a shoe, he asked, "What do you think of my $400 shoehorn?" My eyes widened as he held it up. It was four one-hundred-dollar bills folded into a rectangle. His shoehorn was in his trunk, so he had improvised.

When dressing for a show, Fred never liked to be interrupted—it interfered with his routine. He would dress always in the same order—first the pants (automatically holding the leg so it wouldn't touch the floor—from all the years of filthy backstage theaters), then shoes, shirt, and so on. I never fully comprehended his fanaticism until I toured with the Pennsylvanians. I had three costume changes. The last was a quick one—sometimes I had two numbers to change in, sometimes one—depending on how tired everyone was, the audience response, Fred's whim, or whatever—and several times I found myself on the stage minus a belt or necklace, or wearing the wrong shoes simply because I hadn't trained myself to put them on in order. (Fred was also methodical about house and car keys. He *never* mislaid them. I have driven myself crazy doing just that.) And to think he ended up with me—I who never folded my dirty clothes—or clean ones, for that matter.

When the Pennsylvanians arrived backstage before the concert, everything had been set up in the afternoon—lights, microphones, sound checks. Their only obligation was to take their costumes, shoes, and accessories from where they hung in the large wooden standing boxes to their dressing rooms, and then replace them after the show. Unfortunately, these boxes had to be closed immediately after the concert and put on the truck, which meant they were not aired out. Frequent spraying helped somewhat. Each performer was responsible for seeing that loose threads, buttons, and seams were repaired by the wardrobe mistress. A thread hanging from the hem of a dress catches the light, and Fred has been known to send a girl offstage for such an infraction.

Fans who came backstage after a show were always amazed at the frenetic activity going on. Several Pennsylvanians helped the stagehands repack the equipment in boxes to be loaded on the truck in proper order and in jiffy time because it had to be completed by the time the bus left for the hotel. Fred was usually detained by admirers, so that by the time he donned his street clothes, the loading was complete and the bus could then leave.

On the 1980 "Farewell Tour," we arrived in Independence, Missouri. Several officials and police officers were there, holding a bulletproof vest for Fred to put on. Someone had sent a note to the theater that said: "Mr. Waring, this *is* your farewell tour!" They knew the man, even described him to us, but never had enough evidence to pull him in. In 1980, Fred weighed only one hundred and twenty-five pounds. The weight of the bulletproof vest nearly toppled him over. To make it worse, the stage was an open one with no curtain. Fred never said a word, just went out and performed a two-hour show. I was sorry the police had described the man, because Fred thought he saw him in an aisle seat and had to live with that suspicion for the duration. The Pennsylvanians were behind Fred. But nothing happened. Fred had weathered another hurdle.

Fred's "Farewell Tour" was such an unmitigated success that he completed three more tours after that. There was talk of calling the first of these "Son of Farewell Tour" or "Farewell Tour II," but as I remember, it came out "Hello Again."

．　．　．

While writing about the problems Margaret Mead experienced with being married to another anthropologist, Jane Howard stated, "Perhaps no other endogamous marriages except those of two committed foreign missionaries or two stars of show business, present quite as many hazards. The members of a good anthropological team in a difficult field location are as interdependent as two trapeze artists, or to pick a loftier simile, as Alfred Lunt and Lynn Fontanne."[3] Endogamy—marriage within the same tribe or caste—was what I unwittingly had embraced on my two trips to the altar.

One of the dangers of touring *à deux* lies in the ever-present fatigue that tends to make a person irritable and not so objective. The best hotel solution on the road is connecting rooms. It is injudicious to request a suite—you often end up with a large living room, with no time to enjoy it, and a single cramped bedroom and bath. Two separate rooms ensure individual rest—one person can rise, watch TV, read, sleep, whatever, without disturbing the other. And whoever designed sealed hotel windows should be banished to Siberia. After being enclosed in a bus, restaurant, or auditorium, you're then doomed to spending the night in an airless room that's either too hot or too cold. Fred and I flew ahead on long jumps, but in the end it was almost easier to be taken door to door on the bus than to hassle with the vagaries of air travel—delayed connections, bumpy commuter flights, and long waits.

Backstage after the show Fred would greet fans and sign autographs. He seldom went to the "green" room, the special room where performers customarily greet well-wishers. It is, by the way, rarely painted green. Fred preferred the openness of backstage, although the stage crews weren't too happy with fans milling about as they lowered lights and scrims from overhead. Dog tired by now, we'd finally arrive in a restaurant. Suddenly the whole room would fill with people from the concert. They'd come to our table one by one to tell Fred how much they loved him and how much they enjoyed the show, and almost all would say, as well-wishers invariably say to every performer, "You're my greatest fan," instead of "I'm your greatest fan."

Fine! He'd smile, shake their hands, and thank them. *Then* they would proceed to tell him every detail of when, how, and where they had heard him in the past. They were fervently anxious that he should know the impact he had made on their lives. It was touching. But all we could do was to keep smiling and looking up. They were standing, we were sitting. We'd nod our heads and continue smiling, although after the tenth visitor the smile was frozen, the food was cold, and the body sagged from fatigue.

After-concert receptions were also tiring. For the local residents it's a one-shot, fun event. For the traveling entertainer or musician, it means another show. When you walk into a room full of people, you are *on*. Few laymen realize how tiring it is to meet and socialize with strangers after a two and a half hour concert. That is work! On the other hand, we have had some special fans and relatives throughout the country who realized the nicest thing they could do was to give us a home-cooked meal with *no guests*. It was truly a gesture of love because we could totally relax and unwind.

My notes from a summer mini-tour, Chautauqua, summer 1981: "Long trip getting here but what a crowd, about sixty-nine hundred people! Management says we've broken the attendance record. This fantastic old wooden open air building dates from 1893. Our manager had to take out nearly two million dollars worth of insurance. It's the auditorium's protection against careless entertainers. The show starts at 8:30 but the place has been packed since 6:30—hundreds are seated in the choir loft behind the stage. We arrive at 7:30, the stage is open—no curtains—precludes testing the piano. Darn! Hope the action is tractable. We are sweltering, our costumes are damp and cling to our bodies. A night bug crawled around on the back of my neck during my piano solo.

"Two nights ago we played in another charming Victorian, all-wood auditorium—at Ocean Grove, New Jersey. A crowd of about seven thousand people were there. When Fred and I emerged afterwards to get on the bus, around three hundred fans were waiting for a close-up view of Fred. They all clapped and gazed at him as though he were some delicate treasure. It was really quite touching."

More from my diary: "This mini-tour has been rugged. F.W. and I aren't able to fly because these summer auditoriums lie in inaccessible places and are separated by endless miles. In four consecutive days we performed in Interlochen, Michigan, Columbus, Ohio, Chautauqua, New York, then back to Lakeside, Ohio. It's the zig zagging that wears one out."

Yet in spite of the tedium, the rewarding aspects of live audiences began to seep through. All those beaming upturned faces exuded some sort of magical elixir that was like a swig of oxygen. Fred's step was quicker and his face pinker. It was a mutual giving and taking that flowed back and forth across the footlights. Fred especially loved the Frank Lloyd Wright theaters. The first row of seats lay directly under his nose—no yawning orchestra pit to separate him from his beloved audience, and no aisles—just one solid mass of people.

There was nothing esoteric about his performances. They were easily understood, yet his musicianship was such that the greater the artist, the more they appreciated him. Besides Toscanini and Ormandy, the renowned conductor Georg Solti was also a fan of Fred's. In Chicago's Symphony Hall, Ray Sax was surprised to see Solti backstage watching a Waring performance when he was supposed to be home with a minor ailment. When quizzed, Solti said, "I'm never too sick to watch a Fred Waring show."

· · ·

The difference between playing the piano in concert and conducting is as night and day or black and white. To play well, you must practice constantly. Fritz Kreisler often said, "The first day I don't practice, I know it; the second day, my wife knows it; the third day, my audience knows it."

One is a slave to the instrument. The hundreds of notes artistically executed take an incredible combination of mental and physical coordination. A simple flawless run on the piano entails several factors—each note has to be struck in direct relation to the one before and the one after, that is, a thumb coming under cannot be louder or softer than the forefinger next to it. The notes must be equidistant in time one from the other. Add to that all the other components of nuances, ritards, and crescendos. The eccentric pianist Glenn Gould deemed that a piano recital was one of "the last blood sports."[4] Some say it's akin to being a gladiator in an arena. . . . The joys of listening to music arise from the one chance risk of performance when no one, neither performer nor listener, knows quite how it will come out.

Conducting is different. Bigger muscles are used. The conductor must have the music in his head and know every second where he is taking his musicians, but he can pick up his baton after weeks of layoff and do a credible job. Once the notes are digested, he is then free to concentrate on making the music come alive through arm and hand motions instead of ten disciplined fingers.

The second year I went out with Fred, in the fall of 1981, he hoped I would play "Liebestraum" by Liszt. It sounds like an easy piece, but there are two cadenzas in it that I liken to sand traps on a golf course. You're never quite sure you'll be able to get out of them. Faced with the possible hazards of untested stage pianos, I called up the concert division of Steinway Company. Much to my surprise, their Mr. Rubens not only remembered me from twenty-five years before but also lent me a beautiful concert grand. And so one more piece of equipment went into the truck. Each night the three legs of the piano were unscrewed, and the piano, covered with a thick quilted case, was tipped on its side and then dollied up the ramp into the truck.

Playing the piano onstage after twenty-five years was quite different. My attitude had changed. I still wanted and needed to have the music as perfect as possible, but if I didn't succeed—so what? At the beginning of the "Liebestraum" arrangement, Fred would conduct as the chorus sang along with me and then tacet as I began the difficult first cadenza up the keyboard. Sometimes if my hands were cold, I'd attack it with more caution, but when all felt right, I'd put my ears back, hold my breath, and go for it. (I heard Artur Rubinstein get tangled up in that passage one night.) Fortunately, I succeeded, but whether I did was not so important anymore—not as in my younger years when our two-piano career was blooming. Now at this point in my life I was simply doing my best.

I do regret one thing in looking back over my life with Fred—that I didn't always play the piano for him. Fred never made demands—he hinted once or twice—but I was too dense to realize his deep desire to hear me play or how happy it made him. In 1980 after his stroke, the doctors said Fred must walk every day. Fred loathed the idea, so I struck a bargain. If he would walk, I would practice twice as long as he walked. He agreed. At Shawnee, when he came out for breakfast around 9:30 or 10 A.M., I would sit in the living room and play. My housekeeper told me later that two months before he died, he turned to her with tears in his eyes and said, "Isn't that beautiful? You must promise me to make her practice."

For two seasons I toured with Fred but by the fall of 1983, I reluctantly decided that being on the road again was not for me. Fortunately, I was able to persuade a dedicated Pennsylvanian vet, Pete Kiefer, to watch over Fred on the road.

28

Timing

ALL during the years of train travel, Fred had contributed a few gray hairs and ulcers among his entourage by timing his entrance into his Pullman car just as the train was pulling out. Admiral Dexter said, "Fred used to worry me because we would be set up to leave someplace on a train and I knew that he could not reach the next point in time for a concert unless he caught the train, and at the last minute he would usually come wandering down slowly and make it with a few seconds to spare. He has the uncanny faculty of knowing exactly how much time he has to get from one place to another."

After Fred's stroke, when I was out on the road with him, he and I and young Pennsylvanian Tommy Paterra flew ahead on long jumps, often changing planes in large airports. Fred would go off to buy a newspaper or a cup of coffee, and then come dawdling in at the last moment. I was pretty used to it, but it nearly drove Tommy crazy.

Unfortunately, Fred's delicate sense of timing was impaired by his stroke. There were several close calls, but two stand out in my mind. One is an episode we refer to as Fred's "six-hundred-dollar hamburger."

He was flying alone to Palm Springs, as I had been detained by business. After leaving the road, I had fallen heir to another humongous job—president and CEO of Shawnee Press, our large choral music publishing company, which was almost like being on stage again, only this time in an utterly foreign arena. I had not the slightest clue as to how Shawnee Press was run. I figured my fifty skilled employees knew what they were doing so I, who had never held a job in my life, put on my best bib and tucker and, together with my sales crew, faced the music publishing world at national conventions. At home I sat in on selection sessions where one of our seven editors in charge of our various church, school, and instrumental divisions, would present manuscripts to a committee of fellow editors and marketing people. The group would sing the different parts or listen to performance tapes, and then vote. New music often looked better on paper than it sounded.

At any rate, the Pennsylvanians' stage manager was driving Fred from our home in Pennsylvania to Kennedy Airport, when suddenly Fred announced he would like to detour to mid-Manhattan and stop off at Hamburger Heaven. The driver dutifully did as he was bade. Fred went in, but instead of ordering his favorite medium-rare hamburger (a no-no at home) to go, he stayed inside and ate it there, evidently unaware of the passing minutes. When they finally arrived at the airport, the driver deposited him at the curb, not realizing Fred had missed his plane. Our son Bill called from Palm Springs, saying his father was not on the plane. We finally tracked Fred down in Phoenix, where he had spent a miserable night without his special pillows and other paraphernalia. In all the confusion, Fred's original first class ticket was lost and never refunded, hence the reference to his "six-hundred-dollar hamburger."

In another episode, he and I were in the Allentown airport to take the only commuter flight available for a concert that night. We had a half-hour wait, so Fred headed for the coffee shop while I went to the gate to check in—two escalators and a long corridor away. By the time I got our boarding passes, it was time to board—and no Fred. I begged the officials to hold the plane while I ran back to find him. There he was, sitting peacefully in the coffee shop, reading the paper. His watch had stopped and his inner clock didn't apprise him of the elapsed time—something that never would have happened before his illness.

. . .

Fred's ability to ad-lib funnies onstage was still there despite his stroke. When I came out to play my Gershwin piece, Fred, at center mike, announced to the audience as I sat down at the piano that I hadn't played in twenty-five years. The audience always laughed. It made me a little indignant that they didn't believe him, so I said emphatically, "It's true," and they laughed even more. Then Fred asked me what I was going to play, and I blurted out, "I dug up 'The Man I Love.'" Although surprised, within a second Fred was brushing himself off, saying to the audience, "Well? How do I look?" Then he and I and the Pennsylvanians together produced what *Variety* said was "an exquisite, shimmering version of 'The Man I Love.'"[1] It was this juxtaposition of impudent humor next to music performed with sensitivity that drew fans back year after year. Fred made them feel *good*.

Fred relished catching an audience off guard and making them laugh at themselves. For example, at a concert in Carnegie Hall, New York, in 1980, a special message from Mayor Ed Koch was read to Fred in front of the curtain after intermission. Koch congratulated Fred Waring for his significant contributions to the cultural tradition of New York. Then the curtain rose on the Pennsylvanians looking elegant in their costume change of evening clothes. They had been well rehearsed in a lush, stately Ringwald arrangement of the old jazz tune "Ja-Da."

Fred turned to the audience and said solemnly, "Now, knowing that we are in this center of culture and that you are a discriminating audience and demand only the best (lots of applause here), we prepared something special—a chorale done in all dignity. I trust you will receive it as such. Do not cough, do not sneeze, and above all, do not leave." (Laughter.) "This is a French chorale—'Szha—DA.'" (Nobody laughs or catches on.) Reverently and momentously, the Pennsylvanians sang slowly, "Szh . . . a—da, Szh . . . a—da; szha-da, szh-da, szh . . . ing, szh . . . ing, szh . . . ing." The audience burst out laughing.

Fred could get the same reaction in a small town. When he said, "Now, knowing that we are in this center of culture—" the audience always applauded, glad that their taste, too, was appreciated.

In my family there was laughter, but none of those games of verbal agility that surrounded Fred. Fast repartee and getting the punch lines of jokes are not my forte. In fact, I'm a prime example of what the French call *esprit d'escalier* ("stairway wit," the witty comment that comes to mind after one leaves the scene). I'm also addicted to clichés. I know it shows a paucity of thought and vocabulary, but they just seem to pop out . . . and often slightly askew. For example, I once said, "I'm up a stump!"

While I was on tour in the eighties, ostensibly to spell Fred onstage, one of my duties was to introduce each Pennsylvanian. Fred, instead of taking it easy, kept butting in with smart-aleck remarks that made everybody laugh. Finally, in disgust, I turned to the audience and said, "There's nothing like *uncooked* ham!" The Pennsylvanians joined in on that one.

Fred was given awards, plaques, and keys to almost every city we hit during the 1980 tour. He was grateful, of course, but they were given at intermission with grandiloquent humorless speeches—an abomination!

One night, three men came out together. Each had a plaque and a speech. The first man wore a beard. Before he could open his mouth, Fred asked him if he'd had trouble finding his razor (the audience roared). Fred was merciless. Not one of the three was able to finish his speech properly. Fred's teasing and twisting of their words to bring laughter was merely his way of easing a deadly situation.

It was on a summer tour that Fred met his match. A tall, elderly gentleman came out to present him with a few mementos. When Fred started teasing him, the gentleman retorted as fast as Fred could dish it out—the perfect straight man. Finally, hoping to get a little sympathy from the laughing audience, the man said, "Mr. Waring, you know I'm close to eighty." Fred, who had just celebrated his eightieth birthday, quickly stepped next to him and said, "You certainly are!"

In 1982 Radio City Music Hall celebrated its fiftieth anniversary. Every Sunday a renowned conductor would lead the orchestra in a special overture. Fred was asked to appear. We arrived on the appointed Sunday, and Fred went backstage while I found my seat in the auditorium, filled to capacity. The lights dimmed, as a stentorian voice came over the loudspeaker: "*And now . . . the Radio City Music Hall Symphony Orchestra . . . under the direction . . . of Fred Waring!*"

The audience was applauding as the orchestra, with Fred at the podium, rose majestically from the pit to stage level. An impressive air of sophistication prevailed as Fred, looking quite distinguished with the spotlight on his wavy white hair, gave the downbeat, and the orchestra began a medley of well-known symphony excerpts.

The third number in the medley was the "William Tell Overture." As the familiar rhythmic galloping beat of "The Lone Ranger" theme was heard, Fred suddenly turned to face the audience and, in full voice, yelled out, "*Hi-yo Silver!*" The audience gasped en masse and then howled with laughter. The first violinist nearly fell off his chair while the orchestra smilingly continued, and as the overture ended, it received a tremendous ovation.

Fred was asked to appear with the Reverend Dr. Robert Schuller on his Sunday television show. He agreed, with two stipulations: that he conduct their splendid choir, and that he *not* be quizzed about his religious beliefs. When Fred stood up behind the wide pulpit to be interviewed, he found Dr. Schuller towering over him. Fred was eighty-one and barely five feet, four inches tall, having shrunk two inches in his later years.

Fred disappeared suddenly behind the dais, leaving poor Dr. Schuller talking to the air. When Fred just as suddenly reappeared, he was standing eyeball to eyeball with the flustered minister. Fred had found a box to stand on. The staid church audience laughed heartily.

Then, when the good preacher attempted to draw from Fred his inner feelings of religion, I held my breath. Fred skillfully evaded the issue but later admitted to me, "Dr. Schuller was getting too close and I was about to let him have it."

The only public statement of Fred's on religion I ever found was his quote from the 12th Point of the Boy Scout Law: *He is reverent toward God. He is faithful in his religious duties, and respects the convictions of others in matters of custom and religion.* "I found in that the basis of a daily prayer," Fred said. "I wish I would live up to it."

We both believed firmly that all individuals have the right to worship where and how they please. All the friction, backbiting, and intolerance, not to mention hideous wars, that go on between denominations and sects simply drove us back to our original concept—the Golden Rule—putting oneself in the other person's shoes—and also making each day a positive one not only for oneself and family but for the community.

Fred was irrepressible to the end. In July, 1984, three weeks before he died, he was invited to St. Louis to receive an honorary *lifetime* membership from the Society for the Preservation and Encouragement of Barbershop Quartet Singing in America. He was standing onstage before many thousands in the audience while the presenter was going on and on about the lifetime honor. Fred interrupted, saying dryly, "I'm glad you didn't wait any longer." He always saw the ridiculous side to a stuffy situation.

29

Phaetons, Zephyrs, and Model A Fords

IN 1982 I asked Fred to name some of the cars he owned. They were engraved in his computer memory and, without a moment's hesitation, he reeled them off, from past to present: "An open Cadillac, a four-passenger Cadillac, a Phaeton Cadillac—very classy. [A 1926 edition of the *Pittsburgh Press* ran a photo captioned 'Waring and his faithful Cadillac (Brougham), his third Cadillac.']

"A Model A Ford, then a Lincoln Zephyr—a huge, enormous black sedan. A Lincoln convertible roadster made especially for me with a compartment for golf clubs. A special Ford made by Rolls-Royce—a Ford chassis with extended body—a very classy convertible sedan with an unusual top; made by Brewster Body company, makers of the Rolls-Royce. They made about three of them. I saw one years later in Arlington, Texas. It had almost rotted away.

"In 1932 I had a show car, a one-of-a-kind made for an automobile show. It was a Phaeton with wire wheels, ivory paint, and robin's egg blue leather seats. I took it to Europe, and it was continually mobbed. Everyone stood on the running board to look. I drove it all over France, Switzerland, and Italy.

"A Chrysler convertible with a wood body. It looked like a station wagon, but it was a convertible. A Lincoln Zephyr convertible—the same idea as a Chrysler. A Studebaker station wagon. One of the first Lincoln Continentals, which I purchased in the mid-forties." Liv and I bought this wonderful car from Fred to tour in. Our nine-foot grand pianos, donated by Steinway, went separately in a van.

When we were married, Fred was driving a Chrysler Imperial. Because it had an unusual loping ride that made me queasy, he turned it in for the first push-button Packard. Fred had several Packards in a row, and then suddenly he fell in love with the Citroën. We had several. It had an unusual suspension that enabled one to speed over a pothole with barely a quiver. Fred frequently took unsuspecting guests for a ride on the golf course just to watch their facial expressions as he raced toward a deep rut.

Next for Fred came the original Studebaker Skylark model. Then, in 1955 or 1956, Oldsmobile brought out its first front-wheel drive, the Toronado. The Museum of Modern Art in New York had the automobile on display in its exhibition hall, hailing it as "the first really new design to come out of Detroit in forty years." It's easy to guess who bought the first one. After enjoying a couple of Toronados, Fred joined mainstream America, acquiring a series of Toyotas, Hondas, Mazdas, and Renaults. In his later years, Fred said, "I still dream about these old cars. I park them in a New York garage, and I can't find them later on. It's a repeated dream."[1]

. . .

Fred didn't just love cars—he had a passion for them. In 1906, when he was six, he saw his first automobile:

"It was a little one that looked like a carriage. The back had a center door where you entered. It was one or two cylinders.

"In 1912 I was so car crazy it was pathetic. Dad was kind of strict and wouldn't let me near a car, but our neighbor had a Model T Ford and he taught me to drive it. He had an ulterior motive because he had an orchard up on this mountain, which he wanted to visit twice a week, and he would say, 'Would you like to go up to the orchard?' Of course, I would.

"Well, that meant that I would be driving this Model T up a rickety road. You know the catch—pressing that low gear in there all the way up a mountain. His leg would get tired and he knew I could take it. So he let me drive up the mountain. And then, of course, he would drive down. I can still hear him laughing—it was a great deal of fun.

"I also learned how to turn on the ignition of Dad's Chalmers, using a bent fork for a key, which resulted in a few extracurricular excursions."

In 1923, just before he married, Fred bought his first car, a Willys-Knight coupe, in dark blue. He was arrested for speeding on his honeymoon, and I don't believe he stayed within the speed limit for the rest of his life. Recorded bits of this mania show up here and there. In Springfield, Massachusetts, in 1933, for instance,

Nearly 2,000 persons waited more than an hour last night for the appearance of Fred Waring, leader of the Pennsylvanians, at Riverside Park. According to the officer, Waring (who was late) ran a red light, and was unable to produce his license and registration. He was taken to police headquarters, and Waring defied them to lock him up. So they placed him under arrest. When Waring finally arrived at the Park, boiling mad, he made a speech to the crowd, told them of his arrest, and received a big hand. Earlier in the day, the band had been stopped in Connecticut for a motor vehicle violation and, all in all, it was a tough day for Fred.[2]

From 1938 to 1954, Fred was in New York for five days a week performing his radio and television shows, and in Shawnee on weekends. The state police did not take long to catch onto his routine: Friday night driving west, and Sunday night or Monday morning headed east.

It was always open season on Fred and his automobile, whether it be the police or the press. Actually, he was a tremendously skilled operator who never indulged in races along the highway, and never took what he believed to be chances, although some Pennsylvanians would challenge that statement. He was just always in too much of a hurry.

The eighty-five-mile trip from New York to Shawnee, Pennsylvania, on two-lane Route 46, crossed New Jersey. Fred lived on the Delaware River, which divides the two states. In those days, the speed limit was fifty m.p.h. The police (according to Fred) picked him up when only going two or three miles per hour over the limit—although not one Pennsylvanian remembers any such pedestrian speeds. Office worker Sydney Johnson said the Pennsylvanians were frequently invited to Shawnee on weekends, chauffeured personally by Fred Waring: "It was delightful, with one exception: the excessive speed on the ride up. Patsy Garrett said she used to lie on the floor in the back—she was so terrified."

In Camden, New Jersey, it was noted that Waring had been arrested in New Jersey for speeding, five times in nine years. The commissioner debated but didn't revoke his license. However, by 1954, we all assumed Fred had lost his privilege of driving in New Jersey (no reciprocity existed between states in those days) because an Irishman named Pat was driving him back and forth to New York.

When we were first married, I was surprised when Fred—he who was always the one behind the wheel—asked me if I would like to drive across New Jersey. He later obtained a California driver's license. When I was in the car, Fred did not drive excessively fast. He knew it made me nervous, although I was no slouch myself.

In the summer of 1984 I was driving the two of us to Penn State on Interstate 80. No one was on the highway, so I was zipping along. As I came over the crest of a hill, a cop was standing outside his cruiser, arms folded, waiting for me. When we pulled over, Fred never said a word—just grinned at me.

All our boys and their cousins worked like beavers on the Shawnee Inn golf course every summer to save up money for their first cars—all except Billy, who went into hotel management (he slaved in the hotel kitchen). Finally, we had only one child left at home, Malcolm, who was growing up fast and becoming slightly warped on the subject of cars himself. On his sixth birthday, he leaned back from the table as though he were going to light a cigar and said, "Well . . . in ten years, I'll have my wheels."

In 1976, the year of the United States' bicentennial, Fred acquired a 1964 Cadillac stretch limousine that had belonged to an outstanding and colorful local citizen. "Papa Wyckoff," as everyone called him, was a bit like Fred's father, Frank Waring—very pious and upright. His married children would hide their alcoholic drinks if he happened by. When Mr. Wyckoff died, Fred, for sentimental reasons, bought the Cadillac and painted it a beautiful bicentennial blue with a narrow red and white stripe along the side. The excessive play in the steering wheel made the limo difficult to control on winding country roads, but Fred drove it every summer to Penn State for his music workshops. When the students saw this monstrously long apparition go tooling by, they would let out such loud appreciative remarks as "Holy sh——t!" or "Hot damn!" or whatever other elegant phrases kids used to say when surprised or pleased.

Even after his stroke, Fred would maneuver that Cadillac around the narrow streets of State College without denting a fender. He then decided to have breakfast every day at a little pancake house on a one-way street where the curb was marked in yellow paint: NO PARKING. Every day Fred pulled up, parked in the yellow zone, and went inside. Every day he received a citation. I suggested to the harassed workshop director, who didn't need a daily visit to the police station, that the town might allow a most distinguished alumnus a special two-month, one-hour privilege, but I don't think it worked.

. . .

In the spring of 1984, two and a half months before his death, Fred was returning to the California desert. He was extremely frail by now, and I was concerned about his traveling alone. I couldn't leave for two days. But

Fred was determined to go to Los Angeles, because there was an annual automobile exposition in the Coliseum and he just had to see all the new models.

We arranged for someone to meet him, watch over him, take him to the auto show, and then, the second day, check him out of the hotel and meet me in the L.A. airport, where Fred and I would then take a commuter flight to Palm Springs. It turned out, unbeknownst to us, that Fred was on his own—the aide had been stricken and hospitalized. Undaunted, Fred checked into the hotel and immediately took a cab out to the Coliseum. He tramped all over the place, happy as could be, gathering brochures and studying the cars, but when he came out of the building there wasn't a cab in sight. Finally, in desperation, he flagged down a pretty young lady and asked her where she was going and would she please drop him off at his hotel. When they arrived at the hotel, he invited her in for lunch, and she accepted. Then afterwards he managed to check out with all his bags and pull up at the airport in time to take the flight with me to Palm Springs. I had been standing there wondering what I would do if he didn't show up. But bless his heart, his enthusiasm over the cars he had just seen couldn't have been more intense if he had been twenty-four years old instead of eighty-four. I had to look at every last detail in every single brochure.

Fred maintained a heartwarming freshness in attitude throughout his life. He approached each curtain raising as the debut of the most important night of a lifetime. The anticipation of a favorite golf event made his eyes gleam. He called his friends with real excitement—"The sun is shining out there. Let's go." Every day is the first day of the world. His boyishness came in a startling way, speaking out at an unsuspected moment, "Tom is funny," as if he had never observed it before.

Fred's endearing way of reacting with the unguarded radiance of a five-year-old on Christmas Eve always came as a surprise in an octogenarian. I remember that Aldous Huxley once said, "To carry the spirit of the child into old age is the secret of genius." His observation fit Fred exactly.

30

What Glorious Music

THROUGHOUT the thirty years of our marriage, the only child who caused Fred to worry and spend sleepless nights was his first-born son, Fred Jr. Freddy had considerable potential, but somehow it all went askew.

He was nineteen when I entered the family. He spent many long hours sitting on the foot of my bed, complaining of the handicap of bearing the name of his famous father, yet at the same time using it to his advantage. Freddy had winning ways. People were drawn to him, but he would never allow himself to succeed at anything. He admitted to me years later that this was his pattern. His addiction to alcohol had begun in his teens, but we unfortunately didn't recognize the symptoms. Today, with Alcoholics Anonymous and Al-Anon, families have some guidelines for what their actions and roles should be. But in our ignorance, Fred, like many caring parents, alternated between helping Freddy and then pulling back when Freddy squandered the opportunities given him. He sent him to Penn State—which was not successful. Freddy played the trombone and had always had a band of some sort while growing up, so Fred invited him to tour if he wished. The musicians' union decreed that Freddy's salary be comparable to that of twenty-year veteran Pennsylvanians. Fred had been in the middle of an arbitration meeting with union heads over who was to be unionized in his touring company; he believed in apprenticeships for young or inexperienced craftsmen—be they plumbers or musicians. He said, "Do you think it right that my unseasoned son should receive the same weekly wage as skilled men who have been with me for thirty years?" One VIP from a large and powerful union said, "You're his boss. Don't you make him kick back?"

Even with his exalted salary, Freddy returned from the tour in debt. The creditors were persistent, and Fred paid them off reluctantly. After that he held back, trying not to be a permissive parent. Fred's pattern of helping and withdrawing help was to be the paradigm of his relationship with Freddy down through the years.

Time passed. Freddy seemed to be buckling down, and another opportunity would be offered. When that was blown, Fred would retract. Fred's love for his son was there always, but I don't think Freddy saw it.

Freddy married at twenty-one. The marriage was an uneasy one and he divorced a few years later. He remarried, entered AA, and for several years seemed to be on the right track. Fred decided to give him another chance, and offered him a position at Shawnee Press to learn the music-publishing business. Freddy started work in 1980, the spring I toured alone with the Pennsylvanians. He was forty-four years old.

After the tour I joined Fred in the California desert, and when we returned to Shawnee that June, Ernest Farmer, president and chief executive officer of Shawnee Press, asked to see us. He stated flatly that either Freddy must go or he would go. Freddy was arrogant and claiming unsanctioned business expenses. Even though Farmer had done a most commendable job of running the firm for many years, Fred just couldn't face firing his son. And so Farmer left, and Freddy became the CEO.

Fred formed a governing board consisting of himself as chairman, two men from Philadelphia, a lawyer and a management consultant (both suggested by Freddy), Fred's old publisher friend Cork O'Keefe, and me. We were there ostensibly to help guide Freddy in major decisions.

Freddy first settled his wife in as editor of a division without consulting the board. Then he began spending money on large unauthorized projects. More and more rumors reached us that all was not well at Shawnee Press. I didn't want to hear any of it, being overloaded with responsibilities and Fred's frail health.

By the third year, when we looked into it, it was clear that Fred Jr. had been taking money for his own use in breach of trust. It wasn't a small amount—it had jeopardized the health of the company. Fred agonized over the thought of firing Freddy, in spite of what he had done.

When Freddy learned he would probably be fired, he in turn sued me and the two gentlemen from Philadelphia, saying we had taken the company away from him behind his senile father's back. He and his wife set up a hot-dog stand in view of the building on Interstate 80 with a huge sign: HUNGRY FRED'S. And then they went public. The press, of course, feasted on the poor little rich man's son who said, "My father isn't a nice man. He doesn't want me to succeed, etc., etc." (*"How sharper than a serpent's tooth . . ."*)

The other children were furious. They *knew* and, God knows, I knew the efforts their father had made to help his alcoholic offspring. They told the media the truth, but it was never printed. Freddy's public denunciations cut deep into Fred's heart. Fred, the gutsy battler, who had faced and remained unbowed by seven decades of adversities, was crushed. He had no weapons. As his sister Helen predicted, "Freddy [meaning Sr.] will bleed inside."

The final blow came when *People* magazine published a similar biased article in the spring of 1984.[1] The day it went on the stands, Fred was on the sofa, totally withdrawn. I remember I took his hand and tried to cajole him out of his despair by saying, "You know, my love, what they say in show business—'I don't care what you say about me as long as you spell my name right.'" But nothing helped. The wound was too deep. It was then I think that Fred gave up and lost his will to live. Each passing month of 1984, Fred became more and more frail. A broken heart can do terrible things to a person. He scarcely ate because nothing tasted good to him.

He finished the spring tour, and after a few weeks of rest, we arrived in July at Penn State for his beloved youth workshop sessions. I see now he was totally concentrated on fulfilling his obligations, which ended July 27. Fred had suffered a few health relapses in the four years since his stroke, but had managed to overcome them with renewed vigor and determination. This time it was different. He had lost heart. He had decided to die— without telling us, of course.

I was told later that when he left the desert in June, instead of taking leave of his friends with his customary cheerful "Ta-ta" or "Be seeing you," he said "Good-bye" to all of them. And when he later left Shawnee for the Penn State workshop in July, he also said "Good-bye" to a few close friends.

The Pennsylvanians were already on campus as artists-in-residence when we arrived. Fred conducted them in a short concert in front of the Old Main building. It had been eight weeks since their last performance. Now, once again, he was "playing" his instrument, which made him extremely happy. On the way back to our rented residence, he sighed contentedly and said, "I feel like I've been let out of jail." It reminded me of

Pablo Casals, who sat at his piano each morning playing Bach as a kind of benediction, an "all's right with the world" feeling.

Fred was faced with four weeks of teaching. Two concerts would be given by nearly two hundred youngsters at the end of each two-week session. Fred worked with them every night with the same fierce and unrelenting demands for excellence that he required of his Pennsylvanians. It took almost all of his energy.

During this period, Fred and the Pennsylvanians also gave what was to be their last professional performance, at Penn State's Eisenhower Auditorium. It was televised for PBS.

The second workshop began. Fred had chosen as one of the numbers a beautiful Ringwald arrangement of the spiritual "Were You There When They Crucified My Lord?" He was more obdurate than ever in getting the nuances and inflections exactly right. In fact, he became so infuriated with the singers' lack of response to his directives that he walked out of rehearsals a couple of times.

But the choir's total concentration when they sang that song at the final concert made it the most moving of my musical experience. Fred had taken a ragged group of untrained youngsters and miraculously created a sound so exquisite and celestial that one truly felt caressed by a benign power.

That night, Fred had a massive stroke and died twenty-four hours later, on July 29, 1984. He was eighty-four.

Former Pennsylvanians arrived from all corners of America for his funeral. A few borrowed money for their fare, and one couple sold some bonds. Len Thomas rehearsed them—even the instrumentalists sang. The service was held in an auditorium on the nearby campus of East Stroudsburg University. The Pennsylvanians sang with fervor and inspiration. The musical tribute, as is customary at funerals, was followed by total silence.

I learned later that many of those present had an overpowering impulse to fill the hall with the same ringing cheers and applause that had reverberated from every stage in America for nearly seven decades.

• • •

Fortunately, the Waring legacy lives on. His disciplines and techniques have not been lost but are continuing through various channels. Fred's choral conductors from every generation teach and conduct throughout the country. For five years, with the help of Marlowe Froke at Penn State, I carried out a dream of Fred's—creating a U.S. chorus of one hundred young men and women drawn from all the states. Their performances were aired annually on PBS. And now the television kinescopes are being repackaged for cable consumption and the record albums restored on compact discs so the world can once again hear the Waring sound with, as Fred so often stressed, all of the beauty of all of the sounds of all of the syllables of all of the words.

Notes

Chapter 1: The Victorian Warings

1. Helen Waring Martin interview with Jack Dolph, York, Pa., 1960. This and other interviews, letters, and additional unpublished materials are listed in the Note on Sources at the end of this book. Unless otherwise indicated, all quotations come from these sources.

2. *Town and Gown*, Aug., 1979.

Chapter 2: Entrepreneur

1. *Town and Gown*, Aug., 1979.

2. Jack O'Brian interview with Fred Waring on WOR Radio 710, New York, 1980.

Chapter 4: The Brash Kid from Tyrone

1. Jack O'Brian column, *New York Daily News*, 1982.

2. *Baltimore News-Post*, Jan. 4, 1924; Jan. 16, 1924; *Detroit Free Press*, June 22, 1922.

3. *Billboard*, Aug. 15, 1922.

4. *Milwaukee Journal*, Sept. 16, 1922.

5. Michigan booking agent to Sid Grauman.

6. Grauman to Michigan booking agent, Dec. 11, 1922.

7. Fred Waring to Grauman, Dec. 20, 1922.

8. Grauman to Waring, Dec. 29, 1922.

9. Concert manager to Grauman, Jan. 5, 1923.

10. *Los Angeles Examiner,* Jan. 26, 1923.

11. *Los Angeles Times,* May 16, 1923.

12. *San Francisco Examiner,* May 25, 1923.

13. *San Francisco Bulletin,* June 6, 1923.

14. *Pacific Coast Musical Review,* Feb. 6, 1923.

15. *Los Angeles Times,* 1923. Exact date not known. Article can be found in book 2 of press book archives located at Pennsylvania State University.

Chapter 5: Milk Trains

1. *Washington Post,* Feb. 3, 1924; *New York Evening World,* 1924, Penn State archives, book 2.

2. *Etude* 42, no. 8 (Aug., 1924): 515.

3. *Washington, D.C., Daily News,* Feb. 2, 1924.

4. *Richmond, Va., Ledger,* Sept. 2, 1924; *Richmond Times-Dispatch,* Sept. 5, 1924; *Washington Post,* Feb. 11, 1924.

5. *Baltimore News,* Jan. 16, 1924.

6. "Ah! Waring's Syncopators are 'Golfopators' Also!" *Los Angeles Examiner,* July 1, 1925.

7. *Philadelphia Record,* Mar. 14, 1926.

8. These phrases appeared in various letters written to Hilda Cole Espy from 1978 to 1981, Espy file.

Chapter 6: Stairway to Fame

1. Fred Mertz, liner notes on *Fred Waring Memorial Album,* Stash Records ST126.

2. *Variety,* June 2, 1926.

3. Penn State archives, book 3.

4. *Cleveland News,* Dec. 27, 1927.

5. *Baltimore News-Post,* May 4, 1927.

6. *Columbus, Ohio State Journal,* Sept. 11, 1927.

7. Critic Archie Bell, *Cleveland News,* Dec. 30, 1927.

8. Penn State archives, book 3, Oct., 1927.

9. Edna Gorma, *Philadelphia Record,* 1926, Penn State archives, book 3.

10. Fred Waring memorabilia, 1980.

11. *Buffalo Courier Express,* Aug. 9, 1931.

12. *Variety,* Apr. 7, 1926.

13. Boston interview, 1928, Penn State archives, book 3.

14. "A Slight Similarity—in Name Only," *New York Morning Telegraph,* Jan. 4, 1926.

15. Penn State archives, book 3, 1928.

Chapter 7: Paris

1. *New York World-Telegram,* Nov. 11, 1940.
2. *New York World-Telegram,* Nov. 11, 1940.
3. *Paris Herald Tribune,* June 24, 1928.
4. Ernest Newman quote, Penn State archives, book 3, Aug., 1928.
5. Fred Waring's reply to Newman.
6. "Up and Down Broadway," *New York Evening World,* Dec. 18, 1928.
7. "Waring at $55,000," *New York Sunday Telegraph,* Dec. 9, 1928.
8. *Philadelphia Bulletin,* May 4, 1929.
9. *Milwaukee Journal,* Aug. 22, 1929.
10. *Cincinnati Times-Star,* Oct. 9, 1929.
11. Will Friedwald liner notes for *Fred Waring Memorial Album,* Stash Records ST126, 1984.
12. *Metronome,* Mar., 1928.
13. *Cleveland Press,* Aug., 1929.
14. Victor advertising circular, Paris, 1928.

Chapter 8: Fred Loses His Shirt

1. *Los Angeles Times* interview, May, 1930, Penn State archives, book 7.
2. *New York Times,* Dec. 9, 1930.
3. *New York Telegraph,* Dec. 20, 1930.
4. Ibid.
5. *New York Telegraph,* June, 1931, Penn State archives, book 7.
6. *New York Evening Graphic,* Dec. 26, 1931.
7. *New York World-Telegram,* Nov. 11, 1940.
8. Ibid.
9. *Syracuse Herald,* Aug. 21, 1931.

Chapter 9: Ballet, Classics and the Roxyettes

1. *Boston Traveler,* Aug. 24, 1932.
2. *New York Variety,* Jan. 12, 1932.
3. *New York Daily News,* Feb. 27, 1932.
4. *Orchestra World,* Feb. 1932.
5. "Intimate Glimpses of Interesting People," *New York Evening Graphic,* Feb. 15, 1932.
6. Louis Sobol, "Voice of Broadway," *New York Evening Journal,* Apr. 18, 1932; Walter Winchell, *New York Journal,* Apr. 15, 1932; *New York Morning Telegraph,* June 22, 1932.
7. *Boston Globe,* Aug. 23, 1932.
8. *Billboard,* Sept. 10, 1932.

Chapter 10: Radio Days

1. James Cannon, *New York World-Telegram,* July 6, 1933.
2. "Behind the Mike," New York, July 13, 1933.
3. Lloyd Lewis, *Chicago American,* Sept. 23, 1931.
4. *Chicago Tribune,* Oct., 1933. Penn State archives, book 11.
5. *Washington Daily News,* Apr. 23, 1933; *Washington Post,* Apr. 23, 1933.
6. Jack O'Brian radio interview, WOR, New York, 1980. Recorded interview drawer.
7. Nick Kenny, *New York Daily Mirror,* May 1, 1934.
8. Guy Lombardo and Jack Altshul, *Auld Lang Syne* (Garden City, N.Y.: Doubleday, 1975).
9. Bill Demarest conversation with Fred and Virginia Waring, Canyon Country Club, Palm Springs, Calif., 1968.

Chapter 11: Henry Ford & Co.

1. *Boston Traveler,* May 2, 1934.
2. *Washington Herald,* 1934. Penn State archives, book 16. Poor Evalyn was not only a stage widow but a golf widow as well—she never went on the road or the links.
3. *New York World-Telegram,* Feb. 10, 1934.
4. *Variety* reports from scrapbooks of years 1934, 1935, and 1936.
5. *New York Telegram,* 1935, Penn State archives, book 18.
6. *Variety,* Feb. 14, 1933.
7. John Royal to Jack Dolph, 1960 tapes.
8. Horace Heidt telegram to Fred Waring, June 11, 1935.
9. Johnny O'Connor letter to Heidt, June 20, 1935.
10. Heidt telegram to O'Connor, June 29, 1935.
11. O'Connor letter to Heidt, July 1935.
12. Cole Porter, *Harper's Magazine,* 1935, magazine drawer.
13. Leonard Lyon, "Lyon's Den," *Broadway Gazette,* 1935, undated Penn State archives, book 20.

Chapter 12: The Legalities of Interpretation

1. Opinion of the Supreme Court of Pennsylvania (Stern) and Concurring Opinion (Maxey) in the case of *Fred Waring vs. WDAS Broadcasting Station, Inc;* reprinted by the National Association of Performing Artists and sent to Fred Waring by Maurice J. Speiser, general counsel (Oct. 12, 1937), in the Penn State archives.
2. Harold C. Schonberg, *New York Times,* 1981, Espy file.
3. Charles Champlin, *Los Angeles Times,* Feb. 27, 1967.

Chapter 13: The Waring Blendor

1. "For Men Only," radio interview, Mr. Butell and Fred Waring, Jan. 24, 1938, recorded interview drawer.
2. *American Business,* Sept., 1938.

Chapter 14: Burgeoning Empire

1. *Cleveland Press,* Feb. 18, 1936.
2. *Chicago Times,* Feb. 9, 1936.
3. *Newark, N.J., Star Eagle,* Feb. 10, 1936.

Chapter 15: Hollywood

1. *Time,* June 26, 1939.
2. Milton Caniff told this to Virginia Waring in 1985, Espy file.
3. *New York Sun,* Apr. 27, 1939.

Chapter 16: "A Cigarette, Sweet Music, and You"

1. Fred Waring told this story in the 1960 interview Jack Dolph recorded with him.
2. Lombardo and Altshul, *Auld Lang Syne.*
3. *Buffalo, N.Y., Times,* Feb. 16, 1936.
4. *New York Radio Mirror,* undated, Penn State archives, book 23.
5. Jack O'Brian radio interview, WOR 710, 1980, recorded interview drawer.
6. Maud Howe Elliot handwritten letter to Fred Waring, June 22, 1943.
7. *New York World-Telegram* editors' poll, American Press Clipping Service, Feb. 18. 1941.
8. Lumpy Brannum told this story in the 1978 interview Hilda Cole Espy recorded with him, Espy file.
9. Fred Waring to Donna Dae and Patsy Garrett, undated.

Chapter 17: My Debut

1. *San Francisco Chronicle,* Apr. 27, 1942; *Cleveland Plain Dealer,* July, 1948.
2. Fred Waring, 1978 radio interview, recorded interview drawer.

Chapter 18: For the Sake of One Singer

1. Walter Winchell, "On Broadway," *New York Daily Mirror,* Aug. 16, 1944; Ed Leamy, "Wavelets," Aug. 21, 1944 (paper not named); Jack Lait, "For the Love of Mike, Broadway & Elsewhere," *New York Mirror,* Aug. 6, 1944; Ben Kaplan, New York, July 28, 1944 (paper not named); Kups Column, *Chicago Times,* May 26, 1944.

2. Claudia Cassidy, *Chicago Tribune*, Oct. 1, 1946.

3. *Chicago Daily News,* Oct. 2, 1946.

4. *Detroit Free Press,* undated, 1934, Penn State archives, book 16.

Chapter 19: Music Workshops

1. Fred Waring announced on his first broadcast for Groves Bromo Quinine, Oct. 8, 1938, "Melodies are written to be played; poems are written to be read; songs are written to be sung." He repeated a variation of that theme the rest of his life.

2. "Black Is the Color of My True Love's Hair," arrangement published by Shawnee Press, Delaware Water Gap, Pa., 1948.

3. "America the Beautiful," arrangement published by Shawnee Press, Delaware Water Gap, Pa., 1951; "Havah Nagilah," Fred Waring's America music library, unpublished.

4. Gary Giddens, *Satchmo* (New York: Doubleday, 1988), p. 81.

5. Edgar Williams, Today-Sunday Magazine, *Philadelphia Inquirer,* Jan. 8, 1978.

6. *Washington Post,* Mar. 4, 1947.

7. This story was related by Pennsylvanian Sydney Johnson, who wrote to Hilda Cole Espy, Aug. 8, 1980, Espy file.

8. Recollections of Pennsylvanian Marvin Long in 1980, in Espy file.

9. Recollections of Pennsylvanian Lette Rehnolds in Oct., 1980, in Espy file.

Chapter 20: Television

1. *New York Variety,* Apr. 20, 1949.

2. *Newsweek,* Feb. 2, 1950.

3. Bob Banner, conference video, 1985.

4. Mickey Dugdale, "Remembrances," taped interview, Nov. 30, 1980, Espy file.

5. Harry Simeone, 1981.

Chapter 21: The Anti-Semitic Rumor

1. Memorandum from A. Walter Socolow to Fred Waring, Feb. 8, 1983, Espy file.

2. Stephen Birmingham, *The Rest of Us: The Rise of America's Eastern European Jews* (New York: Little Brown & Company, 1984).

3. Sidney Zion, letter undated, Espy file.

Chapter 22: Life with Fred

1. Jack Dolph on tape with John Royal, 1960.

Chapter 23: Golf

1. *New York World-Telegram,* July 29, 1958.
2. Bob Intieri, 1984, Espy file.
3. *Evansville, Ill., Courier,* Aug. 10, 1959; *St. Louis Dispatch,* Mar. 11, 1964.
4. Telephone newspaper interview, 1978, recorded interview drawer.
5. Fred Scrutchfield told this story in the 1985 interview he taped with Virginia Waring, Espy file.
6. Jack Best included this story in the letter he wrote to Hilda Cole Espy, May 29, 1980, Espy file.
7. Nick Kenny, radio editor, *New York Daily News,* undated.
8. Ibid.
9. Ibid.
10. Fred Waring radio interview, recorded interview drawer, 1978.
11. Russ Halford, associate editor, *Country Club Golfer,* Jan., 1978.
12. Howard Richmond, press agent and music publisher, quoted in the *Desert Sun,* Palm Springs, Calif., Feb. 22, 1995.

Chapter 24: "On the Road Again"

1. Dick Cavett and Christopher Porterfield, *Cavett* (New York: Harcourt Brace Jovanovich, 1974).
2. Fred Waring program book.
3. Ty Cobb, *Nevada State Journal,* June 28, 1968.
4. *New York Variety,* Oct. 15, 1955.
5. Ken Winters, *Winnipeg Free Press,* Nov. 1, 1958.
6. Art Rosenbaum, "Fred Waring Perfectionist," *San Francisco Chronicle,* June 26, 1968.
7. *Minneapolis Sunday Tribune,* Aug. 9, 1959.
8. *Ann Arbor News,* Nov. 10, 1978.

Chapter 25: Ike and the Famous

1. Jack Dolph tapes, 1960.
2. Washington correspondent Newman Wright, "Sweetest Music Ever," *Herald News,* Passaic-Clifton, N.J., 1953.
3. Hugh L. Morris, staff correspondent, *Inter News Service,* Oct. 14, 1953.
4. For a fuller account of Floyd Odlum's development of the Atlas missile, see Paul Wellman, *Senator Stuart Symington: Portrait of a Man with a Mission* (Garden City, N.Y.: Doubleday, 1960).

Chapter 26: Crucible of Professionals

1. Kirk Douglas, *The Ragman's Son* (New York: Simon and Schuster,

1988); Nancy Sinatra, *Frank Sinatra, My Father* (Garden City, N.Y.: Doubleday, 1985).

2. Fred Waring to a fan backstage in Des Moines, Iowa, 1976.

3. These sentiments typify many expressed by Pennsylvanians in their 1978 letters to Hilda Cole Espy, Espy file.

4. *Rochester, New York, Democrat and Chronicle,* Mar. 16, 1967.

5. *Fresno, Calif., Bee,* Jan. 8, 1967.

6. Fred Waring radio interview, 1979, recorded interview drawer.

Chapter 27: Stroke

1. Review of show in Sarasota, Fla., Jan. 31, 1980.

2. Fred Waring radio interview, 1982, recorded interview drawer.

3. Jane Howard, *Margaret Mead: A Life* (New York: Simon and Schuster, 1984).

4. Otto Friedrich, *Glenn Gould: A Life and Variations* (New York: Random House, 1989).

Chapter 28: Timing

1. *Hollywood, Calif., Variety,* Mar. 10, 1981.

Chapter 29: Phaetons, Zephyrs, and Model A Fords

1. *Pittsburgh Gazette Times,* July 11, 1926.

2. Springfield, Mass., review, Aug. 25, 1933.

Chapter 30: What Glorious Music

1. *People,* May 1984.

A Note on Sources

IN July, 1984, Fred Waring gave to Pennsylvania State University his vast collection of memorabilia, spanning his nearly seven-decade show-business career. Formally known as Fred Waring's America: A Collection of Memories (FWA), this treasure trove is now administered by the University Libraries Special Collections and is housed in the Special Services Building at Penn State. Sammy Gallu had begun talking with Fred in the late 1970s about donating his collection to the university, and formal negotiations were undertaken by Penn State administrators Richard Grubb and Marlowe Froke. Peter Kiefer, who currently serves as FWA coordinator, continues to organize the collection so that it will serve the needs of future scholars, students, and others interested in this vibrant part of American music, popular culture, and the history of mass media.

At the time it was presented to Penn State, Fred Waring's America included the following materials. I have drawn extensively upon these resources, and on those subsequently added to the collection (such as the videotape described below), in writing about Fred's life and career:

60 filing cabinets full of music scores and vocal and instrumental arrangements for more than 6,400 songs;
7500 pages of scrapbooks containing clippings dating back to 1922;
759 cans of film holding the visual record of TV's *The Fred Waring Show* from 1949 through the 1950s;

8,524 phonograph disks holding 1,161 hours of radio broadcasts from 1933 through 1949;

600 audio tapes, including masters of commercial recordings, concert performances, and workshop sessions.

In 1960 Jack Dolph, Fred's scriptwriter for twenty-five years, interviewed many Pennsylvanians, family members, and friends for a proposed book to cover Fred's life up to that period. In 1978 Hilda Cole Espy began writing a book about Fred. She asked many former Pennsylvanians for their memories, opinions, and other comments. Most of them shared their thoughts in letters to her. She interviewed four people on tape. She also wrote out her own reminiscences.

In 1985, Penn State set up and videotaped an informal discussion of the 1949–54 television shows. Those participating were Bob Banner, director; Nadine Gae Schroeder, dancer and choreographer; Ray Sax Schroeder, production; Pat McBride, cameraman; and myself.

Finally, I have drawn on my own forty-year association with Fred, as well as interviews I conducted with him in 1981 and with several of his friends and colleagues in 1981, 1985, and 1987. Fred's sister Helen also shared her memories with me in a 1980 taped interview.

Unless otherwise indicated in the notes, all direct quotations come from the following sources. Tape recordings are indicated by T, letters by L, the videotape by V, and manuscripts by M. These materials are included in Fred Waring's America.

Hawley Ades (L, 1978)
Leo Arnaud (T, Beverly Hills, Calif., Sept. 14, 1960; L, 1978)
Cora Ballard (T, Waring's New York office, Mar. 8, 1960)
Bob Banner (V, 1985)
Lou Benson (L, 1978)
Jack Best (L, 1978)
Bill Blackburn (T, Shawnee-on-Delaware, Pa., 1978)
Hugh "Lumpy" Brannum (T, Shawnee-on-Delaware, Pa., 1978)
Ferne Buckner (L, 1960)
Pete Buonconsiglio (L, 1960)
Milton Caniff (L, 1978)
Jake Cohen (T, Shawnee-on-Delaware, Pa., 1960; L, 1978)
Don Craig (L, 1978)
Fred Culley (T, Shawnee-on-Delaware, Pa., 1960)
Donna Dae (L, 1978)

Virgil "Stinky" Davis (L, 1960)
Admiral Edwin Dexter (T, Shawnee-on-Delaware, Pa., 1960)
Jack Dolph (L, 1960)
Mickey Dugdale (L, 1978)
Hilda Cole Espy (M, 1978)
Howard Everitt (L, 1978)
Tot Fisher (T, Tyrone, Pa., 1960)
Bill Flick (L, 1978; T, 1981)
Sammy Gallu (T, Shawnee-on-Delaware, Pa., 1978)
Patsy Garrett (L, 1978)
J. L. Gaunt (T, Los Angeles, Calif., Oct., 1960)
Don Gillis (T, New York, 1960)
Bob Harris (L, 1978)
Helen Helwig (T, Waring's New York office, Mar. 17, 1960)
Sydney Johnson (L, 1978)
Hal Kanner (L, 1978)
Nelson "Nels" Keller (T, Shawnee-on-Delaware, Pa., 1960)
Pete Kiefer (L, 1978)
Leonard Kranendonk (L, 1978)
Priscilla [Magillicutty] Lane (L, 1978)
Bill Lear (L, 1978)
Dolly Waring Lee (T, Shawnee-on-Delaware, Pa., Mar. 20, 1960)
Dorothy Lee (T, Ed Lee's Chicago office, Mar. 20, 1960)
Ed Lee (T, Ed Lee's Chicago office, Mar. 20, 1960)
Marv Long (L, 1978)
Murray Luth (T, Shawnee-on-Delaware, Pa., 1960)
Pat McBride (V, 1985)
Poley McClintock (T, Shawnee-on-Delaware, Pa., 1960)
Yvette McClintock (T, Shawnee-on-Delaware, Pa., 1978)
Glenn McGihon (L, 1978)
Russell Markert (T, 1960)
Helen Waring Martin (T, York, Pa., Feb. 5, 1960; T, York, Pa., 1980)
Beverly Mayer (L, 1978)
Lou Metz (T, Waring's New York office, Jan. 1, 1960)
Jim Miller (L, 1981)
Charlie Naylor (L, 1978)
Harry Obitz (T, Shawnee-on-Delaware, Pa., 1960)
Johnny O'Connor (T, New York, 1960)
Tommy Paterra (L, 1978)
Lette Rehnolds (L, 1978)

Roy Ringwald (T, Solvang, Calif., Aug. 12, 1960; L, Mar., 1960; L, 1978)
Clarence Robinson (T, Los Angeles, Calif., Oct., 1960)
Norman "Puss" Ronemus (L, 1978)
John Royal (T, NBC office, New York, Mar. 15, 1960)
Evalyn Nair Waring Santiago (T, Solana Beach, Calif., 1960)
Nadine Gae Schroeder (V, 1985)
Ray Sax Schroeder (T, Shawnee-on-Delaware, Pa., 1960; V, 1985)
Fred Scrutchfield (L, 1978; T, Shawnee-on-Delaware, Pa., 1985)
Robert Shaw (L, 1978)
Ruth Sibley (L, 1978)
Harry Simeone (L, 1978)
Walter Socolow (T, New York, 1960)
Bill Townsend (L, 1960)
Jackie Mayer Townsend (L, 1978)
Dorothy "Dot" McAteer Waring (T, San Diego, Calif., 1960)
Fred Waring (T, Shawnee-on-Delaware, Pa., 1960; T, Shawnee-on-Delaware, Pa., 1981)
Tom Waring (T, Shawnee-on-Delaware, Pa., 1960)
Virginia Waring (V, 1985)
George Webb (L, 1978)
Linda Wheeler (L, 1978)
Al Wilson (T, Shawnee-on-Delaware, Pa., 1987)
Dixie Waring Wilson (T, Shawnee-on-Delaware, Pa., May 26, 1960)
Jane Wilson (L, 1978)
Danny Winkler (T, Beverly Hills, Calif., Aug. 9, 1960)

Index

The relationship of each Waring family member to Fred Waring is indicated in parentheses.

Popular song, 111, 305
Porter, Cole, 2, 80–83, 86, 87, 94, 98, 135–36, 346
Porter, John, 14
Powell, Dick, 159
Precision drills, 42, 74–75, 102
Presser, Theodore, music company, 51
"Pretty Blue Eyed Sally," 46
Prohibition, 7, 119
Punxsatawny, Pa., 346
Purdue University, 188, 301

Rachmaninoff, Sergei, 240
Racial issues, 41, 45, 51, 61, 297–99
Radel (Pennsylvanian in 1924), 55
Radio, 2, 42, 58, 70, 78, 85, 103, 113, 114, 133–34, 135, 138–43, 152, 161, 163, 229
Radio broadcasts, 102, 138–40, 144, 153, 157, 161, 215, 223
Radio City Music Hall (New York), 122, 358
Radio Mirror, 180
Radio Pictures, 89
Radio stations, 139–43
Rah Rah Daze, 96, 98
"Ramona," 88
Rapsey, Bud, 30–31
Ravel, Maurice, 85, 225, 240
Reagan, Nancy, 317, 330
Reagan, Ronald, 213, 236, 317, 330
Recording companies, 138, 140, 142
Recordings, 2, 52, 85, 139, 161, 175. *See also* Pennsylvanians
Rehnolds, Lette, 265, 300, 328, 381
Reiner, Fritz, 139
Reinhardt, Aurelia, 196
Renault, 361
Reno, Nev., 321
Restaurants, use of recordings, 141, 321
Revolta, Johnny, 110
Rhine, Jules P., 329
Rhythm, 84, 93
Rialto Theater (Chicago), 45
Rialto Theater (Omaha, Neb.), 61–62
Richardson, Johnny, 207, 216
Richmond, Howard, 291

Richmond, Va., 162
Right of Interpretation, 139
Ringwald, Roy, 134–37, 162, 169, 170, 182, 183, 342, 368, 382
RKO (Radio Keith Orpheum), 89, 91
Robin, Leo, 59
Robinson, Clarence, 31–32, 382
Rochester, Minn., 300
Rochester, University of, 188
Rocky Mountain tick fever, serum for, 150
Rodgers, Richard, 2, 136, 198, 220, 222, 241
Rodgers and Hammerstein, 183, 228
Rogers, Buddy, 59, 99, 331
Rogers, Will, 40
Rolls-Royce, 360
Rolph, B. A., and his Lucky Strike Band, 95
Ronemus, Norman "Puss," 116, 382
Roosevelt, Franklin Delano, 31, 119, 137, 157–58, 214, 312
Roosevelt, Theodore, Jr., 306
Rose, Billy, 171
Rosenberg (union representative), 166
Rosenkavalier, Der, 240
Rothschild, Baron, 83
Roxy Theater (New York), 105–8, 111, 128, 204, 205, 225
Roxyettes, 105–6
Royal, John, 39, 65, 69, 71, 84–85, 113, 117, 132, 141, 145, 165, 168, 203, 225–26, 246, 269, 382
Royal Connaught Hotel (Toronto), 40
Rubenstein and Pasternack band, 42
Ruber, John, 121
Runyan, Damon, 180
Runyan, Paul, 164
Rusk, Dean,, 196–97
Ruston, La., 298–99
Ryan, Mary, 185
Ryden, Jean, 195

Salk, Jonas, 151
Salle Chopin, 197
Salle Pleyel, 84
Salton Sea property, 287–88
Salvation Army, 139, 270, 311

Valéry, Paul, 197
Vallee, Rudy, 70, 118, 128, 148–50, 180, 241
Vanderbilt, Alfred Gwynn, 320
Vanderbilt, Jeanne, 320–21
Vanderbilt Theater (New York), 1, 168, 175–76, 190, 198, 199
Variety, 71, 73, 76–77, 80, 94, 107–8, 131, 303, 357
Variety Managers Protective Association, 101–2
Varsity Show, 159–60, 163
"Varsity Show Case," 297
Vaudeville, 2, 38, 88, 89, 91, 92, 95, 100, 112, 113, 157, 163
Verdi, Giuseppe: *Requiem,* 182
Victor Talking Machine Company, 37, 38, 69–70, 94, 139, 320
"Victory Tunes," 183
Vietnam War, 312
Vinson, Fred M., 313
Violin, 24, 26, 27, 32, 40, 41, 67, 78, 136, 167, 195, 207, 208, 325
Visions of Sleep, 51
Vochestra, 162
Voght, Emma, 22
"Voice of Broadway" column, 109
Volstead Act, 7
Voorhees, Don, 139

Waggoner, Lyle, 178
Waldorf-Astoria (New York), 150
Walker, Jimmy, 173
Wall, Art, 282
Wallis, Hal, 160
Walzer, Winnie. *See* Palmer, Winnie
Wanamakers, 146
Warfield, David, 173
Warfield Theater (San Francisco), 64
Waring, Dixie (first child; married Al Wilson), 126–27, 165, 168, 210, 261–62, 272, 274, 282, 287, 295, 342, 382
Waring, Dolly (sister; married Ed Lee), 5, 8, 9, 12, 16, 18, 20, 22, 76, 92, 174, 212, 227
Waring, Dorothy "Dot" McAteer (first wife), 35, 47, 49, 55, 65, 76–77, 81, 84, 86–87, 92, 153, 164, 283
Waring, Evalyn Nair (second wife; later,

Santiago, Evalyn), 89, 92, 110–11, 126, 152, 153, 159, 164, 172, 204, 205, 209, 210, 227, 255, 261, 275
Waring, Frank (father), 5–12, 14–20, 21, 27–28, 29, 61, 165, 173–74, 209, 275, 306, 361
Waring, Fred, Jr., "Freddy" (second child), 142, 153, 168, 210, 295, 331–32, 340, 365–67
Waring, Frederic Malcolm "Fred"
—ability to nurture others' talent, 43, 121–22, 123, 162, 193–94, 200
—aesthetic of music to be enjoyed, 24, 63, 79, 111–12, 122, 201, 338
—aloofness, emotional, 92, 152, 153
—athletics, love of, 15, 25, 57, 83, 90
—attitudes about music, 93, 122, 133, 222
—audience, love of, 25, 63, 111–12, 122, 236, 293, 312, 353
—aversion to cigars and cigarettes, 116–17, 156
—birth, 5
—as a Boy Scout, 3, 13, 14, 19, 22, 23, 26, 29, 48, 186, 187, 191, 359
—business sense, 28–29, 103, 108, 124, 131–32, 152, 154–55, 229–30
—campaigner for "Ike," 307–9
—cars, 50, 62–63, 109, 110, 360–64
—childhood performances, 6–7
—children, relationship with his, 126, 153, 165, 209, 210, 255, 261, 274, 287, 331–33
—clothes, 108, 262–63
—college songs, composer of, 178, 184
—conducting, 39, 50, 83, 98, 105–7, 159, 325
—crisis management, 45, 125, 142, 160, 206, 275–79
—death, 368
—divisive relationship with Tom, 3, 10, 12, 16, 68–69, 99, 118, 127, 162
—as emcee, 78, 122, 177, 239
—engineering and architecture, love of, 6, 25, 27, 34, 36, 49, 99, 272, 274
—extrasensory perception, 156, 216–17, 328
—failure, sense of, 99
—financial losses, 97, 142

A Note on the Recording

This CD represents excerpts from radio shows and commercial recordings dating from 1923 to 1963—a smorgasbord of music intended simply to give a taste of these four decades and to add an aural dimension to the biography. Songs marked with an asterisk (*) were shortened, by judicious editing, from the original recording.

1. *Sleep,* by Adam Geibel and Tom Waring (Victor Talking Machine 19172–A, New York City, Feb. 15, 1928). The master for the first recording of "Sleep" in 1923 is now lost, but this 1928 performance was made from the same arrangement.
2. *Collegiate,* by Nat Bonx and Moe Jaffee, arr. Leo Arnaud (Victor Talking Machine 19648–A, Camden, N.J., Apr. 4, 1925).
3. *Wobally Walk,* by Warren and Green (Victor Talking Machine 21099–A, New York City, Nov. 10, 1927). Fred Waring, soloist.
4. *Love for Sale,* by Cole Porter, arr. Don Sebesky (Victor Talking Machine 22598–A, New York City, Dec. 24, 1930). The Three Waring Girls, soloists.
5. *Sing! Sing! Sing!* by Louis Prima (New York City broadcast, Oct. 6, 1936).
6. *Mama Don't Allow,* by Sammy Kahn and C. Davenport (New York City broadcast, Mar. 3, 1936).
7. *Comin' through the Rye,* traditional (New York City broadcast, Dec. 10, 1940).
8. *Baseball,* by Tom Waring, Gibbons, Leitch (New York City broadcast, July 21, 1939). Paul Douglas, announcer.
9. *Battle Hymn of the Republic,* by Howe and Steffe, arr. Roy Ringwald (New York City broadcast, Oct. 10, 1945). Gordon Berger, soloist.
10. *Smoke Gets in Your Eyes,* by Jerome Kern and Otto Harbach, arr. Roy Ringwald (New York City broadcast, Nov. 24, 1947).
11. *I Got Rhythm,* by George and Ira Gershwin, arr. Livingston Gearhart (New York City broadcast, Nov. 28, 1947). Virginia Morley and Livingston Gearhart, piano soloists.
12. *Sometimes I Feel like a Motherless Child,* traditional spiritual, arr. Roy Ringwald (New York City broadcast, Feb. 2, 1948). Don Craig, soloist.

13. *Funiculi, Funicula,* by Luigi Denza and G. Turco, arr. Harry Simeone (New York City broadcast, Feb. 4, 1948). Leonard Kranendonk, soloist.
14. **So Beats My Heart for You,* by Pat Ballard, Tom Waring, and Henderson, arr. Roy Ringwald (Decca #72301 [78 rpm], June 26, 1944). Jack Wilson, soloist.
15. **So Long, Mary,* by George M. Cohan, arr. Harry Simeone (Shawnee-on-Delaware, Pa., broadcast, July 4, 1947).
16. *Dry Bones,* traditional spiritual, arr. Livingston Gearhart (New York City broadcast, Mar. 1, 1948). Paul Whiteman, guest host; he agreed to fill in for Waring, but only if "Dry Bones" was on the show, too.
17. **Bali Ha'i,* by Oscar Hammerstein and Richard Rodgers, arr. Hawley Ades (New York City, Langworth Transcription No. LW-23, Apr. 29, 1949). Joanne Wheatley, soloist.
18. *Fanny,* by Harold Rome, arr. Roy Ringwald (Capitol LP WBO-1079, May 16, 1958).
19. **Stars and Stripes Forever,* by John Phillip Sousa, arr. Harry Simeone and Hawley Ades (Shawnee-on-Delaware, Pa., broadcast, Aug. 1, 1947).
20. **Remember,* by Irving Berlin, arr. Roy Ringwald (New York City broadcast, Feb. 23, 1948). Gordon Goodman, soloist.
21. *Mr. Frog a Courtin' He Did Ride,* traditional folk song, arr. Livingston Gearhart (New York City broadcast, Jan. 3, 1947).
22. *September Song,* by Kurt Weill and Maxwell Anderson, arr. Hawley Ades (Capitol LP WBO-1079, recorded at Delaware Water Gap, Pa., May 18, 1958). Joe Marine, soloist.
23. *Hora Staccato,* by Grigoras Dinicu, transcribed by Jascha Heifetz, arr. Harry Simeone and Eric Siday (Capitol LP W-845, recorded in New York City, Jan. 30, 1957).
24. *Some Enchanted Evening,* by Oscar Hammerstein and Richard Rodgers, arr. Roy Ringwald (Capitol LP T-992, recorded in New York City, Jan. 23, 1958).
25. *Without a Song,* by Vincent Youmans, Billy Rose, and Edward Eliscu, arr. Roy Ringwald (Capitol LP WBO-1079, recorded at Delaware Water Gap, Pa., May 9, 1958). Frank Davis, soloist.
26. *All the Things You Are,* by Jerome Kern and Oscar Hammerstein, arr. Roy Ringwald (Capitol LP WBO-1079, recorded at Delaware Water Gap, Pa., May 18, 1958).
27. *Give Me Your Tired, Your Poor,* by Irving Berlin, arr. Roy Ringwald (Reprise LP F-2020, recorded in Hollywood, Calif., Dec. 4, 1963).
28. *Sleep,* by Geibel and Waring, arr. Don Walker and Frank Hower (Capitol LP W-845, recorded in New York City, May 20, 1957).

Produced by Virginia Waring (author) and Peter Kiefer (coordinator of Fred Waring's America, The Pennsylvania State University Libraries)

Engineering and digital editing by Peter Kiefer, Kerry Trout (WPSX-TV, Penn State), and Jennifer Bortz (WPSX-TV, Penn State)

Disc mastering and manufacture by Digi-Rom, Inc. (New York, N.Y.), Harry Hirsch, owner/manager

Additional information about recordings made by Fred Waring and the Pennsylvanians is available in *The Fred Waring Discography,* compiled by Peter T. Kiefer, Discographies 65 (Westport, Conn.: Greenwood Press, 1996) ISBN 0-313-20010-2.

VIRGINIA WARING is a native Californian who studied in Paris with Robert Casadesus and Nadia Boulanger. For fifteen years she toured as the Morley half of the famed duo-pianists Morley and Gearhart. She was married to Fred Waring from 1954 until his death in 1984. From 1983 to 1989 she was president and owner of Shawnee Press, founded by Fred Waring, and from 1985 to 1991 was artistic director of the Fred Waring U.S. Chorus at Pennsylvania State University. A prestigious international piano competition now carries her name and takes place in California's Coachella Valley at the College of the Desert and the Palm Desert campus of California State University, San Bernardino.

Pistol Packin' Mama: Aunt Molly Jackson and the Politics of Folksong   *Shelly Romalis*

Sixties Rock: Garage, Psychedelic, and Other Satisfactions   *Michael Hicks*

The Late Great Johnny Ace and the Transition from R&B to Rock 'n' Roll
James M. Salem

Tito Puente and the Making of Latin Music   *Steven Loza*

Juilliard: A History   *Andrea Olmstead*

Understanding Charles Seeger, Pioneer in American Musicology   *Edited by Bell Yung
and Helen Rees*

Mountains of Music: West Virginia Traditional Music from *Goldenseal*   *Edited by
John Lilly*

Alice Tully: An Intimate Portrait   *Albert Fuller*

A Blues Life   *Henry Townsend, as told to Bill Greensmith*

Long Steel Rail: The Railroad in American Folksong (2d ed.)   *Norm Cohen*

The Golden Age of Gospel   *Text by Horace Clarence Boyer; photography by
Lloyd Yearwood*

Aaron Copland: The Life and Work of an Uncommon Man   *Howard Pollack*

Louis Moreau Gottschalk   *S. Frederick Starr*

Race, Rock, and Elvis   *Michael T. Bertrand*

Theremin: Ether Music and Espionage   *Albert Glinsky*

Poetry and Violence: The Ballad Tradition of Mexico's Costa Chica
John H. McDowell

The Bill Monroe Reader   *Edited by Tom Ewing*

Music in Lubavitcher Life   *Ellen Koskoff*

Zarzuela: Spanish Operetta, American Stage   *Janet L. Sturman*

Bluegrass Odyssey: A Documentary in Pictures and Words, 1966–86
Carl Fleischhauer and Neil V. Rosenberg

That Old-Time Rock & Roll: A Chronicle of an Era, 1954–63   *Richard Aquila*

Labor's Troubadour   *Joe Glazer*

American Opera   *Elise K. Kirk*

Don't Get above Your Raisin': Country Music and the Southern Working Class
Bill C. Malone

John Alden Carpenter: A Chicago Composer   *Howard Pollack*

Heartbeat of the People: Music and Dance of the Northern Pow-wow   *Tara Browner*